Phia Sing, drawn by Soun from a photograph.

ປື້ມຄົວກິນລາວຂອງເພັຽສິງ

Traditional Recipes of Laos

being the manuscript recipe books of the late Phia Sing,
from the Royal Palace at Luang Prabang, reproduced in
facsimile and furnished with an English translation

TRANSLATORS Phouangphet Vannithone and Boon Song Klausner
EDITORS Alan and Jennifer Davidson
DRAWINGS by Thao Soun Vannithone

PB

PROSPECT BOOKS

2013

This edition published in 2013 by Prospect Books, 26 Parke Road, London, SW13 9NG. Reprinted 2022.

Originally published in 1981 by Prospect Books Ltd, London. A subsequent edition in smaller format and without the Lao text was published in 1995 by Prospect Books, Totnes.

About 90 of the 99 drawings in the book are by the Lao artist Thao Soun Vannithone. The remaining 9 or so drawings, slightly modified where appropriate, are by two other artists from Laos, Elian Bleton Souvannavong and Thao Singha. Their contributions have not been identified separately, because all three artists worked together in Vientiane and cannot now recall with certainty in every instance who did which drawing.

British Library Cataloguing in Publication Data:
A catalogue entry of this book is available from the British Library.

Design consultant, Phillip Wills.

Printed in Britain by the Short Run Press, Exeter.

ISBN 978-1-903018-95-8

Contents

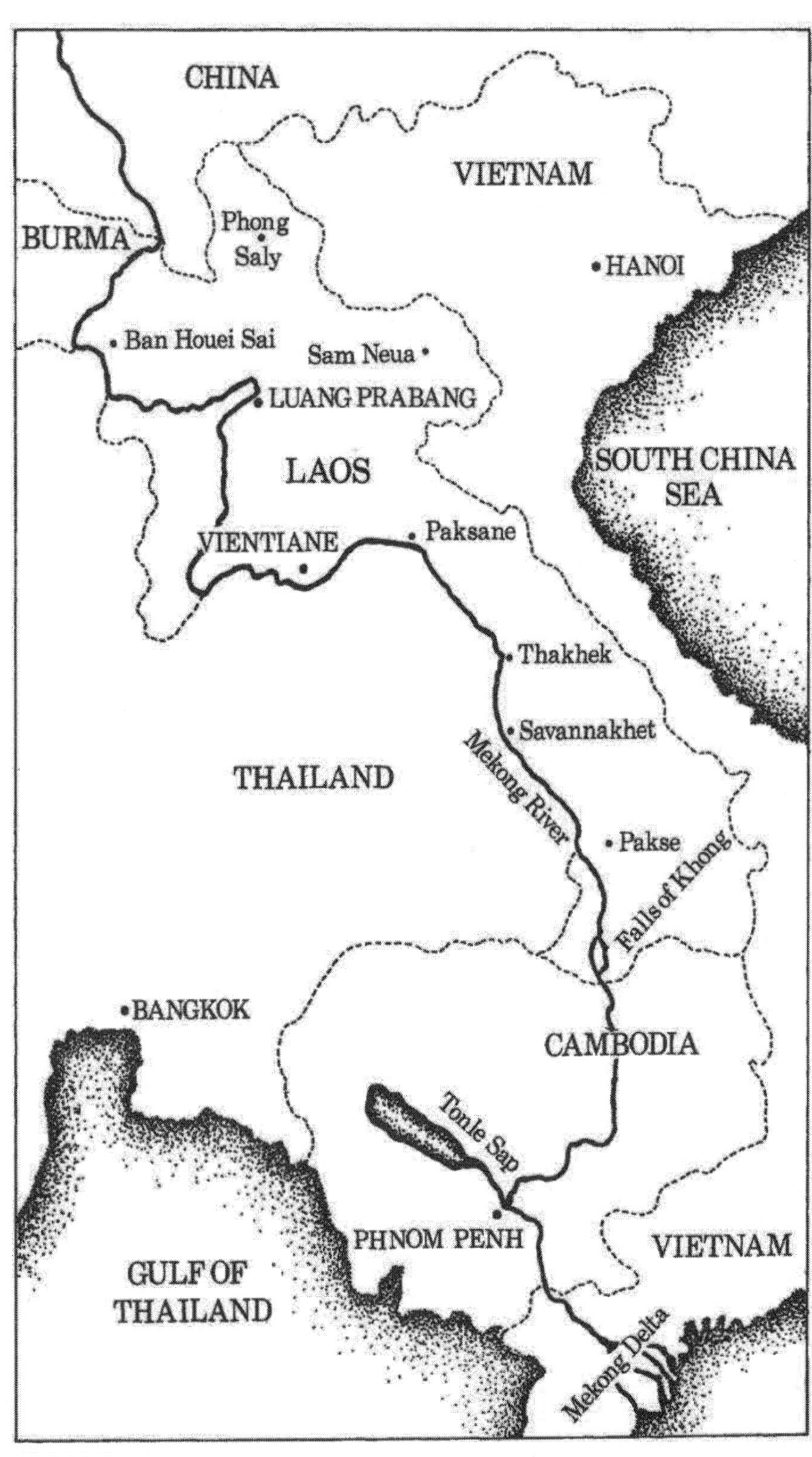
CHINA
VIETNAM
BURMA
Phong Saly
HANOI
Ban Houei Sai
Sam Neua
LUANG PRABANG
LAOS
SOUTH CHINA SEA
VIENTIANE
Paksane
Thakhek
Savannakhet
Mekong River
THAILAND
Pakse
Falls of Khong
BANGKOK
CAMBODIA
Tonle Sap
PHNOM PENH
VIETNAM
GULF OF THAILAND
Mekong Delta

Introduction

In 1974 I called on the then Crown Prince of Laos in his house at Luang Prabang, the royal capital. I was writing a book about the fish of Laos, and wished to discuss it with H.R.H., who was renowned for his interest in fishing. We talked for half an hour and I made many notes, especially of the anecdotes which the Crown Prince related about the giant catfish of the Mekong, PANGASIANODON GIGAS.

When my audience drew to a close, I rose to take leave, but paused in the doorway to mention one last matter, which I had meant to bring up sooner. I told the Crown Prince that I was having difficulty in collecting authentic Lao recipes for fish, the written sources being almost non-existent, and oral accounts less precise than I would have wished.

For two or three seconds the fate of this book hung in the balance. The Crown Prince hesitated, as though searching his memory. Then he asked me to wait a moment, went upstairs and came down again with two little notebooks such as French schoolchildren use. He told me that they were the *cahiers* in which the late Phia Sing, who had been Master of Ceremonies and Chef at the Royal Palace, had recorded his recipes. I was welcome to borrow them. He thought that there were three of them altogether, but he had only been able to find two.

In the Dakota in which I flew back to Vientiane I sat beside a senior official of the Royal Government and asked him to look through the notebooks and tell me what they contained. I feared that they would be an anthology of western dishes, since all Lao cooks were used to relying on oral tradition for making their own dishes but had to write down the details of foreign ones. However, my companion assured me that what I had was a collection of authentic Lao recipes, including many for fish dishes.

I arranged for the fish recipes to be translated, and published many of them in *Fish and Fish Dishes of Laos* (Vientiane, early 1975, and Charles Tuttle and Co. of Tokyo and Vermont, late 1975). Learning in the meantime that the widow of Phia Sing was still living in Luang Prabang, I arranged to call on her with an interpreter in order to inform her, as an act of courtesy, of what I was doing. She was a frail and dignified lady, with the naturally beautiful manners which are a Lao characteristic. In response to the homage which I paid to the quality of her late husband's work, she replied with an expression of gratitude to myself. She revealed that Phia Sing's dying wish had been that his collection of recipes should be published and that the proceeds should go towards building the new shrine which was to protect the Prabang, the most venerated Buddha statue in Laos, which had come from Ceylon many centuries ago and which was housed in the precincts of the palace. She had given the notebooks to the Crown Prince, thinking that he was in a position to have this wish executed. She was glad to hear that some at least of the recipes were now to be published, albeit in a foreign language.

These revelations made a deep impression on me; all the more so since I knew by what a slender thread of chance I had paused on leaving the Crown Prince's house, and how he had hesitated before recalling the existence of the notebooks. I told the old lady that she could count on me to do my best to see that the whole collection of recipes was published. 'Then,' said she, 'the soul of my husband will rest in peace at last.'

When this conversation took place the (Communist) Pathet Lao forces were already established in both capitals of Laos, and their representatives in the Coalition Government were manoeuvring towards an eventual takeover of the country. Soon afterwards Saigon fell to the Communists in Vietnam, and Phnom Penh to the Khmer Rouge in Cambodia. When my tour of duty in Laos ended in the autumn of 1975, it was clear that effective power had already passed into the hands of the Pathet Lao and their North Vietnamese patrons, although the façade of a coalition government was still in being and H.M. The King was still on his throne. I and my wife were probably the last western visitors whom he entertained to a family lunch at the Palace in Luang Prabang. I took the opportunity to tell the Crown Prince that I was returning to him by safe hand the notebooks of Phia Sing, but that I had taken xerox copies, one for the National Library and one for myself. I kept my word and saw to it that the notebooks went back to the Crown Prince, although I feared that they would never be seen again in the original by anyone else.

Now, years later, I have been able to arrange for publication of the recipes in the notebooks. In present circumstances in Laos it would not be feasible to devote the proceeds of this book to the preservation of a Buddhist shrine, as Phia Sing had wished. I came to the conclusion that, in default of this, he would have wished the money to be used to help Lao refugees. These refugees are scattered in many countries. As I am in Britain, and know at first hand what splendid work is being done by the British Council for Aid to Refugees, I proposed that the money be given to them, to be used specifically for the Lao whom they are helping to start a new life here. Since forming this plan, I have had the opportunity of consulting Phia Sing's eldest son, in Paris. He assures me that his late father would have been entirely content with this interpretation of his original wish.

Alan Davidson
September 1980

Phia Sing and his Recipe Books

Chaleunsilp Phia Sing, who was born at Luang Prabang in about 1898, was an extraordinarily versatile man, a sort of Laotian Leonardo da Vinci. He appears here in his capacity as the royal chef at the Palace in Luang Prabang, of which a view from the hill behind it is shown on the next page. But he was also the Royal Master of Ceremonies, at a court of many and beautiful ceremonies, a physician, architect, choreographer, sculptor, painter and poet. In addition, he had been the mentor of the youthful Princes Souvanna Phouma and Souvannavong, and accompanied them when they went to Hanoi to pursue their studies at the university there in the 1920s.

Phia Sing died in 1967. He had been ill for some time and knew that death was approaching. It was in these circumstances that he wrote out his recipes in the two little notebooks referred to in the Preface to this book.

These notebooks were of the French kind, with the pages marked out in tiny squares rather than left blank or with nothing but ruled horizontal lines. When the pages were photocopied in Vientiane this unwanted 'grid', being printed in light blue, came out very faintly or even, in some instances, disappeared altogether. In most of the recipes, however, it could still be seen, especially at the numerous points where vertical and horizontal lines crossed. The photocopies had therefore to be 'doctored', a task which was appropriately carried out by Lao refugees who were temporarily in hospital in London, by whiting out the unwanted marks. This was a laborious task. Moreover, the quality of the photocopies was poor. Some of them were so smudgy that the only possible method of making them reproducible again was to make tracings of Phia Sing's actual writing, a task which was mainly performed by the artist Soun, in a most meticulous fashion.

The end of recipe 106 and the beginning of recipe 107 turned out to be missing in the xerox copy. The National Library in Vientiane confirmed that the same applied to the copy in their possession. No attempt was made to fill these gaps in the Lao text, but what seemed to be the appropriate additions were made to the English text, after careful consultation with an expert cook from Luang Prabang. These additions are clearly indicated in the text.

The numbering of the recipes calls for two comments. First, Phia Sing's relations are all of the opinion that these were added by another hand; and that he himself, even if he had intended to number them, did not do so. Secondly, whoever did the numbering made a mistake and, after reaching number 57, went back to 48 and continued again from there. So there are two each of recipes numbered 48 to 57 inclusive. We have distinguished the second ones bearing these numbers by adding B after the number.

The principal translators received much help and advice from other qualified persons. In doing the translations, they sought to be fairly literal and kept to the sequence of ingredients and that of instructions which Phia Sing himself followed. In some instances the recipes would have been made clearer and

The Royal Palace at Luang Prabang, viewed from the Phousi hill.

easier to follow if the order had been changed; but it was thought better to eschew editing and stick to translating.

However, certain steps were taken to make the recipes easier to use. Equivalent quantities were given, and some necessary explanations, and a few obvious additions (such as putting water in the pot with the ingredients before bringing them to the boil!) were made. All these are in brackets. So are the few additions which had to be made, e.g. because Phia Sing had omitted an ingredient from his list (the omission being apparent from a reference to the ingredient in the instructions). Note, however, that all punctuation marks are additions (Lao writing is not punctuated) and that for obvious reasons these have not been bracketed.

Phia Sing himself added explanatory notes at the end of certain recipes. These appear under the heading 'Note'. Any similar notes added by the editors appear under the heading 'Editors' Note'. All footnotes are by the translators or editors.

By all these means the text and its translation have been presented with complete accuracy (save for the fallibility which must affect all translators) and no distortion; but the work of Phia Sing has been rendered more easily comprehensible by the discreet addition, in a manner clearly identifiable, of a little information to supplement his and of certain comments which at least some readers are likely to find useful.

Lao Eating Habits and Attitudes to Food

The country of Laos includes about sixty ethnic groups, mostly hill tribes in the north. The ethnic Lao who inhabit the north bank of the river Mekong and its attendant plains and valleys are by far the largest group, and are also to be found in the south of China and the north of Thailand. Indeed, even before the exodus of refugees following the Communist takeover at the end of 1975, the majority of ethnic Lao lived outside Laos. When we talk about 'the Lao' it is members of this ethnic group whom we usually mean (Laotian being the corresponding adjective which refers to citizenship of Laos, irrespective of ethnic factors).

Vientiane, the governmental capital of Laos, is on the banks of the Mekong and lies fair and square in ethnic Lao territory. Luang Prabang, which was the royal capital, lies up in the mountains to the north, with many other ethnic groups in or near it. Luang Prabang was where Phia Sing lived and worked; but, as befitted the person in charge of the royal kitchens, his cuisine was almost entirely Lao, and his recipe books contain only occasional references to the culinary practices of other ethnic groups and make only minor use of imported ingredients.

The Lao are famed for their amiable characteristics and tolerant, easy-going attitudes. The dominant religion is Buddhism, mixed up with elements of spirit worship in various forms. Until the last few years one of the most noticeable features of daily life was the morning procession of Buddhist monks around the towns, accepting offerings of food from the willing population. In this respect, food had an important role in the religious practices of the Lao.

Eating at home, the Lao give the impression of being completely relaxed; hospitable, informal, and free of any feelings of hurry, anxiety or ostentation. Such, at least, is the impression which an occidental visitor will receive. In fact, however, the relaxed atmosphere invests procedures which are surprisingly formal. These have been described to me by Dr Amphay Doré, formerly of Luang Prabang, with the proviso that the concepts and traditions to which he refers are those of the older generations and would not necessarily be familiar to younger Lao (although still implicit in certain features of their table manners).

Briefly, one has to understand that two of the important concepts in Lao life are *piep*, which may be roughly translated as prestige, and *lieng*, which means feeding, giving nourishment. The concept of *lieng* gives rise to what might be called contractual obligations. Both concepts apply to Lao meals.

This means, in practice, that at a family meal the father and mother, being the persons of highest rank in the family unit, take the first mouthfuls, followed by the other family members in descending order of age. Once this 'first tasting' has been accomplished, the meal appears to be free for all, but in fact is still subject to rules, for example that no-one should help himself at the same time as anyone else or go in front of a person of higher rank, which would cause that person to lose *piep*.

A guest must observe the same rules, and also additional ones. If he begins to eat without first being invited to do so by his host or hostess, he will be deemed to have no *piep* at all. (The logic here is that it is only someone who has nothing who is entitled to appropriate what belongs to others.) He may not continue eating after the others have finished. If he is still hungry, it will be necessary for at least one member of the household to continue eating with him. However, even so, he cannot go on indefinitely, for custom requires that he should leave something on his plate. If he were not to do so, the host's *piep* would suffer, since it would seem that he had not provided enough.

It follows from this last point that the Lao practice is to prepare more food than will be consumed. This practice is not effected by serving a large number of successive 'courses', as in the west, but by laying out a wide variety of foods at once, in such abundance as to ensure that everyone will have as much as he or she may fancy of anything. This ideal situation may not always be achieved; but it is always the aim.

The significance of certain foods

This is a very complex subject, and can only be touched on here, to show that the various foodstuffs have their own special kinds of status and that this fact has to be kept in mind when considering Lao recipes.

I am emboldened, and indeed, enabled, to touch on the matter as a result of the publication of an interesting comparison between the peppers (the fruits of the genus CAPSICUM—see page 34), black pepper (the condiment), and ginger.*

It emerges from this study that all these three spices (to use the term in its broadest sense) have one thing in common, namely that they belong to the first of three classes of plants which the Lao distinguish for medicinal purposes. This is the class of 'hot' or 'chauds' plants, for which the Lao term is *hon*. The second class is that of the 'cold' (*yen*) plants, which produce a cooling and refreshing effect instead of a heating and fiery one. The third class consists of those plants which are neutral in this respect.

However, although our three spices are thus classed together, they occupy very different places in Lao cookery. Pepper, the condiment, is used, but seems to have come to Laos as a result of Chinese and Thai influences. Pepper, the fruit, in contrast, is one of the essential elements in traditional Lao cookery, almost as important as rice and fish sauce. Ginger, according to M. Pottier, is the next most important flavouring, but is much more besides. Unlike the other two plants, it has a ritual significance and is an important element in offerings to the spirits. It is deemed, in the world of spirits, to represent gold; while its relation ZINGIBER ZERUMBET is taken to represent silver.

I found for myself that there is a similar mystique surrounding the giant catfish of the Mekong, PANGASIANODON GIGAS, on which see Davidson, *Fish and Fish Dishes of Laos*. The fishery for this noble creature, the largest freshwater fish in the world if one excepts anadromous sturgeon, used to be attended by rituals of such complexity that it seems a wonder that the fishermen ever succeeded in catching any. Now, alas, the rituals are but a memory and the fish itself is in danger of extinction.

* See 'Le Piment, le Poivre et le Gingembre. Leurs Usages alimentaires et médicinaux au Laos' by Richard Pottier, in *Langues et Techniques Nature et Société*, Tome II, Approche ethnologique et naturaliste, Editions Klincksieck, Paris, 1972.

Food and the *baçi* ceremony

A *baçi* ceremony is such a charming Lao institution that it deserves mention here, although the presence of symbolic foods are only one aspect of it, albeit an important one. Eggs are the principal symbolic foods used, but rice is almost always in evidence also.

A *baçi* is a highly informal ceremony which may be held to mark any important occasion, such as a birthday, a wedding, the start or conclusion of a major journey (e.g. if someone is going abroad) or for greeting a distinguished visitor. It represents a mixture of Buddhism and spirit worship; and the person officiating may accordingly be either a monk or a 'magic-man'. In either event the centrepiece is a 'tree' which is usually made from banana leaves and flowers but may be composed of artificial materials. Symbolic foods surround it. The monk or 'magic-man' intones prayers and benedictions appropriate to the particular occasion. Then, after the person being honoured has had some symbolic food placed in his hand, white cotton strings are tied round his or her wrists, to the accompaniment of further benedictions. After this, all the participants, who have been sitting round the 'tree', are allowed to tie more strings around his or her wrists, while expressing their own specific good wishes; and are also permitted to tie strings around each other's wrists, so that the whole affair develops into a free-for-all from which everyone emerges with at least some strings. These strings must never be cut, and should not be removed for three days. Many people leave them on for longer, to be on the safe side; some indeed until they finally disintegrate months later.

Lao Culinary Terms and Equipment

The definitions and illustrations given in this section are intended for reference, and to supplement the descriptions and explanations given in the English texts of the recipes. We deal in sequence with the preparation of raw food, cooking utensils, culinary processes, and the serving of food.

Preparation of food

Chopping and pounding are the main processes of preparation, and have quite an elaborate vocabulary.

Chopping is normally done with a knife. *Chak* is a verb meaning to chop, especially when you are holding in one hand the thing to be chopped, and using a knife held in the other hand to chop it.

Soi also means to chop. *Fak* means to chop very finely, or mince.

Khood means to grate, and *fan* (or, again, *soi*) to slice.

The adverbs *laep* or *mun* are used to indicate 'finely'. Thus *soi laep* would mean something like 'to shred'.

Pounding is done with a pestle and mortar, as shown on the right.

Tam means to pound. *Kheuang* means ingredients. So *kheuang tam* means pounded ingredients. *Kheuang hom* means fragrant or aromatic ingredients, which may or may not have been pounded or finely chopped. *Kheuang nai* means giblets.

Lap is a noun which refers to meat or other flesh which has been finely chopped and pounded. The meat is usually raw; but partly cooked meat can also be used to make a *lap*. *Sa* is a term rather like *lap*, but indicates meat which has been sliced or roughly (not finely) chopped.

Nian is a verb meaning to make something into a homogeneous sticky mass, whether by pounding it or mashing it with the back of a spoon or by using your hands.

Dip is an adjective with two meanings: either raw (uncooked) or unripe. *Souk* is its opposite in both senses, meaning either cooked or ripe.

Cooking utensils

The typical Lao 'stove' is the charcoal-burning apparatus shown in the drawing below. It is called *tao-lo*. If a cook were using a wood fire, of logs instead of charcoal, the 'stove' would consist of three stones arranged to form a shelter and support (like a camper's fire in the west) and would be called *kon sao*; or an iron tripod, called *kiang*.

The wok, used throughout South-East Asia and probably of Chinese origin, is *maw kang* in Laos, or *maw kat-ta* or (as in Thailand) just *kat-ta*.

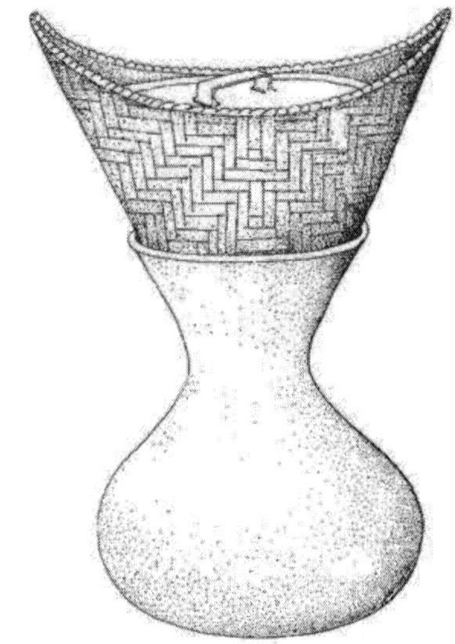

The word for a steamer (the upper part) is *houad*. The drawing shows the traditional kind of steamer used in Laos. The name for its lower part is *maw nung* (*maw* meaning pot, and *nung* meaning steam). A modern steamer, made of aluminium, would be called *houad lek*, and may have one or two steaming compartments set over its lower part. When Phia Sing gives instructions for steaming something he usually says that it is to be steamed in a *houad* or by means of what he calls a steaming rack. We have omitted this last phrase in the translation, when it is simply mentioned as an alternative, to avoid constant repetition of something which might sound mysterious. However, we must explain here what he meant. His 'steaming rack' (*lang tung*) is not traditionally Lao, but Chinese, and is to be seen in Chinese restaurants the world over. It consists of a stack of circular bamboo recipients, fitting on top of each other and permitting the passage of steam all the way up, so that different dishes can be cooked simultaneously in the various 'layers'.

A soup pot (or 'marmite', as the French would call it) is known as *maw keng* in Laos, *maw* for pot and *keng* for soup. The traditional Lao soup pot is made of pottery and has two raised handles. However, many Lao families now use aluminium soup pots. A soup pot with a lid on it would be called *maw keng mee fa ad*. Lao cooks make much use of a heavy iron, general-purpose cooking pot, such as would be called a pot-roaster in the west. The name for this is *maw lutee* (or *maw rutee*—it is difficult to distinguish the r from the l in the second word, and some say that the word is derived from the French rôtir, which became successively rotee, lotee and lutee). A small such pot would be called *maw lek noi*.

Maw kan is the name for an ordinary frying-pan of the western kind; and *maw kan noi* refers to a small pan of this sort.

Much use, naturally, is made of bowls, whether for mixing ingredients or serving such things as sauces. *Tuay* is bowl; *tuay nyai* a large bowl; *tuay noi* a small bowl; and *tuay keng* a soup bowl, an individual one of the Chinese kind, as shown on page 163. See also page 50, on Lao measures, for further uses of the word *tuay*.

A ladle is called *jong*. Examples of ladles made from coconuts are shown below. They vary greatly in capacity. One of them, the upper of the two, would be used as a 'dipping cup', i.e. a person would dip it into a liquid and drink from it.

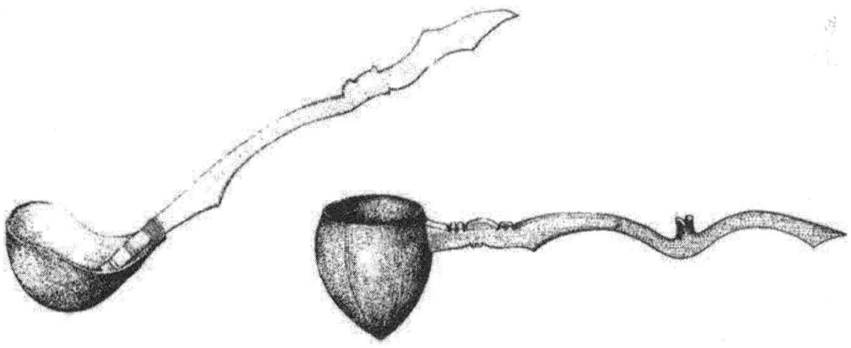

A strainer is known as *antong*. An example of one made from finely woven strands of bamboo is illustrated, below left, together with the different and specialised strainer which is used for lowering *padek* (see page 23) into something which is cooking, in such a way as to ensure that the padek liquid circulates in the dish while the solids remain in the basket.

Terms for the various culinary operations

Mok means to sear or cook by placing something directly into the glowing embers and hot ashes of a charcoal fire. What is put in may or may not be protected by a wrapping of banana leaf. For searing, as in the initial preparation of chilli peppers or shallots for many dishes, there would be no wrapping.

Nung means to steam. Food is often steamed after being enclosed in banana leaf wrappers, but it may also be steamed unwrapped. A *houad*, the Lao sort of steamer, is illustrated on page 16. *Mawk* is the name for something which has been steamed.

Or means to stew, or a stew. This is only an approximate translation. An *or* is less liquid than a western stew. But the proportion of liquid to solid matter varies; *Or Sod* has more than *Or Lam* (cf. recipe 4 and the notes at the end of recipes 23 and 24). *Or* might often be best translated as 'to braise'. The cooking vessel used would be a *maw keng* (see page 17).

Ping means to grill; and so does *kang*. The word *kanab* is a noun which denotes a food wrapped in a banana leaf package and grilled in it, usually by placing it over or in a charcoal fire. The drawing below left shows a *kanab*. The one on the right shows the different shape of the package which is used when the grilling is being done with the aid of a *mai heep neep*, the split bamboo device which is gripping it.

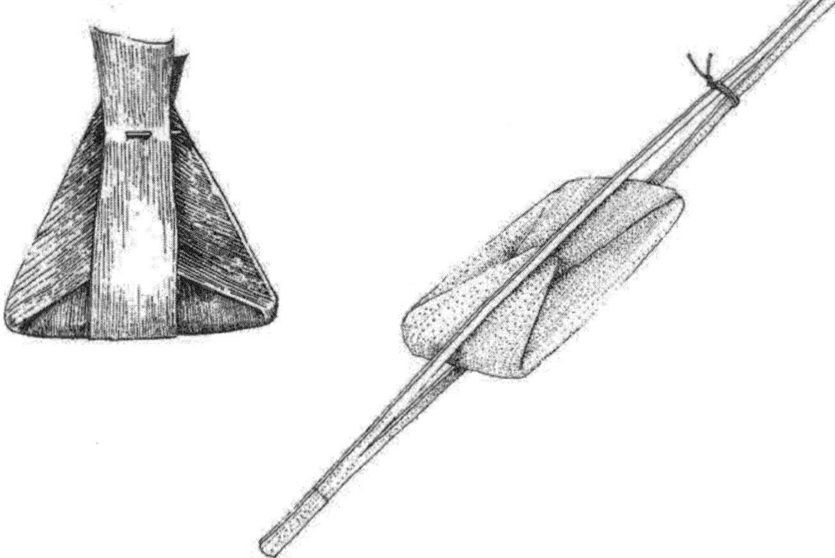

Keng is the noun meaning soup. A *tom keng* is a 'hot' (i.e. peppery) soup. A *keng som* is a sour soup. Some Lao soups contain a relatively high proportion of solid matter, e.g. meat or fish and vegetables, and are close to what we might call a stew in the west.

Hum means to cook in a pot over a low fire, very slowly. *Om* has the same meaning. So *keng om* means a soup cooked thus, over a low fire.

Kiaw means to go on cooking, in order to reduce the liquid in a dish.

Tom is to boil; not a common cooking method, but used in, for example, the preparation of *Tom Jaew* (recipe 112).

Khoua means either to 'fry' without fat, i.e. to toast or 'parch' in a hot dry pan, as you do with sesame seeds for example; or to fry with fat, in the usual way. *Pad* means to fry in the latter sense only, and is commonly used when a number of ingredients are being fried together. The general Lao term for 'to fry' is *jeun* (one of those words which are hard to transliterate—it may also be written *joun* or *tchoun* or *chun*) and this is the word which would be used for a deep-frying operation.

Ua indicates a stuffed dish, for example *Ua Nok Noi*, Stuffed small birds.

Yam refers to a mixture, sometimes like what we in the west would call a salad. The Lao term has, however, a wider meaning, as can be seen from studying recipes 106 to 109.

Baking in the western sense of the term does not occur in traditional Lao cookery, since the Lao did not have ovens. But see page 307 for a description of how they improvise one for baking cakes.

Tasting

Phia Sing bids the cook, in almost every recipe, to 'taste and check the saltiness'. He uses two different words for 'taste', *jae* and *sim*. The former is appropriate when tasting uncooked mixtures. It means to touch the ingredients with your finger tip and then put the finger tip to your lips, thus tasting only a very small amount. The latter is normally used for tasting cooked ingredients, when it would be usual to take a tiny spoonful.

Phia Sing sometimes indicates what should be done if a mixture is insufficiently salty, for example to add some *padek* liquid. If he gives no such indication, one may assume that the remedy is just to add more salt. He does not tell us what to do if the mixture is too salty. Modern practice would be to add a little sugar. But Phia Sing hardly ever used sugar; so we are left to speculate about what he did in such a situation.

Serving foods, and tableware

It is not part of the Lao tradition to sit round a high table, in western style, and to eat successive courses. Instead, they have the food put out all at once, often on low tables of bamboo, such as the one shown below, help themselves and dispose themselves comfortably while they eat.

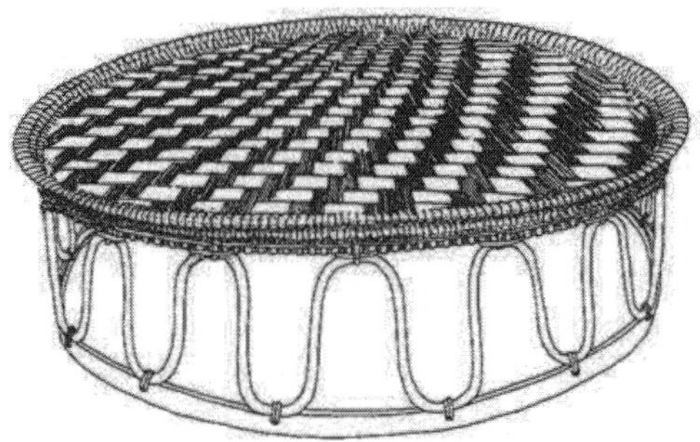

They have a range of platters and plates which vary from a very large round platter—what we would call a tray—which fits on to one of the low, circular bamboo tables and is called *taat* to middle-sized platters and small plates. The name for these last two categories is *chan* (or *tian*, as it is sometimes transcribed). Phia Sing uses this term to refer both to small plates and to large platters; but in translating his recipes we have said 'plate' or 'platter' according to what he meant.

There are in fact some epithets which can be applied to *chan*. *Chan luk* is a fairly large oval serving-dish, fairly deep and with a rim. *Chan noi* is a small plate, for use by one person. *Chan nyai* is a large plate or platter, suitable for serving food.

Soup bowls are used. *Tuay keng* is an individual soup bowl.

Chopsticks are not part of the Lao tradition. A spoon (*bouang*) is used for soups and dishes with more liquid than can conveniently be mopped up with sticky rice.

Sticky rice itself almost counts as a piece of tableware, since it is used both as a 'pusher' for bits of food and to sop up liquids. Each person usually has his or her own little basket of sticky rice, which may be of various patterns, as shown in the drawings opposite.

The person eating will take some sticky rice between the fingers, knead it slightly together and then use it as described above.

It is also common to eat with the fingers. This can be done delicately by wrapping up mouthfuls of food in edible leaves. *Phan* is a verb which indicates the use of such leaves to wrap up morsels of food, or a mixture of morsels, before eating them. The Lao often have one platter of edible leaves, another or others of meat or fish or vegetables, and a bowl of sauce for 'dunking'. The leaves enable them to eat the food, with the sauce, without employing any cutlery.

Ingredients and Other Practical Information for the Cook

Let it be said, before we embark on what may seem like a daunting catalogue of exotic ingredients, that those which are essential to Lao cookery are few and can be obtained without great difficulty in any place where reasonably comprehensive food shopping facilities exist, and especially where there are Chinese groceries.

One problem is *padek* (page 23). But other fermented fish products may be used instead; or plain fish sauce.

A second problem is lemon grass. It is best to use fresh lemon grass, and this can be grown in a wide range of climates. Failing this, buy dried lemon grass, or use powdered lemon grass. The latter is often sold as *sereh* powder, *sereh* being its Indonesian name.

We have taken some pains to identify as exactly as possible some of the more obscure ingredients used in Phia Sing's recipes. This is in the interests of presenting his work in its authentic form; it is not meant to imply that failure will attend the efforts of any cook who cannot conjure up everything which he lists. He himself was well aware of the possibilities of substitution, for he takes care to point out, on the few occasions when this is necessary, that substitution, e.g. of one kind of fish for another, will not do.

Minor differences in flavour or texture are of little consequence. Major differences, such as would change the character of a dish, can almost always be avoided. Lao people themselves, in exile, offer a shining example of how to overcome incidental problems of supply and to maintain their culinary traditions in a different environment.

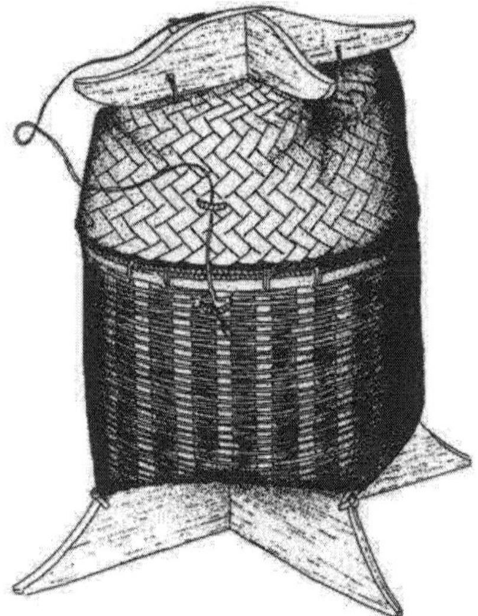

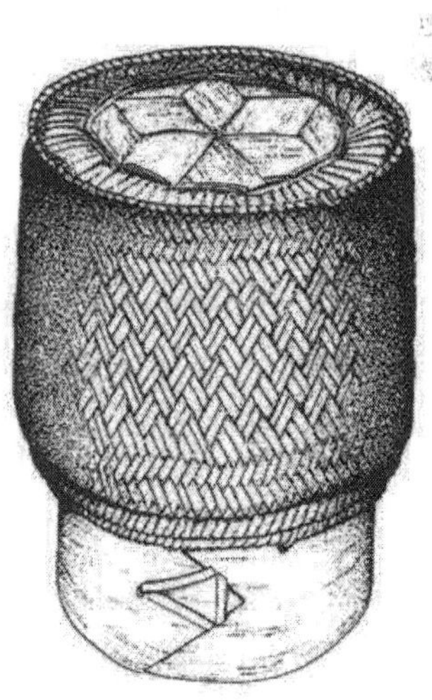

Sticky-rice containers. The one on the left comes from Luang Prabang. The other one is typical of the kind used at Vientiane.

Rice and pasta-type products

The Lao are notoriously partial to sticky or glutinous rice; but contrary to the belief sometimes encountered outside Laos they do not eat it exclusively. About a third of the rice consumed in Laos is ordinary, non-glutinous, rice. (The distinction, incidentally, is not clear-cut. There is a more or less continuous spectrum of varieties of rice from the markedly non-glutinous to the markedly glutinous. All varieties of rice belong to the species ORYZA SATIVA. The Lao name for glutinous rice is *khao nyao*; and for non-glutinous rice *khao chao*.)

Peng khao is the name for rice flour, in large quantities such as would be used for making cakes etcetera. A rice-grinding mill is shown on page 312.

Khao beua is rice, either sticky or ordinary, which has been soaked in water and then pounded to make a sort of rice flour, for use when small quantities are needed.

Khao khoua is rice, either sticky or ordinary, which has been toasted in a hot dry pan until brown and then pounded.

Khao jee is cooked sticky rice which has been mashed and then grilled, in small quantities, to a golden colour. It is an alternative, which some Lao prefer, to *khao beua*. The name *khao jee* is also used by the Lao for western-type bread.

Khao khob, rice cakes, are sold in Lao markets. They are made by cooking sticky rice, moulding it into small cakes, letting these dry and then deep-frying them. See the drawing.

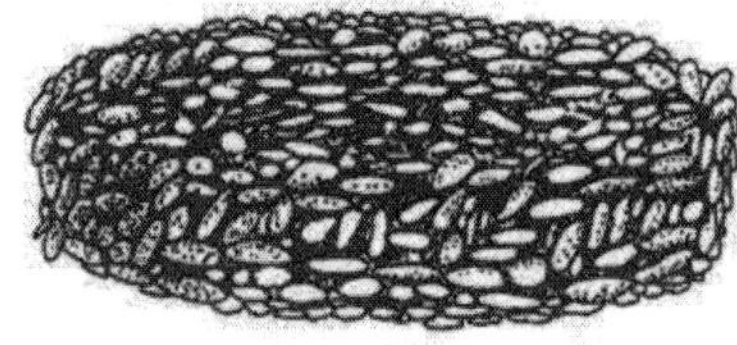

The most popular pasta-type product in Laos is *khao poon*, rice vermicelli. This is the main ingredient in the national dish, which goes under the same name (see recipe 97). *Khao poon* is sold in the markets in Laos in bunches which are arranged round a circular bamboo tray, each bunch overlapping with the next, and each circle of bunches constituting one of what may be many layers piled on top of each other. One layer, for which the Lao word is *na*, would comprise about 8 to 10 bunches and would weigh about half a kilo or one pound.

Khao poon Chin refers to the transparent Chinese-type vermicelli which is manufactured from green bean starch and which is sometimes referred to in the west as 'cellophane noodles'. The last word in the Lao name may be found transcribed as *tien*.

Fish sauce and *padek*

Nam pa, fish sauce, is an ingredient found in almost every recipe. Every South-East Asian country has its own fish sauce: *nuoc mam* in Vietnam, *tuk trey* in Cambodia, *nam pla* in Thailand, *ngan-pya-ye* in Burma, and so on. Fish sauce plays the same role in this region as soy sauce in China and Japan. It is prepared by steeping fish in brine for a long time (in Laos, far from the sea, a mixture of 20 per cent sea fish and 80 per cent freshwater fish used to be the norm) and draining off the liquor which is formed. This is brown in colour, rather like a peaty Scotch whisky, and is usually sold in bottles.

Padek is a related product, but more specific to Laos and northern Thailand. It can best be described as fish sauce with chunks of the fermented fish still in it; also rice 'dust' and rice husks. The whole mixture may be used in cookery; or the pieces of fish alone, with the rice dust and husks cleaned off them; or the liquid (*nam padek*, literally 'water padek') without any of the solids. *Padek* has a very strong smell and the large pottery jar (see drawing) which contains a household's supply is usually kept out on a verandah. Most *padek* is home-made. The real thing is not available in the west, but jars of fermented fish from the Philippines are one acceptable substitute. And I was once told that the Lao bride of an Englishman, on being offered canned anchovies for the first time, exclaimed: 'But this is *padek*—rather salty *padek*, but good!'

Fish

Fish, for which the Lao word is *pa*, are plentiful in Laos, not only in rivers, lakes and ponds, but also in the wet paddy fields and the irrigation canals and ditches. *Fish and Fish Dishes of Laos* by Alan Davidson gives details of the 80 or so species which are most commonly marketed and eaten in Laos. The recipes of Phia Sing refer to a surprisingly small proportion of these, perhaps because they reflect what were the personal preferences of the Royal Family among those available in the area of Luang Prabang. The species used in his recipes are listed below. (*Pa nang*, incidentally, means any scaleless fish, such as catfish; and *pa ked* is the general name for scaly fish.)

Pa ling, probably PANGASIUS NASUTUS, a catfish which sometimes reaches a length of 60 or 65 cm in Laos, but is more commonly found in the markets at a length of about 25 or 30 cm. A drawing of it accompanies recipe 53.

Pa gnon, PANGASIUS SIAMENSIS, which has a maximum length of about 30 cm and is illustrated with recipe 10.

Pa sa ngoua, KRYPTOPTERUS BLEEKERI, a sheatfish (still in the catfish tribe) which may attain a length of 60 cm. It is shown with recipe 34.

Pa leum, PANGASIUS SANITWONGSEI, another catfish, but much larger; its maximum length is 3 metres, although 1 metre is a common market length. It is reputed to enjoy eating the carcases of dogs floating in the river, and its flesh is rather fat and indigestible. A drawing of it accompanies recipe 113.

Pa beuk, PANGASIANODON GIGAS, the king of Laotian fish—both the biggest and the best. It is a vegetarian catfish, with very fine flesh; and is also the source of Laotian 'caviar', a great delicacy. As mentioned on page 13, this magnificent fish seems to be on the verge of extinction. Phia Sing does not give a recipe which specifies this fish, perhaps because even in his days few were being caught in the vicinity of Luang Prabang; but his recipe 102 calls for the Laotian 'caviar' made from the eggs of the *pa beuk*.

Pa va, LABEO DYOCHEILUS, is a kind of carp which is well-known in parts of India and in Burma also. A drawing of it is shown with recipe 37. In the rivers near Luang Prabang it attains a maximum length of 45 cm, although to hear Luang Prabang fishermen talk you would think that it was closer to the maximum size which it reaches in India, 1 metre. The *pa va* was the favourite quarry of H.R.H. The Crown Prince when he went fishing at Luang Prabang. He described to the senior editor of this book how a fortunate fisherman may sometimes catch three at once while they are performing their 'danse d'amour' (in which two males rub themselves, one on each side, against a female, in order to squeeze out the eggs). This happens when the *pa va* come down the tributaries, in July and August, to spawn in the Mekong. The eggs, incidentally, are among those most prized for making 'caviar', which is done by salting them.

Pa keng, OSTEOCHILUS PROSEMION, is a barb and one of the best known fish at Luang Prabang. Its maximum length is about 25 cm. In appearance it is very close to OSTEOCHILUS MELANOPLEURA, a larger relation, of which a drawing is shown with recipe 29.

Pa kho, OPICEPHALUS STRIATUS, is one of the four species of 'snakehead' fish which are eaten in Laos. Its common length is around 50 cm, but it can attain a maximum length of 1 metre. It is depicted with recipe 11.

Pa fa lai, DASYATIS sp., is a sting ray which has adapted to life in fresh water (the sting rays are normally marine fish) and is found in the Mekong. See recipe 48 for a drawing of it.

Other aquatic foods

Kung (sometimes transliterated as *koung*) means shrimp. The freshwater species commonly taken in Laos is shown with recipe 51.

Kob is the Lao name for frog. Frogs figure in more than one of Phia Sing's recipes and are a popular food in Laos. It is likely that several species are eaten, but clear information is lacking.

Hoi pang, the only freshwater mollusc to occur in Phia Sing's recipes, is a univalve, a sort of water-snail whose scientific name we have not been able to establish.

Finally, this seems to be the place to mention water algae. In the market at Luang Prabang one used to see white enamel bowls full of a dark green semi-liquid stuff, which was algae collected from ponds and other stagnant waters during the rainy season. The name at Luang Prabang was *thao*; at Vientiane *phak thao*. These algae apparently belong to the genus SPIROGYRA. But the matter is uncertain. Vidal, in his *Les plantes utiles du Laos*, refers also to two kinds of algae in the north of Laos, both known as *khai*. The first of the two is described as a mixture including CLADOPHORA spp. and also SPIROGYRA spp. Vidal believes that the second sort, which he identifies as DICHOTOMOSIPHON TUBEROSUM, is much rarer and found mainly in the vicinity of Luang Prabang.

Water-buffalo

This animal, BUBALIS BUBALIS, is greatly prized in Laos, both for the work it does and the meat which it provides. Its Lao name is *kuai*. A drawing of one appears at the top of the next page.

Water-buffalo meat may be consumed raw (in a *lap*, as in recipe 80), dried (*sin kuai haeng*), or cooked in various ways. Those who are in a position to make the comparison often declare it to be as good as beef (which is hardly known at all in Laos, although there was an experimental station for rearing cows and bulls, in the early 1970s, in the northern part of the Plain of Vientiane).

One very popular ingredient in Lao cookery in Luang Prabang is dried water-buffalo skin (*nang kuai haeng*). The drawing below shows how pieces of the skin appear when sold in the markets. Each section is called a *sae*, translated as strip in the recipes.

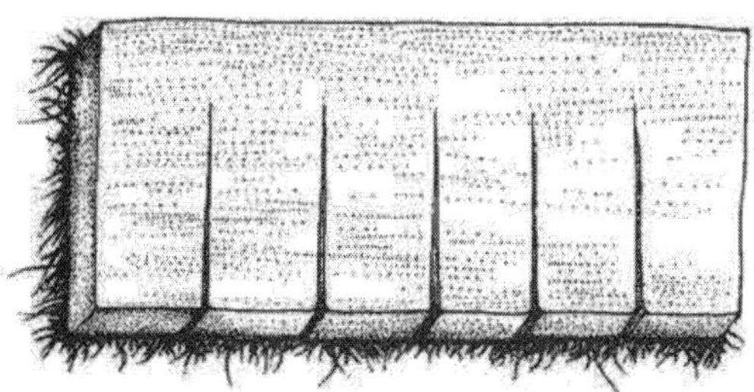

A Lao water-buffalo, often referred to simply as 'buffalo'.

Pork

Moo is the Lao name for pig. Families living in villages usually have their own pigs, and everyone enjoys pork meat. However, many other parts of the pig are eaten also, such as the trotters (*teen moo*) and tripe (*poung na moo*).

Sin moo ping is the name for pork which has already been grilled, whether bought thus in the market or prepared at home.

Moo pin (literally, 'pork turned') refers to a whole small pig which has been spit-roasted.

Fried pork skin is an ingredient in many dishes. It comes in two forms. *Khiep moo* is crisp-fried pork skin. *Khiep moo houm* is moist fried pork skin. Lao refugees in Britain have discovered that they can buy in pubs little packets of 'pork scratchings', which are quite like *khiep moo* although chopped up small, whereas in Laos the product is sold in sizeable pieces (as shown on page 139).

Another ingredient in many Lao dishes is *moo sam san*, 'three-layer pork'. What it looks like, on sale, is shown in the drawing below. It is rather like an unsliced piece of bacon, comprising skin, fat and lean meat.

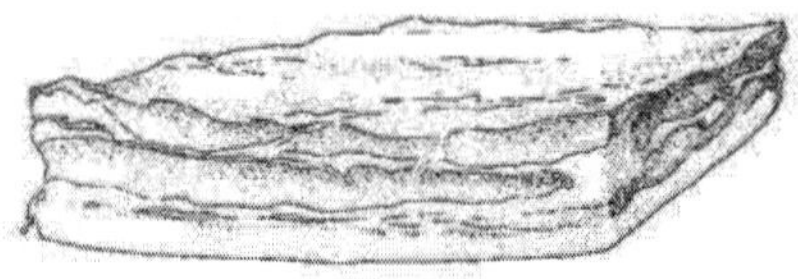

Poultry and game

Chicken is a food which is highly esteemed by all the Lao people. Some cooked chicken often appears as one of the symbolic foods which are used at a *baçi*, the charming Lao ceremony which is described on page 13. Chicken is a main or subsidiary ingredient in many of Phia Sing's recipes. One part of the chicken which he mentions frequently is the gizzard, known as *tai*. All chicken giblets are regarded as delicacies. Even the feet of the chicken are used in Lao cookery.

Ducks are less common in the markets, but are also prized as food. Lao families often raise their own ducks, for which the name is *ped*, in their gardens (i.e. the land round their houses—formal gardens are almost unknown in Laos, except for those belonging to palaces and the relatively small number of large villas or European-type houses which are to be found mainly in the two capital cities). The esteem in which duck meat is held is illustrated by a Lao superstition, that one should never serve duck to a visiting relation, since this might be thought to imply that you were presenting an honorific dish as a final farewell gesture to the visitor.

Turkeys have been introduced into Laos and are—or were—to be seen in the markets. But they are not traditional Lao fare and do not appear in Phia Sing's recipes.

As for game birds, the Lao commonly eat three. The first is the wild chicken, *kai pa*. The second is a quail, *nok kho*, of which a drawing appears on the right. The third is really a category rather than a single species, the Lao name being *nok noi*, which simply means small birds and embraces all such creatures which can be caught and eaten.

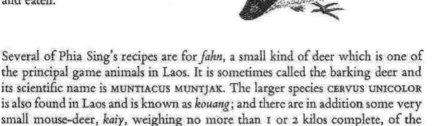

Several of Phia Sing's recipes are for *fahn*, a small kind of deer which is one of the principal game animals in Laos. It is sometimes called the barking deer and its scientific name is MUNTIACUS MUNTJAK. The larger species CERVUS UNICOLOR is also found in Laos and is known as *kouang*; and there are in addition some very small mouse-deer, *kaiy*, weighing no more than 1 or 2 kilos complete, of the genus TRAGULUS.

Less conventional kinds of game, not mentioned by Phia Sing but often eaten in Laos, include water-monitors and snakes. Other such surprises are in store for anyone visiting Lao markets.

Coconut

The coconut, *mak phao*, occupies a place of primary importance in Lao cookery, and provides a range of products which need to be carefully distinguished.

First, there is the liquid which you can hear slopping about inside a coconut before it is opened. It is normally used for the preparation of soft drinks—it is very refreshing if drunk just as it comes, but may also be mixed with other fruit juices—rather than in cookery. The Lao name for it is *nam mak phao*.

Coconut oil is prepared from the white meat inside the coconut. It is usual to buy it ready-made. It may be used as an oil for frying.

However, the main use to which the white meat of the coconut is put is the preparation of coconut cream (or coconut milk—both terms are used, and they are virtually interchangeable). The first requirement is of course to extract the meat, and this operation is combined with grating it, by the use of the device shown at the foot of the page—a *ka-tai* or 'rabbit'. Half a split coconut is worked to and fro over the projecting sharp edge, and the meat allowed to fall into a container below. The grated white coconut is then mixed with water and squeezed through a muslin or other suitable cloth to produce what is called the first extraction of coconut cream (*kati nam kok*). The process is repeated (same white coconut meat, fresh water) to produce the second extraction (*nam ti song*), which is, naturally, less creamy than the first. A third extraction (*nam pai*) may also be taken; it is even thinner.

When Phia Sing lists a coconut as an ingredient, he usually describes it as 'mature'. In practice, any coconut mentioned in any of the recipes should be taken to be a mature, i.e. ripe, one unless otherwise described.

Given the importance of the coconut, and the fact that it is not always easy or inexpensive to buy fresh coconuts in the west, it is a blessing that desiccated coconut and creamed coconut (in tubs or cans) are available as an easy source of perfectly acceptable coconut cream. Follow the directions on the package. Add more or less water according to whether you want a thick extraction (equivalent to the first extraction mentioned above) or a thinner one (like the second extraction).

When cooking with coconut cream, be careful to keep stirring as the liquid approaches boiling point; otherwise it will curdle. But in some recipes you should let it do so; this is when the instructions refer to the oil 'separating'.

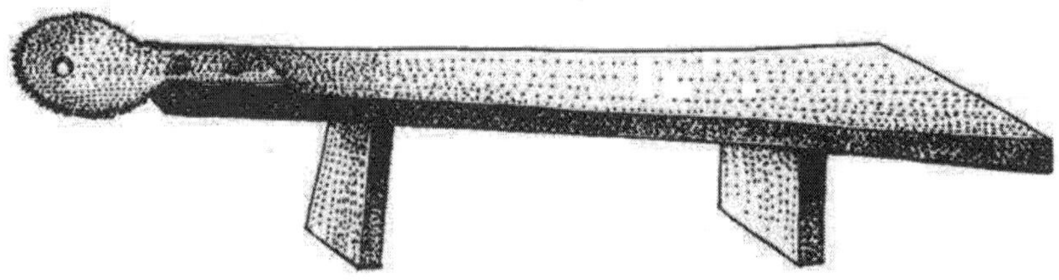

Some acid and sour-tasting ingredients

The lemon itself is not available in Laos. As usual in tropical areas, the lime, which is too well-known to require description here, takes its place. But another member of the citrus family, commonly used in Lao cookery, does require identification. This is the Kaffir lime, CITRUS HYSTRIX, which the Lao call *mak khi hout*. Its leaves, broken into two or into small pieces, are used in many recipes. They play the same role as bay leaves do in western cookery, and do not have a sour taste. But the juice of the Kaffir lime, which is occasionally used, does.

One ingredient which is frequently used to give a sour or acid taste to dishes is the tamarind, TAMARINDUS INDICUS, shown in the drawing below right. Its tiny leaves are used in some recipes, but it is the pulp of the fruit which is most commonly employed. It is available in Chinese grocery stores in small transparent packets, so there is no need to search for a substitute. The Lao name for tamarind is *mak kham*.

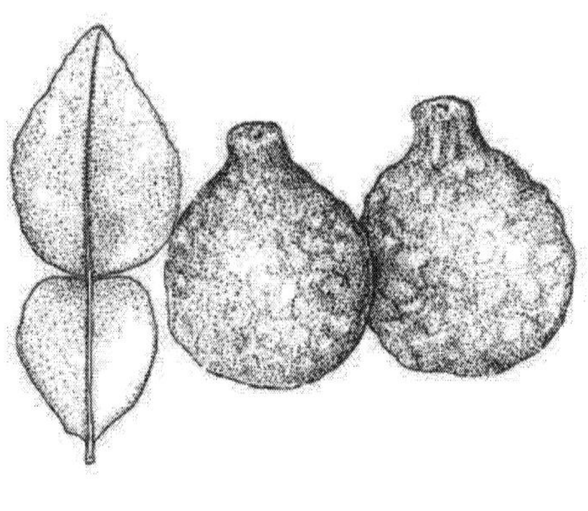

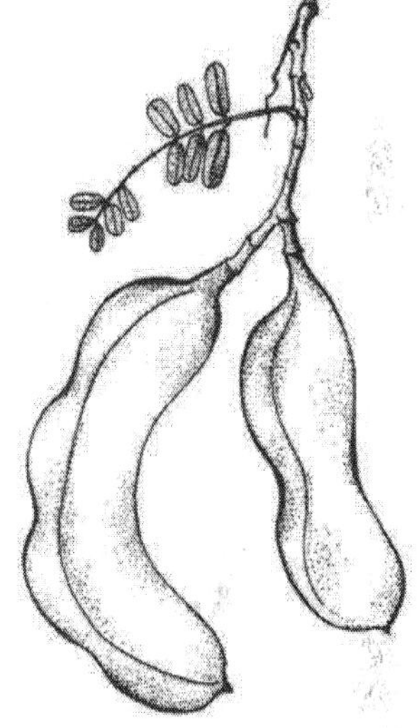

Although the lemon is not present in Laos, something which has the flavour of lemon is. This is lemon grass, sometimes called citronella. The principal edible species is CYMBOPOGON CITRATUS, which may be of Malaysian origin but is now found in many subtropical parts of the world. (CYMBOPOGON NARDUS is a similar plant, but one which is normally reserved for external use, rather than as a food flavouring.) It is used throughout South-East Asia, often but not exclusively as an ingredient in fish dishes, for which the lemon flavour makes it especially suitable. People in parts of the world which lack this valuable plant can survive without it either by using dried lemon grass powder (often sold as *sereh* powder, after the Malaysian and Indonesian name), or dried stalks of lemon grass, or (where the lemon flavour is the only requirement) the rather obvious alternative of lemon, lemon peel or lemon juice. But there are some dishes, for example crab steamed on a bed of lemon grass, for which fresh lemon grass is essential. It can be grown from imported root stock in countries with temperate climates, such as Britain, if it is kept under glass in the winter. The Lao name for it is *sikhai*, and a drawing of it appears overleaf.

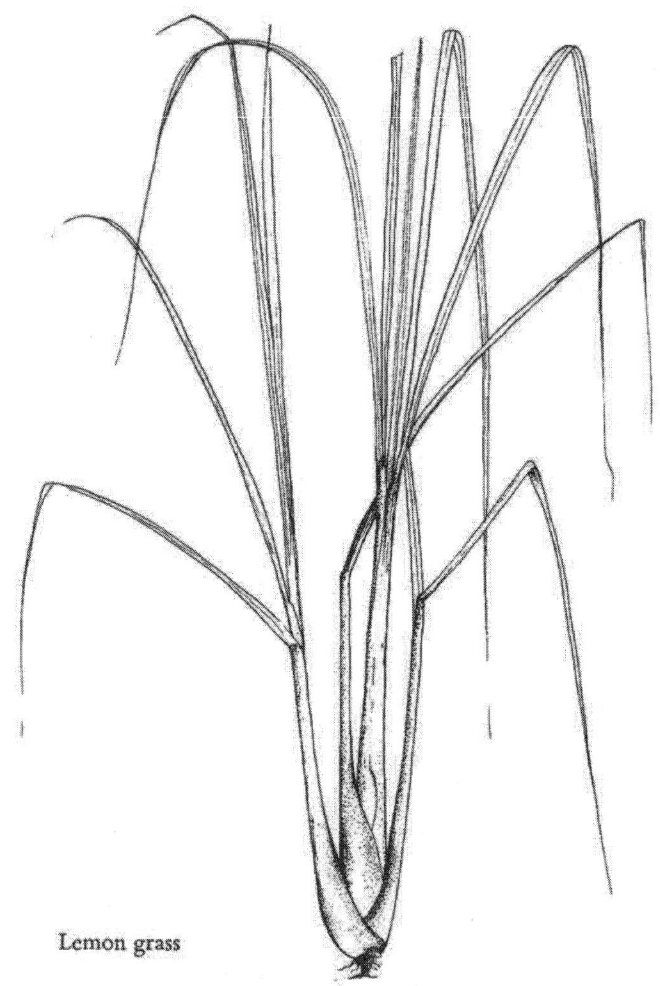
Lemon grass

There are two types of star-fruit, the sour and the sweet. The latter, AVERRHOA CARAMBOLA, is eaten for dessert. The former, for which the Lao name is *mak feuang*, is an ingredient often used for providing a sour taste. It is shown below. Alongside it, on the right, is another fruit used in cookery, ELAEOCARPUS MADOPETALUS, which the Lao call *mak kawk*. It too has a bitter, sour taste.

Other fruits used in cookery

Most edible fruits in Laos are eaten as dessert or for snacks. But there are some, not already listed under acid and sour ingredients above, which are used, in their immature state, for cookery.

The banana is one such fruit. The Lao name for banana is *kuay*, and for unripe banana *kuay dip*. The Lao have their own preferences among the many varieties of banana which grow in Laos, but in practice any banana will do in a recipe which calls for one. The variety known as *kuay tanee*, referred to in recipe 60, is about 5 or 6 inches long, has lots of seeds and is suitable for cookery only. For banana 'flowers', see the next page.

The jackfruit, shown below, is another fruit which is used in cookery while still in its unripe state. See, for example, recipe 93. Jackfruits, which belong to the genus ARTOCARPUS, can grow to an enormous size; but it is best to buy one weighing only a kilo or so. In countries such as Britain, where fresh jackfruit is hardly ever obtainable, canned jackfruit can be used; but this is a second-best solution since the jackfruit which are canned are often riper than they should be for cooking purposes. (When possible, buy a can of 'green' jackfruit, which is less ripe.) If using fresh, unripe jackfruit, peel off the thick skin and remove the hard core before cutting up the flesh into suitable pieces; and take care not to allow the sticky juice to stain your clothes, since the stains cannot be removed.

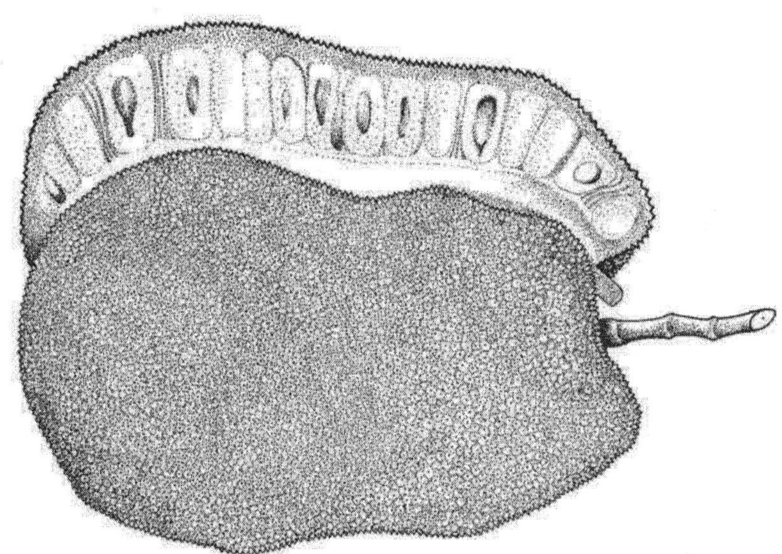

Edible flowers

Reference was made on the preceding page to banana 'flowers'. The Lao name for these is *nam wah*, and they are not, strictly speaking, flowers, but rather the 'heart' of the banana, i.e. the male bud with its fibrous outer bracts removed. See the drawing below left.

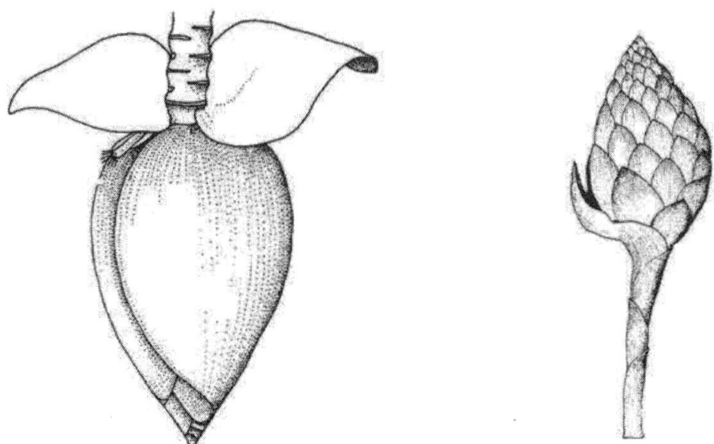

Dok khing, the flowers of the ginger plant, are used in Lao cookery. See the drawing above right of a flower in bud. (Ginger itself is treated on page 47.)

Dok khae ban, the flowers of the cultivated plant AGATI GRANDIFLORA, also used, are illustrated below left. (For *dok khae*, a wild plant, see page 161.) Below right is a drawing of the flowers of the plant CAESALPINIA MINOSOIDES, for which the Lao name is *nam panya*.

The above are not all the flowers which occur in Phia Sing's recipes. He also refers to *man neng*, ELETTARIA CARDAMUM, the cardamom plant. This grows in parts of Laos and is an export of some value. Besides using it as a spice, the Lao use the flowers of the plant in cookery; but both on a small scale. In addition, they sometimes use the 'heart' of the lotus flower, as well as its stems and leaves; see the drawing of this plant on page 35.

Eggplants and tomatoes

Mak kheua is the general Lao name for eggplant. The elongated purple kind familiar to Europeans and Americans is known as *mak kheua hamaa*, but it is not grown much in Laos. What the Lao use in their cooking most often is a round eggplant, for which the general name is *mak kheua poy*. When fully mature, its seeds are hard and are not used. Phia Sing sometimes refers to 'old' eggplants, and this is what he means. We have not translated the word 'old', partly because to western ears it might suggest fruit that was too old for use. So a reference to a round eggplant, without any additional epithet, just means a mature one, as one would expect. There are, however, other epithets which are applied to eggplants, and these have been translated, as follows:

mak kheua waan on is a sweet, young, round eggplant (not yet ripe)
mak kheua waan noi is the same
mak kheua waan kae is a sweet, round eggplant (not as young as the preceding but still not fully mature)

These round eggplants are most often green in colour, but they may also be found in white, yellow and other hues. Those below left are green. A white variety is shown on page 297.

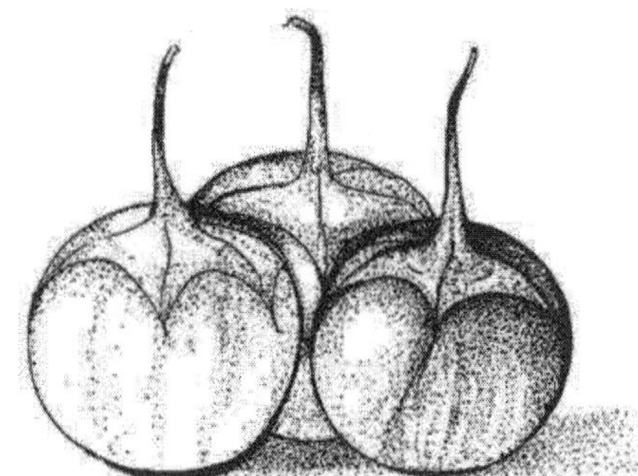

One kind of round eggplant, which has a thinner and hairy skin, is called *mak kheua khuen*. The last word means bitter, in contrast to the sweet varieties referred to above. See the drawing above right.

Mak kheng, sometimes called *mak kheng Thai* (the last word meaning from Thailand), is the very small eggplant, about the size of a cherry or large pea, shown on the right. *Mak kheng khom* is an even smaller variety, and a very bitter one.

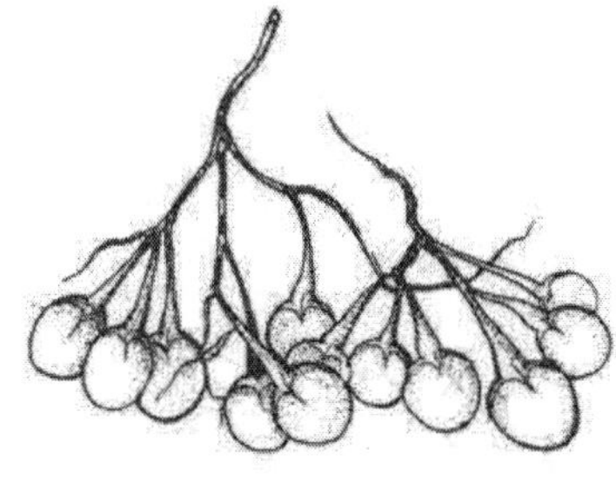

Tomatoes are not indigenous to Laos, but are grown there and have won themselves a place in Lao cookery. The general name for a tomato is *mak kheua khua*, or *mak len*. The adjectives *nyai* and *noi* may be added to indicate large and small. Tomato paste, in cans, is known as *mak kheua bom*. It is not, of course, a traditional ingredient, but Lao cooks have been quick to see its advantages and it appears in some of Phia Sing's recipes.

Chilli and other peppers

Pepper is a thoroughly confusing name. There are four plants, or groups of plants, involved. One (PIPER LONGUM and PIPER OFFICINARUM) bears small fruits called long pepper and need not concern us here (being used neither in Lao nor western cookery). The second, PIPER NIGRUM, is a vine-like plant which bears small round fruits which are what we know as peppercorns. Peppercorns can be either white, green or black, depending on their state of maturity and on the treatment which they have undergone. Phia Sing uses ground black peppercorns in most of his dishes.

The third pepper is the fruit of an annual plant, CAPSICUM ANNUUM. This is what we know as the sweet pepper, the green pepper or the pimento. (The term 'green pepper' is misleading. All fruits of the capsicum peppers are green first and then orange or red later.) It is eaten in Laos, but is of far less importance than the chilli peppers to which we now come.

CAPSICUM FRUTESCENS is a perennial plant, bearing fruits which are smaller and more elongated than those of CAPSICUM ANNUUM. These fruits, which are a beautiful pale jade green when marketed young and fresh, are red when fully ripe, and very dark red when dried. They come in many varieties and sizes. Those common in Laos and their Lao names are as follows:

mak phet dip, fresh chilli peppers, usually still green
mak phet deng, the same, when they have turned red
mak phet nyai, large chilli peppers
mak phet kuntsi, small chilli peppers
mak phet kinou, tiny chilli peppers (*kinou* means rat droppings)
mak phet haeng, dried chilli peppers (always red)
mak phet pun, ground or powdered chilli pepper

Drawings of the three sizes appear below.

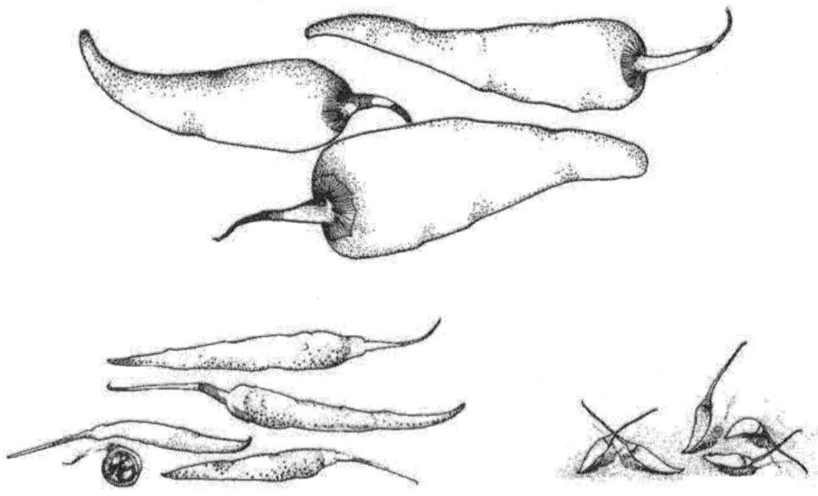

Dried chilli peppers can be prepared for use in two ways. Sometimes Phia Sing directs us to grill them over a charcoal fire until they are crisp and brittle. In other recipes he bids us soak them first in water until they become soft.

Salad leaves, the cabbage family, and other edible leaves

The familiar lettuce, *phak salat*, is often used to provide leaves for wrapping up morsels of food before eating them. Another popular salad leaf, mildly pungent, of the genus PIPER, is known as *phak i leut* and is shown below left. *Bai boua*, lotus leaves, shown below right, are also often used as edible wrapping leaves.

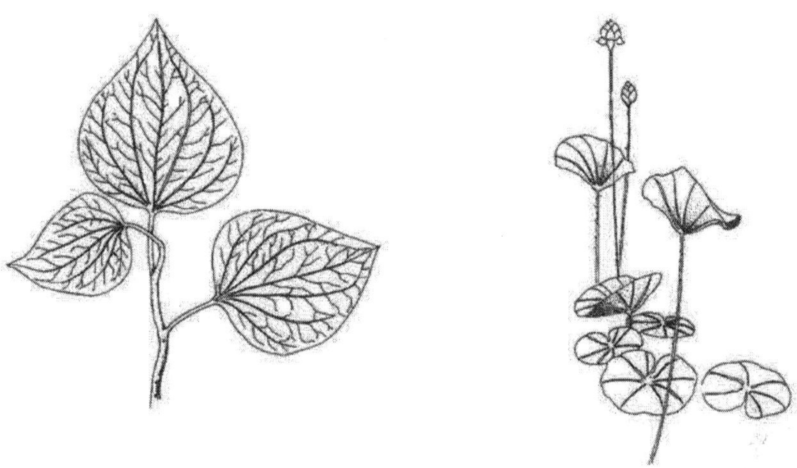

The cabbage family, mainly BRASSICA spp., is well represented in South-East Asia, and some species have a bewildering number of varieties or cultivars. *Phak kad* is the general Lao name for cabbage. *Phak kad kieo* is green cabbage, or mustard greens. The Chinese 'white' cabbage, of which there are many cultivars, is called *phak kad khao*. Its young leaves are shown below left. Beside this drawing is one of BRASSICA JUNCEA var. RUGOSA, sometimes known as Chinese or Swatow mustard. Its Lao name is *phak kad Meo* (the Meo hill tribe, now known as Hmong, being especially partial to it). When pickled, it is *som phak kad Meo*.

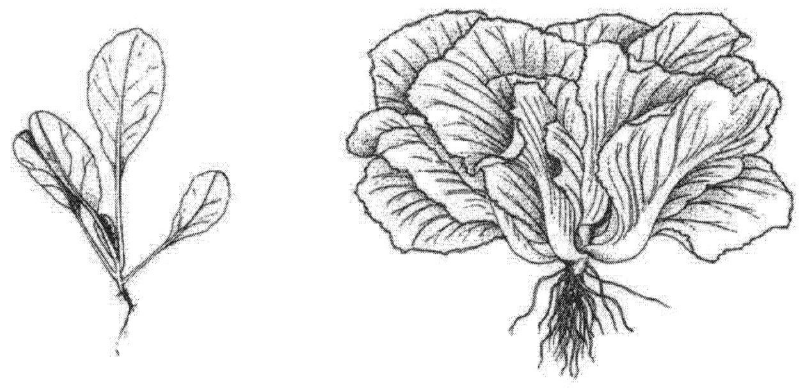

There are many other edible leaves in Laos. Some such as spinach, *phak hum*, are familiar. Incidentally, what is sometimes called water spinach (or swamp cabbage), *phak bong* in Lao, is not related to the true spinach; its scientific name is IPOMOEA AQUATICA, and it is shown below right. Below it is a drawing of *phak kadone*, CAREYA SPHAERICA.

The plant shown below left is *phak hai kai*, CENTIPEDA MINIMA, a leafy vegetable which grows on moist ground such as river banks. Its stem is reddish and its leaves have a bitter taste. Below it is a drawing of ACACIA CONCINNA, known as *som pon* at Luang Prabang. Its leaves impart a sour taste; it is used in soups and for marinating fish before drying them.

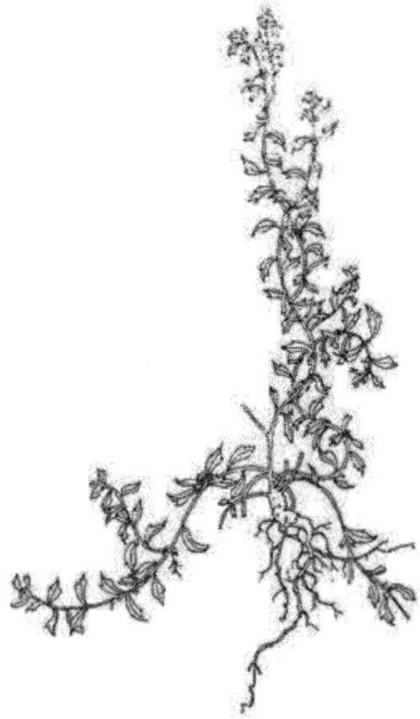

The plant climbing gracefully up the right-hand side of the page is what the Lao call *phak tam ling* (or *phak tam nin*), MELOTHRIA HETEROPHYLLA, whose leaves are eaten. Another climbing plant (not shown) with a rather woody stem is *yanang*, TILIACORA TRIANDRA, whose leaves are often cooked with bamboo, to help rid the latter of its bitter taste.

Another edible leaf, shown on page 233, is *phak khom kadao*, AZADIRACHIRA INDICA.

Phak kan tan, not shown, is a sort of edible broad-bladed grass.

Below right is a drawing of *mak deed*, ARDISIA (?) CRISPA, of which both leaves and fruit are eaten.

Immediately below is a drawing of *phak kaab pi*, COMMELINA COMMUNIS, another edible leaf.

Bon is a plant which exists in more than one form, of which there is a bad, itch-provoking kind known as *bon waan* and several good kinds. See the beginning and end of recipe 17 for the use of bon leaves in Lao cookery. A drawing of *bon waan tao*, COLOCASIA ANTIQUORUM var. ESCULENTUM, the taro plant, appears below left. This is the sweet *bon* referred to in the recipes.

Toon is a plant which belongs to the same family as *bon*, but is larger, the English name being giant taro. There are two species, ALOCASIA MACRORRHIZA and ALOCASIA INDICA. The *toon* eaten in Laos is probably the latter, the leaves of which are shown below right. They are normally used only for wrapping up foods, as in recipe 51B, but their stems may be eaten.

We should also mention *phak sa-ao*, and *waan pai*, mystery plants which we have been unable to identify, but whose leaves are eaten.

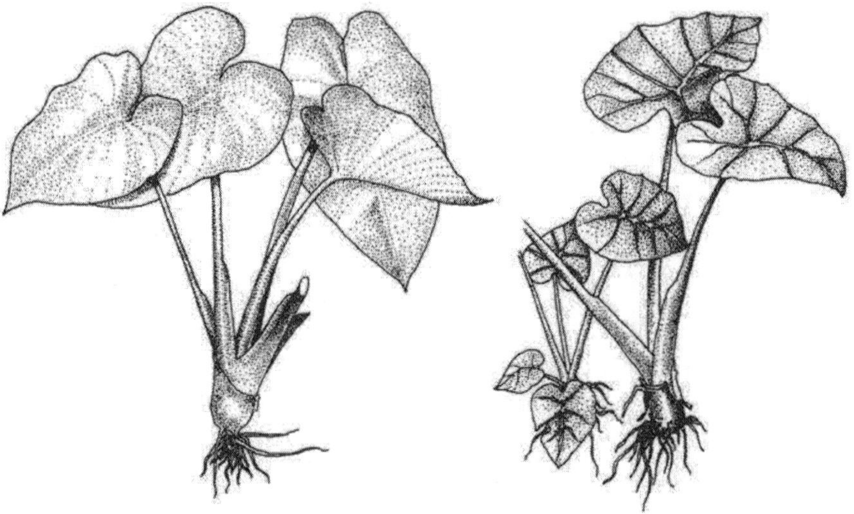

The onion family

ALLIUM CEPA is the scientific name of various onion plants. The general Lao name for these is *phak boua*. The common large onion is known as *phak boua nyai*.

Shallots are used in Lao cookery far more than big onions. The shallots obtainable in Laos are smaller than European or American ones, so a larger number is needed. We have reminded the reader of this in the translations of Phia Sing's recipes. by adding '(small)' before shallots when he specifies a number. The Lao name for the shallot is *hom boua haeng*, or *phak boua houa pom*, or *houa phak boua*. Shallots are always sold dried (hence *haeng* in the first name cited) and have a purplish skin. The dried bulbs of spring onions (see next page), which are sometimes used instead, have a brown skin.

ALLIUM SATIVUM is the familiar garlic, *phak thiem* in Lao. What is said above about the size of shallots applies equally to the size of cloves of garlic. Lao recipes almost always call for dried heads of garlic; but fresh garlic and the leaves of the plant are occasionally used.

A different sort of onion, which we know in the west as the spring onion or scallion, is used in one way or another in most Lao dishes. Spring onions are what you see growing outside almost all Lao houses, often on a little table raised on stilts, as shown on page 302.

The Lao name for the spring onion is *phak boua sot*, or simply *phak boua*. The leaves alone are *bai phak boua*; and the head alone is *houa phak boua*, whether fresh or dried.

A different variety of spring onion, which never develops a rounded bulb, and which is shown on the right, is called *phak boua lai leui* or by the old-fashioned name *phak boua lai leung*. It is cultivated mainly by the Kha (or Lao Tung) tribes, and is well known at Luang Prabang. It is noticeable that in his recipes Phia Sing is always careful to specify it when he thinks it preferable to the ordinary kind.

Bunches of dried spring onions may be seen for sale in Lao markets. As noted on the preceding page, they may be used as a substitute for shallots; but they are commonly sold for replanting. A bunch is shown on the far right.

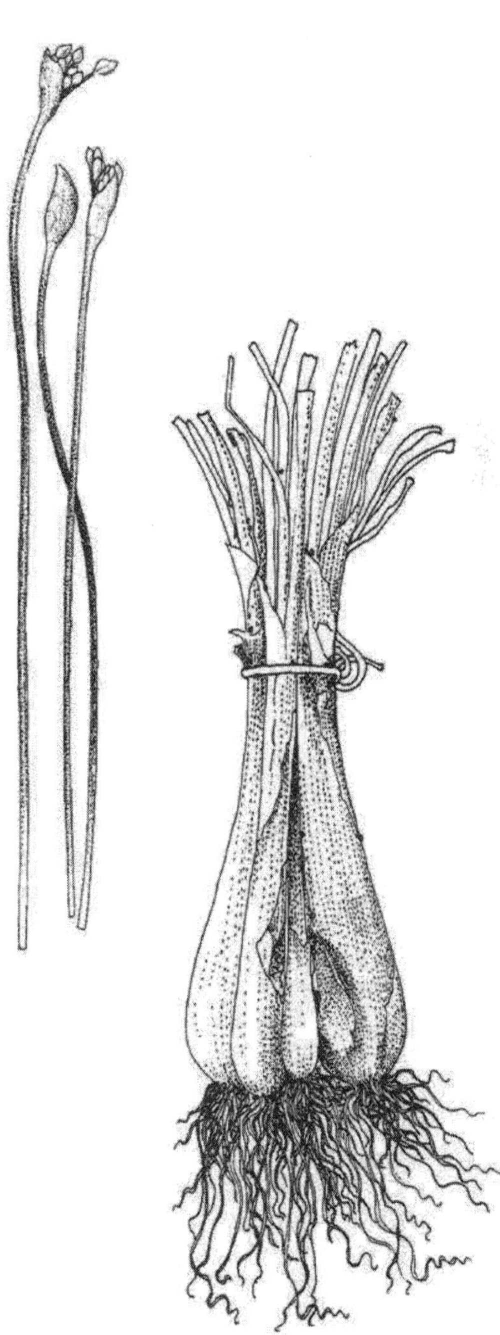

Beans

Mak thua beu is the Lao name for the familiar French or runner bean, usually eaten whole, like mange-tout beans.

The yard-long bean (or long-podded cow bean, as it is sometimes called) is *mak thua nyao* in Lao. Its scientific name is VIGNA UNGUICULATA. It is not often as long as a yard, but it is a very long bean indeed, as the drawing below suggests.

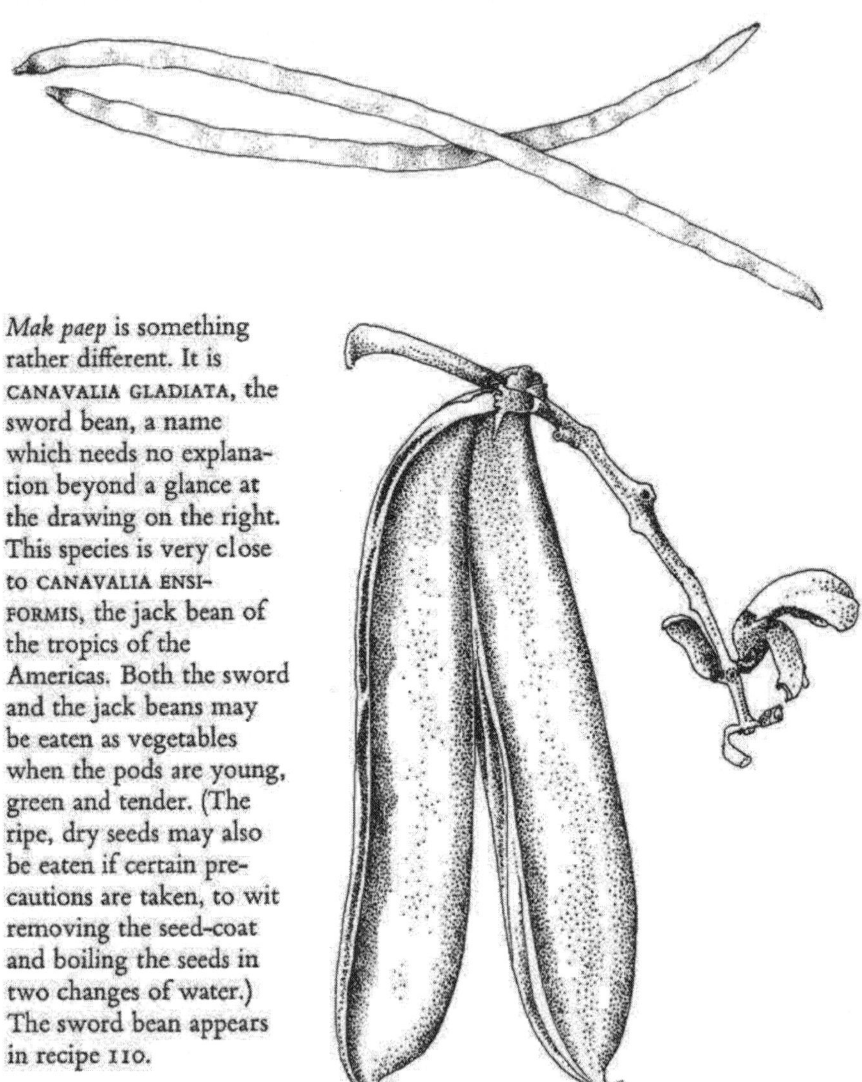

Mak paep is something rather different. It is CANAVALIA GLADIATA, the sword bean, a name which needs no explanation beyond a glance at the drawing on the right. This species is very close to CANAVALIA ENSIFORMIS, the jack bean of the tropics of the Americas. Both the sword and the jack beans may be eaten as vegetables when the pods are young, green and tender. (The ripe, dry seeds may also be eaten if certain precautions are taken, to wit removing the seed-coat and boiling the seeds in two changes of water.) The sword bean appears in recipe 110.

Bean sprouts are usually grown from mung beans and may be bought fresh or canned. The Lao name for them is *mak thua ngork.*

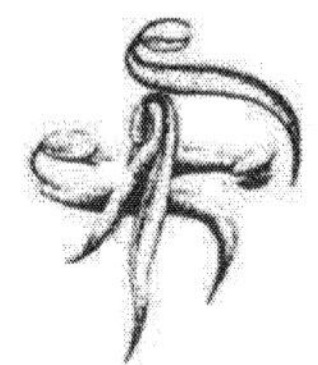

Bamboo and rattan

Three species of bamboo are used as food in Laos:

- GIGANTOCHLEA NIGROCILIATA, *no mai lai,*
- BAMBUSA TULDA, *no mai bong,* and
- DENDROCALAMUS HAMILTONII, *no mai hok.*

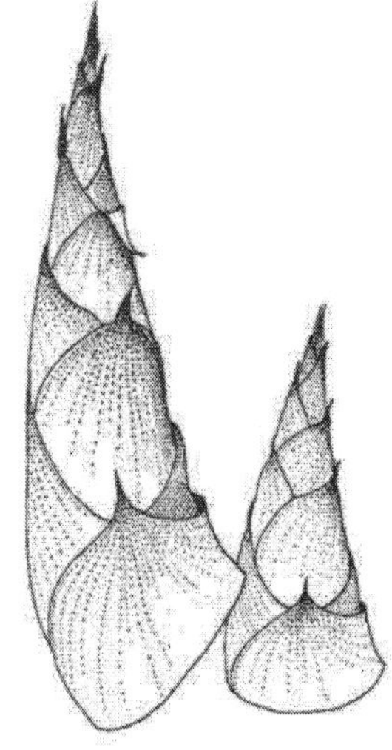

What people eat are the young bamboo shoots, prepared for consumption by being boiled or pickled. *No so* are pickled bamboo shoots which have been chopped fairly finely. *No sae* is the same product, but sliced instead of chopped. *No mai sum* refers to bamboo shoots which have been preserved by chopping them up and storing them dry, with rice and salt, for about a year in large earthenware jars. An alternative technique is to store the chopped shoots wet, in rice-washing water. They keep well either way.

Wick wai is rattan, of the genus CALAMUS. It is shown below left.

Sa-khan is another woody stem, this time with a spicy flavour, which belongs to the genus PIPER. It is shown below right.

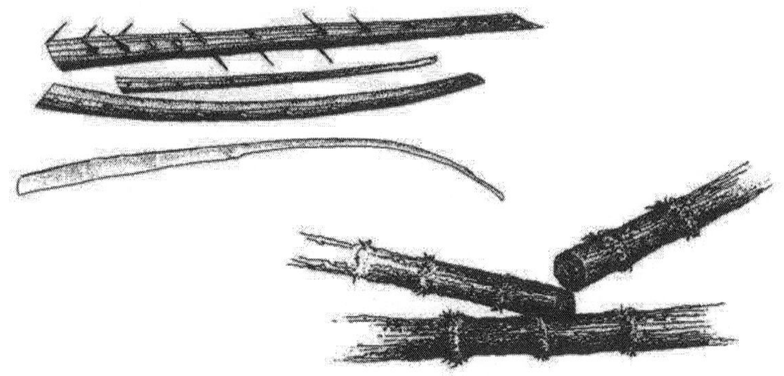

Miscellaneous vegetables

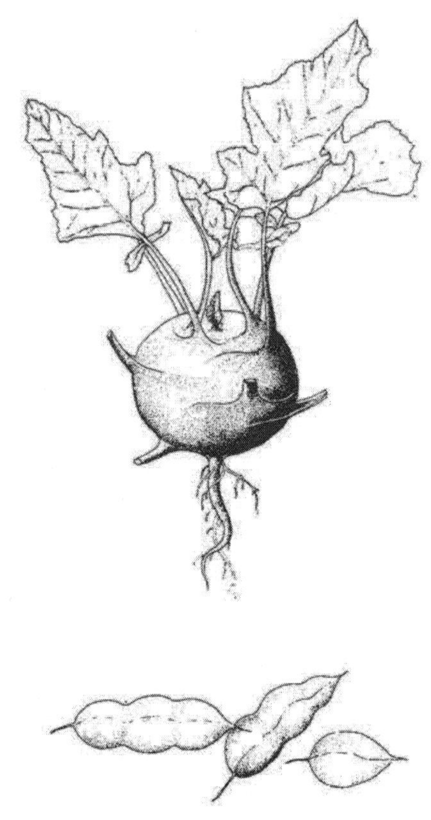

Kohlrabi, BRASSICA OLERACEA var. GONGYLODES, belongs to the cabbage family (page 35) but appears here because it is the swollen root which is usually eaten, rather than the leaves, as with the other family members.

Another swollen root which is eaten is the Chinese (or oriental or giant) radish, *houa phak pheuk* in Lao, RAPHANUS SATIVUS var. LONGIPINNATUS to the scientist. It has become a sufficiently familiar sight in oriental grocery stores to need no illustration here. However, what are less familiar are the seed pods which form on the plant if it is not dug up. The tender young pods, shown on the right, are eaten in Laos as *mak phak poom*, with the hard tips cut off.

In the realm of gourds, the cucumber, CUCUMIS SATIVUS, is a common vegetable in Laos, and more than one variety is available. There is one very small one, used for garnishing; and another which is large and has to be seeded as well as peeled before use. Another familiar kind of gourd, the pumpkin, is used for some Lao desserts. It is called *mak fak kam*, and seems to be of the species HODGSONIA MACROCARPA.

Two other gourds used in Lao cookery are shown below. The upper one is the bottle gourd, *mak bouab*, LAGENARIA SICERARIA; and the lower one is the loofah, *mak noi*, LUFFA ACUTANGULA (the ridged version of a gourd which also occurs as a thin-skinned species, LUFFA CYLINDRICA).

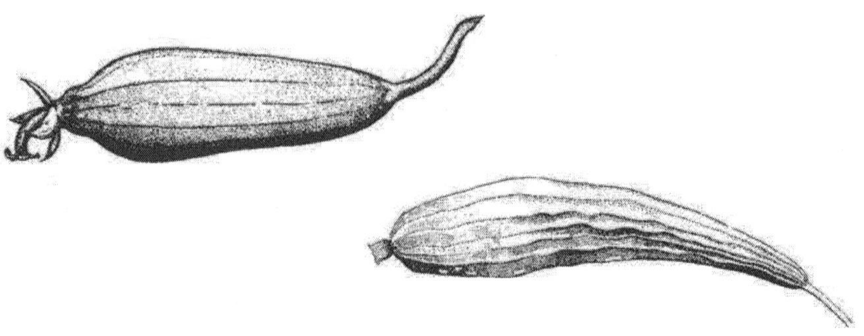

Mushrooms and other edible fungi

It would be impossible here to give a full list of edible fungi in Laos. In *Les plantes utiles du Laos* (1ére Série) Jules Vidal lists dozens and explains how much doubt exists about their scientific classification and vernacular names. Here, however, are the most important nine, six of which fall conveniently into pairs.

Hed khao is the white mushroom, which does not seem to be listed by Vidal, but is commonly eaten. *Hed bod* is a similar mushroom, but pale brown in colour. It appears to be the same as Vidal's *hêt bôt*, which he describes as being common in the Vientiane market in November and for which he gives the scientific name LENTINUS KURZIANUS.

Hed khon is a kind of mushroom which grows on dead, decaying trees or in other damp places. Another rather similar mushroom is *hed pouak*, illustrated below. Both these names have to do with termites' nests. *Khon* refers to the base of such a nest; and *pouak* means termite. The former of these two has been identified by some naturalists as AGARICUS INTEGER. Others would assign both of them to the genus AMARITA or the genus LEPIOTA.

The third 'pair' are *hed sanoun* and *hed huark hai*. The former is commonly known as the jelly mushroom, or Chinese jelly mushroom, since it is a favourite Chinese food and has a jelly-like consistency. (It is usually bought dried, and then soaked in water.) A drawing of it appears on the next page. Another Lao name, *hed hou*, meaning mouse's ear, seems to apply to it. *Hed huark hai* is also a Chinese jelly mushroom, but thicker, which no doubt accounts for the vernacular names *hed hou nou* (rat's ear mushroom) and *hed hou ling* (monkey's ear mushroom). The name *hed huark hai* itself means, literally, mushroom-palate-water-buffalo. The name *hed tan* (flat mushroom) seems also to be applied to the species, and its scientific name appears to be AURICULARIA POLYTRICHA (but there are several species in this genus, not easy to distinguish).

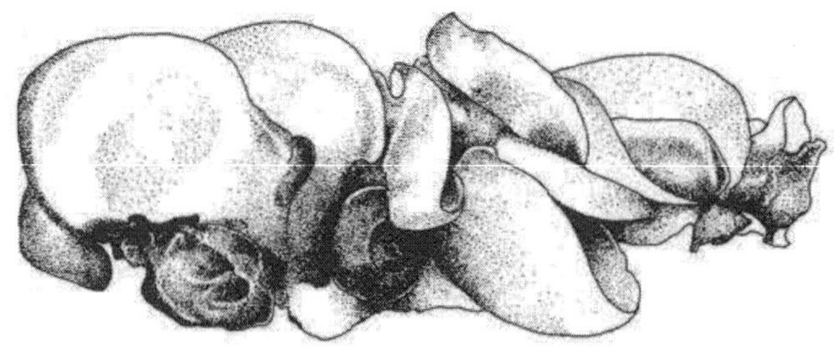

Jelly mushrooms

Hed hom, also known as *hed foun fai*, is the 'fragrance' mushroom. This is another kind which is well known and highly appreciated in China. A drawing of it appears below left. *Hed khaen* is a very small mushroom which grows in clusters. A drawing of it appears below right.

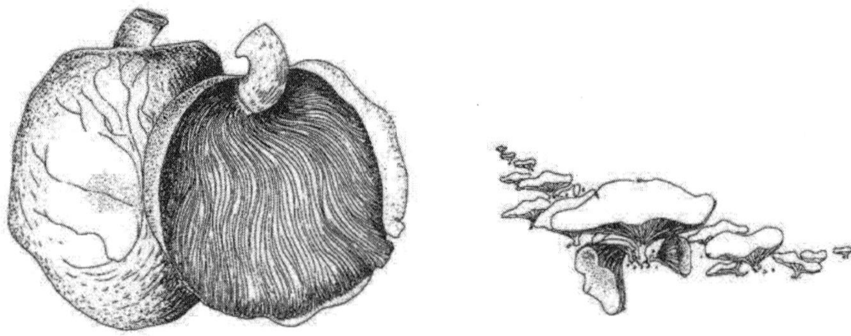

Hed saed is the orange mushroom, one of the species used in Phia Sing's recipes. The illustration below is of it.

Herbs

Ordinary French parsley, PETROSELINUM CRISPUM, has been introduced to Laos and is used, but very little. What the Lao do use in large quantities is coriander, sometimes called 'Chinese parsley'. This plant, CORIANDRUM SATIVUM, is known as *phak hom pom.** Its leaves appear as a garnish in a large number of Lao recipes, and their strong flavour is often too much for Europeans and Americans. (Note, however, that many people who recoil from a dish heavily flavoured with coriander would appreciate it if only a very small quantity of coriander had been added.) Stems and roots may also be used. See the drawing below left.

Dill, ANETHUM GRAVEOLENS, is shown below right. Its Lao name is *phak si*, and it is quite often used in fish cookery. Another species of dill, ANETHUM SOWA, is grown in India and Indonesia, for example; but we believe that what is grown in Laos is always the species already named, which is that of the Near East and Europe.

* The name *phak hom*, sometimes shortened to *hom*, may cause confusion. It is a general name for aromatic herbs and is to be interpreted according to the context as meaning mint, coriander, dill, spring onion, basil etcetera, or a mixture of some of these.

Mint is used in Lao cookery, and there are at least two varieties of MENTHA spp. which grow there, one of which is very close to and possibly identical with the common mint of Europe. It is shown in the upper drawing. Lao names for mint are *phak hom ho* and *phak kankam* (*kan* means stalk and *kam* means darkish). The other mint usually available in Laos is probably a sort of mint-leaved basil, OCIMUM MENTHAEFOLIUM, but we have not been able to establish this definitely.

What is certain is that the genus OCIMUM does provide other plants which are used by Lao cooks. Sweet basil, OCIMUM BASILICUM, is known as *phak itu Lao* and is shown below left. Below centre is OCIMUM GRATISSIMUM, called *phak boua la pha*. It may also be called *phak itu Thai*, as may its relation, OCIMUM SANCTUM, below right.

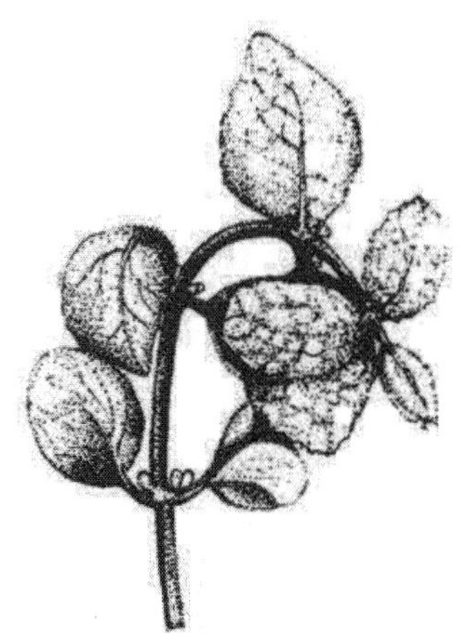

While all these herbs are used, it would be true to say that Lao cookery makes use of a rather limited range of them by comparison with, say, French cuisine. Coriander, mint and basil; and that's about it. The aromatic ingredients which are used to supplement these few herbs are the various forms of *kheuang hom* (page 15) and rhizomes of ginger and kindred plants, to which we now come.

Ginger and Galingale

The ginger plant, ZINGIBER OFFICINALE, is a native of Asia. The parts which are eaten (excepting the flowers, for which see page 32) are the irregular rhizomes, shown in the drawing on the right, which form just below or at the surface of the soil. Fresh ginger is normally used in Lao dishes. When slices of it are specified, these would be about as thick as a large coin. The Lao name for ginger is *khing*; and, in the currency of the spirit world in which many Lao believe, it is gold.

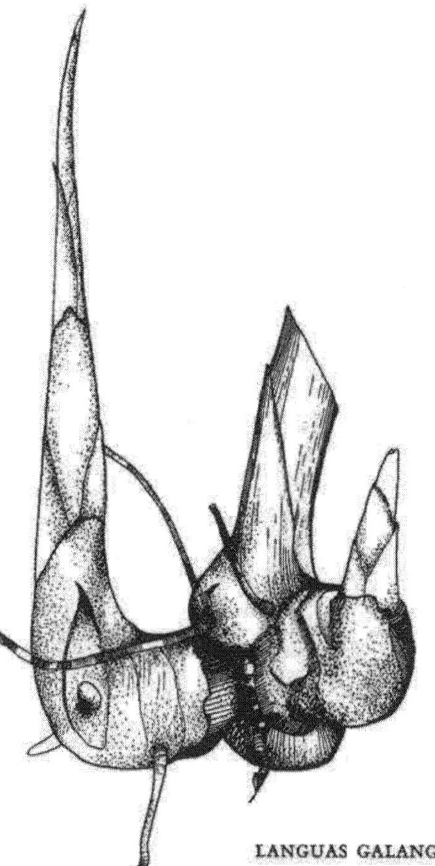

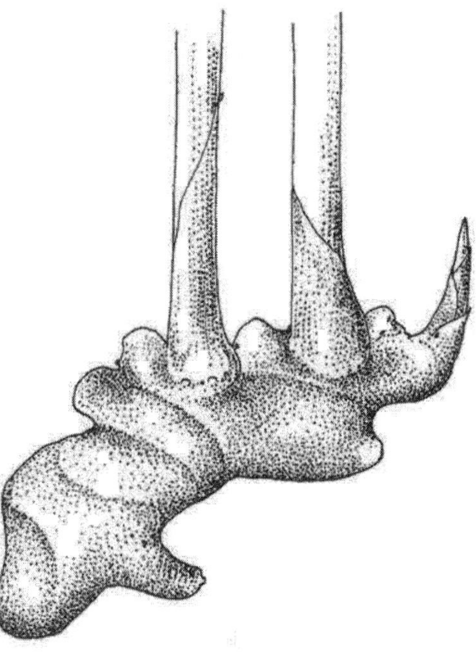

LANGUAS GALANGA (or ALPINIA GALANGA, as it is sometimes known) is galingale (or, to follow older English usage, galangal). As with ginger, it is the rhizomes which are eaten. They are a very popular ingredient in South-East Asia. The Lao name is *kha*, or *kha ta deng* (*deng*, red, refers to the pinkish colour of the base of the old flowering stem). The rhizomes of this plant are a little harder than those of ginger, and have a somewhat different flavour, but are used in the same way. Powdered galingale, as well as the dried rhizomes, are available in the west, often under their Indonesian name of *laos* (which has nothing to do with the country Laos).

Sauces and Relishes (with a note on MSG)

The Lao word for a sauce is *jaew*. That, at least, is one way of representing it in English characters. It is a particularly intractable word for transliteration, and may appear as *tchéo* or *jéo* or in kindred forms.

Phia Sing often says at the end of a recipe what sauce should accompany the dish. The sauce is often an uncooked mixture, which we would be just as likely to call a relish or a dressing. Phia Sing gives recipes for *Jaew Som Mak Nao* (recipe 57B) and for *Jaew Bong* (recipe 64), but otherwise assumes that readers will know how to prepare the sauces. All those to which he simply alludes in this way are explained below.

Jaew Som, one of the basic sauces, is not always made in exactly the same way. As noted above, Phia Sing gives a recipe for one special kind (*Jaew Som Mak Nao*). The basic kind, to be eaten with rice, is made by mixing together pounded garlic, chilli peppers, fish sauce and coriander leaves. If, however, the sauce is to accompany a *phan* dish (e.g. recipes 58, 60 and 77) a small amount of salt might be added instead of the coriander leaves, and pounded roast peanuts might be put in as well.

Nam Jeem, which is a name of Thai rather than Lao origin, is virtually identical with the last kind of *Jaew Som* described above. But it too occurs in various special forms. Thus *Nam Jeem Mak Phet* is a mixture of, say, 6 small chilli peppers (red or green, fresh or dried) and 2 heads of garlic (all of which may first be given the *mok* treatment, page 18, if desired) pounded finely together, with 2 teaspoonfuls of sugar and 2 to 3 tablespoons of fish sauce. *Nam Jeem Mak Phet Deng*, despite its longer title, is simpler; it is just a mixture of fish sauce, to which lime juice may be added, and chopped small fresh red chilli peppers.

Jaew Kapi is made as follows. Sear 2 heads of garlic and 2 shallots in a charcoal fire, then peel them and pound them together with 2 teaspoons of *kapi* (shrimp paste, a product of Thailand) and 8 to 10 small red chilli peppers. Add a tablespoon of fish sauce, the juice of a lime, and 2 teaspoonfuls of sugar. If boiling water is to hand, add a tablespoon of that too.

Jaew Kha is a very hot sauce, named after the Kha tribe, the ethnic group with which it is primarily associated. It is made thus. Cook in a charcoal fire 1 head of garlic, 2 shallots and 5 large (green or red) chilli peppers, then blow the ashes off them and peel the garlic and shallots. Then put all the ingredients in a mortar and pound them fairly finely.

Jaew Mak Phet Dip is the same as *Nam Jeem Mak Phet* (see above), except that the chilli peppers would always be fresh, not dried.

Relishes play the same sort of role as sauces, but are solid or nearly so.

Som moo is a mixture of minced pork and sour ingredients, wrapped in pieces of banana leaf and allowed to mature for several days before consumption.

Som pa keng is a mixture of minced fish (*pa keng* is one of the favourite fish at Luang Prabang, as explained on page 24) with rice and sour ingredients. It is usually prepared in a shallow bowl (*aeng*) and covered with a piece of banana leaf.

. . .

MSG stands for monosodium glutamate, a substance which occurs naturally in various foods. Around the turn of the century it was isolated by scientists and then manufactured synthetically by the Japanese, who gave it the name *aji-no-moto*. They used it as an additive to foods, on the ground that it heightened existing flavours in a pleasing way. The Chinese adopted the new product with enthusiasm and have for long been using it as *vetsin*. It arrived later in western countries, where it has been marketed under brand names such as Accent. Its use as an additive to such products as canned soups is now very widespread, but is controversial, since it seems to have been established that some people suffer bad reactions, collectively known as the 'Chinese restaurant syndrome', if they ingest more than a trace of it. Your editors have encountered this phenomenon sufficiently often to be convinced that it is a real problem, and would not themselves recommend adding MSG to any dish. Nor is it a part of the ancient Lao culinary tradition, since MSG as such did not exist until fairly recent times as a possible ingredient in cookery. Although the Lao have taken to using it (albeit on a much smaller scale than the Chinese, the Vietnamese and the Japanese) it does not occur in Phia Sing's recipes. We suggest that readers who are trying out the recipes should abstain, as he did, from using it as an added condiment.

Lao Measures

Lao cooks do not often use precise measures. They judge the quantity of liquid to be added to a dish, for example, from experience and by eye. But there are Lao measures, and Phia Sing uses them in his recipes. Here they are, with their (approximate) imperial and metric equivalents. The most important are repeated, with the addition where necessary of American measures, on the bookmark which accompanies the book.

LAO	ENGLISH	IMPERIAL	METRIC
kang buang	½ spoonful	(teaspoon)	5 ml
tem buang	1 spoonful	(tablespoon)	15 ml
tem buang keng	1 soupspoonful	(soupspoon)	10 ml
jong (page 17)	ladleful (various)	6 tbsp–½ pint	100–285 ml
jawk	beaker	½ pint	285 ml
jawk kéo nam	glass beaker	½ pint	285 ml
jok	jug	1 pint	570 ml
jok kateun	medium-sized jug	⅞ pint	500 ml
jok noi	small jug	¾ pint	425 ml
jok lik	metal jug	1 pint	570 ml
jok tong	bronze jug	1 pint	570 ml
tuay	bowl (various)		
tuay kateun	medium-sized bowl	⅝ pint	350 ml
tuay keng noi	small soupbowl	½ pint	285 ml
tuay keng (page 163)	soupbowl	¾ pint	425 ml
tuay keng nyai	large soupbowl	1¼ to 1½ pints	700–850 ml
*tuay mak toom**	ricebowl	¼ pint	140 ml
tuay mak toom noi	small ricebowl	6 to 7 tbsp	90–105 ml
khai ped	duck's egg	4 to 5 tbsp	60–75 ml
khai kai	hen's egg	3 tbsp	45 ml

Miscellaneous

kaang, used of ginger, for example in recipe 105, is not a measure—it means a single rhizome of the plant

na, used of rice vermicelli, means a 'layer', as sold in the market (see page 22), which is about ½ kilo of just over 1 lb

* So-called because it is about the size of a scooped-out *mak toom* fruit (see page 51).

THE RECIPES OF PHIA SING

ປື້ມຄົວກິນລາວຂອງເພັຽສິງ

Mak toom fruit

1= ໄກ່ແກງຮ້ອນເຂົ້າປຸ້ນຈີນ ສຳລັບ ໑໐

ເຄື່ອງປະສົມ

ໄກ່ ປອກໜັງອອກ ເຈາະໃສ່ລາງ ຕົ້ມໃສ່ສະອາດ ແລ້ວ ໑ ໂຕ
ເອັນໄກ່ຄ່ອງ ຕາມລ້າງສະອາດ ແລ້ວສ່ວນ ຍາວ
໑ ຊົ່ວ ແມ່ວກາຄານນີ້ ຜັກບົ່ວປອກ ແລ້ວ ໑ ຖ້ວຍນ້ຳ
ປາ ນ້ຳກ້ອງ ນາກ ຕຳ ໃຫ້ສະອາດ ແລ້ວ ໑ ຕົວ ມັນເຜືອກ
ປອກລ້າງ ນາກ ສະອາດ ຊອຍໃສ່ຈານ ເມັດກາລາ ເຄື່ອງ ໑ ຖ້ວຍ
ຖົ່ວ ໃສ່ ສອງ ນ່ອງ ປົ່ນ ແລ້ວ ຫຼືຍາວ ສອງ ຊອງ ໃສ່ ໃຫ້ ແລບ
ໃສ່ຈານໄວ້ . ເສັ້ນຫອນສອນ ດອກ ຕຳ ນ້ຳ ໃສ່ ໃສ່ຈານ ໃຊ້
ໃບຜັກບົ່ວ ໃສ່ພໍ ສວນ ຜັກຫອມ ໃສ່ພໍ ຄວນ ເກືອ ນ້ຳປາ
ພໍຄວນ ຜັກບົ່ວໃບ ມີຫົວພ້ອມ ຊອຍໄວ້
ຮວມຜັກຫອມ ຂ້າງ ນີ້ . ເຂົ້າປຸ້ນຈີນ ຕຳ ນ້ຳ ຊຸບ ແລ້ວ ໑ ຊົ່ວ

ວິທີປະສົມ – ເມື່ອເຮົາ ທາງ ເຄື່ອງ ແພງ ການນີ້ ແລ້ວ ຕໍ່ ແລ້ວ
ຈຶ່ງເອົາ ໝໍ້ ຂຶ້ນ ຕັ້ງໄຟ ເອົານ້ຳ ໃສ່ ປະມານ ລິໂຈກ
ເຄິ່ງ ແລ້ວ ເອົາ ເກືອ ພໍຄວນ ຜັກບົ່ວ ທັງ ຫົວ ແລະ
ໃບ ຮາກ ຜັກຫອມ ໃສ່ ລົງໄປ ຕາມ ໃນ ຈົນເດືອດ ຈຶ່ງ ເອົາ ໄກ່
ທີ່ ລ້າງ ສະອາດ ແລ້ວ ນັ້ນ ໃສ່ລົງໄປ ຕົ້ມ ພໍ ສຸກ ຕາມ ໃນ ຈະ
ໃຫ້ ເປື່ອຍ ພໍ ສົມ ຄວນ ແລ້ວ ຈຶ່ງ ຍົກ ລົງ , ແກະ ເອົາ ໄກ່
ອອກ ໃສ່ ຈານ ໄວ້ ແລ້ວ ເອົາ ແຕ່ ນ້ຳ ອັນ ມາ ຈັກ ໃຫ້
ເປັນ ເສັ້ນ ໃສ່ ຈານ ໄວ້ ສ່ວນ ນ້ຳ ຕອງ ໃຫ້ ສະອາດ ຍົກ
ເອົາ ຂຶ້ນ ຕັ້ງ ໃສ່ ໄຟ ແລ້ວ ນ້ຳປາ ໃສ່ ຫົວ ຜັກບົ່ວ ປອກ

ເຄື່ອງ ... ເຕົ້າ ສອງ ໃສ່ ເມື່ອ ຫົວ ຜັກ ສຸກ ແລ້ວ ຈຶ່ງ ເອົາ ມັນ
ປອກ ແລະ ຈຸລີ ໃສ່ ເຂົ້າ ປຸ້ນ ຈີນ ປາ ນ້ຳ ໃສ່ ສ່ວນ ແລ້ວ ວຸ້ນ ເສັ້ນ
ແກງ ຈາກ ການ ໂຈ ຊຸບ ແລ້ວ ເຖິງ ລາ ເອົາ ໃສ່ ໃສ່ ໝໍ້ ໃສ່ ຖ້ວຍ
ແລ້ວ ເອົາ ຜັກ ຫົວ ຜັກ ຫອມ ແພງ ນີ້ ໃສ່ ເຫັດ ພິກ ເມັ່ນ ຄື ໃຫ້
ມີ ທາງ ສູບ ແລ້ວ ທາະບີ ./.

ໝາຍເຫດ – ຢານີ້ຈະແກ້ ແກງ ຮ້ອນ ຈູ ນີ້ ພູມ ສ່ວນ ເຄື່ອງ ປະສົມ
ມັນ ກໍ ຄື ກັນ ຕາງ ແຕ່ ຕາງ ໃຊ້ ການ ພາສາ ໃຫ້ ຫຼາຍ ວຸ້ນ
ເສັ້ນ ລວມ ນີ້ ເພື່ອ ຈະ ກິນ ເອົາ ມາ ຈຸ້ມ ເປັນ ວຸ້ນ ແກງ ນອກ
ນັ້ນ ແມ່ນ ເພື່ອ ກັນ ທັງ ໝົດ ແຕ່ ລະ ອັນ ບໍ່ ພາ ໄລ ໃຊ້ ເຄື່ອງ
ຫຼາຍ ຢ່າງ ສະອາດ ເປັນ ສອງ ເພາະ ວ່າ ນີ້ ຕ້ອງ ຮີບ ແລ້ວ ເອົາ
ຕຳ ການ ເຊື້ອ ໃຫ້ ໝູ ກ່ອນ

Kai Keng Khao Poon Chin **Recipe 1**

HOT CHICKEN SOUP WITH CHINESE VERMICELLI

Ingredients

1 chicken, washed and gutted
1 small rice-bowl (4 tbsp) of jelly mushrooms (see page 43), washed and sliced lengthwise
1 small rice-bowl (i.e. about 4 to 5) shallots, peeled
1 dried squid, soaked and washed, beaten to soften it, and sliced thinly
1 bowl (i.e. 3 to 4 large) potatoes, washed and peeled and cut into cubes of 0.5 cm
2 hen's eggs—make them into a thin omelette, fold the omelette, cut it into strips of 2 cm, then slice the strips thinly, lengthwise
3 fragrance mushrooms (page 44), soaked and thinly sliced
spring onion, the green parts only, chopped
coriander leaves, chopped
salt, fish sauce, ground black pepper
1 whole spring onion, bulb included
3 bunches of coriander roots
1 rice-bowl Chinese vermicelli, soaked and cut up

Method

After preparing all the above ingredients, put a soup pot on the fire. In it put three metal jugfuls (3 pints) of water. Add a sprinkle of salt, the whole spring onion and the coriander roots. Place the lid on the pot and leave it until the contents come to the boil. Then put the whole chicken into the pot. Keep the lid on and leave it until the chicken is well cooked.

Take the pot off the fire. Remove the chicken to a platter. Take off the breast meat only, shred this and put it on a plate.

Pour the broth through a strainer. Place the pot of strained broth back on the fire and leave it until it comes to the boil. Then add the fish sauce, shallots and mushrooms. When the shallots are cooked, add the potatoes, the shredded chicken breast, Chinese vermicelli and squid. When all these are cooked, taste and check the saltiness. Take the pot off the fire and add the sliced omelette.

Serve the soup in a bowl and garnish it with the chopped spring onion leaves and coriander leaves, and the ground black pepper. Serve with *Jaew Kapi* (see page 48).

Notes

If you wish to make *Keng Hon Sin Moo* (Hot soup with pork) you would need the same ingredients (but substituting pork for chicken). The difference in preparation is that a lot of pork bones should be used to make the broth; and in addition there should be slices of pork to put in the soup. The rest of the method is the same.

One must not be too lavish in adding other ingredients, or else the dish will turn into an *Or* (see page 18). If it is called a *Keng*, this means that we want to eat the soup more than the meat.

໒໕ ແກງປາໃສ້

ເຄື່ອງປະສົມ

ໝາກຍມສົບ ໝາກມັນ ຂອງລາວ ໃບກ້ອນ ລາວ ໝາກກະຫຼ້ຳ ຕົ້ນອົບ ທີ່ການສົ້ມ ຫອມ – ປາທີ່ໃຈອັກ ເຄືອ ໑ ກ້ຽນນັ້ນ ຕົວເຜັດ ຫົວປລົ້ກ ໑ ກ້ຽນນັ້ນ ເຫຼືອ ເນື້ອ ຄ້າວງູ ຕາມີ ສະຫຼາ ມູ ເຄືອ ຈາກ ກ້ຽນນັ້ນ ໃຫ້ໄກ່ ສາມນ້ຽ ປາມ ເຄື່ອງ ຫຼັງຍາວ ສອງ ວຽງ ໃບກ້ ຕລອງ ໃຈ ຈານ ໃຫ້ ໃບເຜັດ ບົວ – ໃບເຜັດ ຫອມລາ, ໃບຮົ້ນ ສານໃບ ລູ ໃຫ້ຕົ່ງ ເຜັດ ນ້ຳປ່ນ ລາວ ມາກປາ ເຜັດ ຫົວ ລຽງ ເລື້ອ ຫົວ ຄົ້ນ ເຜັດປາຈານ ສາງ ນ້ຳ. ຕົ້ວ ປຸ່ນ ຈົນ ແກ່ແລ້ວ ~~…~~ ໝາ ໃຫ້ສັ້ນ ໑ ກ້ຽນນັ້ນ

ວິທີເຮັດ

ຍັງທີ່ນຳ ແກງ ຕົ້ກ ໄຟ ລາວ ນຳ ໃຈ ປະມານ ສາມ ໃຈ ສະໝຸກ ເຄືອ ລາວ ລາວ – ເຜັດ ຫົວ ລາງ ເລື້ອ ເຜັດ ປາມ ເກື້ອ ວາກ ຄາ ແລະ ໃຫ້ ໃຈ ໝີ້ ນຳ ຜູ້ ເຄິ່ງ ຈາ ລາວ ໝາກ ຫາ ກ ລາ ສະຫຼາ ເຄືອ ໃຈ ໝູ ເປົາ ຕຳ ມີ ຕົ້ງ ໃປ ຈົນ ຄກ ໃຈ ຈາກ ວິ ມີ ຈູ ປາ ລາ ທາວ ຕົ້ນ ລອກ ຕອງ ລາວ ແກ່ ນຳ ໃສ ກ້ າ ມີ ສັ ກ ໃຫ້ ສົ ປ ໜອ ຈົນ ມູ ເຄື່ອງ ຫຼູ ຄືນ ລາກ ກຸ ອກ ໃຈ ນັ້ນ ແກງ ຍັງ ຄູ ມີ ຕົ້ກ ໄຟ ລາວ ຫົວ ເຜັດ ຫົວ ປລົ້ກ ເຫຼືອ ເນື້ອ ຄ້າວງູ ນຳ ປາ ໃຈ ນໍ ຫົວ ເຜັດ ຫົວ ລີ້ງ ຈົ່ງ ລາວ ເຂົ້າ ປຸ່ນ ຈົນ ໃຈ ນໍ ສາ ຈູ ມີ ເລົ້າ ຄາວ ອ ກ ຕານ ຈູ ມ ປາ ລາ ລາວ ໄກ່ ລູ ໃອ ~~…~~

ແລະ ປາທີ່ໃຈອັກ ເຄືອ ໃຈ ກາມ ໃຫ້ ຫົວ ຕົວ ໃຈ ກ້ຽນ ລາວ ຫອມ ລາ ເຜັດ ບົວ ເຜັດ ນ້ຳ – ໃບ ຫົ້ວ ຍັງ ເລື້ອ ຕຳ ໃຫ້ ຍັງ ນາ ກ ນ ຕາ ໑໐ ນາ ທີ ແລະ ເຜັດ ທາງ ຕ່າງໆ ໆ.

Keng Pa Sai **Recipe 2**

CLEAR FISH SOUP

Ingredients

pork bones, trimmed of any fat and washed
1 small rice-bowl (i.e. about 200 g) grilled fish, deboned
1 small rice-bowl (i.e. about 4 to 5) shallots, peeled
½ small rice-bowl (i.e. about 2 tbsp) jelly mushrooms (see page 43), cleaned, boiled and sliced
2 hen's eggs—make them into a thin omelette, then fold the omelette, cut it into strips of 2 cm, slice the strips thinly lengthwise and put them on a plate
spring onion, the green parts, chopped
coriander leaves, chopped
3 Kaffir lime leaves, finely chopped with a knife
ground black pepper, salt and fish sauce
6 straight-bulbed spring onions
2 bunches coriander (1 bunch consists of 2 or 3 sprigs)
1 small rice-bowl Chinese vermicelli, soaked in water and cut up small

Method

Put 3 metal jugfuls (3 pints) of water in a soup pot. Place the pot on the fire. Add salt, the 6 spring onions, and the bunches of coriander leaves with their roots. When the water boils, add the pork bones and put the lid on the pot. Leave it until the bones are cooked sufficiently for the meat to fall off them. Take the pot off the fire and spoon out the meat. If there is still any fat left, cut it all off.

Strain the broth and return it to the pot. Add the meat and return the pot to the fire. Add the shallots, the jelly mushrooms and the fish sauce. When the shallots are cooked, add the Chinese vermicelli. When all is done, taste and check the saltiness.

Take the pot off the fire. Add the prepared strips of omelette and the dried fish. Serve in a bowl and garnish with the chopped spring onion leaves, the chopped coriander leaves, the finely chopped Kaffir lime leaves and the ground black pepper. Accompany the dish with *Jaew Kapi* (see page 48) and fried vegetables.

ຈີ: ແກງກະລໍາປີຈີນ

ເຄື່ອງປະສົມ

ຊີ້ນໝູມີມັນບໍ່ຫຼາຍ ໃຫ້ສັບລີ້ ທຸບກໍ້ສີ່-ຫ້າ ແກ້ວ ກາບສາມ ຫອມ ຜັກບົ່ວລາບຕົ້ນ ຫົວຜັກທຽມ ຜັກຫອມສອງຕົ້ນ ຜັກຫົວ ຫົວປະກາ ແກ່ວ ປລອງ ຍາວ ໑໐ ຫົວ ຈຸ້ມີຫາ ແລ ເມັດໃຫ້ຄົ້ນ ທໍ່ບ່ວງ ໃຊ້ຝ້າໃຫຍ່ ຫົວຜັກກະລໍາປີໃຫ້ຄາຍ ດອກອ່ອນ ຕົວ ແຕກໃຫຍ່ ໃບຜັກຫອມ ຜັກຢ່າປັ້ນ ແລ້ວນໍ້າປາ ໃສ່ໃຫ້ ຮອງນ່ອງ.

ວິທີທໍາ – ເອົາໝໍ້ໃສ່ນໍ້າຕາມປະສົງ ໃຈການເລີຍຈື່ໃຫ້ ໃຫ້ ແລ້ວ ເອົາຊີ້ນໝູ ເປົ່ານຶ່ງ ຜັກບົ່ວ ເລົ້າ ທີ່ປາງ ໃສ່ໃຫ້ສຸກ ເມື່ອແລ້ວໄປຈົບດຸກ ໂຮ່ຍ ລາກລູ້ ຈ້າງບ້ານ ໃຕ້ ບ່ວງ ບໍ່ໃຫ້ມີ ດາຍໄຈ ຕົ້ມແລ້ວ ເອົາມາໃສ່ໝໍ້ ແກງໃຫ້ຍໍ່ນໍ້າເດືອດ ແລ້ວເອົາ ກະລໍາປີຜັກ ຫົວໃນຜັກບົ່ວ – ນໍ້າປາ. ຈຸ້ມີຫາ ຜັກ ເອົາ ຂອງທີ່ຕາກໄວ້ ໃຫ້ສົມຕ່ອນເປັນ ພໍ້ຜັກເປື່ອຍ ຈຸ້ມີເບິ່ງ ການຈາງ ລາກຈູບ ແລ້ວເຖິງໃສ່ໄຫ້ໄດ້ ລາ ໄດ້ໃສ່ແຕ່ງ ແລ້ວຕັກໃສ່ຖ້ວຍ ໂຮຍຜັກບົ່ວ ແລະ ຜັກຫອມ ໃນໜ້າ ພ້ອມໃສ່ໃຫ້ຫຼາຍ %.

Keng Kalampi Jak **Recipe 3**

CHOPPED CABBAGE SOUP (WITH MINCED PORK)

Ingredients
pork bones, washed and trimmed of all fat
6 straight-bulbed spring onions
2 bunches coriander
10 (small) shallots, peeled and sliced
minced pork, the red meat only, a quantity equivalent to a duck's egg (4 to 5 tbsp)
1 large soup bowl (capacity about 1½ pints) sliced cabbage
coriander leaves, finely chopped
ground black pepper, salt, fish sauce
2 hen's eggs

Method
Put 2 metal jugfuls (2 pints) of water in a pot. Put the pot on the fire. Put the prepared bones, the spring onions, the coriander and salt in the pot, cover it and leave it to boil until the meat separates from the bones. Take the pot off the fire. Strain the soup, return it to the pot and put it back on the fire. Let it come back to the boil, then add the cabbage, the shallots and fish sauce. Use a fork to add in the minced pork a little at a time. When the vegetables are cooked, taste and check the saltiness. Break the hen's eggs into the soup and stir to mix them in.

Serve the soup in a bowl, garnished with the chopped coriander leaves and the ground black pepper.

43 ເອາະຫຼາມມັນຕົ້ນ

ເຄື່ອງປະສົມ

ມັນຕົ້ນ ຊີ້ນປີ້ງຊີ້ນລາວ ໑ ຫໍ່ ຈະກີເປັນຕ່ອນການສ່ວນ
ອື່ນໆ ແລະ ຂາວ ລ້າງນ້ຳໃຫ້ສະອາດ ໃສ່ຈານໄວ້ ໝາກ
ເຂືອຫອມທັງອ່ອນ ຂີ້ນ່ອຍ ໝາກເຜັດໃຫຍ່ ຂີ້ນ່ອຍ
ສີໄຄ ໑ ຫົວ ຜັກບົ່ວລຶ້ງເຄີ້ງ ລີທີມ ຂີດ ແລ້ວ
ມີ ຍ່າ ຂອມີລ້າງນ້ຳໃຫ້ສະອາດ ສະຄ່ານ ເຖົ່າຈະກີ
ຕາງ ອອກ ຢູ່ ຍາວ ຂີ້ ຊີດ ແລ້ວພ່າເປັນສີ່ ໝາກຊີດ
ປະມານ ໑໐ ທ່ອນ ລ້າງນ້ຳ ຍອດທອງ ມີ ຍອດ
ຜັກ ໃບສວກ ແລ້ວ ປາກ ເອົາ ແຕ່ຍອດອ່ອນ ຍາວສຶກ
ຊີດ ລ້າງນ້ຳ ຜັກຕຳລຶງ ເອົາ ແຕ່ ໃບ ແລະ ຍອດ

ການປຸງແຕ່ງ — ~~ຫມີ~~ ລ້າງນ້ຳ ຜັກຊີ ລ້າງນ້ຳ ແລ້ວ ຍ່ ເປັນ
ທ່ອນ ຍາວ ສີ່ ຊີດ ~~ລ້າງນ້ຳ~~ ໃບ ຜັກບົ່ວ ຍ່ ຍາວ ສີ່ ຊີດ ລ້າງນ້ຳ
ຜັກອີ່ຕູ່ ເອົາ ແຕ່ ໃບ ພໍ ຄວນ ລ້າງນ້ຳ . ໝູ່ ນົ່ມ ຮອນ
໑ ທ່ອນ ຍ່ ເປັນ ຕ່ອນ ປີ້ງ ຊີດ ໃສ່ ຖ້ວຍ ໄວ້ ປາແດກ ແລ້ວ
ໝາກ ຫອ ຕົ້ມ ເສີ່ງ ໃຈ ຜັກ ຍ່ ຍາວ ສີ່ ຊີດ ລ້າງນ້ຳ

ວິທີເຮັດ — ເອົາ ນ້ຳ ໃສ່ ໝໍ້ ເອາະ ສອງ ໂຈກ ຍົກ ຂຶ້ນ ຕັ້ງ ໄຟ
ແລ້ວ ເອົາ - ມັນຕົ້ນ - ໝາກເຂືອ - ໝາກເຜັດ - ຜັກບົ່ວ ລຶ້ງເຄີ້ງ
ສີໄຄ - ສະຄ່ານ - ເຄື່ອງ - ຊີ້ນປີ້ງ ໃສ່ ລົງ ພ່າ ຕາມ ໄປ ຕົ້ມ ແລ້ວ
ໃຫ້ ເອົາ ປາແດກ ຕອງ ໃສ່ ພໍ ຄວນ ຖ້າ ໝາກເຜັດ ໝາກ
ເຂືອ ເປື່ອຍ ແລ້ວ ຕັກ ອອກ ມາ ຕຳ ໃຫ້ ແຫຼກ ແລ້ວ ຕັກ ຄືນ
ໃສ່ ໝໍ້ ເອາະ ພໍ ຟົດ ໃຫ້ ເອົາ ຜັກຕຳລຶງ ໝາກ ທ່ອ ຕົ້ມ ເສີ່ງ
ໃສ່ ພໍ ເຫັນ ວ່າ ຜັກ ສຸກ ທີ່ ເອົາ ໝູ່ ນົ່ມ ຜັກຊີ ອີ່ຕູ່
ໃສ່ ຊີ້ນ ເປື່ອຍ ແກ້ ນ້ຳ ຕາມ ຄວາມ ຊອບ ແລ້ວ ຕັກ ໃສ່ ຖ້ວຍ ຜັກ
ບົ່ວ ໂຮຍ ໜ້າ ເພື່ອ ຕົກ ແຕ່ງ ໃຫ້ ງາມ ກິນ ກັບ ໝາກ ແຕງ ອ່ອນ ແລະ
ໝາກ ເຂືອ ແລະ ຜັກ ຕ່າງໆ %.

ໝາຍເຫດ — ເອາະຫຼາມນີ້ຈະເອົາຊີ້ນກະບືອ ຊີ້ນລາວ ແລ້ວ
ໃສ່ນ້ຳກໍໄດ້ ຖ້າບໍ່ມີ ຊອຍ ທີ່ ແຕ່ງ ຜັກ
ຕ່າງໆ ກໍ ເພີ່ມ ຈະ ຕົ້ມ ໃສ່ ກໍ ໄດ້ ແຕ່ ຄວນ ລະວັງ ຢ່າ
ໃຫ້ ຫຼາຍ ຄວນ ເພາະ ບໍ່ ມີ ກິ່ນ ຫອມ ຄືກັບ ເອາະ ມັນ
ຕົ້ນ ຈະ ເປັນ ເອາະ ຊີ້ນ ຫຼື ເອາະ ຜັກ ໄປ

Or Lam Nok Kho **Recipe 4**

QUAIL STEW

Ingredients

1 dried quail, matured until almost mouldy, divided into separate breast and leg parts, washed and put on a plate

7 round eggplants (see page 33)

5 large fresh green chilli peppers }
1 stalk lemon grass } all washed
3 straight-bulbed spring onions }

sa-kahn (an aromatic plant, used in stews—see page 41), cut into pieces about 5 cm long and 1 cm thick—about 10 pieces—washed

3 young shoots rattan, cooked by being placed directly on a charcoal fire and peeled so as to leave only the soft part, which is to be cut into pieces 2 cm long and washed

1 bunch *phak tam nin* (an edible leaf, see page 37), picked over, keeping only the leaves and tops, which are to be washed

dill, washed and cut into pieces about 2 cm long

spring onion, the green parts, cut into pieces about 2 cm long and washed

sweet basil leaves, washed

1 piece of crisp-fried pork skin, cut into squares of 1 cm and put on a plate

padek (page 23)

salt

2 yard-long beans, cut into pieces about 2 cm long

Method

Put 2 metal jugfuls (2 pints) of water in a pot and place it on the fire. Add the prepared bird, the eggplants, the chilli peppers, the spring onions, the lemon grass, the *sa-kahn* and salt. Cover and let it boil. Add the *padek* in a padek basket suspended in the soup. When the eggplants and the chilli peppers are done, spoon them out and pound them. Put this mixture back in the pot. When it returns to the boil add the *phak tam nin* and the yard-long beans. When all is done, add the pieces of pork skin and the chopped coriander leaves, taste and check the saltiness.

Serve in a bowl, garnished with the chopped spring onion leaves. Accompany the dish with young cucumbers and older eggplants and other fresh vegetables (e.g. salad leaves, watercress, etc.).

Note

In cooking this *Or Lam*, you can also add *Duk Moo Sam La* (pork bones which have been kept for some time in the broth) if you fear that it will not be '*nua*' (flavoursome enough).

You may also add other kinds of vegetables (when you are cooking the stew), but be careful not to use too many because the *Or Lam Nok Kho* will then turn into *Or Moo* (Pork stew) or *Or Phak* (Vegetable stew).

ຈະໄກ່ພັ່ງຈີ

ເຄື່ອງປະສົມ — ໄກ່ປອກ ໑ ໂຕ ຈັກເອົາສອງຈີ້ສອງວາງອອກ
ສ່ວນຂາໃຫຍ່ ແຫ້ກຕາມຂໍ້ ຕໍ່ອອກ ເປັນສອງທ່ອນ ແລ້ວ
ແຫ້ກ ຕາມຂໍ້ ຫົວເຈົ້າອອກ ສ່ວນປີກ ປາຍປີກໃຫ້ແຫ້ກ
ອອກຕາມຂໍ້ ຕໍ່ຄືກັນ ແຕ່ງປີກ ໃຫ້ເປັນສອງທ່ອນ
ແລະຄອ ຫົວ ກໍໃຫ້ຍູ້ເປັນຕ່ອນໃຫຍ່ ຢ່າໃຫ້ມີດູກ
ມົນ ເປັນອັນຂາດ ສ່ວນໂຕ ກໍໃຫ້ປັ້ນເກົ່າຄວາມສະອາດ
ສ່ວງ ນອງ ຊຸ່ມແລ້ວ ແລະ ພັກ ມັ້ນໃສ່ ລວມໄວ້
ໝາກເຜັດ ເຜົາ ຫົວ ໑ ບ່ວງ ຜ່າ ຫຼຸງ ຄັ້ນເອົາ ນ້ຳ ກະທິ
ນ້ຳ ກະທິ ແລະ ຕາງ ໄວ້ ໃຊ້ ປາ ລະ ບໍ

ວິທີ ເຮ-ຄົວ - ຈັກເຄື່ອງ ປຸງ ນ້ຳ ອອກ ເອົາ ຈົມ ນ້ຳ ມາ ເປ
ພໍ ຫອມ ແລ້ວ ໃສ່ ໄວ້ ພັກ ບົວ ຫົວ ປອກ ຫົວ ຫຼາຍ
ເລືອ ເອົາ ໄປ ຈືນ ພໍ ຫອມ ແລະ ເຍື່ອງ ຕາກ ອອກ ໄວ້ -
ຄ - ງົວ ໝາກ ຂາມ ໃຫຍ່ . ພັກ ບົວ ຫົວ ໃຫຍ່ ໑ ຫົວ ຊອ ສອງ
ຂວາງ ໃສ່ ງົບ ໄວ້ ໃບ ພັກ ບົວ ລາງ ເຄີ່ງ ຕາງ ເອົາ ຈ່ຳ ຫົວ ລາງ
ນ້ຳ ຕາງ ຍາວ ສອງ ຂຸງ ໄວ້ ພັກ ຫຼຽນ ແລະ ເປັນ ມື ມ ຫົວ
ໃສ່ ໝາກ ຂຽງ ຫຼຽ ໃຫ້ ຫາກ ເລືອ ພັກ ໄວ້ . ລາວ - ນ້ຳ ປາ.
ໃບ ພັກ ຫອມ ຊຸ ພໍ ຄວາ ພັກ ມັ້ນ ປ່ນ

ວິທີ ຄົວ - ເອົາ ໝໍ້ ຂາງ ເຕົາ ໄຟ ແລ້ວ ເອົາ ນ້ຳ ມັນ ໝູ ໃສ່ ເຫຼົ່າ ຈອງ
ເອົາ ພັກ ບົວ ຫົວ ໃຫຍ່ ຊຸ ໄວ້ ຈືນ ພໍ ຫອມ ຈຶ່ງ ເອົາ ໄກ
ແລະ ພັກ ຫຼຽນ ຫຼຽ ລົງ ຄົນ ໃຫ້ ທົ່ວ ເພີ່ມ ໃປ ຈົນ ເປື່ອ

ໃສ່ ຫອມ ຈຶ່ງ ເອົາ ນ້ຳ ປາ ໃສ່ ແລ ໃຫ້ ທົ່ວ ຄານ ຖ້າ ມີ ນ້ຳ
ມັນ ຫຼາຍ ກໍ ໃຫ້ ໂຄ ຂັ້ນ ອອກ ແລ້ວ ເອົາ ກະທິ ນ້ຳ ຕາງ ສົ່ງ
ໃສ່ ຜ່າງ ຫຼູ ແຕ່ງ ໂຮມ ໃປ ຈົນ ໃກ່ ເປື່ອຍ ຈຶ່ງ ເອົາ ກະທິ
ນ້ຳ ກະທິ ຕາມ ລົງ ໃປ ພໍ ເພັ່ມ ຝູ່ ແລ້ວ ໃຫ້ ເອົາ ຫົວ ພັກ ບົວ
ຈືນ - ຈົ່ງ ຈືນ . ໃສ່ ຊຸມ ເກົ່າ ແກ່ມ ຈອງ ຕາມ ງູ່ ໃບ ພັກ
ບົວ ຕາງ ໃສ່ ແລ ໃຫ້ ທົ່ວ ຕັກ ໃສ່ ຈານ ພັກ ມັ້ນ ປ່ນ ຫອມ
ຊຸ ໃຊ້ ເໝາະ ເມື່ອ ຕຽ ໃຫ້ ງາມ ./.

Kai Pad Khing **Recipe 5**

FRIED CHICKEN WITH GINGER

Ingredients

1 chicken, cleaned and gutted—divide it first into two breast pieces and two leg pieces, then cut and divide the legs from the drumsticks; as for the feet, they should be cut off at the knee joints; the wings should also be separated at the shoulder bones, and each breast cut into two parts; the remaining carcase should be cut into large pieces—do not cut bones into small pieces
1 chicken gizzard, turned inside out, washed, salted, sprinkled with ground black pepper and left on a plate
1 fully grown coconut, opened, the meat grated and two extractions of coconut milk squeezed out, only a little from each extraction
2 pieces ginger, thinly sliced; squeeze out the liquid and fry it in pork fat until it gives off a good aroma, then remove it from the fat and leave it on a plate
shallots, peeled—fry them until they give off a good aroma and are nice and golden, then leave them on a plate—you should have enough to fill a large rice-bowl
1 large onion, peeled and finely chopped and set aside in a bowl
straight-bulbed spring onions—the green parts only, cut into pieces 2 cm long
3 (small) heads garlic—take off the outer skin and peel each clove, then crush them on a chopping-board
salt, fish sauce
chopped coriander leaves
ground black pepper

Method

Put a wok on the fire, and 1 ladleful of pork fat in it. Add the chopped onion and fry it until it gives off a good smell and has turned golden. Next, put in the chicken and the crushed garlic. Turn the pieces of chicken frequently, add the fish sauce and mix everything together. If there seems to be too much fat, pour off some of it. Then add the second extraction of coconut milk and put the lid on the pan. When the chicken is tender, add the first extraction of coconut milk. When this comes to the boil, add the fried shallots and the fried ginger. Taste and check the saltiness. Then add the chopped spring onion leaves. Dish up on a platter and garnish with ground black pepper and chopped coriander leaves; then serve.

ⓧ **໒ = ປາລ້ຽງຊື່ໝ້ຽງ**

ເຄື່ອງປະສົມ — ປາລ້ຽງເອົາປາງອອກຖ້ຽວລອງຂອງໝາ ໑ ງວງ
ລາງນ້ຳສົ້ມເວົາ ຈື່ງນຳມັນໝູໝາຍສາ ແລະເຄື່ອງງາມ
ດີໃສ່ຈາມໃຈ້ ລີ-ດາ່ອນ ໝາກພິກເທົາງແລະເອົາ
ທ່າສ້າງກຸ່ນກໍ ຊົມຢູ່ ພິກບໍ່ຫາວປາມີຕູຫ້ວ ໒໑
ສອງຢາ່ງບໍ່ໃສ່ຕ້ອງເກົ່າໃຫ້ປະຊູມ (ນີ້ເອີ້ນວ່າເຄື່ອງຫອມ)
ໝາກກາແຫ້ວທ້ວວ ໑ ໝູ່ນອກສົມສີ່ກາຫຼຸ່ນ ເຫຼືອຄືນເອົາລະທີ
ນ້ຳສົ້ມກິໃວ້ນ່ອນເທື່ອ ນ້ຳກາໃຈ້ນອນເທື່ອ ພາບໍ່ໃຫຍ່
ໃຫ້ຫຼວງ ໃນພິກຫອມລຸ ເທົ່າ ນ້ຳປາ ພິກປົ່ນ-ໃຫ້ຈືງ
ວິທີທຳ — ເອົາລະທີນ້ຳສົ້ມໃສ່ຫ້ນອາງ ຈື່ນຕົ້ນໄປ ຊິ້ວໃປຈົນແຕກ
ນີ້ ເຫຼືອຕກເອົາເຄື່ອງ ຫອມໃສ່ຂົວໃຫ້ຫອມ ຈື່ງຕັກເອົາ
ນ້ຳຕົ້ມດາເມ ໃທື່ງນ້ຳແລງໃສ່ລ່ຽມໃນອ່ອນ ... ຈົນຫອມ
ວ່າແຫຼ່ງເລົ່າມີເອົານ້ຳປາໃສ່ ແລະລະທີນ້ຳກາໃສ່ນ ຕອນ

ເຫຼືອຈື່ງເອົາປາທີ່ຈືນໄວ້ນັ້ນໃສ່ ລໍ່ໃຫ້ໄປໃຫ້ມາ ໃຫ້
ນ້ຳຖືກເກົວກັນ ເຫຼືອງມີເຍື່ອງແກມຄາງ ໃນຈືງາ ພິກ
ຫອມໃສ່ ຕາກລ້ຽງຈອມ ພິກປີ້ ຫອມປ່ຽນໂຫວ ນາ
ເສີ່ງຕາ ໃຫ້ຈູງແທ ./.
ໝາຍເຫດ ລ້ຽງໝ້ຽງນີ້ລອມລະລາບໍ່ໃຫ້ມີນ້ຳຫຼາຍ
ແນງສົ່ງໃຫ້ຕ່ອນປາລຸ່ມຊື້ນ ແລະນ້ຳລ້ຽງຈອມພໍໃຈ
ຈື່ງມີຊື່ວ່າ ໝ້ຽງ ./.

Pa Ling Sousi Haeng **Recipe 6**

PIQUANT FRIED CATFISH

Ingredients

6 slices of *pa ling* (a name applied to two members of the pangasid family of catfish, one of which, PANGASIUS NASUTUS, is shown on page 157, with its belly full after feeding)—scrape off the mucus from the skin of the fish and cut slices about 1 cm thick—wash and salt these, fry them in pork fat until they are a good golden colour, then set them aside on a plate

5 dried red chilli peppers—pick off the stems, take out their cores and soak them in water
7 (small) shallots (peeled)
} to be pounded finely in a mortar to make your *kheuang hom*

1 fully grown coconut, split open—grate the meat and squeeze two extractions of coconut milk from it

chopped spring onion leaves

chopped coriander leaves

salt, fish sauce, ground black pepper

Kaffir lime leaves

(pig's-bone broth or any other clear soup)

Method

Put the first extraction of coconut milk in a wok on the fire and leave it until the cream separates. Add the *kheuang hom* and leave simmering over a hot fire stirring occasionally, until the ingredients give off a good aroma. Then add the pig's-bone broth or other clear soup and leave the wok over a low fire until the liquid has reduced somewhat.

Next, add the fish sauce and a considerable quantity of the second extraction of coconut milk, followed by the fried slices of fish. Push the fish slices back and forth so that they absorb the liquid. Add the Kaffir lime leaves and the chopped spring onion leaves. Transfer the contents of the pan to a platter, garnish them with ground black pepper and chopped coriander leaves, and serve.

Note

Sousi Haeng should not have much liquid or juice. There should only be enough to keep the slices of fish moist. When dished up, the liquid should cover the bottom of the platter, just enough so that when the platter is tipped the liquid will flow from one side to the other. That is called *haeng* (dry).

ວິທີເຮັດຄ້ຳຮົ່ມໃສ່ກະລໍາປີ

ເຄື່ອງປະສົມ —

ໝ່ອຕ່ຳຊີ້ນ ໑ ຫົວລັກກະທຽມເຄາະ ໃສ່ລ່ວງ ໝາກສົ້ມ ເຄື່ອງເລາະ
ເນີຍນ້ຳ ເອົາພິກທ່ອລ່ຽງເຄື່ອງ ຊີ ຫົວຫອມ ໃສ່ຫົວ
ມັນກຫົວເລາະໃບ ເຫຼືອເອົາເຄື່ອງ ກະທຽມນ້ຳ ໃຫ້ຂາວເລາະປົກ
ແມ່ງທຽມ ຫົວ ເຄັ່ນມ ໃສ່ຈວນໄວ້ ໝາກມັນເພີ້ ທໍ່ມ່ອງ
ໃຈໄກ່ ໑ ກະລໍາປີ໑ ຫົວຜ່າລອງ ນາວ ເປັນຕົວທ່ານ
ໄວ້

ວິທີເຮັດ — ເອົາໝາກມັນເທີ່ ໃສ່ໝໍ້ ໂລທີ ຍັດໃຈປີ້ ຕໍ່
ໄຟ ພໍ່ໝາກມັນຮ້ອນ ຈຶ່ງເອົາເນີ້ ໃສ່ ພຸກໄປພໍ ມາ
ຈົນພິກເຫຼືອ ຕໍ່ງາມ ດີ ທ່ອສາເຫຼືອ ຈຶ່ງຕັກເອົາໝາກ ເຕາ
ໜື່ ໝາກ ດອກ ເມ ຮອງ ພໍ່ ກູ້ອົ່ມ ໝໍ້າ ເຫຼືອ ເອົາ ກະລໍ່າ ປີ ລຸ່ມ
ໃສ່ ຊຸ່ມ ເປົ່າ ຕອມ ໄປ ລົມ ໝາກ ເຫັດ ເລາະ ໝ່ອ ພິກ ເປື້ອນ ດີ ແລ້ວ ພໍ
ໃຫ້ ມັນ ໝາກ ລູກ ໝ່ອ ເລັກ ນ້ອຍ ຈຶ່ງ ຕັກ ໝ່ອ ອອກ ຈັດ ເປັນ

ຄັ້ງ ເປັນ ຂາວ ອອງ ລຸ່ມ ໃສ່ ກາງ ຈານ ເອົາ ຫົວ ພິກ ຈອມ ຕັກ
ລູກ ຮອງ ພັກ ນ້ຳ ປົ່ນ ທາອມ ງວ ໃຫ້ ງາມ ເນົາ ນັກ ເພື່ອ ຕັ້ງ
ເຂົ້າ ຮັບ ທານ ໄດ້ ຕໍ່ ອ ສົ້ນ ./.

Nok Kho Hum Sai Kalampi **Recipe 7**

BRAISED QUAIL WITH CABBAGE

Ingredients

1 fresh quail, plucked, gutted, washed and sprinkled with salt and ground black pepper
5 straight-bulbed spring onions, crushed and stuffed into the bird (tie the bird's feet and wings to its body using wire)
butter, the size of a hen's egg
1 cabbage, cut into quarters
(ground black pepper)
(chopped coriander leaves)
(pig's-bone broth)

Method

Put the butter in a cast-iron pot and put the pot on the fire. When the butter is hot, put in the bird. Turn it from side to side until it is nicely golden all over. Then add enough pig's-bone broth or other clear soup to cover the bird. Put in the quarters of cabbage, cover the pot and leave it until the broth has largely evaporated and the bird and cabbage are well cooked. The liquid remaining should be just enough to keep the bird from drying out.

Take the bird out of the pot and divide it into the breast and leg parts. Dress these on the centre of a platter and arrange the quarters of cabbage around them. Use the liquid left over in the pot as sauce, and garnish the dish with ground black pepper and chopped coriander. Serve it with *Jaew Som* (page 48).

ອາຫານລາວ

ຊື່ : ກະລີ່ໄກ່ – ແບບລາວ

ເຄື່ອງປະສົມ – ໄກ່ປອກໜັງ ໑ ໂຕ ຈະກໍໃຊ້ຂອງໄກ່ປົນຕ່ອນ ...
ຊອຍແລ້ວ ... ແລະ ເພີ່ມ ... ໃສ່ຈານໄວ້ ໝາກເຜັດ ...
ຕ່ອນ ... ໃຫ້ ... ຜັກ ຫົວ ຫົວບົ່ວ ... (...
...) ກະລີ່ ... ໝາກພ້າວ
ຫົວ ... ຕາມ ... ກະທ່ຽມ ...
... ກະທິ ... ໄວ້ ...
... ກະປ໋ອງ ... ໝາກເຜັດ ...
... ໃສ່ຈານໄວ້
ເກືອ – ນ້ຳປາ – ຜັກບົ່ວປົ່ນ – ພິກໄທປົ່ນ –

ວິທີເຮັດ – ເອົາກະທິມາຕົ້ມ ... ໄຟ ... ກະທິ
... ຈຶ່ງເອົາ ເຄື່ອງ ... ໃສ່ ...
... ເອົາມາ
... ກະລີ່ ... ໃສ່ ... ເອົານ້ຳກະທິ ...
... ໃສ່ ... ແລະ ... ເຄື່ອງ ...
... ຕໍ່ໄປ
ຮັບທານ ./.

Kalee Ped **Recipe 8**

DUCK CURRY*

Ingredients

1 duck, plucked, gutted and cut into pieces as desired—these to be washed, sprinkled with salt and ground black pepper and left on a plate

dried chilli peppers, soaked in water until soft } pounded finely in a mortar to make your *kheuang hom*
7 (small) shallots }

3 tablespoons of curry powder

1 fully grown coconut, opened and the meat grated by using a *ka-tai kood mak-pao* (a 'rabbit' for grating coconut, see page 28)—then make the first extraction of cream, followed by the second and third extractions of milk, approximately enough to fill a large soup bowl

10 potatoes, peeled and cut into pieces of the size which you think would be beautiful, then washed and left on a plate

salt, fish sauce, ground black pepper

chopped coriander leaves

Method

Put the coconut cream in a wok and place it on the fire. Leave it until the cream separates, and then add the *kheuang hom*. Stir until it gives off a good aroma.

Next, put in the salted pieces of duck and stir until they have shrunk a bit. Add the fish sauce and curry powder. Stir some more and then add the second extraction of coconut milk and the potatoes. Put the lid on the wok. When the duck and potatoes are well done, taste, then dish up in a bowl, garnish with ground black pepper and chopped coriander leaves, and serve.

* Editor's Note. Phia Sing added the words 'Lao style' to the title, but then crossed them out.

໑= ໝູປີ້ງ

ເຄື່ອງປະສົມ – ໝູປ່ອຍເກ້ຍນ ໑ ໂຕ ເອົາໄສ້ອອກ ແລະ
ແຍກຂາປັ້ນເປັນສອງຂາ ສ່ວນຫົວກໍໃຫ້ຜ່າເປັນສອງ
ອັນ ໃຫ້ເອົາມາກໍມັນເທົ່າເຈາະ ຈູ ອອກ ແລ້ວ ຫັ້ນເປັນ ຕ່ອນ
ນ້ອຍ ສ່ວນດາງ ອນີ້ ກໍຫັ້ນເປັນຕ່ອນໃຫຍ່ ລາງ ນາກາເຣີອ
ເທົ່າຫົວຫົວໃຫຍ່ 6 ເທື່ອ ຄູລອງ ຍາວໄດ້. ໝາກພ້າວ
ໜ່ວຍ ໑ ພ່ອງປອກ ເປືອກອອກ ທັງໝົດ ຕົ້ມເອົານ້ຳ ກະທິ
ນ້ຳກາກ ແລະ ນ້ຳປະສົມ ກາບ ເນື້ອ ກູ ແຕກ ໃຫຍ່ ກະລີ
ຫ່ອ ນ້ຳໃສ່ ໃນ ຫໍ່ ນ້ຳໃສ່ ແກ່ນ ຜັກ ປອກ
ນ້ຳລາງ ໑໒ ຫົວ ໝາກເຜັດ ໃນຫ່ອງ – ເກືອ – ນ້ຳປາ
ນ້ຳຕານ – ພິກໄທປົ່ນ – ໝາກ ສີ້ງ ສົ້ມ ໑ ກະປ໋ອງ

ວິທີເຮັດ – ເອົາໝູທີ່ຕາມີ ເກືອ ໄວ້ ໃສ່ແນ່ ເຕົາໄຟ ຈົ່ງ ໄປ
ຈົນມີ ກິ່ນ ຫອມ ເກື່ອ ປາ ເຮວາ ... ໃຫ້ ນຸ່ມ ເປັນ ສີ ເຫຼືອງ
ກໍ ໃຫ້ ເນື້ອ ມັນ ນອກ ເອົາ ນ້ຳ ໝາກ ພ້າວ ໃສ່ ແນ່ ... ເຕົາ ໄຟ
ເພື່ອ ນ້ຳ ມັນ ຮ້ອນ ດີ ຈຶ່ງ ເອົາ ຫົວ ຫອມ ໃຫຍ່ ປອກ ໃສ່ ກາງ
ເມື່ອ ມີ ກິ່ນ ຫອມ ຈຶ່ງ ເອົາ ໝາກ ເຂືອ ສົ້ມ ກະລີ ທີ່ ຕຳ
ໄວ້ ໃສ່ ແກ່ ຫອມ ເອົາ ນ້ຳ ກະທິ ໃສ່ ເບີ ໃຫ້ ສຸກ ແລ້ວ
ຈຶ່ງ ເອົາ ເນື້ອ ໝູ ທີ່ ປີ້ງ ໄວ້ ແລ້ວ ໃສ່ ເຕົາ ໄຟ ນ້ຳ ກະລີ
ທີ່ ຂົ້ວ ກັບ ໃສ່ ພ້ອມ ກັບ ນ້ຳ ກະທິ ຫາງ
[illegible] ຈຶ່ງ ເກືອ ນ້ຳ ໃຫ້ ສຸກ ໃສ່ ຈານ ໝູ ພ້ອມ ເນື້ອ ໄປ ນຳ ໝູ
ຈະ ເປື່ອຍ ຈຶ່ງ ເອົາ ມັນ ຝະລັ່ງ ແລະ ໝາກ ເຜັດ ໃສ່
ໃສ່ ແກ່ ນັ້ນ ເປື່ອຍ ຊີມ ເບິ່ງ ເຄັມ ຈາງ ຕາມ ຈຸດ ແລ້ວ ຕັກ
ໃສ່ ຖ້ວຍ ແກ່ ນ້ຳ ຫອມ ຈຸ ໄປ ໃຫ້ ເມື່ອ ກໍ ໃຫ້ ຮັບ ທານ ກັບ ເຂົ້າ
ຈ້າວ ./.

ໝາຍເຫດ – ກະລີ ຝາ ກໍ ມີ ບໍ ຄອນ ຈະ ໃຫ້ ນ້ຳ ໃສ ເຊື່ອ ວ່າ
ກະລີ ຂອງ ລາວ ແທ້ ຕ້ອງ ກະ ນ້ຳ ໃຫ້ ຂຸ່ນ ເປັນ ກັນ ກັບ ນ້ຳ
ເຂົ້າ ປຸ້ນ ນ້ຳ ແກງ ໃຫຍ່ ນັ້ນ

Kalee Ped **Recipe 9**

DUCK CURRY*

Ingredients

1 duck, plucked and gutted—cut off the legs and divide the breast into two pieces; cut off the tail end; cut other parts (such as the wings) into large pieces; wash all the pieces and sprinkle them with salt
2 large onions, thinly sliced
1 coconut, opened and the meat grated—make two extractions of coconut milk and combine them, then leave the mixture in a large soup bowl
6 tablespoons of curry powder
2 tablespoons of butter
12 potatoes, peeled, soaked in water and washed
2 large red chilli peppers
salt, fish sauce
chopped coriander leaves
ground black pepper
1 small can tomato paste

Method

Put the pieces of duck in a pot and place this on the fire. Stir until a good aroma is given off. Add the fish sauce and take the pot off the fire. Pour off some of the duck's fat if there seems to be too much.

Put the butter in a wok and put it on the fire. When the butter is hot, add the onion. When this starts to smell good, add the tomato paste and curry powder. When these ingredients give off a good aroma, add the coconut milk. Stir until the cream separates, then take the wok off the fire.

Put the pot with the pieces of duck back on the fire and pour the curry sauce from the wok on to it. If some of the coconut milk had been left over, add it to the pot at this stage. Cover the pot and leave it until the duck meat is well cooked, then add the red chilli peppers and the potatoes. When the latter are thoroughly cooked, taste.

Serve the dish in a bowl, garnished with ground black pepper and chopped coriander leaves and accompanied by rice.

Note

This *kalee falang* (curry for foreigners) should not have as clear a soup as our Lao curry. One must try to make it as thick as the sauce for *Khao Poon Nam Phik* (page 115).

* Editor's Note. Phia Sing had added to the recipe title 'French style', but then crossed out the addition.

(7) ~~ຢາ~~ ຢາປົວຍອມ

ຕຳລາປະສົມ – ປົວຍອມທັງຫົວ ນຳເອົາໃບຄ້ອງຂອງຍາຄູ
ຫົວຖູຫາງ ຈົກໃສ່ລ່ວງ ແລ້ວໃຫ້ກະຈູ້ ທາຄື່ໄວ້
ໝາກພ້ອງ ທ້ອງ ປລົກ ເປືອກ [illegible] ຕົ້ມ ເອົາແກ່ນຕະທິບກໍ
ຈົກຕະລະແກ່ນຄາງ ໃວ້ ຈັບລະຄູ່
ໝາກກລ້ວຍ ຕົ້ມແກ່ ແລ້ວໃຫ້ແປ້ງ – ໃບຍູ້ – ຫົວໝາກພ້ອ
ຫົວປລົມ ຈູ ຫົວ (ຂອງສາຍປ່າງໃສ່ ໃສ່ ຕົກຕ່ ໃຫ້ [illegible])
ຕົວແກ່ນປົວ ໃບຂີ້ຫູ – ໃບໝາກພ້ອງ – ໃບໝາກຫອມສຸ
ເພີ່ມແປ້ງປົວ
ວິທີທຳ – ເອົາຕະຫົບແກ່ນກາໃສ່ເຫຼັ້ມ ຈາງຈິ້ມ ຄ້າງຈົມ ຕົ້ມ ແລ້ວ
ຈື່ ຕກ [illegible] ທີ່ຕົ່ງໄວ້ ຈີ່ໃສ່ຈໍ້ ໃປ ຈົບ [illegible] ເປີ ທາຂອງ
ຕ້ລວ ເອົາຄູ່ ປ່ອງ ໃສ່ ຄົນ ແປ່ ເກື່ອວັນ ແກ່ປາຮອງ ແລ້ວຕະທິ
ແກ່ຈາງ ກູມາໃສ່ແປ່ ກ້ອນ ຕ່ອປົດ ພົປາ [illegible] ຕົ້ມ ຈາງ ຕາມ
ຮູມ (ຫົວໃສ່ຄາມ ໃບໝາກພ້ອງ ຫອມສຸ ເພີ່ມ ແປ້ງປົວ ໂຮງເຫັດ
ໃບຂີ້ຫູເພີ່ມ) ສົມ ຕຸ້ ໃຫ້ ຮູ້ [illegible] –/.

Sousi Pa Gnon **Recipe 10**

A 'HOT' DISH OF SMALL CATFISH

Ingredients

6 *pa gnon*—(see illustration below)—scrape off the mucus from the skin, gut the fish, cut off and discard the heads and tails, wash the fish and salt them

1 fully grown coconut, split open—grate the meat and squeeze two extractions of coconut milk from it, keeping the first extraction separate from the second one—quantity, one soupbowl of each

2 dried chilli peppers soaked in water
7 (small) shallots, peeled
} pounded together in a mortar to make your *kheuang hom*

salt and fish sauce
Kaffir lime leaves
spring onion leaves, chopped
coriander leaves, chopped
ground black pepper

Method

Put the first extraction of coconut milk in a wok on the fire until it becomes creamy. Then add the *kheuang hom* and fry it until it gives off a good aroma. Add the fish gently, stir thoroughly, then add fish sauce and the second extraction of coconut milk. When the fish are cooked, taste and check the saltiness. Add the Kaffir lime leaves. Transfer to a serving-dish, garnish with the chopped spring onion leaves and coriander and ground black pepper, and serve.

Pa gnon, PANGASIUS SIAMENSIS

11: ເຮັດໝົກປາຄໍ່

ເຄື່ອງປະສົມ — ປາຄໍ່ ໑ ໂຕ ເຄາະເກັດ ຄວັກໄສ້ອອກ ລ້າງ
ລອງ ຊອງ ແຫງ ປະມານ ສອງ ຈອກ ຫຼັງ ນໍ້າ ໃຈ ງານ ຫົວ
ສີໄຄຊອຍ ສອງ ຫົວ ໑ ຫລືອ ຜັກຫອມຊອຍ ຫລືອ ຜັກບົ່ວ
ຊອຍ ຫລືອ ໃບຂີ້ຫູດ ຊອຍ ໃບ ~~[illegible]~~ ໃບຜັກທ່ອ
ຊອຍພໍປະມານ ໃບພິກຫອມຊອຍພໍປະມານ ເຂົ້າສານຈ່ວ
ປົ່ນ ມີດ ໃຫ້ ພິກ ແຫ້ງ ຢ່າງ ປາ ແດກ

ວິທີເຮັດ — ເອົາປາ ແລະ ເຄື່ອງໃສ່ທັງໝົດ ໃຫ້ ນຳມາ
ປົນ ຈຶ່ງ ເອົາປາ ແລະ ເຂົ້າຈ່ວໃສ່ ແລ້ວ ປາ ສະອາດ ເລືອ
ກໍໃຫ້ເອົາ ປາ ແລະ ສີໄຄຊອຍ ຜັກຫອມຊອຍ ຫົວຜັກ
ບົ່ວຊອຍໃສ່ ພໍສົມຄວນ ເອົາ ເກືອ ຫຼາກ ຫວານ ຊອຍ ແລວ
ຕາກໃສ່ ຖ້ວຍ ເຄື່ອງ ໃບ ຫອມ ຊອຍ ພິກ ໃຫ້ ຫົວ ປັກ ເມືອ
ຫໍ່ ໃບ ຕອງ ແຫ

ໝາກແຕງ ຕ້ອງ ຊອຍ ສົ້ມ ຈະ ປຸງ ນຳ ແຫງ ວ່າງ ໄຟ
ຮອງ ລາ ໃບ ກໍ ໄດ້

Keng Tom Yum Pa Kho **Recipe 11**

FISH SOUP MADE WITH SNAKEHEAD AND CHOPPED LEMON GRASS, ETC.

Ingredients
1 snakehead (the fish known as *pa kho*, illustrated below)—scale it, gut it, slice it into pieces about 2 cm long, wash these and put them on a plate
1 stalk lemon grass, chopped crossways
2 (small) heads of garlic, (the cloves peeled and) chopped
5 spring onions, bulbs only, chopped
coriander leaves, chopped
rice—1 large 'pinch' (about 1 tbsp)
ground black pepper, fish sauce and salt

Method
Put some water and salt in a pot on the fire. When the water has come to the boil, add the fish and rice. When the fish is cooked, add the fish sauce and chopped lemon grass, garlic and spring onion. When these are cooked, taste and check the saltiness, then transfer everything to a serving-bowl, garnish with the coriander leaves and the ground black pepper, and serve.

Note
If you like the dish sour, squeeze some lime juice on it.

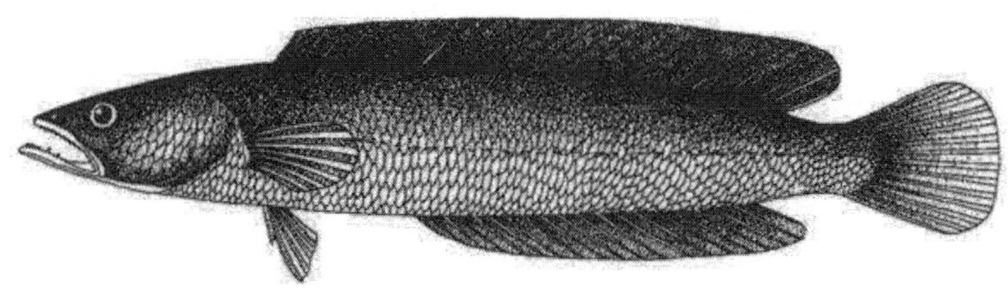

Pa kho, OPICEPHALUS STRIATUS

12. ເປັດຕົ້ມຄ່າ

ເຄື່ອງປະສົມ — ເປັດປອກຂົນ 1 ໂຕ [illegible] ຈັກໄສ້ອອກ ແລ້ວ ແຍກກະດູກ ອົກ ໃຫ້ຫຼຸດ ເຫຼືອແຕ່ສ່ວນປາຍປີກ ນັ້ນ ໃຫ້ຕັດອອກ ຈາກກັນ ວາງກໍ ແຍກກອອກ ໃຫ້ເປັນ 2 ວາ ຕົ້ມຕຸ້ມ ອອກ ສ່ວນດາກ ໃຫ້ຕັດເປັນຕ່ອນໃຫຍ່ ແລະ ເອົາ ມັນ ຈຸນຸກ

ກັບ ອອກ ລ້າງນໍ້າ ໃຫ້ສະອາດ ເຄື່ອງ ໝາກກາ ຜ່າວຫົວ ໝາກ ນ້ອຍ ປອກ ເປືອກ ຫົວພຽງ ເອົາ ນໍ້າກະທິ ນໍ້າກາກ ໄວ້ຕ່າງ ຫາກ ສ່ວນ ນໍ້າ ຕານ ນໍ້າປາ ເອົາ ປະສົມກັນ ໄວ້ພໍສົມ ຄວນ ຄ່າຜ່ານ ເປັນເມັດ ອ່ອນ 60 ພ່ານ ແລ້ວ ບໍ່ ຫາ ປອນ ປອກ ເປືອກ ແລ້ວ 1 ກ້ອນ ໝາກ ກາ ແລ້ວ ປອກ ເປືອກ ອອກ ແລ້ວ ກາງ ກ້ອນ ໝາກ ກາ ໃບ ພາກ ບົວ ແລ້ວ ໃບ ພາກ ຫອມ ແລ້ວ ພໍ ຄວນ ພິກ ນ້ອຍ ຕ່ຳ ນໍ້າ ປາ

ວິທີ ເຮັດ — ເອົາເປັດ ທີ່ ຕັດ ແລະ ຜ່າ ທີ່ ຜ່ານ ໄວ້ ໃສ່ ໝໍ້ ຕັ້ງໄຟ ຈົນ ໄປ ພໍ ເປື່ອຍ ຈຶ່ງ ເອົາ ນໍ້າ ປາ ລົງ ພໍ ຄວນ ແລ້ວ ເອົາ ນໍ້າ ກະທິ [illegible] ນໍ້າ ຕານ ແລະ ນໍ້າ ປາ ພາກ ບົວ ປອກ ພາກ ຫອມ ປອກ ໃສ່ ອ່ອນ ໄຟ ຈົນ ນໍ້າ ແຫ້ງ ແລະ ເປັດ ເປື່ອຍ ຈຶ່ງ ເປີດ ຕັກ ເອົາ ຕອນ ກ່ອນ ເຫຼືອ ໄວ້ ໂລກ ນີ້ ແລ້ວ ຈຶ່ງ ເອົາ ກະທິ ນໍ້າ ກາກ ໃສ່ ພໍ ເດືອດ ກະທິ ແຕກ ມັນ ຊີມ ເບິ່ງ ແກ້ ລົດ ຊາດ ແລ້ວ ຕັກ ໃສ່ ຈານ ໃບ ພາກ ບົວ ໃບ ພາກ ຫອມ ແລະ ພິກ ນ້ອຍ ໜ້າ ເວລາ ເມື່ອ ຕັກ ໃຫ້ ມີ ແກນ ຂອງ ເຫາ - ເປັດ ຕົ້ມ ຄ່າ ນີ້ ບໍ່ ໃຫ້ ມີ ນໍ້າ ຫຼາຍ ໃຫ້ ມີ ແຕ່ ແຫ້ງ ຂຸ່ນ ຕອນ ແລະ ນໍ້າ ຄວນ ຈະ ຕົ້ມ ຫາງ ເຄື່ອ ກ່ອນ ເປັດ ແລະ ຫອບ ຫອມ ຈະ ຫຼົ່ນ ໃຫ້ ເປື່ອຍ ໄປ ອ່ອນ ໆ ເອົາ ຈາກ ການ ດີ ທາງ ຍ່າງ

Ped Tom Kha **Recipe 12**

DUCK AND GALINGALE SOUP

Ingredients

1 duck, plucked, cleaned and gutted—slip the knife down the rib cage on each side of the breast bone in order to lift off the breast meat (with the wing attached) in one piece; cut off the legs, discard the feet and the tail (which is smelly) and cut the carcase into large pieces; wash all the pieces and salt everything

1 fully grown coconut, split open—grate the meat and squeeze three extractions of coconut milk from it, keeping the first extraction separate from the other two

20 slices of young galingale

1 rice-bowl (i.e. 7 to 8) shallots—remove any dried or withered leaves and peel them

½ rice-bowl (i.e. about 12) peeled cloves of garlic

spring onion leaves, chopped

fresh coriander leaves, chopped

ground black pepper, salt and fish sauce

Method

Put the salted pieces of duck and the sliced galingale into a pot. Put it on the fire. Stir until the duck meat has shrunk a little, then add fish sauce. Next, add the second and third extractions of coconut milk, followed by the peeled shallots and garlic. Boil gently until the coconut milk has been reduced and the duck meat is well cooked. Then take out the slices of galingale, all but a few.

Now add the first extraction of coconut milk. Leave it on the fire until the cream separates. Taste and check the saltiness. Pour the soup into a dish. Garnish it with the spring onion, coriander and ground black pepper, then serve it.

Note

There should not be too much liquid in *Ped Tom Kha*. There should be just enough to cover the meat.

One should not stir the dish too much, lest the pieces of meat be broken up.

The fire should be low so that all the ingredients remain in good condition (i.e. not overcooked).

13ະ ຄູສາໄກ່

ເຄື່ອງປະສົມ — ໄກ່ປະທູກຫຼາຍ ໑ ໂຕ ເພາະກັນຈັກໃສ່ຂອງກາ
ລ່າງແກ່ ຫາແພກາປີແລະເຄື່ອງໃນ ຫົວພິກປອກ
ຫຼາຍ ໑ ຊີ ຫົວ ພິກຫຼາຍ ຊີ ຫົວ ເພາະເປັນມີປອກເອົາ
ແກ່ເນື້ອ ໝາກພ້າວຫົວ ໑ ບ່ວງ ປອກເປືອກອອກຫຼາຍ
ຂັ້ນເອົາແຕ່ກະທິແກ່ ກາກ ໑ ຖ້ວຍ ໝາກເໝັນ
ໝາກເໝັນເຄື່ອງໃນບ່ວງ ເພາະເອົາແຕ່ກ້ຽງກາແກ່ໂຕເປັນ
ພິກບົດຄົວປົ່ນ ຊີ ຫົວ ໝາກເໝັນຫຼາຍພິກບົດຊີກ
ສາຍປ່ຽນໃສ່ຄົ້ນແກ່ຈົບແຍກ ແລ້ວເອົາຖົ່ວງອນ
໑ ຖ້ວຍ ມາເພາະເອົາບັກມັນເຫົ້າຂອງ ເອົາແຕ່
ໝູ່ເກົ່າໃສ່ແກ່ແດງຫອມໄວ້ ຫົວຫອມຫົວ
ແລ້ວແຊ່ໄຟໂຫໃໝ່ແລ້ວ ຫຼູເປັນຕ່ອນນ້ອຍ
ກວາງເຄື່ອງ ໝາກສາມແລ້ວແກ່ໂຕ ອ່ອນເຄົ້າ
ງູບໜູແລະ ມັນໝາກໂຫ້ແຍກທໍ່ບ່ວງໃສ່ເປັນ ໃສ
ພິກຫອມ ຊູ ເກືອ ນ້ຳປາ ພິກປົ່ນ

ວິດທີເຮັດ

ໂຕໄກ່ເອົາເຄື່ອງທີ່ແກ່ໃຈລົງໃສ່ກວຍ ແລ້ວເອົາພິກ
ບົດ ພິກຫຼາຍ ຫົວຫອມ ມັນໝາກພ້າວ ທີ່ຫ່ຽວໄວ້ໃສ່
ແກ່ປາເກືອລວງ ແກ່ກະທິໃສ່ເຄື່ອງປົ່ນຮ່ວມເຄື່ອງ
ເພາະເນື້ອໂຫ້ອ່ອນແລ້ວໄວ້ ແລ້ວເອົາໝູໃສ່ໃນ
ທ້ອງໄກ່ໂຫ້ເຕັມ ຫຍິບປິດໄວ້ໃຫ້ສະໜິດໂຕໄກ່
ເອົາໃບກ້ວຍມາຫຸ້ມໄວ້ ເອົາໃສ່ໝໍ້ນຶ່ງໄຟອ່ອນໆ
ໄປຈົນງູບໄກ່ເປື່ອຍ ຖ້າແກ່ເຫັນກໍເອົາແກ່ກະທິເຖ
ໄວ້ໃສ່ ບ່າໂຫ້ແຫ້ງ ຫຼຸດໂຫ້ມີແກ່ພໍສົມຄວນ ແລ້ວ
ຕັດໄກ່ອອກເປັນຕ່ອນ ເພາະເອົາເຄື່ອງຈາກ
ກາງຈານກ່ອນ ຈຶ່ງເອົາຊີ້ໄກ່ວາງໃສ່ ແຕ່ງໂຫ້
ງາມ ງູບນ້ຳແກ່ຮ່ມໄກ່ທີ່ເຫຼືອປົ່ນ ເຫມາະສົມ
ຕັກອອກລວງຕ່ອນໄກ່ແລະເຄື່ອງຈົວໄກ່ໂຫ້ທົ່ວ ແລ້ວເອົາ
ພິກປົ່ນຫອມໃສ່ ມາເຊີນແຂກກິນ

ໝາຍເຫດ — ຄວາໄກ່ນີ້ຈະເອົາໃສ່ລົງໃນໝໍ້ເອົາກໍໄດ້ ແຕ່
ວ່າເຄື່ອງສ່ວນປະສົມຕ້ອງລົງມາເລືອ ສີຮູ່ມເອົາກໍໄດ້ເພາະ
ຮູ້ວ່າອາຫານນັ້ນຫອມດີ ທັງແກ່ຄວາເອົາກໍໄດ້ເຊີນໂຫ້
ການແຕ່ງອາຫານທີ່ຕ້ອງດີກວ່າງ່າຍໆ ອື່ນໆ

Kula Kai **Recipe 13**

CHICKEN KULA

Ingredients

1 chicken, gutted, washed, salted and sprinkled with ground black pepper
15 (small) shallots, peeled
5 (small) heads of garlic, the cloves to be peeled
1 coconut, to produce 1 rice-bowl of coconut cream (*nam kok*, meaning the first extraction, with no water added)
2 dried chilli peppers, to be prepared by cutting out their cores and then soaking them in water until they are soft
5 (small) shallots, (peeled and) pounded in the mortar with the chillis
1 piece of crisp-fried pork skin of the kind called *khiep moo sorn* (i.e. with some fat on the inside)—remove and discard the fat and pound the skin with the shallots and chillis until all three are well mixed
1 piece of dried buffalo skin, to be put in the fire until its outside is burned—then scrape off the burned surface, cut the pieces into strips of 2 cm by 5 mm and 3 mm thick, and soak these in water until soft
minced pork, to include some fat—a quantity the size of a duck's egg
fresh coriander, chopped
salt, fish sauce and ground black pepper

Method

Put the pounded ingredients into a bowl.

In the same bowl combine the shallots, garlic, buffalo skin and minced pork. Season with fish sauce and salt. Add some of the coconut cream a little at a time to the mixture, stirring it, just enough to make the mixture moist. Take care that it does not taste too salty (i.e. you should have been sparing in adding salt with the fish sauce).

Stuff this mixture into the chicken until it is full. Wind sewing-thread (round the chicken) to keep the wings and legs as close as possible to the body.

Put the chicken in a cast-iron pot (with some water). Leave the pot on the fire, the heat being very low, until the chicken is done. If the water dries out, add some of the remaining coconut cream. Do not let the liquid dry out; there should always be enough to keep the chicken meat from drying.

Take out the chicken and divide it into breasts, wings and legs. Place the stuffing, first, in the centre of a serving-platter and then put round it the breasts, wings and legs.

Taste the liquid remaining in the pot and correct the seasoning according to your liking. Use it as a sauce to pour over the chicken and the stuffing together with the chopped coriander and the ground black pepper. Serve.

Note

It is possible to use a steaming rack (see page 16) for steaming this *Kula Kai*, but if you are cooking fewer than three chickens you should use the above method since the chicken will taste and smell better, and so will the sauce, and it will be easier to control the saltiness of the sauce.

14- ແກງໄກ່ໃສ່ເຂົ້າເບືອ

ເຄື່ອງປະສົມ— ໄກ່ປອກຂົນ ໑ ໂຕ ແລະໄສ້ອອກ ລ້າງນ້ຳ ໃຫ້ສະອາດ ເຂົ້າໜຽວ ມື ໑ ຂອດ ລ້າງນ້ຳ ຂູດ ຕົບ ເຈົ່າ ໃຫ້ລະອຽດ ໝາກເຜັດ ລຽງ ເຄີ່ງ (ໃຕ້ນີ້ ເອົາຫົວ ແລະໃບ ຕົ້ນຮາກ ກິນ ລ້າງນ້ຳ ຜັກຫອມ ເອົາຮາກ ເອົາໃບ ຊອຍ ລ້າງນ້ຳໄວ້ ໃບໝາກບົ່ວ ຂູ ເກືອ- ນ້ຳປາ

ວິທີເຮັດ— ເອົານ້ຳໃສ່ໝໍ້ ຕັ້ງໄຟ ສອງໃຈພໍເດືອດ ແລ້ວເອົາ ເກືອ- ໝາກບົ່ວ ກັບຜັກຫອມ ທີ່ຫາໄວ້ໃສ່ ພໍນ້ຳ ຟົດ ຈຶ່ງເອົາໄກ່ໃສ່ ຖ້າໄກ່ສຸກດີ ແລ້ວໃຫ້ເອົາ ນ້ຳປາ ເຂົ້າເບືອ ໃສ່ລົງ ພໍໃຫ້ເປື່ອຍ ມີເນື້ອເຫຼືອ ຈາງ ທານ ອູບ ແລ້ວ ຕັກ ເອົາ ມາ ຈັດ ເປັນ ເປັນ ຊາມ ໃສ່ ຈານ ຫມໍ້ ສ່ວນ ນ້ຳ ແລະ ເຂົ້າ ກໍ ຕັກໃສ່ ຖ້ວຍ ຜັກ ບົ່ວ ໃສ່ ຜັກ ຫອມ ເທິງ ຫົວ ນ້ຳ ແກງ ແລະ ຕ່ອນ ໄກ່ ຕ້ອງໃຫ້ ມີ ທາມ ສົມ ພໍ ສົມ.

Keng Kai Sai Hed Khon **Recipe 14**

CHICKEN SOUP WITH MUSHROOMS

Ingredients
1 chicken, washed and gutted
30 mushrooms, (*hed khon*, page 43), washed
2 straight-bulbed spring onions, the roots trimmed off and the onions washed
7 sprigs coriander, stems and leaves, washed
spring onion leaves, chopped
salt and fish sauce

Method
Put 2 metal jugfuls (2 pints) of water into a pot. Add salt, the straight-bulbed spring onions and the coriander. Bring to the boil, then put in the chicken. When the water comes back to the boil, add the mushrooms and the fish sauce.

When the chicken is done, taste and check the saltiness. Then divide the chicken into breasts, wings and legs, and put them on a serving-plate. Put the broth and mushrooms in a bowl, and garnish with the chopped spring onion leaves.

Serve the chicken meat and the broth separately, accompanied by *Jaew Som* (see page 48).

15- ສ້າໂຄນຊີ້ນງົວ

ເຄື່ອງປະສົມ — ຊີ້ນສັນງົວລ້ຽງ ເອົາເນີນຂອງກາຍນໍ້າ - ແລະ ກາມ
ມະຂູບລາງເຂືອງ - ເຂືອ 3 × ເຂືອ 2 × 0 ະແດງ ແລ້ວຊູບຫຼຸງ ແລ້ວເອົາໃສ່
ຈານ ຊອດແກ້ວ ເຄື່ອງຫຼີ້ ມັກແມງກາ ນອດ ຮອງ ຜັກບົ່ວ
ຂີ່ງ ຖາວ ໃຫ້ແດ່ງ ກັນ ລາຍ ເກືອ ຫຼາປະໄວ້ ສາກ ຊີ້ອ ໃສ່ ມີ ໃສ່
ມີ ຕາວ ~~[illegible]~~ ພັກຫອມ ໃບຫອ ທົວພັກບົ່ວ ກັງ
ພາກຫອມ ແຕງ ປີ ມ່ອງ ສ່ວນ ສັກ ໂນ ຂອງ ເອົາ ປ່າ ຊີ້ ຊູ
ປະສົມ ກັນ ໃຫ້ ຫຼາ ເປັນ ເສັ້ນ ຫອມ ຜັກ ງົວ- ແມ່ ຜັກ ງົວ-
ທົວ ໃຈງົວ- ສົມ ພາງົວ - ຂາງ ອີ ປ່ານີ້ ຜັກ ສະ ຫຼີ ເກີດ ເຂົ້າ
ເອົາ ປ່າ ລະ ເປັນ ແລວ ໄປ ແຊ່ ມ້ຳ ມັກ ແລງ ເຫຼື້ ແລ້ວ ເອົາ
ອອກ ມາ ຊູ ເປັນ ແຜ່ນ ເປັນ ງາມ ໃສ່ ຈານ ໄວ້ ປ່າ ແລ ກາ ເງາະ
ໜໍ່ ຊູ ປົງ ແກ້ວ- ໃບ ພັກ ພ້ອ ຊູ- ພັກ ຫອມ ຊູ ໃບ
ຂີ້ ຊູ ຊີ

ວິທີເຮັດ — ໃຫ້ ເອົາ ເຫຼື້ ຫອມ ທົ່ວ ປູ ໃສ່ ໄສ່ ຫ່ອ ເອົາ ເຄື່ອງ ໂຮງ ເລີກ
ຝັກ ເຫຼືອ ລ່ວນ ແມ່ ເຂົ້າ ໜັກ ຈູ່ ເອົາ ຊີ້ນ ທົ່ວ ແນນ ສົມ ໃສ່ ນັ້ນ
ອອກ ມາ ຟັ່ນ ມັກ ເຫຼື້ ໃຫ້ ມູ່ ແລ້ວ ເອົາ ມັກ ເຫຼື້ ໄປ ເລາະ ໄຟ
ໃຫ້ ສຸກ ສ່ວນ ຊີ້ນ ສ້າ ເອົາ ມາ ປະສົມ ເຂົ້າ ກັບ ເຫຼື້ ຫອມ
ມັກ ປາ ແລະ ຮອງ ແລ້ວ ມັ້ງ ຖາວ ໃຫ້ ທົວ ຕູງ ໂຕ ແກ້ ໂນ
ໃສ່ ຫ່ອ ເປັ້ ກາອນ ສ່ວນ ມັກ ເຫຼື້ ທີ່ ຈະ ມັ້ນ ໃຫ້ ເຫົ້າ ໝັ້ນ
ມັກ ໃສ່ ອອກ ເອົາ ເກ່າ ມັກ ຊູ ມາ ໃສ່ ຮອງ ໃສ່ ສ້າ ພັກ ບົ່ວ
ຂີ້ ຕູ ຊູ ໃສ່ ຊີ້ນ ເຫຼື້ ແກ້ ຈາງ ຫາມ ຊູ ປູ ຕາກ ໃສ່ ຈານ ແລ້ວ
ໃນ ໃບ ຫອມ ຊູ ໂຮງ ເກົາ ນາ ເມື່ອ ຕ່າ ໃຫ້ ຮູ້ ແທນ ຫຼີ ແທງ
ອ່ອນ ແດກ ງົວ .

Sa Ton Sin Ngua **Recipe 15**

BEEF SA TON

(This recipe and number 16 are complementary. They should be read and executed together.)

Ingredients

400 grams beef sirloin, sliced into pieces measuring 2 cm by 3 cm and 3 mm thick, salted and marinated for two hours in the juice of 6 limes

3 stalks lemon grass 2 (small) heads garlic 7 (small) shallots 3 dried chilli peppers galingale (3 to 5 slices)	sliced into small pieces and mixed together—the result is called *kheuang hom*
liver spleen heart tripe	to be boiled in the meat broth from recipe 16, sliced into small pieces and set aside on a plate

1 small bowl (¼ pint) *or padek**

salt

spring onion leaves fresh coriander Kaffir lime leaves	all finely sliced or chopped

Method

Put the *kheuang hom* into a bowl and add salt.

Squeeze out the liquid from the marinated beef, and set the liquid to cook on a low heat.

Mix the pieces of beef with the *kheuang hom*. Add the *or padek* little by little, mixing the ingredients continuously as you do so. Mix in also half the sliced offal, the reduced liquid from the beef, the spring onions and the Kaffir lime leaves. Mix well. Taste and check the saltiness. Place the mixture on a serving-plate and garnish it with the remaining sliced offal and the coriander. Serve with *Keng Om Duk Ngua* (recipe 16).

* Editor's Note. *Or padek* is produced by cooking *padek* until it is almost dry; then adding water and bringing back to the boil; and then straining out any remaining fish bones. The result is a sauce which is used for adding flavour, as in this recipe.

16– ແກງອ່ອມເນື້ອງົວ

ເຄື່ອງປະສົມ — ກະດູກອ່ອນຫາງງົວ ຫຼື ເອົາໃຈງວກໃຫ້ພໍ ໝູ່ປັ່ນ ຕະອ້ນ ລ້າງນໍ້າໃຫ້ສະອາດໄວ້ ຕາມແຕ່ງ ຂີງ ສີໄຄ ດອກກະ ຫົວຜັກບົ່ວ ໃບຫອມ ໝາກເຜັດ ເກືອ ນໍ້າປາ ໃບຜັກອີ່ຕູ່ ໃບລາງ ເຂົ້າຈ້າວສານ ແລ້ວ ນໍ້າປາ ໃບຜັກບົ່ວ

ວິທີເຮັດ — ໃຫ້ເອົາ [illegible] ລ້າງ. ເຂົ້າຈ້າວ ແລະ ເຄື່ອງປັ່ນ ໃນໃສ່ [illegible] ແລ້ວ [illegible] ໃສ່ [illegible] ໝາກ [illegible]

Keng Om Duk Ngua **Recipe 16**

SOUP OF BOILED BEEF BONES

Ingredients

beef spare ribs—take off and discard the fat and cut the bones into pieces

1 rhizome of ginger 1 stalk of lemon grass 2 (small) shallots	all to be placed in the hot ashes of a charcoal fire until the aroma is brought out, then to be crushed just enough to break them—the result is known as *kheuang mok fai*

5 *phak i leut* (salad leaves, see page 35)

some plain uncooked rice, washed (and drained)

salt and fish sauce

spring onion leaves, chopped

Method

Put two bronze jugfuls (2 pints) of water, salt, the rice and the *kheuang mok fai* into a pot. Put it on the fire until the water comes to the boil. Put in the bones and continue boiling until the meat on them is done. Add the fish (sauce). Skim off the foaming fat from the surface. Add the salad leaves, chopped. Taste and check the saltiness.

Put (the contents of the pot) into a soup bowl and garnish with the chopped spring onion leaves. Serve with *Sa Ngua* (recipe 15) or *Jaew Mak Phet Dip* (see page 48).

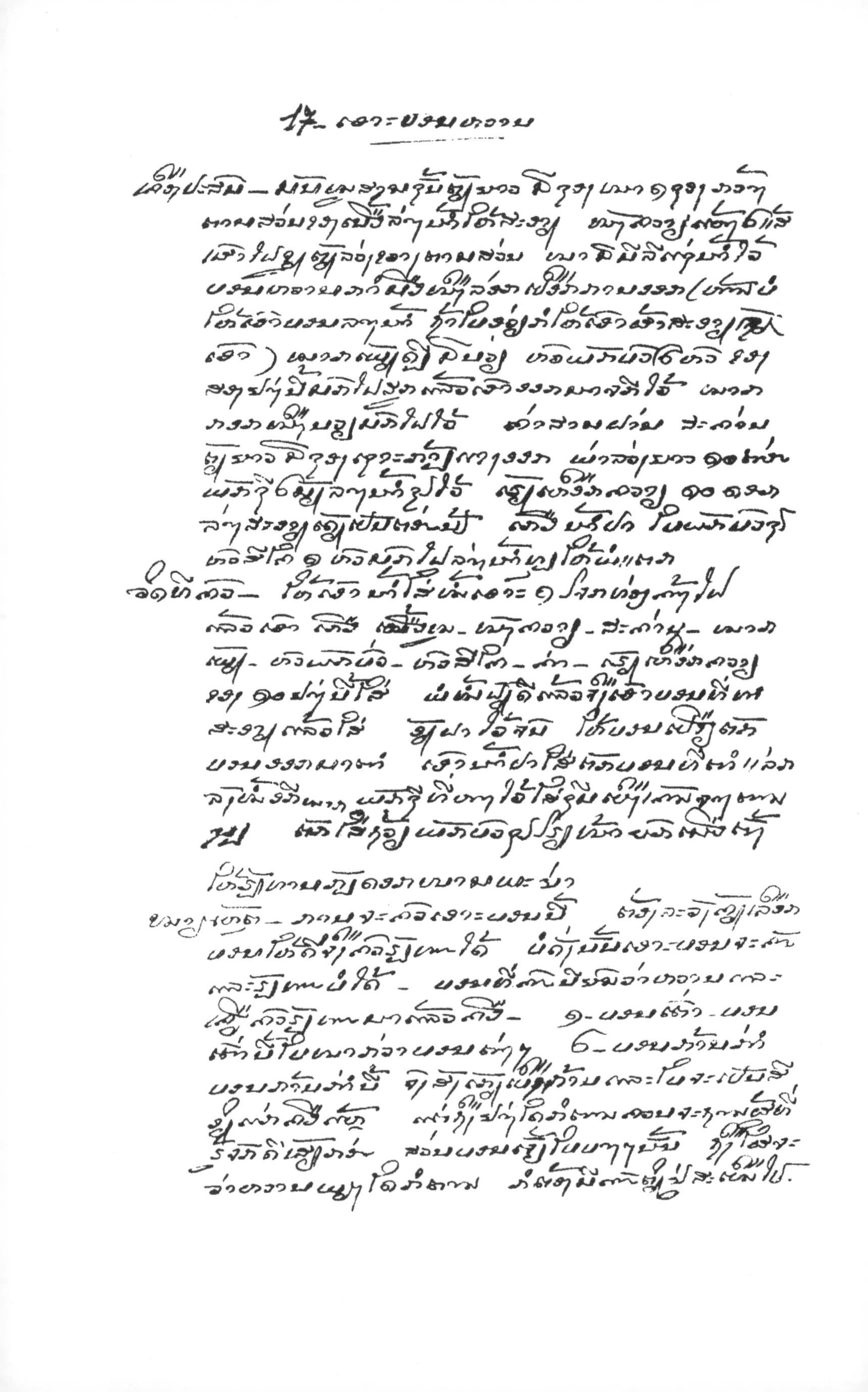

17- ເອາະບອນຫວານ

ເຄື່ອງປະສົມ – [illegible]

ວິທີເຮັດ – [illegible]

ໝາຍເຫດ – [illegible]

Or Bon Waan **Recipe 17**

A STEW MADE WITH SWEET BON

(*Bon* is the name of a plant, but it may be applied either to *bon waan*—a general name referring to any *bon* which is sweet and edible—or to *bon kan*, an itchy or scratchy *bon*, which should not be eaten since it will cause puffing and itching of the skin. Sweet *bon* in its cultivated form is taro. The drawing of a sweet *bon* on page 38 is of the species called *bon tao*—see end of recipe.)

Ingredients

a piece of three-layer pork (see page 26), cut into strips about 3 cm thick and 1 cm wide

a handful of *bon waan* (i.e. presumably a bunch as sold in the market, about five stalks)—peel off the outer skin, but do not wash the *bon*—if it is dirty, use a clean cloth to remove the dirt

2 pieces of dried buffalo skin—put them in a charcoal fire until they are a bit burned on the outside, then scrape off the burned part, cut the pieces into strips 3 mm wide and soak them in water

3 fresh chilli peppers } seared in a charcoal fire, then torn
2 (small) shallots } into small pieces

1 *mak kawk* (the fruit illustrated on page 30) treated like the chilli peppers and shallots

3 slices of galingale

sa-kahn (an aromatic plant used in making stews—see page 41)—cut a section 3 cm long of its (thick) stem, then take off the hard outer skin and divide the section vertically into 10 slices

2 bunches (about 6 sprigs) of dill, washed and chopped

10 jelly mushrooms (page 43), washed and divided into small pieces

salt and fish sauce

spring onion leaves, chopped

1 stalk of lemon grass—sear it in a charcoal fire, then wash it and crush it (with the flat of a heavy knife or with a pestle) just enough to bring out the aroma

Method

Put 1½ beakers (¾ pint) of water in a pot on the fire. Add the following: salt, pork, buffalo skin, *sa-kahn*, fresh chilli peppers, shallots, lemon grass, galingale and mushrooms.* When the mixture comes to the boil, add the cleaned *bon waan*, cover the pot and leave it until the *bon waan* is completely cooked. Then spoon out the *bon waan*, pound it, add fish sauce to it and return it to the pot. Add the *mak kawk* and the dill. Taste and check the saltiness. Transfer everything to a serving bowl, garnish it with the chopped spring onion and serve.

The dish should be accompanied by *dok nam panya*. (This name, which has no English equivalent, refers to CAESALPINIA MIMOSOIDES, illustrated on page 32, and means 'thorny flower of the Panya'. The Thai name is *phak pu ya*, meaning 'grandparents' vegetable'.)

Note

In cooking *Or Bon* we must be cautious in selecting the *bon*, since otherwise

18- ແກງສົ້ມກະລໍ່າປີ

ເຄື່ອງປະສົມ — ກະດູກໝູ ຫົວໝີ້ນ ເນື້ອໝູເທົ່າໃດ ກໍ່ໄດ້ ຕັດເປັນຕ່ອນຕາມຕ້ອງ
ການມີຫຼາຍລາຄາກໍ່ໄດ້ ກະລໍ່າປີທ່ອນຫົວ ເພາະຕຸ່ມລ່າ
ກໍ່ໄດ້ ຫົວພັກບົ່ວ ມີຫົວ ສີໂຄ 1 ຫົວ ໝາກເຂືອ
ເກືອເຂົ້າຈືນ ປາໂຕ ແລະສຸກາ ຫຼອງ 6 ບ່ວງລາກກໍ່ດີລອງ
ມາດຕາມ ບ່ວງໃດ້ ເກືອ — ນ້ຳປາ — ໃບພັກຫອມ
ວິທີເຮັດ — ເອົາໝໍ້ກໍ່ໃສ່ນ້ຳໃສກະທາ ມາໃສ່ຂຶ້ນໄຟ ແລ້ວເອົາ
ເກືອ- ຫົວພັກບົ່ວສີໂຄໃສ່ ແລ້ວກໍ່ຜັດຈົນເຂົ້າກັນໝົດ
ສຸກ ແລ້ວເອົານ້ຳປາກະລໍ່າປີໃສ່ ໝາກເຜັດ ສຸກາ ແລະ
ເປັນຕາມຕ້ອງການ ແລ້ວ ຈົນເຂົ້າ ໝາກເຂືອໃສ່

ຈຶ່ງເຕີມນ້ຳ ຈາກ ຕາມຕ້ອງ ປົງລົງ ໃສ່ຖ້ວຍ ພັກຫອມ
ຈຶ່ງຈະ ມາກິນ ນຳເຂົ້າໜຽວ ແລະ ສຸກາ ແລະ
ຈຶ່ງຈະດີ

(i.e. if we chose the wrong sort of *bon*—see introductory remarks) the dish would cause itching and would be inedible. Different types of *bon waan* which are popularly used in cooking for their sweet flavour are:

Bon tao,† whose special characteristic is that the leaves are thicker than those of other types; and

Bon kan kam, which one can easily recognise by the colour of its leaves and stems—the colour of which is purplish.‡

Anyway, one should consult those who know these types of *bon* (before making the dish). As for the common *bon* with thin leaves, no matter how much people admire its sweet taste, its juice causes itching.

Editors' Notes

* In the Lao text a superfluous sentence appears here, repeating the instruction to put these 'ten ingredients' in. The figure of ten was no doubt reached by counting the water as one ingredient.

† *Tao* means turtle, and the scientific name is REMUSATIA VIVIPARA.

‡ *Kai* means stalk and *kam* means dark-coloured. The scientific name is CALADIUM BICOLOR. Another Lao name for this species is *Bon deng*.

Keng Som Kalampi **Recipe 18**

SOUR CABBAGE SOUP

Ingredients

pig's bones or pork meat—the desired quantity, cut according to your wishes and washed
½ cabbage, cut up into pieces (of bite size, or bigger) and washed
3 spring onions, the bulbs only (but you will need the leaves too—see below)
1 stalk lemon grass
2 fresh tomatoes, washed and sliced
salt and fish sauce
chopped spring onion leaves

Method

Put 1 bronze jugful (1 pint) of water into a pot and place the pot on the fire. Add salt, spring onion bulbs and lemon grass. When the water comes to the boil, add fish sauce and the pieces of cabbage. When the vegetables are done, add the tomatoes. (A minute or two later) taste and check the saltiness. Transfer the contents of the pot to a serving-bowl and garnish with chopped spring onions.

Serve the dish with *Jaew Bong* (see recipe 64) and *Sin Dawd Chi* (sometimes called *Sin Lawd Chi*—it consists of thin pieces of beef or water-buffalo meat which have been cooked into a curling shape by placing them direct on the glowing embers of a charcoal fire).

19– ກະປຸ່ງປາແດກ

ເຄື່ອງປະສົມ — ປາແດກ 6 ຕ່ອນ ເລືອກເອົາຕ່ອນມີຊີ້ນປາຫລາຍ ໃສ່
ລ້າງແກ້ເອົາເກັດແລະຂ້ຳຂອງອອກໃຫ້ໝົດ ຟັກໃຫ້ແຫລກໃສ່
ຈານໄວ້ ຫົວຜັກບົ່ວປອກແລ້ວ 30 ຫົວ ຫົວຜັກ
ທຽມ 6 ຫົວ ເພາະງົມອອກ ປອກເອົາແຕ່ເນື້ອ
ສີໂຕ 2 ຫົວ ຜັກບົ່ວລາງເຄື່ອງ 6 ຫົວ ຊອຍໝາກສອນ
ແລະເອົາແກ້ວນ້ຳກໍ່ບົມຂອງ 6 ຕ່ອນ ຂອງສາມຢ່າງນີ້
ທຳໃສ່ກັນໃຫ້ແຫລກ ຂົມສາມຈຸ່ມ ຟັກໃຫ້ແຫລກເຫັນບ່ອງ
ໃສ່ເນີ້ ໃບຜັກບົ່ວຈີນ ໃບຫອມດູໃບ ຕາກຕ້ອງເປື້ອ
ຈອນມ່ວງໝາກ ໝາກຄອງ ເຂົ້າໜຽວ ໜຶ່ງເສັ້ນ ເອົາໄຟໃຫ້ໄໝ້ ຊຸເອົາຕ້ອງກອ
ຂອງ ຈຶ່ງເປັນທ່ອນ ນີ້ແລະບາງໆ ແງ່ນກໍ່ເອົາໄວ້ໃຫ້ເປື້ອງ
ວິທີເຮັດ — ຕັດເອົາເຄື່ອງຕຳລົງໃສ່ຄົກ ແລ້ວເອົາ ປູນຟັກ
ປາແດກຟັກ ຜັກບົ່ວປອກ ຜັກທຽມປອກ ໝາກຄອງ
ທີ່ແງ່ໄວ້ໃສ່ ຕຳໃຫ້ເຂົ້າກັນ ຈຶ່ງເອົາໃບຜັກບົ່ວຈີນ
ແລະໝາກດ ເນີ້ງຕົ້ນນີ້ໃສ່ຂາວໃຫ້ທົ່ວ ເພາະເປັນແພ
ເກັນຈາງ ຖ້າຕຳເອົາມາປາແດກຂອງຂີ້ ໃຫ້ກະເຍົາ
ພໍງາມດີ ຈຶ່ງເອົາໃບຫມາກອ່ອນ ຈຶ່ງເອົາຕາກຕ້ອງຈີ່
ແຕ່ງເມື່ອເປື້ອນບໍ່ກວ່າໄຟ ໃຫ້ສຸກແລະຫອມດີແລ້ວ
ຈຶ່ງເອົາມາໃສ່ຈານ ພ້ອມເນື້ອດັ່ງໃຫ້ຊິ້ນກາຍໝາກ
ແຕງ ອ່ອນແລະຜັກທີ່ຢາງໆ

Kanab Padek **Recipe 19**

A FERMENTED FISH MIXTURE GRILLED IN BANANA LEAF CONTAINERS

Ingredients

2 pieces of fish from the *padek* pot (see page 23)—choose pieces with a lot of meat, wash them and get rid of all the dust and rice husks, then mince the meat and leave it on a plate

30 (small) shallots, peeled

2 (small) heads of garlic—remove the outer skin and peel each clove

3 stalks of lemon grass

2 straight-bulbed spring onions

2 pieces of crisp-fried pork skin, the fat removed and the remainder pounded with the lemon grass and spring onions until the three ingredients are completely mixed (to constitute what is called the *kheuang tam*)

a piece of three-layer pork (page 26), minced, to produce a quantity the size of a duck's egg

chopped spring onion leaves

1 *toon* leaf (*bai toon*, see page 38)

pieces of banana leaf

1 piece of dried water-buffalo skin—sear it in the charcoal fire, then scrape off the burned parts, cut the remainder into small, thin slices and soak them in water until soft

10 small chilli peppers (*mak phet kuntsi*, page 34)

Method

Put the prepared *kheuang tam* in a mixing bowl. Add the minced pork, minced *padek*, shallots, garlic and soaked water-buffalo skin. Mix, then add the chopped spring onion leaves and small chilli peppers and mix some more. Taste and check the saltiness. If the taste is not strong enough, add more *padek* liquid. Make sure that the mixture is moist enough but not too watery.

Wrap the mixture in the *toon* leaf and then in outer wrappings of banana leaf. (Several such outer wrappings, probably four or five, should be used.) Grill the wrapped mixture in a bamboo holder (see the drawing on page 18) over a charcoal fire until it is cooked and smells good. Then set it on a platter and serve it with young cucumbers and various steamed vegetables.*

* Editors' Notes. These latter might be some or all of the following: sliced cabbage; gourds, halved, or cut in three if big; the flower and young leaves of *khae ban*, AGATI GRANDIFLORA (drawing on page 32); leaves of *phak bun*, IPOMOEA AQUATICA, known as swamp cabbage or water spinach (drawing on page 36); and leaves of *phak kad khao*, 'greens' of the cabbage family (see the drawing on page 35).

20 - ຕົ້ມຈືດທ່ອນລີ້ນ

ເຄື່ອງປະສົມ - ຊີ້ນສັນງົວລຸ່ມ ເອົາເອັນອອກໃຫ້ໝົດ ໜຶ່ງລອງຂາງ
ຕາງມສ່ວນ ມັນໃຫຍ່ ໝາກ ໑ ງວຍ ມີຕ່ອນ ໜຶ່ງໃຫ້ນຳ
ອອມ ແຫ້ງ ມັນໃຫຍ່ ເຫົ້າໃສ່ຈານໄວ້ ໝາກເຜັດເຄື່ອງສັບ
ມັນ ໑ ຊັ້ນ ຜັກທ່ອນທອງໃຫຍ່ ໑ ຫົວ ຜັກຫອມ 6 ຕົ້ນ
ສະລຸ ມີຕ່ວນ ນ້ຳມັນລ່ຽ ເຄື່ອ ເກືອໝັ້ນ - ນ້ຳຕົ້ມຊີ້ນງົວ
ວິທີເຮັດ — ເອົາໝໍ້ຕົ້ມນ້ຳໃສ່ໄຟ ນ້ຳມັນ ເຄື່ອງໃສ່ 6 ບ່ອງ ເມື່ອນ້ຳ
ມັນຮ້ອນເອົາ ຜັກທ່ອມ ທ່ອງໃຫຍ່ ງົວລົງ ບາງໃສ່ ຈົນໃຫ້ເປັນ
ຫອມ ຈຶ່ງເອົາໝາກເຜັດເຄື່ອງສັບ ໃສ່ ຂົວໃຫ້ຫອມ
ແລ້ວເອົານ້ຳຕົ້ມງົວໃສ່ພໍ ສົມຄວນ ແລະ ຮຸ່ມໄຟອ່ອນໆ ທ່າ
ນັ້ນ ສະລຸ ໃຫ້ເປັນໃບ ໃຫ້ງາມ ລຸ່ມ ອອມ ແຄມຈານ
ໃຊ້ ເມື່ອເຫັນວ່າ ຊ່ວງນີ້ ບາງ ຮ່ອງ ແລ້ວ ຈຶ່ງເອົາໝໍ້
ຂວາງຕັ້ງໃສ່ ນ້ຳມັນໃສ່ໃນໝໍ້ບ່ອງ ເມື່ອນ້ຳມັນ
ຮ້ອນເປັນຕອນ ຂື້ນ ຈຶ່ງເອົາຊີ້ນງົວລົງປ່ຽນ ຜັດ ເພື່ອງັນ
ເບື່ອມີ ນຳໃຫ້ ເຫັນ ແຕ່ ອອກ ແລ້ວເອົາເຄື່ອງ ໃສ່ ຕາມ
ອອກ ໃສ່ຈານ ຜັກ ສະລຸ ນ້ຳ ເພາະ ເຄື່ອງ ໃສ່ ຕ່າງ
ເກືອ ມັນ ຜັກຫອມ ໃສ່ ເຫົ້າ ຍັງ ເພື່ອ ຕັງ ໃຫ້
ຫາມ ລົງ ນ້ຳ ສົ້ມ ໝາກ ເພາ -

Nua Ngua Tod Som **Recipe 20**

SOUR FRIED BEEF

Ingredients

beef—take the meat and trim off all the tough part (gristle or tendons) and slice it into three pieces 1 cm thick
ground black pepper—sprinkle it on the pieces of meat and put them on a plate
1 small can of tomato paste*
1 large onion
2 sprigs of coriander
3 lettuces
butter*
salt, ground black pepper
meat broth

Method

Heat 2 tablespoons of butter in a sauté pan (*maw kan noi*). When the butter is hot, put the large onion, which has been sliced, into it. Fry until it smells good. Open the can of tomato paste and put its contents into the pot. Keep frying until the mixture gives off a good aroma. Then add the meat broth, only enough to keep the mixture from becoming dry. Cover and leave on a low heat.

Prepare the lettuces by separating the leaves and placing them in a circle on a platter.

After these two preparations, heat a tablespoon of butter in a wok. When the butter has melted and is smoking hot, brown the pieces of meat in it, turning them back and forth. Sprinkle them with salt and place them on the prepared lettuce. Then pour the sauce which you have made over the meat and sprinkle ground black pepper on top. Pick off the coriander leaves and use them as a garnish. Serve with *Nam Jeem Mak Phet* (an uncooked mixture of fish sauce, garlic, lime juice, sugar and chopped small green chilli peppers—see page 48).

* Editors' Note. The use of canned tomato paste and butter shows clearly that this is not a purely Lao recipe, but one which combines Lao techniques with western ingredients.

21- ຝຸ່ນຮົ່ມໃສ່ຫົວຜັກເພີ່ມ

ເຄື່ອງປະສົມ — ຝຸ່ນປອກຫ້ອນ ໑ ຕອນ ຝຸ່ນຫົວ ຝຸ່ນຄວາຍ ປຽງປີ້ງ
ຂອງ ເພາະວ່ານີ້ຈະໃສ່ຂອງລ່າງນັ້ນເອົາມົນປຽງວ່ານີ້
ຝຸ່ນຂອງໃຫ້ສຸກ ຕົ້ນເດີມແລະພືດ ນໍ້າໃຈ ສ່ວນຝຸ່ນຝຸ່ນ
ຜັກໃຫ້ລະອຽດ ໂດຍຝຸ່ນນໍ້າໃຫ້ທ່ານລອງເອົາເຄື່ອງ ຂອງຂອງ
ລ້າງນໍ້າໃຫ້ສະອາດແລ້ວເອົາມາວາງໄວ້ເປັນໆ ໃຊ້ນໍ້າຝຸ່ນ
ຜັກຍັງຫົວປອນ ໑໐ ຫົວ ຕາກໃຫ້ແຫ້ງ ແລ້ວທ່ອງຫົວໃຫຍ່
ທ່າງ ຫົວຈຸລອງຂອງ ໃຫ້ນາງແລ້ວຜັກຈົນແຫ້ງ ໃນເຂົ້າ
ໜຶ້ງປຸ້ຍນໍ້າ ນອງໃນຝຸ່ນ ຜັກໃຫ້ແຫ້ງ ໃບຜັກຫອມ ມີຕົ້ນ
ຜັກໃຫ້ແຫ້ງ ແລ້ວເພີ່ມ ໆ ຫົວປຸ້ຍຫົວນໍ້າປອມເພື່ອ
ລ້າງນໍ້າໃຊ້ ເຄື່ອງ - ນໍ້າປາ - ທົ່ວນໍ້າປ່າ - ຜັກຫອມໄວ
ນໍ້າມັນພືດ ຝຸ່ນແມສອນສອງຕ່ອນຈຸເອົາມາຂອງຕາກໃຫ້
ແຫ້ງ ເພື່ອອຸ່ມສາມວັນ ຜັກໃຫ້ແຫ້ງ ເກົ່ານອງ
ໃຊ້ໄດ້

ວິທີທຳ — ໃຫ້ເອົາເຄື່ອງຕ່າງໆຄື — ຝຸ່ນ - ໃຕ - ແຫ້ງຍ່ອຍນໍ້າ - ຜັກ
ບົ່ວຜັກ - ໜຶ້ງປຸ້ຍນໍ້າ - ໃບຜັກຫອມຜັກ - ຝຸ່ນແມສອນ -
ຈຸບີແມຜັກ 2ທາງ ພໍສົມຄວນນີ້ໃຫ້ເອົາລວມຄົນໃສ່ແຫ່ງ ແລ້ວ
ນໍ້າປາລວງ ແລະເພີ່ມເຕີມຈາງຕາມຈຸດ ແລ້ວເອົາຝຸ່ນ
ໃສ່ທັງໝົດ ສູນເຄື່ອງໃນຝຸ່ນໃຫ້ໝຸ່ນ ເພື່ອບ້າງເປັນ
ນີ້ໃຊ້ດີແລ້ວ ຈຶ່ງເອົາເສັ້ນລວດ ຂົນເຫຼັກໄຟນໍ້າມັນເພ
ໃສ່ສອງບ່ອນ ແລ້ວເອົາຝຸ່ນລົງຈົນ ແລ້ວໄປພືດມາຈົນເປັນ
ເນື້ອງານດີ ຈຶ່ງເອົາຫົວຜັກໃສ່ຈົນປຸ້ມໃຫ້ທົ່ວ ຖ້າມີ
ມັນຝຸ່ນຂອງບາງທໍາໃຫ້ປຸ່ງປ່ອຍເພາະນໍ້າມັນກຸ້ມໃຫ້
ຝຸ່ນ ແລ້ວເອົາເຫຼັກໄຟຕີພື້ນຕາກເອົາມດຕົ້ນດາຍມໃສ່
ຈົນກ້ອນເປັນແລະຫົວຜັກສຸກຟ່າເຄີ້ນໄປ ຈົນຝຸ່ນເປື່ອຍນໍ້າ
ແຫ້ງເຫຼືອໃຊ້ປະມານສາມອາທິດ ປາສຽງຕາກເອົາເປັນຂອງ
ນາ ຈົນເປັນກ້ອນແລະ 27 ແລ້ວຈຶ່ງເອົາເຄື່ອງອື່ນໃສ່ຂອງ
ໃສ່ຕາກງາມ ເພື່ອຝຸ່ນອາງລົງຂອງມເຄື່ອງຫົວ ຫົວຜັກ
ເອົາລົງມສົມຕາມງາມ ແລ້ວນໍ້າຫອມວຽກຫຼາຍເປົ້າ
ນອກເພື່ອສົ່ງໃຫ້ຝຸ່ນງາມ ຝຸ່ນນໍ້າຈຶ່ງແນວຄົນເປັນອັນດຽວ

Ped Hum Sai Houa Phak Peuk **Recipe 21**

STUFFED DUCK WITH HORSERADISH

Ingredients

1 duck, cleaned and gutted—cut off the head, the feet and the wing-tips; open the duck up, take out the intestines and remove the fat from the tail end; salt it and add a sprinkling of ground black pepper
the duck's liver, minced
the duck's gizzard—slit it open, discard any food in it, peel off the inner lining, slice the gizzard thinly and put it with the prepared liver on a plate
10 (small) shallots, pounded finely
½ onion, thinly sliced and finely chopped
the soft part of French bread—size of a duck's egg—chopped
3 sprigs of coriander, the leaves only, finely chopped
8 small Chinese radishes, peeled and washed
salt, fish sauce and ground black pepper
coriander, chopped (for garnishing)
butter (2 tbsp)
2 pieces of crisp-fried pork skin—remove and discard the fat and pound the skin
three-layer pork (see page 26), minced—size of a hen's egg
(pork broth)

Method

Put in a mixing bowl the minced liver, sliced gizzard, pounded shallots, chopped onion, chopped bread, chopped coriander leaves, pounded crisp-fried pork skin and minced pork. Add salt and fish sauce. Taste and check the saltiness. Then stuff the mixture into the duck and wind thread tightly round the bird. After thus preparing the duck, put a cooking pot on the fire. Put 2 tablespoons of butter in it. Then put in the duck to fry. Turn it over and over until it becomes a nice golden-brown. Add the Chinese radishes. Continue to fry. If there seems to be too much duck fat, take the pot off the fire and pour out all the fat; then put the pot back on the fire. Add enough pork broth to cover the duck and the vegetable. Cover the pot and leave it to cook until the duck is well done and the liquid has been reduced to about 3 ladlefuls.

Open out the duck, separating the breast part from the leg parts. Take out the stuffing and put it in the middle of a platter. Arrange the duck meat around it, then place the Chinese radishes around the outside. Garnish with chopped coriander and sprinkle with ground black pepper. Serve with *Nam Jeem Mak Phet Deng* (see page 48).

22– ແກງຜັກຫົມອ່ອນ

ເຄື່ອງປະສົມ – ປານອນປີ້ງ ສິຕ້ອງລ້າງເນົ່າໃຫ້ດີ ຜັກຫົມ
ອ່ອນ ຫຼືຮ່ວາກລ້າງໃຫ້ສະອາດ ຕາມຄວນ ຫົວຜັກ
ບົ່ວ ຫົວປອມ ສີຫົວ ໃບຜັກບົ່ວ – ເກືອ – ນໍ້າປາ
ວິທີຄົວ – ໃຫ້ຕົ້ມນໍ້າ ໃຈກຸ [illegible] ເກືອເລັກນ້ອຍ ຫົວຜັກ
ບົ່ວ ປານອນ [illegible] ໃສ່ໝໍ້ [illegible] ໄຟ [illegible] ນໍ້າ [illegible]
ປາ [illegible] ເກືອ [illegible] ຜັກຫົມໃສ່ [illegible]
[illegible] ເປີດ [illegible] ໃສ່ [illegible] ໃບຜັກບົ່ວ [illegible]
[illegible] ເມື່ອ [illegible] ໃຫ້ [illegible] ແກ້ວ 2 [illegible]

Keng Phak Hum On **Recipe 22**

YOUNG SPINACH SOUP

Ingredients

3 dried *pa gnon* (PANGASIUS SIAMENSIS, a species of catfish illustrated on page 71), washed
young spinach, (several bunches) with the roots cut off, and washed
3 (small) shallots
spring onion leaves, chopped
salt and fish sauce

Method

Put 1 metal jugful (1 pint) of water, salt, the shallots and the dried *pa gnon* into a pot. Put the pot on the fire. When the soup boils and the fish is done, add the spinach. When the soup comes back to the boil, taste and check the saltiness, then pour it into a bowl. Garnish it with the chopped spring onion leaves. Serve with *Jaew Kha* (see page 48).

໒໓. ເອາະຫລາມຊີ້ນຄວາຽ

ເຄື່ອງປະສົມ — ຊີ້ນຄວາຽແຫ້ງ ມີ ທ່ອນນຶ່ງໃຫ້ເປັນທ່ອນນ້ອຽປີ້ງ ນຳໃຫ້ສະອາດໄວ້ ໜັງຄວາຽແຫ້ງ ໒ ແຜ່ນ ເຜົາໄຟໃຫ້ໄໝ້ ຂູດ ແລະ ຫັ່ນ ຊຸ່ມ ໃຫ້ນ້ອຽ ເຄິ່ງ ຂອບໃສ່ຂອດ ຖ້ວຍເປັນທ່ອນ ບາງໆ ພໍຄວນ ແຊ່ນ້ຳໄວ້ ຜັກເຜັດ ຮອນ ໑ ຕ່ອນ ຜັກເປັນທ່ອນ ນ້ອຽໄວ້ ສະຄ້ານ ຜັກຍາວເທົ່າຂໍ້ ເຄາະ ... ເປັນ ທ່ອນນຶ່ງ ໑໐ ທ່ອນ ໝາກເຂືອ ... ສີໂກ ໑ ຕົ້ນ ຜັກໃບ ... ນຳໄວ້ ໝາກເຂືອ ບາວ ... ໗ ໜ່ວຍ ໝາກເຂືອ ... ຜັກທ່ຳລີ ໑ ກຳມື ... ໝາກເຂືອ ... ກຳມື ໃບ ຜັກອີ່ຕູ່ ຜັກສົມຄວາຍ ຜັກ ຊີ ... ໑ ກຳມື ໃບ ຜັກ ... ... ປາແດກ

ວິທີເຮັດ — ໃຫ້ເອົາ ນ້ຳ ໑ ໝໍ້ ... ໃສ່ເຄື່ອງ ເອາະ ... ໄຟ ແລ້ວ ເອົາ - ... - ສີໂກ - ຊີ້ນຄວາຽ - ໜັງຄວາຽ - ຫົວ ຜັກບົ່ວ - ໝາກ ເຜັດ ໝາກເຂືອ - ສະຄ້ານ - ... ໃສ່ ... ນ້ຳ ... ແລ້ວ ຈຶ່ງເອົາປາແດກ ໃສ່ ... ... ໄປ ... ໝາກ ... ໝາກ ... ແລ້ວ ... ... ແລ້ວ ... ... ໃສ່ ... ... ແລ້ວ ເອົາ ... ... ໃສ່ ... ... ປາແດກ .

ໝາຽເຫດ — ເຣື່ອງ ເອາະຫລາມ ນີ້ ຈະເອົາຊີ້ນ ໄປ ... ໄດ້ ... ເພາະ ... ... ບໍ່ມີ ... ... ເອາະ ... ... ໄດ້ ... ເອາະຫລາມ ນີ້ ... ... ເອາະໂຣະ ເອາະໂຣະ ... ... ເອາະໂຣະ
... ເອາະຫລາມ ... ...
... ... ເອາະ ... ...

Or Lam Sin Kuay **Recipe 23**

'OR LAM' OF WATER-BUFFALO MEAT

Ingredients

3 pieces of dried buffalo meat, sliced into smaller pieces and washed
2 strips of dried buffalo skin (see page 25)—cook it by putting it directly into the charcoal fire and then scraping off the burned parts, after which cut it into smaller pieces and soak them in water
3 or 4 (small) shallots, peeled
1 piece of crisp-fried pork skin, sliced into smaller pieces
1 piece of *sa-kahn* (an aromatic plant, see page 41) 5 cm long—peel off and discard the rough outer skin and divide it into 15 small parts
3 straight-bulbed spring onions
1 stalk of lemon grass—sear it in hot ashes, then wash it and crush it
7 young round eggplants (see page 33)
7 fresh chilli peppers (large ones)
1 bunch *phak tam ling* (an edible leaf, see page 37)
1 bunch of young shoots (stems and leaves) of a chilli pepper plant
a considerable amount of sweet basil leaves
1 bunch of dill, chopped
a considerable amount of chopped spring onion leaves
salt and *padek*

Method

Put $1\frac{1}{2}$ metal jugfuls ($1\frac{1}{2}$ pints) of water into a pot and place it on the fire. Add salt, the crushed stalk of lemon grass, the buffalo meat, the buffalo skin, the shallots, the chilli peppers, the eggplants and the *sa-kahn*. Wait for all this to come to the boil, then add some *padek* by using a small-meshed strainer (as shown on page 17). Leave it boiling until the chilli peppers and eggplants are done—then take out these ingredients, pound them finely and return them to the pot.

Next, add the *phak tam ling* and the young shoots of chilli pepper. Taste and check the saltiness. Then add the crisp-fried pork skin, the chopped dill and the sweet basil leaves. Take the pot off the fire. Transfer the contents to a bowl. Garnish the dish with chopped spring onion leaves and serve it with *Som Moo* (page 49) or *Som Pa Keng* (page 49).

Note

There is no one definite recipe for *Or Lam* because there are no fixed rules about how to make it. Some people put in a very large quantity of fresh vegetables and mushrooms, until the dish is more like an *Or Phak* (a vegetable *Or*). In fact, there are two types of *Or Lam*. One is called *Or Ho*: and this is made by putting in meat or fish and vegetables and mushrooms—everything edible—in large or small quantities. That is why they call it *Or Ho*. ('*Ho*' in Lao means to put in. So '*Or Ho*' is the result of putting in whatever you have.) The real *Or Lam* is the one I have explained above. The tastes and smells of the two types of *Or Lam* are different.

໒໔ ເພາະລູກໄມ້

ເຄື່ອງປະສົມ — ໄມ້ປ່ອງຫຼາຍຫ້ອນ ໑ ທ່ອນ ເຈາະກົ້ນຈັກໄສ້ອອກລຽງກໍ່
ໃຫ້ສະອາດ ຫຼືເປັນທ່ອນທໍ່ມະດາໄວ້ ໝາກເຫຼືອງຫວານ
ທ່ອນຂູດລ່ອງຍາວພໍງາມ ຈົນບ່ອງ ໝາກເໝືອງເປີດບ່ອງ
ທ່ອເພາະບໍ່ ໒ ທ່ອ ສີໂຄງອ່ອນ ໑ ທ່ອ ຂອງສາລະ
ຢ່າງນີ້ໃສ່ຕົ້ນທໍ່ ໃຫ້ແຫຼກໄວ້ ເອົາເຂົ້າໝຽງໝໍ້ມາ
ມຽງໃຫ້ແໜ້ນ ເຂົ້າທັງແຜ່ນເມື່ອຂາງໃນພໍເຫຼືອງໄວ້ ໝາກ
ເຫຼືອງໃຫ ອອນບ່ອງ ເພາະທ່ຳລົງໆ ທ່ຳມື ເຫຼືອງເມັ່ນປູເຫຼືອ
ເສັ້ນຂາວ ໑ ທ່ຳມື ເຫຼືອ (ເຫຼືອງແກວ) ປາແດກເຫຼືອ ນຳປາ
ໃບອີ່ຕູ່ ເພາະພ້ອງປ
ວິທີທຳ — ໃຫ້ເອົາເນົ່າໃສ່ເພ ໑ ໂຈກ ຍາກາ ທ່ອງ ຂຶ້ນຕົ້ນໃຜ
ພໍເນົ່າຝົນ ຈຶ່ງເອົາໄປທີ່ຕູ້ໄວ້ ເຫຼືອ ເພາະເຄື່ອງທຳໃສ່
ພໍໄດ້ສຸກ ໃຫ້ເອົາໝາກເຫຼືອງປ ເສີ້ງ ເວົ້າຈົ່ ນຳປາ
ເຫຼືອປາແດກ ຕາຍໄວ້ ໝາກເຫຼືອງໃຫເພາະມາ
ເມື່ອເພາະວ່າ ໝາກເຫຼືອເປື່ອຍແລ້ວ ຈຶ່ງເອົາເພາະທ່ຳລົງ
ໃສ່ ສຸກແລ້ວງມເຟື່ອງເຕັມຈາງແກມງຸປ ເພາະອີ່ຕູ່
ໃສ່ທັງລົງຕອກໃສ່ຖ້ວຍ ເພາະພ້ອງປໂງ ໝາກ ນາກເມື່ອ ຕັ້ງໃຫ້
ມີທາມ ຝາ ເພາະທ່ຽງໆ
ໝາຍເຫດ — ເຂາະລູກນີ້ ກຸບພະໂທມີນຳບາງ ເພື່ອໃຫ້ຜົ
ມີທາມ ໄດ້ເອົາບ່ອງລູກນຳຕອງ ຈຶ່ງໄດ້ຊື່ວ່າເຂາະລູກ
ຕາມທີ່ຕານທາງບາງໆ ເອີ້ນວ່າເຂາະລູກມັນພໍ່ໄປ ເພາະ
ບໍ່ມີລັກສະນະເພາະພໍ ສ່ວນເຂາະລູກນັ້ນລັກສະນະມີ
ວ່າ ແຜ່ນຂາວທາ ນຂອງນ້ຳຕົ້ມທານນຳ ເພາະເຂົ້າ
ໃປກັ່ງທີ່ນອນຕົ້ນໃນ ຈຶ່ງຕາວເຂາະລູກໄມ້ຕາງໆຕາງໆມີ
ທານເພື່ອຕົ້ນຕານຕາຍເຂີວ

Or Sod Kai **Recipe 24**

CHICKEN STEW

Ingredients

1 chicken, plucked, gutted, washed and cut into pieces
3 sweet young round eggplants (see page 33), sliced vertically
2 large fresh chilli peppers }
2 (small) shallots } (chopped small and) pounded finely
1 stalk of lemon grass }
cooked sticky rice—a quantity about equal to your thumb—mash it together and grill it until it is golden (this is called *khao jee*)
20 very small eggplants (*mak kheng*, see page 33)
1 handful *phak tam ling* (an edible leaf, see page 37)
1 handful *hed bod* or *hed khao* (the mushrooms described on page 43)
salt and *padek* or fish sauce
sweet basil leaves
chopped spring onion leaves

Method

Put 1½ metal jugfuls (1½ pints) of water in a pot and place it on the fire. When the water comes to the boil put in the chicken pieces, with salt and the pounded ingredients. When the chicken pieces are done, add the sliced eggplants, the mushrooms, the piece of grilled rice, and either fish sauce or *padek* in a small-meshed strainer (as shown on page 17). Add the very small eggplants when the larger eggplants and the *phak tam ling* are cooked. Taste and check the saltiness, then add the sweet basil leaves and take the pot off the fire.

Serve the dish in a bowl, garnished with the spring onion leaves and accompanied by a variety of fresh raw vegetables (such as cabbage, cucumber and yard-long beans).

Note

Or Sod should have lots of liquid so that people can '*sod*' it (*sod* being a Lao verb which means to eat soup out of a soupspoon), and that is why it is called *sod*. There is some evidence about how this '*Or*' received the name *sod*.* Apparently it originated as a dish for traders travelling by boat. When such people get home, it is usually late at night, so they make this *Or Sod*, instead of a *keng*, because it is easy to swallow with rice.

* Editors' Note. As Phia Sing implies, an '*or*' would usually have little liquid; and people would not use spoons to pick up meat and vegetables, nor for the sauce, which they would sop up by dipping sticky rice into it. With *Or Sod*, however, a spoon would be needed because of the greater quantity of liquid.

25- ລາບປາແດງ

ເຄື່ອງປະສົມ— ປາແດງ ໑ ໂຕ ເອົາມາຂວາະເກັດແລ້ວທ້ອງຈັກ ເອົາໄສ້ອອກ ຖ້າໄສ້ຂາວສະອາດດີ ກໍໃຫ້ເອົາໃສ່ນຳ ກໍ ແລະບີໃສ່ຕ່າງຫາກ ລ້າງນ້ຳເອົາຕາໜ່າງຂ່ວງມາຈໍ່ເຜົາໄຟ ໄວ້ ເພື່ອມີໄຂ່ປາກໍໃຫ້ຈໍ່ຕາໜ່າງເຜົາໄຟໄວ້ຕ່າງຫາກ ແລ້ວ ຈຶ່ງເອົາແຕ່ຊີ້ນປາ ໜັງປາເອົາອອກໄວ້ຕ່າງຕໍ່ ລ້າງນ້ຳ ແລ້ວຟັກໃຫ້ແຫຼກໆໄວ້ ສ່ວນໜັງປາທີ່ລື່ນອອກນັ້ນ ກໍໃຫ້ເອົາລວກນ້ຳແດງໃຫ້ພໍສຸກ ແລ້ວເອົາອອກມາຊອຍ ເປັນຕ່ອນນ້ອຍໆໄວ້ ໝາກເຂືອຂາວ ໒ ໜ່ວຍເຜົາໄຟໃຫ້ໄໝ້ ເປືອກນອກ ຢ່າໃຫ້ໄໝ້ຮອດແກ່ນ ແລ້ວເອົາອອກໃສ່ຖ້ວຍ ຫຼືຈານໄວ້ ໝາກເຜັດແຫ້ງ ໒໗ ໄພໃຫ້ສຸກດີນ່ອງ ຜັກ ຫອມ ໒ ຫົວເຜົາໄຟ ຜັກບົ່ວຫົວປອມ ໒ ຫົວເຜົາໄຟ ຂ່າສອງພ້າງ ແຕ່ງເຜົາທັງໝົດນີ້ເອົາໃສ່ຄົກຕຳໃຫ້ ແຫຼກໆ ແຕ່ຕ້ອງແລ້ວເອົາໄວ້ ຜັກຫອມ ໒ ຫົວຊີ ລ່ວງຂວາງ ຈືນ ນ້ຳມັນໝູ ພໍເຫຼືອງ ແລ້ວຕັກໄວ້ ຜັກຫອມຊີ ຜັກບົ່ວ ຊອຍ ນ້ຳປາແດກເຈາະ ເກືອ ກ້ຽງ ໝາກນາວ ນ້ຳສົ້ມປາ ໑ ກ້ຽງ ກະເທີຍມ ເທື່ອ

ວິທີຕ່ອງ— ໃຫ້ເອົາປາທີ່ຟັກໄວ້ມາໃສ່ຄັກແທືອງເຜົາ ແລ້ວ ບອກຈົນເຂົ້າກັນດີ ຈຶ່ງເອົານ້ຳປາແດກເຈາະ ເກືອ-ເທື່ອ ໃສ່ຄົນໄປຈົນເຂົ້າກັນ ນ້ຳແດງເຮືອງ ແລ້ວຄົນໄປຈົນດາບ ບ່ອນເຫຼວນັ້ນ ສົມຄວນແລ້ວຈຶ່ງເອົາໜັງປາໃຫ້ຜັກ ຫອມ ໃສ່ປາມັດ ໃສ່ປາມາໃສ່ ຈຸ້ມເຫຼືອເກືອມ ຈາງ ຫອມຊອຍ ແລ້ວຕັກໃສ່ຈານ ຜັກຫອມຈົນເຫຼືອງເຕົາ ຜັກຫອມຊອຍ ຍັງ ນັ້ນແມ່ນຕ້ອງໃຫ້ມີໝາກຖົ່ວແຫ່ງ ສົ້ມຫົວປາແດກ ແລະຜັກຕ່າງໆ

Lap Pa Keng **Recipe 25**

MINCED RAW FISH

Ingredients

1 *pa keng* (a barb, see page 24), scaled, gutted and washed—keep the intestine, if it is clean, and eggs, if any, wrap them together in pieces of banana leaf and grill them on the fire until cooked—take half only of the flesh of the fish, wash it and chop it finely—put the fish skin in the soup (see recipe 29) until it is just enough cooked, then take it out and chop it into small pieces

5 sweet young round eggplants (see page 33)—place them on a charcoal fire until their skins are burned, but do not let the seeds inside burn—then place them in a bowl
3 dried chilli peppers—grill them until soft
3 (small) heads of garlic—sear them on a charcoal fire
3 (small) shallots—sear them on a charcoal fire
2 slices of galingale

} put these five ingredients in a mortar and pound them all together finely

5 (more small) heads of garlic, chopped and fried until golden, then removed from the pan

spring onions, chopped

coriander, chopped

1 rice-bowl (½ pint) of *or padek* (cooked *padek*, see page 81)

1 medium-sized bowl of *nam keng* (the liquid part only of the fish soup described in recipe 29)

salt

Method

Put the chopped fish in the mortar with the five pounded ingredients and pound until thoroughly mixed. Add some *or padek* and salt. Then add some *nam keng* and continue stirring. Whether it is thick or not is according to your preference. Next, add the chopped fish skin, the chopped spring onions, and the fish intestine and eggs. Taste and check the saltiness.

Dish up on to a platter and garnish with the fried garlic and chopped coriander. Serve with *Keng Som Houa Pa Keng* (Sour soup made with the head of a *pa keng*, recipe 29) and some vegetables.

໒໖- ໄສ້ອົ່ວ

ເຄື່ອງປະສົມ – ຊີ້ນໝູ [illegible] [illegible] [illegible]
[illegible] ເຄື່ອງເຈົ້າ [illegible] [illegible] [illegible]
[illegible] [illegible] [illegible] ຫົວ
[illegible] ໑໐ [illegible] ຂອງສາມຢ່າງນີ້ ເອົາໃສ່ຄົກຕຳ
[illegible] [illegible] [illegible]
[illegible] ໃສ່ [illegible] [illegible] ແລ້ວ [illegible]
ວິທີທຳ – [illegible] [illegible] [illegible]
ໃສ່ [illegible] [illegible] ນ້ຳປາ ໃສ່ [illegible] [illegible] ແລ້ວເອົາ
[illegible] [illegible] [illegible] ແລ້ວ [illegible]
[illegible] [illegible] ແລ້ວ [illegible] ໃສ່ [illegible]
[illegible] [illegible] [illegible] [illegible]
[illegible] [illegible] [illegible] [illegible]
[illegible] [illegible] [illegible]
ເປັນໄສ້ ແລ້ວເອົາໄປ [illegible] [illegible]
[illegible] [illegible] [illegible]

Sai Ua Moo **Recipe 26**

PORK SAUSAGES

Ingredients

400 grams pork meat, including some fat, washed and minced
150 grams pork fat, washed and minced
2 dried chilli peppers, soaked in water until soft ⎫
10 (small) shallots ⎬ pounded together finely
10 black peppercorns ⎭
coriander leaves, finely chopped
salt and fish sauce
1 pig's intestine, turned inside out and washed and then turned right side out again

Method

Place in a bowl the pounded ingredients, the minced pork, the minced pork fat and the chopped coriander leaves. Add the fish sauce and mix all together. Take a very small sample portion of the mixture, wrap it in pieces of banana leaf and grill it until cooked. Taste it and check the saltiness. (If this test is satisfactory you can proceed to make the sausages. If the taste of the grilled sample is not right, adjust the seasoning.)

Stuff a section of the pig's intestine with the mixture from the bowl, taking care not to include any air bubbles. If there are any, use a needle to let them escape.

Tie the intestine into portions as you stuff it, each portion to be 15 cm long. There should be two knots between each section with a space in between for cutting them apart. Use a bamboo holder (see page 18) to grill them until they are done. Then transfer them to a platter.

Serve with *Jaew Bong* (recipe 64).

31.- ປາຜ່ອມ

ເຄື່ອງປະສົມ.— ປາຄາວໃຫຍ່ ຄືວ່າ ເຊາະເກັດປູ່ສີວ ສົບເອົາໄສ້
ອອກ ປາສອງຂາງລາງບໍ່ໃຫ້ດີ ແລ້ວເອົາປ່ອງນຸ້ມ ເອົາໄສ້
ເນື້ອປາ ພິກບົດຕອງປຸງ ດູຊີດີ ແຜ່ນ 10 ແຜ່ນ
ແກ່ເກືອກັນໃຫ້ເຂົ້າ ແລ້ວເອົາປາທີ່ມູນໃສ້ໃສ່ຄືໄປຈົບໃຫ້
ເນື້ອປາໜຽວໃສ້ ໃສ່ 10 ບ່ວງ ໝາກພ້າວເກົ່າ
1 ບ່ວງ ປະສົມເຂົ້າກັນ ຄັນແລ້ວແຕ່ງກະທຳບໍ່ວາງ ໜາກູ່
ພິກແຫ້ງໃຫຍ່ 7 ເມັດ ສວນ ແລ້ວ ບໍ່ປາ
ວິທີເຮັດ.— ເອົາປາທີ່ຕຳໃສ້ລົງໃສ່ຄອງ ຄັນແລ້ວບໍ່ປາ
ກະທຳໃຫ້ຈົບເຂົ້າກັນດີ ຈຶ່ງໃຫ້ໃສ່ໃຫ້ຕາເກືອໃສ້
ລົງໄປ ຖ້າບໍ່ກໍເຕີມ ບໍ່ກະທຳໃສ່ຄົນໃຫ້ຕາກ ແລ້ວ
ເອົາພິກແຫ້ງໃສ່ ຕັກໃສ່ຕອງກ້ວຍໄປແກ່ໃຫ້ສຸກແລ້ວ
ຈຶ່ງເອົາຕີ້ ຕາມຈາງຕາມດວງ ແລະກ້ວຍເຟື່ອງບໍ່ໃຫ້ເນົາ
ພໍສົມຄວນ ຖ້າບໍ່ໃຫ້ຕີ້ບໍ່ກະທຳໃສ່ ຖ້າແລ້ວ
ກໍໃຫ້ຕີ້ມໃສ່ໃສ່ ແລ້ວຕັກໃສ່ໃບຕອງກ້ວຍໜ້າຕູ້
ກໍໄດ້ ສະກິດແລ້ວ ບໍ່ກໍຂ້ອໃສ່ຈານກິນຕາງເຂົ້າ ຕອນ
ສູ່ກັນບໍ່ມີກິນເນື້ອຕູ້ໃຫ້ຮູ້ເທາ

Pa Fok **Recipe 27**

A MINCED FISH MIXTURE, COOKED IN PACKETS

Ingredients

1 *pa keng* (a barb, see page 24)—scale it and cut off the fillets only, from both sides—wash the fillets and use a spoon to scrape out all the remaining meat (from the skin)

15 (small) shallots } these two ingredients to be pounded together finely
10 black peppercorns } and then pounded with the fish meat until the mixture becomes sticky

10 hen's eggs

1 mature coconut, the husk removed and the meat grated—then make only one cup of the first extraction of coconut milk from it

a considerable amount of chopped coriander

salt and fish sauce

Method

Put the pounded fish mixture in a bowl. Add salt, fish sauce and some of the coconut milk. Mix all together thoroughly. Then break the eggs, beat them and add them to the mixture. If the mixture is too thick, add some more coconut milk. Continue to mix thoroughly, then add some of the chopped coriander. Wrap a small sample portion of the mixture up in pieces of banana leaf and put it on the fire. When this is cooked, taste and check the saltiness and consistency. If it is too thick, add some more coconut milk to the mixture in the bowl; and if it is not thick enough add more beaten egg. Then put the mixture into banana-leaf containers and steam them in a steaming-rack (see page 16). When they are cooked, transfer them to a platter, garnish with chopped coriander and serve.

28 — ໄກ່ໜຶ້ງໃສ່ໝາກດອງ

ເຄື່ອງປະສົມ — ໄກ່ປອກ ໑ ໂຕ ເອົາໄສ້ອອກ ແລ້ວ ຟັກ [illegible] ປາຍປີກ ແລະຕີນ ຈົກເອົາກະດູກຂາງອອກມາ ຟັກເປັນສອງທ່ອນ ສ່ວນຕາກຳ ຟັກໃຫ້ເປັນທ່ອນໃຫຍ່ ແລ້ວນຳໄປລ້າງນ້ຳ ຕາເຫລືອ ແລະແມງໝູ່ ຈື່ງໆ ຕອງນ້ຳມັນໝູໃຫ້ເຫລືອງ ຕາມໃຈ ລາງເພາະດອງ ໑ ຈອກ ແລ້ວກຸງວາງນ້ຳກຸ້ມ ເອົາແຕ່ເນື້ອມາໃສ່ ຈານໄວ້ ພັກ [illegible] ບົວທ່ອນໃຫຍ່ ໑ ຫົວ ປູລອງ ບາວໄວ້ ພັກ ນໍ ທ່ອນປ້ອນປອກ ແລ້ວ ໒໐ ຫົວ ພັກຫອມ ຕຽງ ເອົາແຕ່ ໃບ ອິດໜີ ໃບພັກຫອມ ຈູ ໑ ໜໍ້ ແປ່ງສາລີ ໖ ບ່ວງ ນ້ຳມັນ ເບີ ໜຶ່ງ ນ້ຳມັນໝູ ໖ ບ່ວງ ໝາກເພັດຫຍາບ ປັ່ນໃຫ້ລະອຽດແລ້ວ ເກືອ- ນ້ຳປາ- ແປ້ງນົວ

ວິດທີທຳ — ໃຫ້ເອົາໝໍ້ຂາງ ຕັ້ງໄຟ ນ້ຳມັນໝູໃສ່ ເອົາພັກບົວ ທັງສອງ ປ່າງລາງຈີນ ຫົວຫອມ ຕາກໄວ້ ເອົາແປ້ງສາລີ ສູງ ຫອງຈືນ ຈືນເຫລືອງ ຈຶ່ງເອົາຫົວພັກບົວທີ່ຈືນຂອໃສ່ຕາມ ໃຫ້ທົ່ວ ແລ້ວໃຫ້ເອົານ້ຳຕົ້ມໝູໃສ່ [illegible] ເກືອ ລະປົ້ ຕົ້ນໄປຈົນແປງແລ້ວເອົາກະດູກນ້ຳດີແລ້ວ ປຸງລົງ ຈຶ່ງເອົາໄກ່ ທີ່ຈືນໄວ້ໃສ່ຫມໍ່ ທີ່ມີຟາງ ນັ່ນ ໃຫ້ [illegible] ຕັ້ງໄຟ ກຸງອາເຄິງ ຫອມາທີ່ຈືນໄວ້ ນັ້ນໃສ່ ຊ້ຳນ້ຳປົກໃຫ້ເອົານ້ຳຕົ້ມຕົງ ໝູ ຕົ້ມລົງຈົນກຸ້ມ ຕອນຫຼັງໃບພັກຫອມລົງ ເກືອນ້ຳ ປາໃສ່ ໝາກເພັດປັ່ນແລ້ວນັ້ນຕາມຕ້ອງການ ແລ້ວຈຶ່ງ ໄຟອ່ອນໆ ຢູ່ພາໄວ້ຈົນນ້ຳເຫລືອໄກ່ເປື່ອຍ ຊີມເບິ່ງແຕ່ງ ຈາງຕາມໃຈ ແລ້ວຕັກໃສ່ຈານ ພັກປົ້ ຫອມຈູໃສ່ໜ້າ ນຳເອົາໄປໃຫ້ຮັບທານ

ໝາຍເຫດ — ຫຼັງໃສ່ໄກ່ແລ້ວນີ້ ຕອນລະວັງໄຟບ່າໃຫ້ ແຮງ ບໍ່ຈະໄໝ້ນັ້ນ ເພາະມີແປ້ງ ແຍກຈະຕ້ອງຄອນ ລາຍ ແປ້ງນ້ຳນໍ ກຸ້ມຕ່ອນ ຈຶ່ງງາມດີ ສ່ວນໝາກປັ່ນນັ້ນ ຕັ້ງບໍ່ຕ້ອງການ ຄວາມເຜັດແລ້ວຈະບໍ່ໃສ່ກໍໄດ້

Kai Pad Sai Hed Dong **Recipe 28**

FRIED CHICKEN WITH CANNED MUSHROOMS

Ingredients

1 chicken, gutted—cut off the tips of the wings and of the feet, then divide each leg and each breast into two parts, and cut the carcase into large pieces; wash all the pieces and rub salt and ground black pepper into them, then fry them in pork fat until golden
1 can of mushrooms—open it and drain the mushrooms, discarding the liquid
1 large onion, sliced lengthwise
20 (small) shallots, peeled
3 sprigs of coriander, the leaves only, not chopped
1 sprig of coriander, the leaves only, chopped
2 soupspoonfuls of cornflour
2 soupspoonfuls of butter or pork fat
a little ground, dried red chilli pepper
salt, fish sauce and ground black pepper
(pork broth)

Method

Put a wok on the fire and put the butter (or pork fat) in it. Add the sliced onion and the shallots. Fry these until they give off a good smell, then remove them. Add the cornflour to the fat in the wok and fry it until it is golden. Then return the fried onion and shallots to the wok. Stir until all these ingredients are thoroughly mixed, then add pork broth a little at a time and keep stirring until the cornflour is thoroughly mixed with the other ingredients.

Take the wok off the fire. Put the fried chicken pieces in a pot with a lid, put the pot on the fire and add the fried mixture from the wok. If it is too thick, add some pork broth, just enough to cover the meat. Next, add the mushrooms, the whole coriander leaves, salt, fish sauce and ground dried red chilli pepper according to your taste. Leave the pot on a low fire until the liquid is reduced and the chicken pieces are tender. Then arrange the contents of the pot on a platter, sprinkle with ground black pepper and the chopped coriander leaves, and serve.

Note

Be careful not to use a high heat, because this would burn the cornflour. And check that the liquid is just enough to cover the meat when you transfer it to a platter. If you don't like the dish piquant, leave out the ground, dried red chilli pepper.

໒໙- ແກງສົ້ມຫົວປາແກງ

ເຄື່ອງປະສົມ— ຫົວ-ຫາງ-ດູກປາແກງ ລ້າງນ້ຳໃຫ້ສະອາດໄວ້
ມີໂຕ ໑ ຫົວໃຫຍ່ແລ້ວຂອດໄວ້ ຜັກບົ່ວລາບ ເຄື່ອງມີຫົວ
ສົ້ມປອມ ໑ ໜ່ວຍ ປາແດກ ເຄື່ອງນ້ຳປາ- ເກືອ- ຜັກບົ່ວບົ່ວ,
ວິທີເຮັດ — ໃຫ້ເອົານ້ຳໃສ່ໝໍ້ແກງ ຕັ້ງໃສ່ເຕົາໄຟ ຖ່ານ- ຜັກບົ່ວ
ມີໂຕ ທີ່ທາງໄວ້ ເທົ່າໃສ່ ພໍນ້ຳຂື້ນແກງ ໃສ່ຫົວປາ ແລ້ວຈຶ່ງ
ເອົາປາໃສ່ ປາສຸກແລ້ວຈຶ່ງເອົາປາແດກ ເຄື່ອງນ້ຳປາ
ໃສ່ລົງໄປ ແລ້ວຈຶ່ງເອົາສົ້ມປອມມາຈຸ່ມລົງ ແລ້ວຊີມເບິ່ງ
ອີກ ຈັກສົ້ມ ເມື່ອຈືດ ເບິ່ງສົ້ມ ແລະເຄັມ ຈາງ ຫານ ຈູ່
ຕັກໃສ່ຖ້ວຍແກງ ຜັກບົ່ວໂຮຍໜ້າ ພັກເມື່ອຈຶ່ງໃຫ້ຮ້ອນ ຈູ່
ລວງປາແດກ

Keng Som Houa Pa Keng **Recipe 29**

SOUR SOUP MADE WITH THE HEAD OF A BARB

Ingredients

the head, tail and bones of a *pa keng* (a barb, see drawing and caption below), washed
1 stalk of lemon grass, bruised and tied into a loose knot
3 straight-bulbed spring onions
1 bunch *som pon* (an edible leaf, see page 36)
padek or fish sauce
salt
spring onion leaves, chopped

Method

Put $1\frac{1}{2}$ metal jugfuls ($1\frac{1}{2}$ pints) of water into a soup pot. Put in the chopped spring onions and the lemon grass and salt, and put the pot on the fire. When the water comes to the boil, add the fish head, tail and bones. When these are cooked, add the *padek* or fish sauce, and put in the *som pon*, dipping it in and out of the soup about three times. Taste and check the sourness and the saltiness. Transfer the soup (with the fish head, etc.) to a soup bowl and garnish it with the chopped spring onion leaves. Serve it with *Lap Pa Keng* (recipe 25).

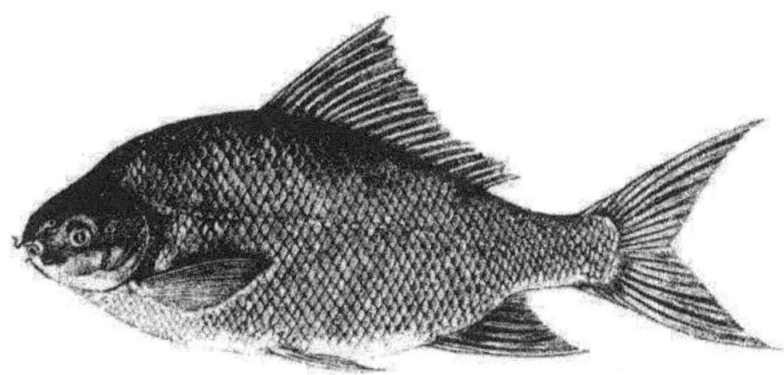

OSTEOCHILUS MELANOPLEURA, a barb which is closely related to, although larger than, the *pa keng*, OSTEOCHILUS PROSEMION. The former species is better known at Vientiane, the latter at Luang Prabang.

80 - ງູບົ້ເບ ຊຸຊີ່ຫາງ

ເຄື່ອງປະສົມ — ວັນເພງ ຕາມ ຜົນ ປູ ພອ ຮ ຊຸ ງ ກອ້ງ ຂ ຊຸ ງ ພາ ໑ ຊຸ ງ

1. ຈອນ ຫຼາກ ລ່າງ ແກ່ ຜົ່ນ ເກີ ແລະ ແຜ່ນ ໃວ້ ພາ ພົວ

ເກົ້າວ ໑ ພ່ ປູ ປລີກ ເປີ່ນ ທົ່ງ ຢູ່ ເກັ່ນ ເລີວ ກະ ທໍ່ ແກ່ ກາ ກາ ແລະ

ແກ່ ງາ ໃວ້ ເລີ ລະ ແຜ່ນ ທາ ກາ ເຫຼັງ ເຕັ້ງ ມີ ພ ອູ່ ໆ ແກ່ ໂກ້

ເປີ່ງ - ແພັກ ປອ ລວງ ເຕົ່ງ ຮິ ຫາວ ຫຼີ ເກົວ ປວນ ກາ ໃດ ກ່ ເຕີ່ງ

໑໐ ຫົວ ຮ ໆ ສາ ມ ປ່ ໆ ມີ ໂທ ດ່ ໃສ່ ກາ ບ ຈັບ ເຕັ່ງ ດີ ໃນ ຊີ ທງ

ແກ່ ປດ ລີ່ ໃນ ແພັກ ປອ ຊູ ແພັກ ທາ ວ ມ ຊູ ແພັກ ນັ້ ປັບ

ວິດທີ ຫຼິ້ນ — ໃຫ້ ເຮົາ ເຫັ່ນ ຂວງ ເຕັ້ງ ໃນ ກະ ທໍ່ ແກ່ ກາ ໃສ່ ຢູ່ ໄປ ຈົບ ແຕາ

ແມ່ນ ຈີ່ ເລົາ ເຕີ່ງ ທາ ວ ມ ທີ່ ເກ່ ໄວ້ ໃສ່ ວ ໄປ ຈົນ ທາ ວ ມ ເຫຼືອ

ເລົາ ວຸ ນົ່ ແມ ໃສ່ ແກ່ ປາ ຮວງ ຮ ຕໍ່ ໄປ ກ່າວ ເປີ່ງ ແພ ຈະ ຈະ ທາ ວ່ມ

ດີ ເຫຼືອ ງ ໆ ເລົາ ແກ່ ເຕັ້ ດ ກາ ແພ ຮວງ ແລັກ ປັ ອ ອ່ມ ໃປ ຈ ບ

ເຕັ້ງ ເລີ ກະ ທໍ່ ແກ່ ງາ ໃສ່ ເພ ເລີ້ ອູ່ມ ຊູ ມີ ເປີ່ ແທວ

ຈາງ ຫາ ພ ວ ຊູ ເລີວ ແພັກ ປອ ຊູ ໃສ່ ແມ່ ລີ ແລະ ໃສ່ ຈາວ

ແພັກ ນັ້ ທາ ຮ ມ ຊູ ໂຮງ ເກົ້າ ແມ່ ເຫຼືອ ເກົ່າ ໂທ ຮຽນ ແທ

Sin Moo Sousi Haeng **Recipe 30**

A PIQUANT 'DRY'* PORK DISH

Ingredients

pork, including fat, sliced into pieces of about 5 cm by 2 cm by 1 cm, washed and put in a small plate with salt and ground black pepper added

1 fully grown coconut—make both first and second extractions of coconut milk from the grated meat

3 dried chilli peppers, soaked in water until soft } pound finely

5 straight-bulbed or ordinary spring onions, heads only } together

10 dried shrimps

Kaffir lime leaves (about 5)

fish sauce and salt

chopped spring onion leaves

chopped coriander leaves

ground black pepper

(pig's bones broth)

Method

Put a wok on the fire. Pour into it the first extraction of coconut milk and let it boil until the cream separates. Add the pounded ingredients and leave until the mixture gives off a pleasant aroma.

Then add the slices of pork and the fish sauce. Keep stirring until the pork smells good. Add a little pig's bone broth and leave the pot on the fire until the ingredients are drying out, at which point add the second extraction of coconut milk, just enough to keep the meat moist. Taste and check the saltiness. Add the chopped spring onion. Take the pot off the fire and transfer the contents to a platter. Garnish with the ground black pepper and chopped coriander leaves and serve.

* Editors' Note. *Haeng* means dry in the sense of 'without a lot of liquid', not dry in the sense in which 'dried meat' is dry. As Phia Sing says, the meat must be moist.

31- ໝົ່ງສົ້ມງົບໄໝ

ເຄື່ອງປະສົມ — ງົບໄໝ ເອົາມະພ້າວອ່ອນ ລ້າງ ໝາກ ພ້ອງ ເອົາ ມາ ງົບ ເປັນ ຕ່ອນ
໑= ພັນບາງ – 0=05 x 0=03 x 0=01 ຕາມ ໃບເຕີຍ ແລະ ພິກ ມີ ໄວ້
໑ ຈານ ພິກບົດ ຫົວປອມ ປົກ ຄ້ອຍ ລິ້ນ ຫົວ ເອົາໃປຈີ່
ໝາກພ້າວ ໃຫ້ນໍ້າ ເບີດ ໄວ້ ພິກໄລ້ ... ຫົວໃຫ້
ຫຼາຍ ໃບ ໄວ້ ໄລ ... ມີ 60 ... ໝາກ ພ້າວ ປອກ ປາ ...
ໃສ່ ... ເອົາ ... ໝາກ ... ແລະ ໝາກ ... ລະ ມີ , ພິກ ...
... ເອົາ ... ເປັນ ... ຫົວ ... ເຄື່ອງ ...
ເຄື່ອງ - ໝາກປາ - ໝາກມີ້ - ໃບພິກ ... - ...
ພິກ ... - ...
ວິທີເຮັດ — ໃຫ້ເອົາ ... ໄຟ ... ໝາກ ... ໃສ່ ...
... ເອົາ ພິກ ... ໃສ່ ...
ໝາກ ... ໄປ ... ... ພິກ ... ໃສ່
ໃສ່ ໝາກ ... ...
... ... ເອົາ ພິກ ... ໄວ້
ໃສ່ ນໍ້າ ... ແລະ ໝາກ ... ...
ມີ ໝາກ ... ...
ໝາຍເຫດ ... ໃບພິກ ... ...
ໃຫ້ ...

Pad Som Sin Moo **Recipe 31**

FRIED SOUR PORK

Ingredients

1 plateful of pork, washed and sliced into pieces 5 cm by 3 cm by 1 cm,* then sprinkled with salt and ground black pepper and left on the plate
30 (small) peeled shallots, fried in pork fat until golden
20 straight-bulbed spring onions, cut very close to the head, leaving just a little bit of the green part
1 fully grown coconut, to be husked and split open—then grate the meat to produce two extractions, each of small quantity
2 (small) heads of garlic—the cloves separated, bruised and finely chopped
salt and fish sauce
pork fat
chopped spring onion leaves
chopped coriander leaves
ground black pepper
lime (juice, from 1 small lime or half a larger one)

Method

Put a wok on the fire and put a spoonful of pork fat in it. When the fat is hot, add the chopped garlic. Then add the slices of pork and the fish sauce. Fry the mixture until it gives off a good aroma. Next, put in the fried shallots, followed by the coconut milk, enough to cover the pork and shallots. When the pork is well done, taste and check the saltiness.

Add the spring onions and wait until they are cooked and the liquid has reduced to about the same level as the meat and vegetables. Take the pot off the fire. Sprinkle lime juice on top. Transfer the contents to a platter and garnish with the chopped spring onion leaves, the chopped coriander leaves and the ground black pepper; then serve.

* Editors' Note. This is how we interpret Phia Sing's measurements as shown in the Lao text opposite.

32 – ເຂົ້າປຸ້ນນ້ຳພິກ

ເຄື່ອງປະສົມ — ໃຫ້ເອົາປາແດກດຸກອຸ້ຍໝາກຂາມປີມາເຄາະ
ເກືອເອົາໄປຕາກແດດໃຫ້ເຫື່ອແຫ້ງແລະເຫລື່ມນ້ຳໃຫ້ໃສດີໄວ້
ຈຶ່ງບົ່ມແນມ ກຸ້ງສາມໂຕ ຖ້າມຜັກໃຫ້ສຸກ ບັ່ນເປັນທ່ອນໃຫ້ງາມ
ຕໍາເອົາໃສ່ໝໍ້ປາແດກໃຫ້ສຸກ ເກືອຕົ້ມອອກໃສ່ຄົກຕໍາໃຫ້
ລະອຽດໄວ້ ປາແຫ້ງຫຼືປາເຄັງກໍໄດ້ແນວ ແອ່ງຂາມ
ກະດູກແມ 1 ກິໂລກາມ ຫົວ 10 ສ່ວນ [illegible] ຫົວຜັກ
ບົວລາຍເສີ້ງ 10 ຫົວທ້າໄບ ໃຫ້ເອົາມາໃສ່ນ້ຳ 6 ໂຈກເຄີກ
ຂຶ້ນຕັ້ງໄຟ ເກືອເອົາ-ນົມ-ປາ-ຕໍາ-ພັກບົວ-ຄົ້ງໃສ
ເສີນໄປຈົນປາສຸກຕັກອອກມາໃຈ້ອໍ້ໃສ່ຄົກຕໍາໃຫ້ລະອຽດ
ໄວ້ ພັກທຽມ 1 ຊີ ຫົວກະໂລ່ງຂອງ ເອົາໄປຈີ່ນ້ຳມັນແນມ
ພໍເຫຼືອງ ຕັກອອກມາຕໍາໃຫ້ລະອຽດ ພັກເທິງຫົວປອນ
1 ຊີ ຫົວກະໂລ່ງຂອງ ເອົາໄປຈີ່ນ້ຳມັນແນມ ພໍເຫຼືອງ ຕັກ
ອອກມາຕໍາໃຫ້ລະອຽດ ໝາກເຜັດຕາວ ລີ ບໍ່ປອກ
ເປືອກ ທົ່ງໝົດ ລອຽດກະທຽມ ຕົ່ມເອົາມາກະທໍາທັງໝົດໄປຂົ້ວ
ພໍມາຈຶ່ງປ່າໃຫ້ທົ່ວແຕກມັນປັ່ງໄວ້ ໝາກແໜ່ງໂຄງລີ
ບໍ່ໝູເອົາໄປຈອງໃນພໍໃຫ້ພໍ່ [illegible] ເຄາະເອົາເຫ່ນອອກແກ່
ເທົ່າກຼູ ໃຫ້ລະອຽດເມັ່ງທັງສິ້ນ ເກືອຈຶ່ງນໍາເອົາໄປຈີ່ຈີ່ນດຽວ
ນ້ຳມັນໝາກເຜັດແກ່ ພໍທອມປ່າໃຫ້ເກັນເຂົ້າມເພົ້າ
ຈະຄໍາ — [illegible] ຄົ້ງ - ຜັກບົ້ງປ່ອ - ຜັກຫອມຊູ - ໝາກນາວ

ສ່າເຂົ້າປຸ້ນ — ໝາກປີ້ໂລ່ງຂອງໃຫ້ຫຼາຍພໍຄວນ ໝາກເຜັດ
ຫວານອ່ອນ ? ບໍ່ໝູໄລ່ງຂອງຈີ່ນດຽວນໍ້າມັນແນມໃຫ້ເຫຼືອງ
ໄວ້ ພັກທຽມກໍມີຈີ່ນພໍສຸກເກືອຫຼຸ່ນກາວ ລີຊຸງໄວ້
ໝາກຫົວຕຶ່ງເສີ້ງ ຄົບ ພັກຈີ່ນເກືອຫຼູນາວ ລີ ຊຸງໄວ້
ໝາກແໜ່ງໂຄງ ລີ ບໍ່ໝູຈີ່ນດຽວນ້ຳມັນແນມໃຫ້ພໍໄວ້
ເສັ້ນເຂົ້າປຸ້ນລາວ 6 ໝໍ້າ

ວິທີກໍາ — ໃຫ້ເອົາ-ແນມທໍາ-ປາທໍາ-ພັກບົວທໍາ-ພັກທຽມທໍາ
ຕັກລົງໃສ່ຫົ່ງ ເອົາແກ່ປາແດກເຄາະໃສ່ລົງໃຫ້ແຕກເຂົ້າ

Khao Poon Nam Phik **Recipe 32**

RICE VERMICELLI WITH CHILLI PEPPER SAUCE

(First) ingredients
1 small rice-bowl (¼ pint) of *padek*—(add ½ pint of water and) boil the *padek* until it is clear when strained*
300 grams of pork, free of fat, minced, rolled into a big ball, poached in the *padek* liquid until cooked, and then taken out of the pot and finely pounded
400 grams of *pa nang* (a catfish, see page 23) or *pa ked* (any fish with scales)
1 kilo of pork bones (to make pork broth)
10 thin slices of galingale
10 straight-bulbed spring onions, both heads and leaves
(salt)

Their preparation
Put 2 metal jugfuls (2 pints) of water in a pot, and put the pot on the fire. Put in the pork, the fish, the galingale, spring onions and salt. Boil until the fish is cooked. Take it out, debone it and pound the flesh finely.

(Further ingredients and preparation of them)
15 (small) heads of garlic, the cloves to be peeled and finely chopped, then fried in pork fat until golden, and pounded
15 (small) shallots, (peeled and) thinly sliced, fried until golden in pork fat and then pounded
3 fully grown coconuts, husked and split open—grate the meat with a *ka-tai* ('rabbit', see page 28), put the extraction of coconut milk into a pot and boil it until the liquid is reduced, but without letting the cream separate, then take the pot off the fire
6 red chilli peppers, grilled until they are soft—then remove the cores and pound the peppers as finely as possible before cooking them in coconut oil until a good aroma arises—do not let the mixture become overcooked or it will turn black (instead of red)
salt and ground pepper
chopped coriander leaves
lime (juice, to taste)
vegetables to be eaten with the dish:
  banana 'flower' (see page 32) sliced into long slices
  7 sweet young eggplants (page 33), sliced and fried in pork fat
  1 bunch of water spinach (*phak bong*, page 36), fried until done and then cut into pieces about 3 cm long
  13 yard-long beans, fried and cut into pieces 3 cm long
6 dried chilli peppers, fried in pork fat until soft
2 *na* (see page 22—about 1 kilo) of rice vermicelli (cooked)

Method
Put the minced pork, the prepared fish, the pounded spring onions and the garlic in a mixing-bowl. Add the *padek* sauce, previously prepared, and stir until these ingredients are mixed together, then add the pork broth and the

ກັນ ແລ້ວເອົາບໍ່ຕັ້ນ ... ແລະບໍ່ກະທົບຖືກໃສ່ ລົມໃຫ້
ຫົວກັນ ວຸ້ນເພີ້ງແກມ [illegible] ຈາງ ແລະບໍ່ຂົ້ນ ບໍ່ເໜຽວເກີນ
ໄປ ... ບໍ່ເມົາ ... ຮອງແລ້ວ ... ເອົາ ... ໃສ່
ຈົນເຫັນວ່າ ... ບໍ່ ... ບໍ່ໃສ່ ແລ້ວຕັກໃສ່ຖ້ວຍ
ເອົາໄປ ... ໃຫ້ ... ແລ້ວເອົາ ...
... ແລະ ... ມາ ... ໃສ່ ... ຈົນ
... ແລ້ວ ... ເອົາໄປ ... ແມ່ນ ...
ຈົນ ... ເອົາ ... ໃສ່ ... ແລ້ວ
... ໃຫ້ ...

33. ແກງຜັກກາດ ໝ້ອ

ເຄື່ອງປະສົມ — ... ຊີ້ນໝູເປັນຕ່ອນ ... ຕ່ອນ ລ້າງ ບໍ່ໃຊ້. ຜັກກາດ ... ຜັກບົ່ວ ... ຕົ້ນ ... ບໍ່ປາ - ໃບຜັກບົ່ວ

ວິທີເຮັດ — ໃຫ້ເອົາ ... ໃສ່ ... ຂຶ້ນ ... ແລ້ວເອົາ ... ຫົວຜັກບົ່ວ - ... ຖ້າ ... ແລ້ວ ... ~~[illegible]~~ ຜັກກາດ ... ໃສ່ ... ຈຶ່ງ ... ແລ້ວ ... ໃສ່ ... ໃຫ້ ...

ເອົາບໍ່ປາ

ໝາຍເຫດ — ແກງຜັກກາດນີ້ ບໍ່ຄວນຈະໃສ່ ... ເພາະຈະເຮັດໃຫ້ມີ ... ຖ້າ ... ຫຼືປາ ... ກໍ ... ຈະເຮັດໃຫ້ມີ ... ແລະ ... ຄວາມ ...

(reduced) coconut milk. Stir, taste and check the saltiness. Squeeze in some lime juice. Add the fried mixture of red chilli peppers. Transfer this whole mixture to a big bowl. Garnish with ground black pepper and chopped coriander leaves. (The sauce is now ready.)

Put the rice vermicelli on a platter, in the middle. Arrange the cut-up vegetables around it, and place the whole fried chilli peppers on top. Serve the sauce separately.

* Editors' Note. Phia Sing specifies that the straining should be done with a *sua pao* (part of a coconut tree) and *kaen fai* (which means cotton seed), but we are not sure just what he meant. A muslin cloth should do.

*Keng Phak Kad Meo** **Recipe 33**

A MEO SOUP MADE WITH GREENS OF THE CABBAGE FAMILY

Ingredients

5 pork bones, cut into small pieces and washed
1 *phak kad Meo* (a kind of cabbage—see page 35), with the root cut off
3 (small) shallots
salt and fish sauce
chopped spring onion leaves

Method

Bring to the boil one jugful (1 pint) of water in a pot, then add to it the pork bones, shallots and salt. When the water comes back to the boil add the fish sauce and *phak kad Meo*, which you have washed and cut up. When the vegetable is cooked and is no longer smelling of fresh vegetable (i.e. when it has lost its 'cabbagy' smell) taste it and check the saltiness. Then transfer it to a serving-bowl, garnish it with chopped spring onion leaves and serve it with a *jaew* (sauce—see page 48).

Note

This *Keng Phak Kad* should not have too much meat in it (i.e. the pork bones should be fairly free of scraps of meat) because otherwise it will taste and smell bad. If dried meat or dried fish could be used, this would be better (than pork bones). Be careful not to overcook the vegetables; otherwise it will taste slightly sour and its sweetness will be lost.

* Editors' Note. The Meo people are the largest ethnic group after the Lao people, in Laos. In recent years the name Meo has been changed to Hmong.

344— ເອາະ[illegible] ຫົວປາສະລ້ອດ

ເຄື່ອງປະສົມ — ຫົວ - ຫາງ - ປາສະລ້ອດ ຖ້າເປັນຕ່ອນລ່ວງພໍໃຫ້ ສະຫງວນໄວ້ ໝາກເຜັດຫວານ ຂ່ອນ (ໃບ[illegible]) ບາວ ລາງພໍໃຊ້ ຫຼູຂາວ ໑ ກຳມື ຖ້າໃຫຍ່ ຈະກໍເປັນຕ່ອນ ລ່ວງພໍໃຊ້ ຜັກ[illegible] ໑ ກຳມື ລາງພໍໃຊ້ ສີໃສ ໑ ຕົວ - ໝາກເຜັດ[illegible] ຊີ່ ໜ່ອຍ - ຫົວຜັກບົ່ວ ຊີ່ ຕົວ - ເຂົ້າສານ[illegible] ໑ ບ່ວງມື [illegible] ໃສ່[illegible]

[illegible] - [illegible] - ປາແດກ ຫຼືນ້ຳປາ - ໃບຜັກບົ່ວ

ວິທີເຮັດ — ໃຫ້ເອົານ້ຳໃສ່ໝໍ້ເອາະ ໑ [illegible] ໃຫຍ່ [illegible] [illegible] ເອົາເຂົ້າ[illegible] ໃສ່ ພໍ[illegible] [illegible] - ປາ - ໝາກເຜັດ[illegible] - [illegible] ໃສ່[illegible] [illegible] ປາສະລ້ອດ [illegible] ເອົານ້ຳປາ ຫຼືປາແດກ ຜັກ[illegible] ໃສ່ [illegible] [illegible] [illegible] ໝາກ[illegible]

Or Sod Hua Pa Sa Ngoua **Recipe 34**

FISH HEAD SOUP MADE WITH SA NGOUA

Ingredients

the head and tail of a *pa sa ngoua* (a sheatfish—see drawing below) cut into pieces and washed

2 sweet young round eggplants (see page 33), sliced vertically and washed

1 handful white mushrooms, to be washed after the bottoms of the stalks have been cut off, and then torn into pieces

1 handful *phak tam nin* (a climbing plant, see page 37), the young tender leaves only

1 stalk lemon grass
5 large fresh chilli peppers
5 (small) shallots
sticky rice—what you can pick up with the fingers of one hand—uncooked, but previously steeped in water
} to be put in a mortar and pounded together*

salt and *padek* or fish sauce

spring onion leaves, chopped

Method

Put 1 big metal jugful ($1\frac{1}{4}$ pints) of water in a pot. Put the pot on the fire. Add salt and the pounded ingredients. Bring all this to the boil. Then add the pieces of fish, the eggplants and the mushrooms. When the fish is cooked, add *padek* or fish sauce and the *phak tam nin*. Taste and check the saltiness.

Transfer the contents of the pot to a bowl, garnish with the chopped spring onion leaves and serve with young cucumber.

* Editors' Note. The text says that only the last two of these ingredients are to be pounded together, but it seems clear that this is a slip and that all four are meant.

Pa sa ngoua, KRYPTOPTERUS BLEEKERI

35. ສາໂຕມປາຄ່າ

ເຄື່ອງປະສົມ — ຊີ້ນປາຄ່າ ໑ ຕ່ອນ ຍາວ ໒໐ ຊມ ກວ້າງ ໑໒ ຊມ
ໝາກຂາມສ່ວນເນື້ອປາ ຊຸບໃຫ້ບາງໆ ຍາວ ໕ ຊມ ກວ້າງ ໒ ຊມ
ໃສ່ຈານ ດາວເຄືອ ໝາກນາວ ໓ ໜ່ວຍ ໃບຜັກເອົາແຕ່
ຍອດ ປາ ຊາວໃຫ້ທ້ອນປະໄວ້ ສີໃສ ຊຸບໃຫ້ຕຸ້ມໃສ ຫົວ
ຜັກບົ່ວ ໝູ ຊອຍ ຂາວ ໂຕ ຫົວ ຜັກທ້ອງຫົວປົ່ນ ຊອຍ ຂາວ
ໃຫ້ ໝາກເຜັດ ເຫຼືອງ ຊອຍ ຂາວ ໂນ່ງ ຄ່ອນແລ້ວ
ນ້ຳ ໃບໂຫຍ ຊຸບໃຫ້ຕຸ້ມ ສີໃສ ຂາງຜັກຂ້າມທີ່ເອົາປະສົມ
ກັນໄວ້ເປັນເຄື່ອງຫອມ ນຳປາ ແຫນມ ແລະ ຂີງ ໝາກເຜັດ
ນ້ຳ ໃສ່ປາຄ່າ ... ສົ້ມໃຫ້ໂຕສູກ ເທົ່ານ້ອຍໃສ່ເປົ່າ
ໃສ່ປາຄ່າ ຕຸ້ມ ຂາວ ງາມດີ ນຳໂຕ ຜັກໃບ ໝາກປາຄ່າເອົາ
ລອກ ນຳ ແຫນງ ຍໍ ສຸກ ເຫຼືອ ຊຸບໄວ້ ໃບຜັກຫອມ ຊຸບ - ຫອມ ຊຸບ
ເຫຼືອ

ວິທີທຳ — ໃຫ້ເອົາ ມີດ ໝັ້ນປາທີ່ ຫອມ ນຳ ສົ້ມ ໄວ້ນັ້ນ ເອົາຍັນ
ໃສ່ກ້ອງ ນຳ ໄວ້ ຈົນ ສຸກ ແລ້ວ ເຫຼືອ ເຄື່ອງ ຫອມ ເຄົາລາ
ແຕ່ງ ໃສ່ ຖ້ວຍ ໃຫ້ ເຂົ້າກັນ ແລະ ຂ້ອນ ແລ້ວ ນ້ຳ ຈຶ່ງເອົາປາ
ທີ່ເຂົ້າ ນ້ຳ ຂອດ ເຫຼືອ ນ້ຳ ໃສ່ ຕຸ້ມ ຊາວໆ ໃຫ້ ເຂົ້າກັນ
ແລ້ວ ເອົາປາ ແລະ ເຄາະ ຍອດ - ໃສ່ປາ - ໝາກປາ - ໃສ່ປາ
ໃສ່ ຊີ້ນ ເຄື່ອງ ແກງ ຈານ ຕຸ້ມ ນຳ ສົ້ມ ນຳ ໃຫ້ ເຂົ້າກັນ ທີ່
ເຂົ້າ ໄວ້ ໃບ ເຄາະ ໃບ ນາ ໃສ່ ຈານ ຕອງ ງາມ ແລ້ວ
ຕັດ ລົງ ຈານ ຜັກ ຫອມ ຊຸບ ຫອມ ຊຸບ ໃສ່ ໝາກ ຍາ ເຄື່ອງ
ຕາງ ໃບ ... ແຫນງ ສົ້ມ ເຄື່ອງ ເຫຼືອ

Sa Ton Pa Va — **Recipe 35**

A MARINATED FISH SALAD

Ingredients

1 piece of a *pa va* (from the fish LABEO DYOCHEILUS: for drawing, see recipe 37) —with eggs—20 cm long by 12 cm deep (the thickness being whatever the thickness of the fish is), cut up into thin slices each 3 cm by 2 cm and dressed with salt and the juice of 5 limes

<table>
<tr><td>3 stalks of lemon grass, finely chopped
2 (small) heads of garlic, sliced
5 (small) shallots, sliced
2 dried chilli peppers, cut up
1 piece of young galingale, cut up
3 leaves of Kaffir lime, cut up finely</td><td>mixed together to form the kheuang hom</td></tr>
</table>

1 small bowlful of *nam padek* (page 23), cooked

the eggs of the *pa va*—quantity equivalent to a hen's egg—grilled in a wrapping of banana leaf

the intestines of the fish (if clean), similarly treated (and cut up)

the skin of the fish, boiled and then cut up

spring onion leaves, chopped

coriander, chopped

salt

Method

Take the slices of fish which have been marinated in lime juice, squeeze them to remove the liquid, then mix them with the *kheuang hom*. Add the *nam padek*, little by little, and the fish eggs, intestines and skin, all mixed together.

Taste the mixture and check the saltiness. If it is not sour enough, take the lime juice left over from the marinade, cook it and add it to the mixture.

Serve on a platter, garnished with the chopped spring onion leaves and coriander. The soup *Keng Som (Houa Pa Va Sai) Hed Saed* (page 125) is to be served together with this dish.

36- ໄກ່ໜຶ້ງໝາກເຜັດແດງ

ເຄື່ອງປະສົມ — ໄກ່ປອກ ໑ ໂຕ ຈົກໄສ້ອອກລ້າງໃຫ້ສະອາດ
ແລ້ວຕັດເປັນ [illegible] ຕັດສອງທ່ອນ [illegible]
[illegible] ຕັດເປັນສອງທ່ອນ. ສ່ວນຄໍກໍໃຫ້ຕັດເປັນສາມ
ທ່ອນ ແລ້ວເອົາ [illegible] ແລະ [illegible] ໝາກສະ-
[illegible] ໑ [illegible] ປອກເປືອກ [illegible] ເອົາໝາກ
ກະທຽມ [illegible] ແລະ [illegible] ກະທຽມປະສົມ [illegible] ທ່ອນ ຜັກ
ບົ່ວ [illegible] ປອກ ແລ້ວ ໑ ຖ້ວຍ ໝາກເຜັດ [illegible]
[illegible] ຜັກບົ່ວ
ເຄື່ອງ ໑໕ [illegible] ເອົາຫົວ [illegible] ໃບ
[illegible] ໝາກເຜັດແດງ [illegible]
[illegible] ແລ້ວເອົາ [illegible]
[illegible] ໃບຜັກບົ່ວ
ໃບຜັກຫອມ [illegible] ເກືອ - ນ້ຳປາ [illegible]
[illegible] ຜັກບົ່ວຫົວໃຫຍ່ [illegible]

ວິທີທໍາ — ໃຫ້ເອົາໝໍ້ [illegible] ໃສ່ [illegible] ຕັ້ງຂຶ້ນ
[illegible] ໄຟ [illegible] ຜັກບົ່ວຫົວໃຫຍ່ ແລະ
ໄກ່ທີ່ຕັດໄວ້ໃສ່ [illegible] ໄກ່ [illegible] ເອົານ້ຳປາ [illegible]
[illegible] ໃສ່ [illegible] ແລ້ວ [illegible] ໄຟອ່ອນ ໃຫ້ຈົນ
ໄກ່ສຸກດີ [illegible] ເອົາຫົວຜັກບົ່ວ [illegible] ໝາກເຜັດແດງໃສ່
[illegible] ແລ້ວເອົາຜັກ [illegible] ໃສ່ [illegible]
ໃສ່ຈານ ຜັກຊີ ຜັກບົ່ວ ຜັກຫອມ [illegible]
[illegible] ໄດ້ແລ

Kai Pad Mak Phet Deng **Recipe 36**

FRIED CHICKEN WITH RED CHILLI PEPPERS

Ingredients

1 chicken, washed and gutted—cut it into large pieces, the legs and breasts into two pieces each and the carcase into three; salt the pieces and sprinkle them with ground black pepper

1 ripe coconut, the meat grated and squeezed into two extractions of coconut milk—enough to cover the chicken pieces

1 small rice-bowl (i.e. 4 to 5) peeled shallots, fried in pork fat until golden and giving off a good aroma

15 straight-bulbed spring onions—cut off the heads with some of the green parts

8 large fresh red chilli peppers, cut lengthways, cored and seeded and soaked in cold water until they have lost most of their hot taste

chopped spring onion leaves

chopped coriander leaves

salt, fish sauce and ground black pepper

pork fat

½ onion, sliced vertically

Method

Heat 1 spoonful of pork fat in a frying-pan or a wok. When the fat is hot, put in the sliced onion and the chicken. Fry until the chicken pieces turn golden; then add the fish sauce and enough coconut milk to cover them. Leave over a low heat until the chicken pieces are well done, then add the fried shallots and the red chilli peppers. Taste and check the saltiness. Then add the spring onion heads (with some of the green parts attached).

Dish up on a platter and garnish with the ground black pepper, the chopped spring onion leaves and the chopped coriander leaves; then serve.

37 – ແກງສົ້ມຫົວປາຄ່າ ໃສ່ເຫັດເຜິ້ງ

ເຄື່ອງປະສົມ — ຫົວປາຄ່າ 1 ຫົວ ຕັດເປັນຕ່ອນໃຫຍ່ ແລ້ວລ້າງ
ນ້ຳໃຫ້ສະອາດໄວ້ ເຫັດເຜິ້ງ 1 ຖ້ວຍ ຕັດແຄມໃຫຍ່ ຕັດຕີນ
ລ້າງນ້ຳຂັ້ນ ຂຸດິນອອກໃຫ້ໝົດ ສີໄຄ 1 ຫົວ ທຸບແລ້ວ
ລາກນ້ຳ ຮັດໄວ້ ຜັກບົ່ວລຽງເຄື່ອງ ມີຕົ້ນ ລ້າງນ້ຳ ໝາກ ຫົວ
ຂອດໄວ້

ນ້ຳສົ້ມ 1 ຖ້ວຍ ເກືອ ຕຽມ - ເກືອ - ປາແດກ - ຜົງນົວ - ນ້ຳປາ
ໃບຜັກຫອມ

ວິທີເຮັດ — ໃຫ້ເອົານ້ຳໃສ່ໝໍ້ແກງ 1 ໂຈກທ່າງ ແກ່ໃຫ້ແມ່ນ
ໂຈກທຸກໃຫຍ່ ເອົາຂີ້ໄຄ ໃບ-ເຄື່ອງ-ຫົວສີໄຄ ຫົວຜັກ
ບົ່ວໃສ່ ຖ້ານ້ຳມັນກໍແລ້ວ ຈຶ່ງເອົາຕ່ອນຫົວປາລົງ ນ້ຳ
ນ້ຳພິກເຕີມ ຈຶ່ງເອົານ້ຳປາ ຫຼືປາແດກ ແລະເຫັດເຜິ້ງ
ໃສ່ ເມື່ອເປັນສຸກແລ້ວ ໃຫ້ເອົານ້ຳສົ້ມໃສ່ ຊີມີແຫ່
ພໍດີແລ້ວ ປົງລົງ ຕັກໃສ່ຖ້ວຍ ຜັກບົ່ວ ຊອຍ
ໜ້າ ຍັກເຜີງຕົງໃຫ້ມີ ແກງສົ້ມ. ຫົວປາຄ່າ

Keng Som Houa Pa Va Sai Hed Saed **Recipe 37**

SOUR SOUP MADE FROM A FISH HEAD WITH ORANGE MUSHROOMS

Ingredients

1 head of a *pa va* (i.e. LABEO DYOCHEILUS—see drawing below), cut into big pieces and washed

1 soupbowl of orange mushrooms (*hed saed*, page 44)—cut off the bottoms of the stalks and wash them free of soil with warm water

1 stalk of lemon grass, bruised, washed and knotted

3 straight-bulbed spring onions, whole—bruise their heads and knot them

1 rice-bowl (6 to 7 tbsp) of pickled bamboo shoots

salt and *padek* or fish sauce

chopped spring onion leaves

Method

Put 1½ metal jugfuls (1½ pints) of water in a pot on the fire. Add salt, the knotted lemon grass and the knotted spring onions. When the water comes to the boil, add the pieces of fish head. When the water comes back to the boil, add fish sauce or *padek* and the orange mushrooms. When the mushrooms are cooked, add the pickled bamboo shoots, taste and check the saltiness. Take off the fire and transfer to a bowl. Garnish with chopped spring onion and serve with *Sa Pa Va* (recipe 35).

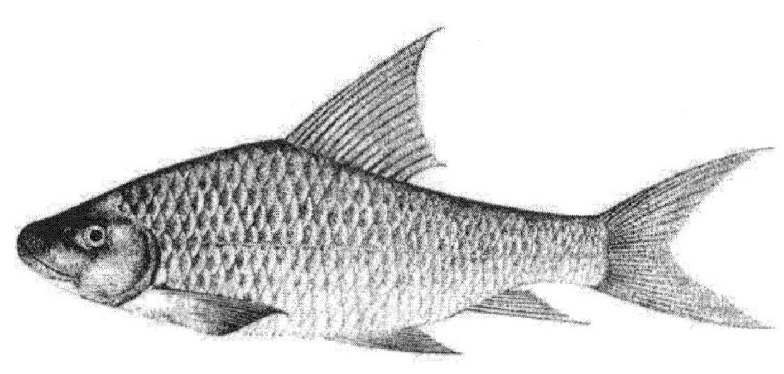

Pa va, LABEO DYOCHEILUS

38 ຕົ້ມເຄື່ອງ ຊີ້ນຄວາຍ

ເຄື່ອງປະສົມ — ຊີ້ນຄວາຍ ຈີ່ ສ່ຳລາງເລືອ ມີຕ່ອນ ຊຸໃຫ້ນາງເກາະ, ຂອມ ຄ່າປ່ອຍເນົ້າເຫຼ່ອນ ມີ ຟາກ່ ເນາວາກ ເຄື່ອງຂອມ ຜັກໃບ ໃຫ້ສາກ ເລືອປະມັກເຂົາ ເປື້ອງງວກ ໂນ່ງໃຈ້ ໝາກຄ່ວຍ ເຊິ່ງຈີ່ ໃນ ໂຕ້ສາກ ມີເນ່ງ ຜັກຫຼາຍມົກ ໂຫວ ຜັກບົ່ວທີ່ວປອນ ມົກ ມີ ຕວວ ຂອງ ເປົ່າ, ມີທີ່ ປະສົມກັນໄດ້ ເກືອ - ປາແດກ ຫຼືນ້ຳປາ ໃບ ຜັກບົ່ວ - ໃບແຄກ [illegible]

ວິທີເຮັດ — ໃຫ້ເອົາ ນ້ຳໃສ່ ໝໍ້ ເຊາະ ຈີ່ນ ເຄື່ອງ ໃນ ຕໍ່ໄຟ ຜັກ ກະທຽມ ເລືອ ເອົາ ເຄື່ອງ ຊີ້ນ ຄວາຍ - ຄ່າ ຂີ້ສົ້ມ ເລີ່ມ ໄປຈົນ ສຸກ ຈຶ່ງ ເອົາ ປາແດກ ຕອງ ໃສ່ ຄາມ ຄອບ ຕົ້ມ ໄປຈົນ ມົກ

ເວລາ ຊີ້ນ ຫອມ ຕ່ອນ ປີ ໄລ ເອົາ ເຄື່ອງ ທີ່ ໃສ່ ຊີ້ນ ເປົ່າ ແກມ ຈາງ ງ ຕາມ ຊູປ ຕັກ ໃສ່ ຖ້ວຍ ຜັກ ບົ່ວ ຊຸ ປ ຕອມ ຊຸໃຈ ເນົາ ເລີ່ມ ຕໍ່ ໃຫ້ ມີ ແກ ກັນ ເນາວາກ ເຄື່ອງ ຕ່າ ຄະ ນາ ສາ ແຕ່ງ ເສີບ

Tom Jaew Sin Kuai **Recipe 38**

HOT BOILED WATER-BUFFALO SAUCE

Ingredients

3 pieces of *ob sam la* (water-buffalo meat which has been partly dried by the sun or over hot charcoal), sliced thinly
3 slices of galingale

<table>
<tr><td>2 young round eggplants (page 33), seared over charcoal and peeled
3 fresh chilli peppers, placed on hot charcoal until cooked
2 (small) heads of garlic, seared over hot charcoal
3 (small) shallots, seared over hot charcoal</td><td>pound these four ingredients* together to form the kheuang tam</td></tr>
</table>

salt
padek or fish sauce
chopped spring onion leaves
chopped coriander leaves

Method

Boil 1 medium-sized metal jugful (just under a pint) of water in a pot. Then add salt, the slices of galingale and the sliced water-buffalo meat. Boil until cooked.

Next, add the *padek*, using a padek strainer (page 17). Continue to boil until the liquid is so reduced that it just covers the meat. Then take the pot off the fire, add the *kheuang tam*, taste and check the saltiness.

Dish up in a serving-bowl and garnish with the chopped spring onion leaves and coriander leaves. Serve with round eggplants and young cucumbers. (These vegetables would be served raw.)

* Editors' Note. Phia Sing's text says that only the last two of these four ingredients are to be pounded together, but it is clear that this is a slip and that he meant all four.

39– ຢາຊຸບຈຸ້ມຝ້າຍ

ເຄື່ອງປະສົມ — ຈຸ້ມຂາວຫຼືຝ້າຍທີ່ເອົາແຕ່ຈຸ້ມອີ່ນໄປຟ່າໃຫ້ມີເງິນ
ປະມານ ໕໐໐ ກຣາມ ມາງາໃຫ້ຫາງ ນາວ 3 ຈຸງ ຫວ້າງ
ໃສ່ຖຸງຂາວເຄື່ອງ ແລ້ວ ຍົກເອົາ ນາວ ໑໐ ມຽງ
ໄປຂາວໃຫ້ທ່ວງ ສີໂກ ມີ ທາວ - ພວກ ຈາກ
ພວກນ້ອຍ ບໍ່ ຫາວ - ເນາ ແນ່ນ - ແລ້ວ
ໃນ ຈໍາ ມີ ໃນ ຂອງ ຕ້ອງ ໄດ້ ລ້ຽງ ພວກ
ໃວ້ ຍົກປາແຕກເພາະ ຈຸ້ມ ຝ້າຍ ໑ ຕ່ອນ
ຍັງ ຫົວໃຈ ຝ້າຍ ທ່ອງ ແລ້ວ ຝ້າຍ ໑ ຕ່ອນ ແລ້ວ
ເນາຝ້ອນ ຂາວ ແລ້ວ ໑ ຕ່ອນ ຂອງ ເປົ່າ ມີ ເອົາ ໄປ
ຍົກ ຕົ້ນ ໃຫ້ ສະອາດ ແລ້ວ ທາງ ມາ ຈຸ ໃຫ້ ໄວ້
ໃນ ພວກ ນ້ອຍ - ພວກ ຫາຍ

ວິທີເຮັດ — ກ່ອນອື່ນໃຫ້ເອົາຈຸ້ມຝ້າຍທີ່ນອນສົມໄວ້ນັ້ນ
ມາງາວໆ ແລ້ວປັ້ນເອົາຍົກເຄື່ອງ ໃສ່ ມີ ໄວ້ ຈົນ
ຍົກ ເຄື່ອງ ໃຫ້ ເອົາ ຍົກ ເຄື່ອງ ມີ ໄປ ເພາະ ໄຟ ສົບ ປີ ໄວ້
ໃຫ້ ແຫ້ງ ຈຶ່ງ ເອົາ ເຄື່ອງ ໃສ່ ແລ້ວ ເອົາ ຈຸ້ມ
ຝ້າຍ ທີ່ ປັ້ນ ໄວ້ ນັ້ນ ມາ ນວດ ໆ ໄວ້ ຍົກ ປາ ແຕກ ແລ້ວ
ໃນ ຂາວ ໄປ ໃຫ້ ທົ່ວ ແລ້ວ ເອົາ ເຄື່ອງ ໃນ ທີ່ ໄວ້ ໃສ່ ຍົກ
ກ້ວາ ທີ່ ເພາະ ໄວ້ ນັ້ນ ໃສ່ ເທິງ ຍົກ ໃສ່ ໄວ້ ກ່ອນ ຈຶ່ງ ເອົາ
ຍົກ ຂຶ້ນ ຂາວ ໃຫ້ ທົ່ວ ກັນ ມີ ເຄື່ອງ ແລະ ຈາງ
ແລະ ສົມ ພຸງ ຖ້າ ສົມ ໃຫ້ ເອົາ ໃສ່ ຂວາງ
ພວກ ນ້ອຍ ໃສ່ ຂາວ ໃຫ້ ທົ່ວ ຕາມ ຈາງ ນ້ຳ ໃຫ້
ໃຫ້ ປີ ແກ ພວກ ຕ່າງໆ ແລະ ຕາງ ຝ້າຍ

Sa Soy Sin Fahn **Recipe 39**

DEER PREPARED AS A SALAD

Ingredients

500 grams meat from the hind legs of a *fahn* (a small deer, see page 27) excluding the tendons, sliced into pieces 2 cm by 3 cm, salted, drenched with the juice of 10 limes and mixed thoroughly therein

3 stalks lemon grass
2 (small) heads garlic
5 (small) shallots
2 dried chilli peppers
galingale (2 or 3 slices)
3 Kaffir lime leaves
} these six ingredients to be chopped finely

1 rice-bowl ($\frac{1}{4}$ pint) of *padek*
(salt)

1 small piece of the deer's liver
half the deer's heart
1 piece of the deer's spleen
tripe from the deer—the thick part, scraped
} these four ingredients to be boiled until well done, then sliced thinly

chopped spring onion leaves
chopped coriander leaves

Method

First of all mix the meat in the lime juice and squeeze out as much liquid as possible. Put this liquid in a small pot, cook it (for a very short time) and leave it to cool. (As it cools, it will separate into a clear part and a thick part.)

Put the chopped ingredients in a small bowl. Add to and mix with these the sliced meat, the *padek* and salt. When all this is thoroughly mixed, add the boiled and sliced liver, heart, spleen and tripe. Next, add to the mixture the liquid which you have previously boiled, little by little, adding the clear part first and the thick part later. Stir the mixture. Taste, check the saltiness and sourness. If it is not sour enough, add more of the clear liquid. Then add the chopped spring onion leaves (and the chopped coriander leaves) and mix again. Dish up on a platter and serve with fresh (raw) vegetables and *Keng Om Fahn* (recipe 95).

40 - ປີ້ງຂາຄວາຍ

ເຄື່ອງປະສົມ — ຂາຫຼັງຄວາຍ ໑ ຂາ — ພິກໄທປົ່ນ — ເກືອ —
ພິກຫຼວງປອກເອົາແຕ່ເມັດ ເຫຼືອຕຳໃຫ້ລະອຽດ ໑ ຫົວ —
ນ້ຳມັນໝູໃໝ່ໆ ເຄິ່ງນ້ຳຖ້ວຍ — ນ້ຳສະອີ້ວ — ພິກຂີ້ໜູ

ຈັດທີສອງ — ໃຫ້ເອົາຂາຄວາຍມາຂູດຂົນອອກ ແລະ ຊີ້ນຕິດກະດູກໃຫ້ເປັນ
ທ່ອນເລັກໆ ທ່ອນນັ້ນນັ້ນ ມາໃຫ້ມີ ເຫຼືອເອົາເກືອ-
ພິກໄທປົ່ນ. ພິກຫຼວງທາໃສ່ຂາຄວາຍໃຫ້ທົ່ວ ແລະ
ເອົາເນື້ອດີ ຈຶ່ງເອົາໄປໃສ່ເຕົາໄຟໃຫ້ໃຊ້ຖ່ານທີ່ບໍ່ມີຄວັນ
ບໍ່ງາມໃຫ້ເປັນຣອຍ ເຫຼືອຫຼາຍໃສ່ລົງໃນປ່ອນໄສ້ຫົວໃຫ້
ແດ່ເຫຼືອດູທອງອອກໄປ ຈຶ່ງເອົາໄມ້ລ່ວງບ່ອງນັ້ນສູງໄສ້ຂາ
ຄວາຍໄປຕາມເລັກ ເຫຼືອເອົາໄມ້ຊີ້ທີ່ກູໄວ້ນັ້ນສູງໃຫ້
ກູ່ທັງບ່ອງໄວ້ເພື່ອຮູ້ນຳໃຫ້ເປັນ ແລະດູໃນຂີ້ໃຫ້ເປັນ
ການຈຶ່ງເອົາຂາຄວາຍເຂົ້າໄປຂາງ ຄັ່ງເປັນໃນເຄື່ອງລະມັດ
ຈົນຈຸ່ມຊຸ່ມ ແລະໃຫ້ມັນເອົານ້ຳມັນທາສະເໝີ
ຈົນກວ່າຊີ້ນຄວາຍຈະສຸກເຂົ້າໄປໃນທຸກບ່ອນ ຈຶ່ງທານ້ຳ
ສະອີ້ວເພື່ອໃຫ້ຫອມ ແລະ ສວຍງາມດີ ເຫຼືອຮັກສາຈົນ
ສຸກລົງຂອງລູກໃສ່ຈານ ພິກຫອມລູກໂຮຍໜ້າ ນັ້ນເພື່ອ
ຫາໃຫ້ຮູ້ວ່າ ສຸກນ້ຳຈິ້ມ ແລະ ສຸກ

Ping Kha Fahn

Recipe 40

GRILLED LEG OF DEER

Ingredients
1 hind leg of a *fahn* (a small deer, see page 27)
ground black pepper and salt
1 (small) head of garlic, peeled and pounded
fresh pork fat, or butter
soy sauce
chopped coriander leaves

Method
Skin the leg and trim it. Rub it with the pepper, salt and garlic. Take a small piece of either *mai lai* or *mai bong* (two special kinds of bamboo) and make a hole in the middle of it. Then sharpen a stick of common bamboo (*mai kib*).* Check that the stick fits easily into the hole in the first piece of bamboo. Push this same first piece of bamboo through the deer's leg, as close as possible to the bone, then push the sharpened stick through the leg (from another angle, so that it passes through the hole in the first piece of bamboo, as shown in the drawing), to make sure that the meat is securely fastened.

Make the fire and roast the leg over it, turning it frequently. Baste it with the pork fat or butter until the meat is well done to a depth of 5 cm inside. Then sprinkle the soy sauce over it to improve its appearance and aroma.

Slice the meat and put it on a platter. Garnish it with the chopped coriander and serve it with *Nam Jeem* (see page 48) and lettuce.

* Editors' Note. *Mai lai* is a young shoot of the bamboo GIGANTOCHLOA NIGROCILIATA and *mai bong* is a piece of the thicker bamboo BAMBUSA TULDA. *Mai kib* refers to the common bamboo or to bamboo generally. This information is offered with some reservation since the nomenclature of the bamboos is a difficult subject.

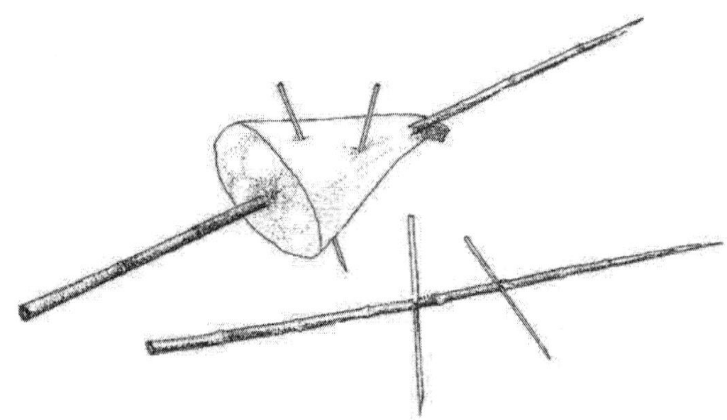

In this illustration, Soun has shown how to secure the leg by using two rather than one stick of common bamboo. The upper drawing is what you would see. The lower drawing simply illustrates how the sticks fit through the holes.

41 — ລາບໄກ່ປ່າ

ເຄື່ອງປະສົມ — ໄກ່ປ່າ ໑ ໂຕ ເອົາລົກຂົນໃຫ້ລ້ຽນດີ ຈົນບໍ່ມີຂົນອ່ອນ ຫຼື [illegible] ແລ້ວ ຕັດທ່ອນ ຈົກໄສ້ອອກ ລ້າງນ້ຳໃຫ້ສະອາດ ມາລຶ້ງເອົາແຕ່ຊີ້ນເອິກ ຊີ້ນຂາ [illegible] ຟັກໃຫ້ລະອຽດດີໆ ໄວ້ ລອກເອົາໜັງ [illegible] ໄກ່ ແລະ ໜັງຕ່າງໆ ພ້ອມ [illegible] ແລະໄສ້ທີ່ລອກສະອາດແລ້ວ [illegible] ສຸກແລ້ວ ເອົາອອກມາຊອຍເປັນເສັ້ນໃຫ້ລະອຽດໄວ້ ໝາກ [illegible] ແກ່ ຫລາຍ [illegible] ເອົາໃບ [illegible] ໄວ້ ຜັກຫອມ ຜັກໃຫ້ສຸກ ມີ ໂຕ ຜັກບົ່ວ ຜັກໃຫ້ສຸກ ໑ ໂຕ ໝາກ [illegible] ໃຫ້ [illegible] ຄ່ວ [illegible] ຂາວ [illegible] ໃສ່ນ້ຳ [illegible] ແຫຼກດີໆ ໄວ້ ເປັນເຄື່ອງ ລາບ ປາແດກ [illegible] ໝາກ [illegible] ນ້ຳ [illegible] ນ້ຳປາ [illegible] ໑ [illegible] ເຂົ້າ ໑໐ ປ່ອນ ສົມ ຄວາມ [illegible] ຜັກຫອມ ມີ [illegible] ແລ້ວ ເຂົ້າໃນ [illegible] ຫາວ ອອກໄວ້

ໃບ [illegible] ໃບ ຜັກບົ່ວ ໃບ ຜັກ [illegible] [illegible]

ວິທີແຕ່ງ — ໃຫ້ເອົາໄກ່ທີ່ຟັກໄວ້ ມາໃສ່ນ້ຳ [illegible] ແລ້ວ ບ່ວກ ໃຫ້ເຂົ້າກັນດີ ແລ້ວເອົາ [illegible] ນ້ຳປາແດກ [illegible] ໃຫ້ເຂົ້າກັນ ຄົວເອົານ້ຳປາແດກ ໃສ່ ປົນສົມ ຄວາມ [illegible] ເອົານ້ຳ [illegible] ໄປ [illegible] ຕາມ [illegible] ເຂົ້າ ໑໐ [illegible] ໃສ່ [illegible] ນ້ຳ [illegible] ໄປ ໝາກ [illegible] ຜັກຫອມ [illegible] ໃສ່ [illegible] ໃຫ້ທົ່ວ [illegible] ຈາກ [illegible] ແລ້ວ [illegible] ຈານ. ຜັກ [illegible] ຜັກບົ່ວ [illegible] ໃຫ້ [illegible] ແລະ ຜັກ [illegible] ຕ່າງໆ

Lap Kai Pa **Recipe 41**

MINCED WILD CHICKEN

Ingredients

1 wild chicken, plucked, washed and gutted; take the meat from the breasts and legs and chop it finely; take the skin, the liver and the gizzard, wash them, tie them together with thread and cook them by boiling them in broth, then slice them thinly

5 round eggplants (see page 33), cooked by putting them in the charcoal fire until their skins are burned 3 (small) heads garlic, seared over a charcoal fire 2 (small) shallots, seared over a charcoal fire 3 dried chilli peppers, grilled until brittle 2 slices of galingale	these five ingredients to be pounded together—we call the result *kheuang lap*, meaning ingredients for the *lap*

1 rice-bowl ($\frac{1}{4}$ pint) of *or padek* (recipe 15)

1 medium-sized bowl of broth to which fish sauce has not been added

an appropriate quantity of ground *khao khoua* (uncooked sticky rice, toasted in a hot dry pan, then pounded very thoroughly)

a young banana flower, sliced

3 (small) heads of garlic, chopped and fried until golden-brown and giving off a good aroma

3 Kaffir lime leaves

chopped spring onion leaves

chopped coriander leaves

salt

Method

Mix the minced chicken with the *kheuang lap*. Add salt and the *or padek*, and mix some more. When the mixture has a sufficiently strong taste of *padek*, add the broth and stir. Then add the *khao khoua* and the sliced banana flower. Add also the sliced chicken skin (etcetera) and the fried garlic. Taste and check the saltiness.

Arrange the ingredients on a platter. Garnish with chopped spring onion leaves, chopped coriander leaves and the Kaffir lime leaves, also chopped. Serve with *Keng Som* (any kind of sour soup, such as those given in recipes 18 and 29) and a variety of fresh (raw) vegetables.

42 ສະນ່ຽນປາຝັກ

ເຄື່ອງປະສົມ — ໃຫ້ເອົາເນື້ອທ້ອງປາ [illegible] ເປັນທ່ອນ ໃຫຍ່ສອງທ່ອນ - ລ້າງໃຫ້ສະອາດ [illegible] ແລະ [illegible] ໄວ້ຈານໃດ ເອົາເນື້ອປາ [illegible] ລ່ວງ [illegible] ໃຫ້ [illegible] ໄວ້ຈານໃດ [illegible] ໜ້າ [illegible] ເຫັດ [illegible] ຜັກ [illegible] ເຫົາ [illegible] ໃຫ້ [illegible] ໃສ່ຈານ [illegible] ຜັກໄວ້ຈານໃດ [illegible] ປາ [illegible] ປາແດກ - [illegible] - ຜັກ [illegible] - ຜັກ [illegible] [illegible] —

ວິທີເຮັດ — ໃຫ້ເອົາເຄື່ອງ [illegible] ແລະ ເນື້ອປາ [illegible] ທີ່ຜັກ [illegible] ໄວ້ນັ້ນ ມາປະສົມ [illegible] ໃຫ້ເຫັດ [illegible] ປາ [illegible] ແລະ [illegible] ແລ້ວ [illegible] ປາ [illegible] ເນື້ອປາ [illegible] ທ່ອນ [illegible] ປາ [illegible] ທ່ອນປາ ທີ່ [illegible] ໃຫ້ [illegible] ໃສ່ [illegible] ໄວ້ຈານ [illegible] ໃສ່ [illegible] ໃຫ້ [illegible] ./.

Kanab Pa Fak **Recipe 42**

GRILLED FISH FILLETS, SANDWICHING MINCED FISH

Ingredients

the lower half (i.e. the belly meat) of a *pa keng* (page 24), cut into two large pieces (i.e. the two lower fillets of the fish)—wash these and rub them with salt and ground black pepper

(more meat from the same) fish—an appropriate amount, minced

minced pork fat, the size of a betel nut

crisp-fried pork skin, a piece the size of a hand

2 fresh chilli peppers }
1 stalk of lemon grass (chopped) } these three ingredients to be pounded together to make the *kheuang hom*
4 (small) shallots }

fish sauce or *padek* (the liquid only)

salt

chopped coriander leaves

chopped dill

banana leaf for wrapping

Method

Mix together the *kheuang hom*, the minced fish and the minced pork fat. Add salt, fish sauce (or *padek* liquid) and the chopped dill. Taste and check the saltiness.

Place one of the two large fillets of fish on pieces of banana leaf, put the above mixture on top of it, and then the second large fillet on top of the mixture (making a sort of sandwich). Wrap it all up tightly in many layers of banana leaf. Use a bamboo holder (page 18) to grill the package until the contents are cooked. Then open the package and transfer the contents to a platter. Garnish with chopped coriander leaves and serve.

43 ຄະນົ່ງດອກງິ້ວ

ເຄື່ອງປະສົມ — ດອກງິ້ວ ເພາະເປັນສ່ວນລາກນໍ່າໄດ້
ຊີ້ນໝູສາມຊັ້ນ ນໍ້າສົ້ມ ດອງລາກນໍ້າກໍ່ດີ
ຄົນໜຶ່ງຜ້າໃຊ້ຈານໃດ
ໝາກເຜັດສາມໜ່ວຍ ສີໃດ ສອງຫົວ
ຜັກຫອມ ຫົວ ບົ່ວ ສາມຫົວ ຂິງສາມຢ່າງ
ມີ້ຊີເກືອ ດາກໍ ໃຫ້ເໝົ້າ ໃບຜັກຫອມ
ນໍ້າສົ້ມ ດອງ ນ້ຳປາ ເລັກ

ວິທີເຮັດ — ໃຫ້ເອົາເຄື່ອງ ນອນທີ່ນາໍໄດ້ ເມັດຊີ້ນ
ຜັກ ແລະ ດອກງິ້ວ ປະສົມ ເຂົ້າກັນ ດອງໃຫ້
ຫົວ ນໍ້າປາ ຮອງເລືອດໃສ່ ເພາະເຍາງ ຕາກໃຫ້ສຸກ
ຊົ່ວໂມງ ຈາງ ຊື່ນແລວ ຈຶ່ງ ພັກໃຫ້ ບອໃນ ວາໄວ້
ນັ້ນໃສ່ ການໃຫ້ ຫົວ ແລວ ນໍ້າ ໃປ ຮໍ ດາງ ປາໃຜ
ຢ່າ ແລວໃດ ໃສ່ ຈານ ມີດ ເມືອ ຄ້າໃຫ້ ຍິນ
ຍິນ ເພາະ ແຕ່ ສ່ວນໆ ~/.

Kanab Dok Khing **Recipe 43**

GINGER FLOWER GRILLED IN BANANA LEAF

Ingredients

1 ginger flower—wash it and separate the petals

a piece of three-layer pork (page 26), washed, minced and mixed with ground black pepper

3 fresh chilli peppers }
2 stalks of lemon grass } these three ingredients to be chopped and then pounded together to make the *kheuang hom*
3 (small) shallots }

chopped spring onion leaves

fish sauce and salt

Method

Mix together thoroughly the *kheuang hom*, the minced pork and the ginger flower petals. Add fish sauce and salt. Taste and check the saltiness. Then put in the chopped spring onion leaves, and mix all together.

Put the mixture on pieces of banana leaf, wrap it up and cook the package over a charcoal fire. When it is cooked transfer the contents to a platter. Serve it with any kind of *Keng phak* (Vegetable soup).

44 ຊະນ່ຽງປາຂອນ (ມີສອນບ່ອນ)

ເຄື່ອງປະສົມ — ປາຂອນ - ຣ ຫົວ ຫຼື ຫາງ ໃສ່ 2 ບ່ ເຄື່ອງຄາວ
ຫົວ ເປັນເຄື່ອງລ່າງ ໝາກ ຫານ ເມື່ອ ໃຊ້ ຈານ ໃຫ້
ສີ ໃສ - 3 ຫົວ - ຫມາກ ເຜັດ ຍີ່ - ຂ ມອງ - ຫົວພັກ
ບົ່ວ - 3 ຫົວ - ເອງ ສາມ ປ່າງ ມີ ໃຫ້ ສາ ເຂົ້າສານ
ຈົ່ນ // ເກືອ ດີ (ເຄື່ອງ ວ່າ ເຄື່ອງຫອມ) - ເກືອ ຈ່ວງ ເຄື່ອງ
ໝາກ ເຜັດ ບົ່ວ ເອົາ ເຂົ້າ ໃສ່ ຄັນ ສອງ ຕ່ອນ ປະໃວ້
ລາມ ຫມສ້ອມ ຈຸ່ມ ຜັກ ໃຫ້ ເຄື່ອງ ລາ ທ່າ ໃຊ້ ໄວ້
ໃບ ແຄ ອີ່ຕູ່ - ໃບ ໜາດ ບໍ່ ລູ - ເກືອ - ນ້ຳປາ

ວິທີເຮັດ

ໃຫ້ເອົາເຄື່ອງຫອມ ແລະ ມາ ມາ ໃນ ຕົ້ນ ເຂົ້າສານ
ໃຫ້ຈົ່ມ ທ່ວ ເມື່ອ ນ້ຳປາຮ້ອນ ແລະ ເຍື່ອງ ແກ່ນ
ຈາງ ນຳ ຈຸ່ມ ເກືອ ໃຫ້ ເອົາ ປາຂອນ ມາ ຄົນ
ເຂົ້າ ຄັນ ໃບ ແກ ບໍ່ ລູ ແລະ ອີ່ ຕູ່ ປະສົມ
ເຂົ້າ ສານ ຄັນ ແລ້ວ ຮ່ຳ ຕາ ຕາ ກີ ທັງ ມາວ ມື
ຫຼື ປິ້ງ ໃນ ໃຫ້ ສຸກ ແລ້ວ ໃດ ໃສ່ ຈານ ຍົກ ເມື່ອ ກິນ
ໃຫ້ ມີ ນານ ຜັກ ແກ ງ ໝາກ ບ້ານ ຂອນ //

Kanab Pa Gnon **Recipe 44**

CATFISH GRILLED IN BANANA LEAF

Ingredients

5 *pa gnon* (the fish PANGASIUS SIAMENSIS, page 71)—cut off their heads and tails, gut them and wash the mucus off them, then make diagonal cuts in their sides, but not right through to the bone, and salt them

3 stalks of lemon grass (chopped) 2 fresh chilli peppers 3 (small) shallots	these three ingredients to be pounded together to make the *kheuang hom*

2 pieces of crisp-fried pork skin, to be pounded with the *kheuang hom*
minced three-layer pork—a quantity the size of a hen's egg
sweet basil leaves
chopped spring onion leaves
salt and fish sauce

Method

Mix thoroughly the *kheuang hom*, the minced pork, salt and fish sauce. Taste and check the saltiness. Add the fish, the chopped spring onion leaves and the sweet basil leaves. Mix again, thoroughly. Then wrap the mixture in pieces of banana leaf, shaped to accommodate the length of the fish. Use a bamboo holder (page 18) to grill the package. When it is cooked, open it and transfer the contents to a platter. Serve with *Keng Phak Hum On* (Young spinach soup, recipe 22).

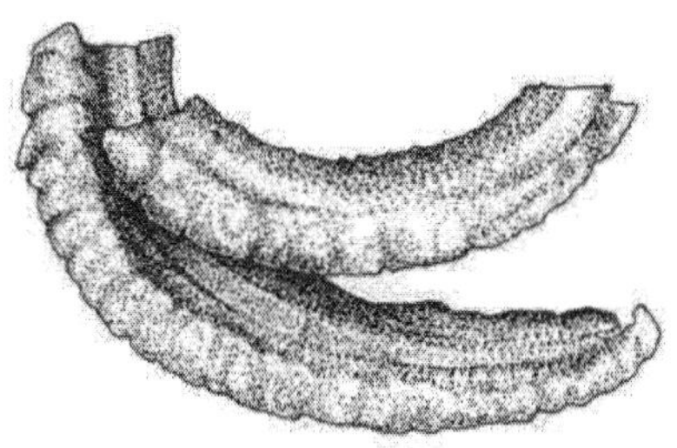

Crisp-fried pork skin

45 [illegible]

[illegible] — [illegible]

[illegible]

[illegible] — [illegible] ([illegible])

Kanab Bon **Recipe 45**

SWEET BON GRILLED WITH OTHER INGREDIENTS

Ingredients

sweet *bon* (see page 38), peeled and steamed in a steamer (page 16) until well done, then pounded finely and put on a plate

2 fresh chilli peppers
5 (small) shallots
1 piece crisp-fried pork skin
} these three ingredients to be pounded finely together

minced three-layer pork—a quantity the size of a hen's egg

salt and fish sauce

(1 soupspoonful pork fat)

chopped spring onion leaves

Method

Put the pounded *bon*, the other pounded ingredients and the minced pork in a mortar and use the pestle to mix them thoroughly together. Add a little salt and fish sauce.

Put a wok on the fire and put a soupspoonful of pork fat in it. Then add the prepared mixture and stir constantly until most of the liquid has dried out. Taste and check the saltiness. Add the chopped spring onion leaves. Place this mixture on to a few layers of banana leaf, and fold them over it tightly. Use a bamboo holder (page 18) to grill the package over the fire. When it gives off a good aroma, open it up and put the cooked food on a platter. Serve it with *Keng Phak Kad* (a soup made with the leaves of a plant of the cabbage family—see recipe 33, where *phak kad Meo* is specified).

46 ມົດປາກາກແໜ່ຄ້າ

ຕົ້ນເຫດປະສົມ — ຕອນ ປາກເຕັດເປົາ ແຕ່ວຸ້ນ ລ່າງ ເປົ່າຮ່ອງຄາຍູ້
ເປັນຕຸ່ມ ມີໃຈ້ຈວມຈື້ (ພູມ ຄ້ານໃຫຍ່) ໝາດ ຕອງ ໃຊ້ເຫຼົ້າ ໃຟ
ສາມແສ້ໃຫ້ ສຸກ ເຄື່ອງ ເຜົາ ຜອດ ມາ ຍູ ບ່ອນ ໃກ້ [illegible] ໂຫມູ
ວຸ້ ເປັນ ຕອນ ນາວ ດ້ວຍ ມືດ ລ່າງ ນັກໃຈ້ ຈວມຈື້
ສີໂຄ ສົດ ຫົວ ເຫົາ ເຫ່ຍ ຍອມ ຮອມ ຕູ … ເປັນ
ຕຸ່ມ ມີ ຍາວ ເຄົ້າ ຂຸດ ແຜັດ ຫົວ ລາວ ເຂົ້າ ຫຼືວ ຫົວ
ປ່ອມ ກໍ ໃກ້ ຫາວ ຫາວ ຍູ ເປັນ ຕຸ່ມ ເຄົ້າ ຂຸດ ຫລາງ
ແຜ່ ໃຫຍ່ ສາມ ນ່ອຍ ຜ່າງ - ໃນ ອີດ ກາ ສາມ ຜ່ານ

ວິທີແກ້ — ເມື່ອ ຫາງ ເຄົ້າ ເຄົ້າ ນີ້ ໃອ້ ຍູ ເຄື່ອ ຈັງ ເຜົາ ນາ
ຮອມ ສັກ ໃຈ ເຄົ້າ ນີ້ ກົບ ໃຫ້ ຫົວ ເຫົາ ນາ ຂອງ ໃຫ້
ພໍ ເຄົ້າ ຂູ ມີ ແກ້ ເຕົ້າ ເຫົາ ຕອງ ກ້ອງ ນາ ຮັ່ ເປັນ ຫາມ
ເຄື່ອງ ໃສ່ ເປີ ນາ ຊີ້ ຫອມ ໃນ ກະ ນຸ່ມ ສູ ລ້ ໃອ້ ຍກ
ໃປ ປີ ໃຟ ສີດ ເຄື່ອງ ໃຊ້ ໃຈ້ ຈວມ ແຜັດ ຫົວ ຂຸ ເມ
ຫລາຍ ເທົ່າ ເມື່ອ ເຕົ້າ ໃຫ້ ຍູ ຫາ ນັ້ນ ຍູ ເຫມ ຮົ່ມ
ເຄາະ ຫມາ ວ ສໍາ ເຄົ້າ ງ ຮອມ ./.

Mok Padek Pho Kha **Recipe 46**

MOK PADEK, MERCHANTS' STYLE

Ingredients

3 pieces of *padek*, fish only, cleaned and cut into small pieces

3 strips of dried buffalo skin—place them in the hot embers and ashes of a charcoal fire, then cut off and discard the burnt skin and cut the rest into pieces about 2.5 cm long

2 stalks of lemon grass, cut into pieces 5 mm long

5 spring onions

3 large chilli peppers, quartered

sweet basil leaves

3 slices of galingale

Method

When the ingredients have been prepared, mix them thoroughly in a bowl. Add some water to keep the mixture moist. (Divide the mixture into two, and wrap it in pieces of banana leaf, making two packages.) Use a bamboo holder to grill them. When they are cooked, transfer them to a platter. Garnish with chopped spring onions and serve with moist fried pork skin (*houm khiep moo*) and cucumber.

44 ແກງເຄື່ອງໃນໄກ່

ເຄື່ອງປະສົມ — ຫົວ . ໃສ້ . ປີກ . ຕີນ . ຄໍ . ໄກ່ [illegible]
[illegible] ລ້າງນ້ຳໃຫ້ສະອາດ [illegible]

ໃສ່ຈານໄວ້ (ມີໃບ [illegible] ໝາກ [illegible] ສາມໜ່ວຍ - ພັກ [illegible] ພັກຫອມ
ສາມຕົ້ນ [illegible])
ໃບພັກ [illegible] ໃບ [illegible] ສາມ [illegible] ລ້າງນ້ຳໄວ້
ນ້ຳປາ

ວິທີເຮັດ — ເມື່ອ [illegible] ນ້ຳ [illegible] ແລ້ວ [illegible]
[illegible] ແລ້ວ [illegible]
ໃສ່ [illegible] ນ້ຳປາ
ໃບ [illegible] ໃບພັກ [illegible] -
[illegible]
[illegible]
[illegible] ພັກ [illegible]
[illegible] ./.

Mok Kheuang Nai Kai **Recipe 47**

CHICKEN GIBLETS GRILLED IN BANANA LEAF PACKETS

Ingredients

the giblets, the gizzard, the wings, feet and neck of a chicken, scraped and washed and sprinkled with salt and ground black pepper

2 stalks of lemon grass
3 fresh chilli peppers
4 spring onions or (small) shallots
3 coriander roots
} pound together finely these four ingredients to make the *kheuang hom*

chopped spring onion leaves
3 Kaffir lime leaves, divided in half
salt and fish sauce

Method

After preparing all the ingredients, put the *kheuang hom* in a small mixing bowl and add the various pieces of chicken. Mix thoroughly and add fish sauce, the Kaffir lime leaves and a little of the chopped spring onion leaves. Pour in a little water, just enough to cover the chicken pieces. Taste and check the saltiness.

Make banana leaf packets of the above mixture and use a bamboo holder (see page 18) to grill it over the fire. When it is cooked, take the contents out of the banana-leaf packets and put them on a platter. Garnish with the remaining chopped spring onion leaves. Serve with *Keng Phak Tam Nin* (a soup made with an edible leaf, MELOTHRIA HETEROPHYLLA—see page 37).

48 ແກງປາຜ່າໃສ

ເຄື່ອງປະສົມ – ປາຜ່າໃສເອົາແຕ່ຕົວໃຫຍ່ພໍສົມຄວນ ມາຂໍອດເກັດ ຄວ້ານຂີ້ປາໃຫ້ ໝົດແລ້ວລ້າງນ້ຳ [illegible] ຊອຍເປັນທ່ອນໆພໍສົມ ຄວນ ຖົ່ວເຂົ້າສານນຶ່ງລາງນ້ຳລາງ [illegible] ຂອກ ຫຼຸເປັນຕອນບໍ່ຜັກໄວ້ ມີໃຄສອງຕົ້ນ ໝາກເຜັດສອງໜ່ວຍ ຫົວຜັກບົ່ວຫົວຫົວ ໃຫຍ່ ສວນນຶ່ງບໍ່ຕ້ອງເອົາເປັນແຜ່ນ [illegible] ໃບຜັກ ບົວ ໃບຜັກຊີ ສອງໃບ ເກືອ ນ້ຳປາ

ວິທີຄົວ – ເມື່ອຕົ້ມເຂົ້າຂົ້ວຄົ່ວແລ້ວ ໃສ່ປາລົງໃຫ້ສຸກ ເຄື່ອງຕຸ່ມໃສ່ ນ້ຳປາລອງເຄື່ອງຄົນໃຫ້ທົ່ວ ພໍສຸກແລ້ວຈາງຕາມຊອບ ໃບຜັກບົວໃບຊີ ບໍ່ໃສ່ແກ່ເພາະມີກິ່ນເໝັນຄາວ ແລ້ວເອົາ ໃບຕາງຄົວມາເຮັດເປັນກະບອກປາກ ຫຼືໃຫຍ່ໃສ່ ລະບຽບແບບ [illegible] ຖາໃສ່ ແລ້ວເຄົ້າໃສ່ ຈານຜັກບົວໃຫ້ເປົາເພື່ອໃຫ້ເຫັນງາມ.

Mok Pa Fa Lai **Recipe 48**

STING-RAY GRILLED IN A BANANA-LEAF PACKET

(The species of sting-ray which inhabits the Mekong belongs to the genus DASYATIS and is illustrated below. It is well-known at Luang Prabang, and it is not surprising that the recipe book of Phia Sing contained a recipe for it, even though sting-rays are usually sea fish.)

Ingredients

1 piece of sting-ray about the size of a man's hand, taken from the underside, cleaned of mucus and cut up into suitable small pieces

2 stalks lemon grass
2 very small green chilli peppers
5 (small) shallots
} chopped and ground together

spring onion leaves, chopped
10 leaves of sweet basil
salt and fish sauce

Method

Put the prepared pieces of fish into a big bowl, add the pounded mixture, mix well and add salt and fish sauce to taste. Add also the sweet basil leaves and some of the chopped spring onion leaves. Mix well together.

Wrap the whole mixture in pieces of banana leaf in a crested shape (see drawing on page 18). Fasten it with a splinter of bamboo. Use a bamboo holder (see page 18) to grill it until it is cooked.

Open the banana-leaf packet, put the cooked mixture on to a plate and garnish it with the rest of the chopped spring onion on top.

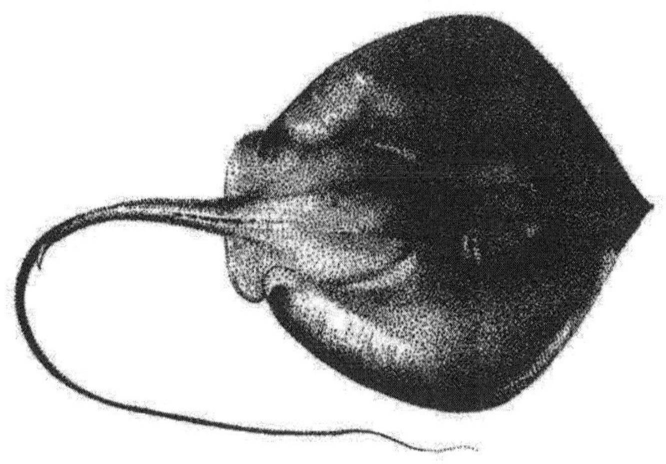

49 ມະກອກ

ເຄື່ອງປະສົມ — ຊີ້ນ ຄວາຍ ໃຫຍ່ ຫຼື ໄກ່ ເຄືອ ສອງສາມ ໃສ່ ຂອງ
ຫົວສີໃສ່ ກໍ່ ເອົາ ອອກ ໄວ້ ເອົາ ຕອງ ກ້ວຍ ລ່າງ ແກ່ ໃຫ້
ສະອາດ ເອົາ ເກືອ ເລັ້ມ ໃສ່ ຊີ້ນ ໃຫ້ ອ້າງ ໄວ້
ສີໄຄ 2 ຫົວ - ເພາະ ຫຍ້າ ຫຼື - 3 ໜ່ວຍ - ຫົວພັກບົ່ວ
5 - ຫົວ 1 ກາ 3 ຢາງ ໃຫ້ ສົ້ມ ໄວ້ ກັບ ຈົນ ແຫຼວ
ໃສ່ ນົມ ເພື່ອ ຕ່ອນ ເກົາ ມາ ຂອງ ຊີ້ນ ເອົາ ສອງ ສາມ
ໃຫ້ ສຸກ ເກົ່າ ເອົາ ອ້ອຍ ແກ້ ຫາ ຕອນ ພ ສາ ມ ນ ນັ້ນ
ໃຫ້ ລະອຽດ ເອົາ ໃສ່ ເປັນ ໃບ ພັກ ບົ່ວ ຮີດ ຢູ່
ໃບ ເກືອ - ນ້ຳປາ

ວິທີເຮັດ — ໃຫ້ ເອົາ ເນື້ອ ເຄື່ອງ ທຸກ ຢ່າງ ກໍ່ ໃສ່ ເຂົ້າ ເກືອ ຈີ່
ເອົາ ຊີ້ນ ທີ່ ຈັກ ເປັນ ຕ່ອນ ໄວ້ ນັ້ນ ໃສ່ ກົ້ນ ໂຖ່
ເຄື່ອງ ຫາ ອອມ ຊີ້ນ ເຂົ້າ ໄວ້ ໃສ່ ລົງ ໄປ ຄົນ ໃຫ້ ທົ່ວ ເກືອ
ນ້ຳ ປາ ຮອງ ນ້ຳ ທ່າ ເປາະ ລອກ ນັ້ນ ອົ່ມ ເພາະ
ເນື້ອ ແຄມ ຈາກ ຕາ ວ ນ ຂົ້ນ ພັກ ບົ່ວ ໃບ ຮີດ ໃສ່
ຄົນ ເຂົ້າ ກັນ ເກືອ ຈຶ່ງ ເຂົ້າ ໃນ ຕອງ ກ້ວຍ ມາ ຮໍ່
ເປັນ ຫາ ອບ ໝົກ ປີ້ງ ຖ້າ ຊີ້ນ ໃນ ລະ ຫຼື ເຂົ້າ ຈີ່
ປີ້ງ ໄຟ ສຸກ ແລ້ວ ໃຫ້ ຈ ວ ນ ພັກ ຫອມ ຈຸ ໄວ້
ແລ້ວ ນຳ ເອົາ ຕັ້ງ ໃຫ້ ຮ້ອນ ກັບ ເຂົ້າ ໜຽວ
ນໍາ ກິນ

Mok Kob

Recipe 49

GRILLED FROGS

Ingredients

2 large grilled frogs, gutted and washed and dismembered
2 stalks of lemon grass } these three ingredients to be
3 fresh chilli peppers } pounded finely together to make
5 (small) shallots } the *kheuang hom*
1 piece of crisp-fried pork skin, the size of a hand—scrape off the fat and pound the remainder together with the *kheuang hom*
minced three-layer pork—a quantity the size of a duck's egg
chopped spring onion leaves
10 sweet basil leaves
salt and fish sauce
(chopped coriander leaves)

Method

Check that all the ingredients have been prepared. Put the pieces of frog into a large bowl. Add the *kheuang hom* and mix thoroughly, then add salt and fish sauce. Sprinkle a little water over the mixture, just enough to keep it moist. Taste and check the saltiness. Then add the chopped spring onion leaves and the sweet basil leaves. Mix all together, then wrap the mixture in banana-leaf containers (page 18) and use a bamboo holder (also page 18) to grill the mixture in these.

When they are cooked, open the containers and place the contents on a platter. Garnish with chopped coriander and serve with *Nung Mak Noi* (steamed small gourds).

50 ນິທານແກ່ນສົ້ມໂອ

ເລື່ອງປະສົມ — ຕອນແກ່ນສົ້ມໂອ. ຈະເປັນລາວກວາງໂງ່ເຫຼືອ
ຫລົ່ນ ເພີ່ນບໍ່ຫາກໍໄດ້ ແນ່ ຕ່ອນ ຜູ້ເອົາສົ້ມໂອມອກ
ໃຫ້ເຂົາມາລອງຍຸ້ງເປັນນປີໃຫ້ຫວານໃຈ້ ຫຼຸມສວນກຸ້ມ
ກູ່ຕາມສ່ວນ ໃຫຍ່ ເມື່ອຂຸມ ແຕ່ໃຫ້ນາ
1 ກໍ. ນາວກີ່ຂອງລູກໝາກ ແລ້ວກັບເມືອເຮົາ
ໄປຈັບແກ່ນມາປົນແນ່ໃຫ້ຕ່ອນ ເຫຼົ່ານັ້ນຈຶ່ງຕາກອອກ
ໃຈ ສີໄດເນື້ອແລ້ວ - ໝາກບໍ່ສວນແລ້ວ - ຂອງຊຸມປ່າ
ມີຕາກໍໄດ້ກັບໃຫ້ເຫຼົາ ໝາກເກົ່າແລ້ວປ່ອຍເພາະ
ໃຫ້ກ້ອນ 10 ແລ້ວ ໝາກງາມເພາະກ້ອນເຈັ້ງມີ
ໝາກເໜຶ່ງກັບມື້ແລງ 10 ໜ່ວຍ ໃບໝາກບໍ່ໃຫຍ່

ວິທີຄື — ເມື່ອຕ່າງເກີດປະສົມນັ້ນຫຼາຍແລ້ວ ກໍໃຫ້
ມາປະສົມເຂົ້າກັນໃຫ້ຫລາຍເທື່ອ ສ່ວນ
ໝາກຫວານກູ່ນັ້ນໃຫ້ໝາກໃຫຍ່ກ່ອນ ເມື່ອເຄີຍ
ເຫັນເລົ່ານັ້ນແລ້ວກັນແລ້ວ ຈຶ່ງເອົາໝາກບໍ່
ກູ່ໃຫ້ແລ້ວຕາເຂົ້າກັນ ເອົາໃບຕາກລົງມາກໍ່
ເປັນຫອມ ເມື່ອປອກກິນໃຫ້ເກະຂຽວເປືອກ
ເອົາໄປປີໃຫ້ໃຫຍ່ ໂຊຕະກອກຕັດໃຫ້ງາມ ໝາກເປັນໃຫຍ່
ເມື່ອຕັ້ງໃຫ້ຮຽບຫາຍ ຊື່ວ່າແນວກາກຕອງຕາມ
ເພາະໝາກລອກຫຼາຍແນວກາກແຕ່ງຂຶ້ນ %

Mok Saen Som Kai **Recipe 50**

PICKLED FISH ROE GRILLED IN BANANA-LEAF PACKETS

Ingredients

1 piece of pickled fish roe, either from the tail end or the middle—squeeze out or scrape off all the roe and cut into small pieces
7 slices of three-layer pork—the thickness of the slices will depend on the thickness of the meat, but the slices should measure 1 by 4 cm—wash the slices and sprinkle them with salt, then fry them in pork fat until they are nice and golden
1 stalk lemon grass } these two ingredients to be pounded finely
3 spring onion bulbs } together to make the *kheuang hom*
10 (small) shallots, peeled
15 (small) cloves of garlic, peeled
10 very small red chilli peppers (*mak phet kuntsi deng*)
chopped spring onion leaves
(chopped coriander leaves)

Method

When all the ingredients have been prepared, mix them together in a mixing bowl. Leave out only the chopped coriander leaves; add in the spring onion leaves.*

Use pieces of banana leaf to wrap up the mixed ingredients (see drawing on page 18), and employ a pin made out of coconut stem or bamboo to fasten the package. Place the parcel of wrapped ingredients in a bamboo holder (page 18) and grill it. When it is cooked, open it and set the contents on a platter. Garnish with the chopped spring onion leaves.

Serve with boiled young eggplants, other boiled vegetables or young cucumbers.

* Editors' Note. The presence or absence of chopped coriander leaves is uncertain. They do not figure in Phia Sing's list of ingredients, nor are they mentioned as a garnish at the end of the recipe; but they are mentioned in this sentence which also contains a puzzling reference to chopped spring onion leaves (puzzling because they appear to have been used already, and are used again later on as a garnish).

51 ກະນ່ອມຍາງໃຫຍ່

ເຄື່ອງປະສົມ — ຢ່າງນີ້ 10 ຕົວ — ເອົາມາເຫລາະ ຕ້ອງຣັດຕົວແນ
ຄົນຫຼາຍຄົນ ສ່ວນທາກຕົວໃຫ້ຜ່າໃຫ້ງໄວ້ຈານໄວ້
ເພື່ອ ວີຕົວໃຫ້ມັດຄົນເຫລັກໄວ້ດາມໄວ້ ມະນຸດນາເສວນ
ວິນນະຫາໄດ້ເຫາກເທົ່າມະນຸດໃຊ້ໄດ້ ສ່ວນຫົວຕົ້ນ
ກໍໃຫ້ເພາະຕົ້ນເອງານຸ່ງເອົາມາກໍມັນຫົວໄວ້ກູ່
ໄວ້ ເມື່ອເພາະມີດາມີທີ່ເປັນກາງຂອງມະນຸດແລ້ວ
ກໍໃຫ້ເອົາໃສ່ດາກແກ່ຈົນເຫຼົ່າແຫກໄວ້ ສີດ
ສອງຫາວ ແຫກບໍ່ເທົ່າຫົວ ໝາກເໝືອງໃສ່ສອງມຸ່ງ
ຂອງສາມຢ່າງນີ້ໃຫ້ມີແລ້ວເອົາໃສ່ດາກແກ່ຈົນ// ປາດດີ
ເຄື່ອ — ມັກບົດ — ໃບແຫກທ້ອງ ໃຫ້ທາວາມາໃນພໍເລື່ອງ
ໝົດໃບວູປໃຫ້ເຫລັກແຫກໄວ້

ວິທີເຮັດ — ເມື່ອຕາມູເປັ່ງເຄື່ອງທີ່ທ້າງໄວ້ມັນມີຜູ້ແລ້ວ
ກໍໃຫ້ເອົາແກອງສາກໍ ເພາະ ຜົດມັນຮອນໃຫ້ເອົາຄານ
ລົງໃສ່ເຄື່ອງປຸອຄູ່ໃຫຍ່ ຄັ້ນໃຫ້ເຂົ້າຄານ ແລ້ວເອົາ
ຜ້າຫໍ່ຍ່ອວໄວ້ໃຊ້ ເຄື່ອງໃຊ້ມາບາຮອງຊາວໄດ້ທ້ອ
ແຫກບ່ອວູປໃບທາອາມໃນຮູ້ໃຊ້ ເພາະເທື່ອງເຄີມ
ຮອງ ຕາມາວູ້ມີແລ້ວ ຮໍໃບຄາຍາງຕ້ອງລອງນາວ
ຄືໃສ່ມີໝູ່ເອົາໄປຢັ້ງໄຟ ສູດແລ້ວໃຫ້ໃຊ້ຕາມເພື່ອ
ຕ້ອງໂຕວົ້ນທາວມ ເມື່ອເທາງແຫກໃຣ່ມ້ /

Kanab Kung Yai **Recipe 51**

LARGE SHRIMPS GRILLED IN BANANA LEAF

Ingredients

10 fresh large shrimps, heads (i.e. the fore parts) and shells removed—then divide them into two piles of 6 and 4, cut the 6 into halves and chop the 4 finely—then take the heads and scrape out the 'fat' and put it in a small bowl—then take the rest of the contents of the heads, except for hard parts, and pound them in a mortar

three-layer pork, minced—quantity the size of hen's egg*

2 stalks of lemon grass
5 (small) shallots
2 fresh chilli peppers
} these three ingredients to be chopped and pounded together finely

salt and fish sauce

chopped spring onion leaves

1 *waan pai* leaf (see page 38), finely chopped

Method

When the above ingredients have been prepared, mix together in a bowl all those which have been pounded and minced. When they are thoroughly mixed, add the shrimps and a sprinkling of salt and fish sauce. Mix again, then add the chopped spring onion leaves and the finely chopped *waan pai* leaf.

Place the mixture on pieces of banana leaf and make a package with a bamboo holder (as explained on page 18), and grill it. When it is cooked, set it on a platter. Serve with *Keng Phak Hai Kai* (a vegetable soup made with *phak hai kai*—see page 36).

* Editors' note. In the original text this ingredient, i.e. the three-layer pork, was inserted in the middle of the instructions about dealing with the shrimps. The order has been changed to avoid confusion.

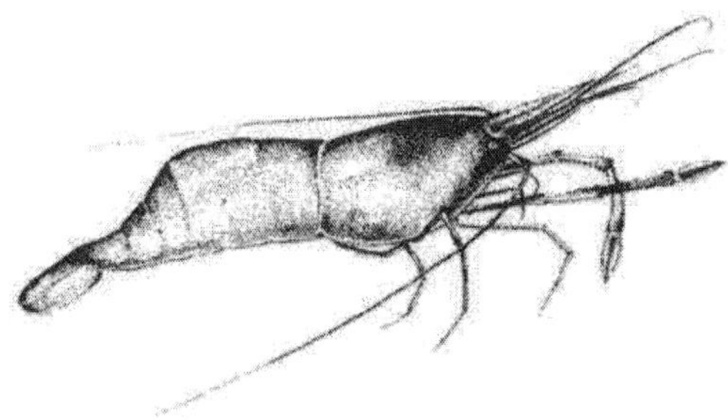

52 ໝົກໄກ່

ເຄື່ອງປະສົມ – ໄກ່ປອກຫນັງອອກ ເອົາລາງບໍ່ໃຫ້ລະອຽດ ເຄິ່ງ
ໃນກໍ່ມູລາງນັ້ນ ແລ້ວ ເອົາມາຍຸ້ເປັນຕາມ ນໍ້າສົມ
ເກືອນ ຫົວສີງຫົ່ວໃຫ້ໄກ່ບໍ່ຍຸ້ ເປັນຕາມແລ້ວກັນ
ເອົາເຄື່ອງພ້ອມ ທັງສັ້ນພັກໄວ້ ໃຫ້ຂາວໃສ່ໃຕ້ສາມ
ຫົວ ພັກທ້ອງໜຸ້ງທົວ ແມ ມາເພິ່ມເທື່ອງຕຸ່ມນໍ້າໃຫ້
ເປື່ອຍ ແລ້ວບໍ່ມີນໍ້າອອກ ເອົາມາເທົ່າຂອມເຂົ້າກັນ
ນໍ້າສີໃສພັກ ທ້ອງໃຫ້ຈືນ ແຕ່ລະອັນ ຕີແລ້ວພັກໄວ້
ເທື່ອ. ນໍ້າປາໃນພັກຫອມ-ໃບຂີ້ ຫູຈົດເປັນສອງງີ
ວິທີເຮັດ – ເມື່ອທາງເຄື່ອງປະສົມ ທັງໝົດນີ້ໄວ້ ລົງແລ້ວ
ໃຫ້ຂາວ ເຄື່ອງຕ່ າ ແລະ ຊຸ່ນໄວ້ ມາໃສ່ເທົ່າຂອມ
ກັນເອົາເຄື່ອງໃສ່ນໍ້າປາຂອງ ຄົນໃຫ້ທົ່ວ ແລະ
ເຄື່ອງພັກນ ຈາງ ນາຄອ ງຸ່ມ ໃນພັກຫໍ່ ໄປໃບຕອງ
ຈັດໃຈລົງໄປ ງາວມ ທົ່ວ ແລ້ວຫໍ່ ຕອງ ຕຽງກັນເປັນ
ທາງນ ໝູ່ປາກ , ຫໍ່ຕອງ ໄມ້ລະ ໃຫ້ແໜ້ນ
ເອົາເປັນສາມອັນ ນຶ່ງ ຕອງລົງ ທຳ ຫຼືຕອງກໍໄດ້
ສຸກແລ້ວ ໃຊ້ໃສ່ຈານ ພັກຫອມໃສ່ ເນາເມື່ອຈະໄດ້
ຢັງທານ ./.

(ໝາຍເຫດ – ໝົກໄກ່ນີ້ ບາງທານ ງຸ່ມ ໃສ່ແລ້ວ
ເທື່ອ ແຄ່ ຄວາມຍັງ ເຄື່ອງ ກໍ່ ຄວາມໃສ່ ເພາະຈະ
ພາງ ເຊັ່ງໄຂ່ຂອງໄກ່ ໄປເປັນຍຸ້ ອື່ນ)

Mawk Kai **Recipe 52**

CHICKEN STEAMED IN BANANA LEAF

Ingredients

½ chicken, gutted and washed—cut the meat and giblets into pieces of medium size, and rub into them salt and ground black pepper

3 stalks of lemon grass (chopped)
7 (small) shallots
(3) dried chilli peppers, soaked in water until soft
} these three ingredients to be pounded together

salt and fish sauce
chopped spring onion leaves
Kaffir lime leaves, each torn into two parts

Method

When the above ingredients have been prepared, mix the chicken pieces and the pounded ingredients together in a bowl. Sprinkle with salt and fish sauce. Taste and check the saltiness. Add the chopped spring onion leaves and the Kaffir lime leaves. Mix thoroughly and wrap the mixture in pieces of banana leaf, securing each package tightly with a pin made out of bamboo or coconut. Make three packages in all.

Steam the packages in a steamer (see page 16). When the packages are cooked, open them and transfer the contents to a platter. Garnish with the chopped spring onion leaves and serve.

Note

In making *Mawk Kai*, some people like to add sticky-rice flour (see page 22). In fact, they shouldn't, because it takes away the flavour of the chicken and makes it taste different.

53 ມອກປາລີ່

ເຄື່ອງປະສົມ — ເນື້ອທາງປາລີ່ ແລະ ລ່າງ ຊຽງ ພ້ອມທັງເນື້ອປາ ແລ້ວມາຍູໄປໃສ່ຕ່ອນນີ້ ໝູ ຊຽງ ທາງ ຢ່າງ ຍູກໍ ໃຫ້ຈູໃສ່ໃນຕ່ອນ ກໍ່ ໃຫ້ເຈືອຫາກ [illegible] ຕາງນກໍ, ໃຫ້ສະອາດ ໜ້ອໄວ້ ສ່ວນຈະຕ້ອນນີ້ ແລະ ປາຍູແທ່ ໃຫ້ນັ້ນ ແລ້ວກົດແລ່ ຕ້ອງການ
ສີໄຄ ສີອງຫົວ ບນາລາ ໝາກເຜັດ ແຊ່ນກໍ ເຂົ້າຍູແລ້ວ ໜຶ່ງບ່ອງ ຫົວຜັກ ຫົວຕະໄຄ ຫົວ ນາລາ ຜັກ ບົວ ສ່ວນຕົ້ນ ຂອງ ດີປາ ໃສ່ໃຫ້ລູ່ ໃຊ້ຜັກ ຍູກໍ ຈນແລ້ວກ ລະອຽດ ເຂົ້າກັນໄວ້ ແປ້ງ - ນກໍ ປາ - ໃບ ຜັກທີ່ ອູ ໃບ ອີຕູ ຊີໃຫ້

ວິທີເຮັດ — ເອົາປາງ ເຕີບ ໃວ້ ລູ ນີ້ ແລ້ວ ກໍ່ໃດ ຕອງ ເຄື່ອງ ຕາວ ແລະ ປາ ທີ່ ຍູ ໄວ້ ນັ້ນ ມາເຈືອ ແຕ່ງ ຮອມ ພອບ ແລ້ວເອົາ ໃສ່ ໝກໍປາ ຮອງ ນກໍ ທ່າ ເພາະ ຜັກ ນີ້ ຊູ ແລ ຈາະ ເປື່ອຍ ແລ້ວ ຈາງ ຕາມ ດູ ນີ້ ໃນ ຜັກ ທີ່ ຈູ ແລະ ອີຕ ໃຊ້ ຮາວ ໃຫ້ ຫົວ ແລ້ວ ຮ່ອງ ໃບ ຕອງ ຕາງ ເມື່ອ ປາ ກໍ ສຸກ ດີ ໃນ ກະ ນ້ຳ ຈະ ໃຊ້ ສາມ ຫຼື ສອງ ນ ບ່ອນ ຕາມ ທາງ ການ ນີ້ ແລະ ໃຊ້ ແລ້ວ ເຈື ປາ ອູ ຫຼື ລາງ ບາງ ນີ້ ສີກ ແລ້ວ ຍກໍ ລົງ ມາ ວາງ ໃສ່ ສາມ ຜັກ ທີ່ ຈູ ໃຊ້ ທັງ ເມື່ອ ທາງ ໃຫ້ ຮ້ອນ ./.

Mawk Pa Ling **Recipe 53**

STEAMED CATFISH

Ingredients

1 *pa ling* (a catfish, probably PANGASIUS NASUTUS—see drawing below)—meat from all its parts including the belly meat cut into pieces of 4 cm and washed —the amount is up to you, according to whether you want to make a lot or just a little

2 stalks of lemon grass
1 dried red chilli pepper, soaked in water until soft
6 (small) shallots
3 roots of coriander
} these four ingredients to be chopped finely and then pounded finely together

salt and fish sauce
chopped spring onion leaves
10 sweet basil leaves

Method

After preparing the above ingredients, put the pounded ingredients and the fish into a bowl and sprinkle them with salt and fish sauce. Taste and check the saltiness. Add the chopped spring onion leaves and the sweet basil leaves. Mix thoroughly, then wrap the mixture in pieces of banana leaf and secure the package with a pin made out of bamboo or coconut. Make two or three of these packages, depending on the size desired. Put them in a steamer (see page 16) and steam them. When they are cooked, open them, put the contents on a platter and garnish them with the chopped spring onion leaves.

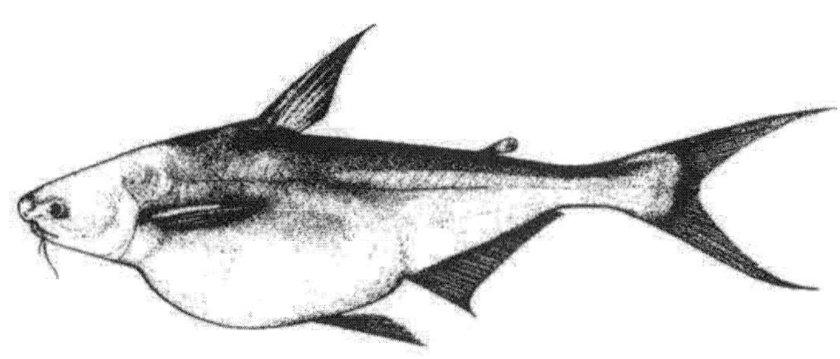

Pa ling, PANGASIUS NASUTUS. The specimen shown has its belly distended. The name *pa ling* may also be applied to at least one other species of catfish.

54 [illegible]

ເຄື່ອງປະສົມ — ປາທີ່ມີ [illegible] ຄືປາ [illegible] ເຊິ່ງໆ ທີ່ຢູ່ໃນ [illegible]
[illegible] ເຜັດ [illegible] ໝາກພິກ [illegible]
[illegible] ໝາກເລັ່ນ [illegible]
[illegible]
[illegible] ແລະ [illegible]
[illegible]
[illegible] ເກືອ [illegible]
[illegible] ໃສ່ [illegible] ເຂົ້າ [illegible]
(ເພີ່ມ [illegible]) [illegible]
[illegible] - [illegible] ເຂົ້າ [illegible]
[illegible] - [illegible] - [illegible] - [illegible]
[illegible]

ວິທີເຮັດ — [illegible] - [illegible] ແລະ [illegible]
[illegible]
[illegible] ແລະ [illegible]
[illegible]
[illegible] ປາ [illegible]
[illegible] ແລະ [illegible]
[illegible]
[illegible] - [illegible] - [illegible]

[illegible]

Mawk Poo Paeng **Recipe 54**

STEAMED STUFFED CRAB

Ingredients

5 crabs of the kind called *poo paeng*, the crab which has yellow matter inside the shell, cooked—lift off their upper shells, remove and discard their aprons (the 'tails' underneath their bodies) and wash the crabs
minced pork, including a little fat—a quantity the size of a duck's egg
1 spoonful (1 tbsp) of sticky-rice flour (page 22)

5 (small) shallots 1 dried chilli pepper, soaked in water until soft	these two ingredients to be pounded together

ground black pepper, salt and fish sauce
spring onion leaves, finely chopped

Method

Mix together in a large bowl the minced pork, the sticky-rice flour and the pounded ingedients. Sprinkle with salt and add fish sauce. Taste and check the saltiness. Then add the ground black pepper and the chopped spring onion leaves. Stuff this mixture into the (upper) crab shells until they are full. Replace these stuffed upper shells on the bodies of the crabs, wrap the crabs in pieces of banana leaf and secure them with bamboo or coconut pins. Then cook them in a steamer (see page 16). When they are cooked, open the packages and transfer the crabs to a platter.

55 ນາງຈາລອງຄາແຄ

ເຄື່ອງປະສົມ — ຂາໄກ່ - 10 - ຂາ ໃຫ້ແກະເອົາແຕ່ ສ່ວນ ຂາ ລ້າງນ້ຳໃຫ້ສະອາດດີ [illegible] [illegible] [illegible] — ຜັກໃຫ້ [illegible] ເຂົ້າສານ [illegible] ໃບ [illegible] [illegible] [illegible] ຫົວ ຜັກ ຫົວ [illegible] [illegible] [illegible] [illegible] - ໃບ ຜັກ ຫົວ [illegible] - [illegible] - [illegible] - [illegible]

ວິທີເຮັດ ໃຫ້ເອົາເຄື່ອງ [illegible] ແລະ ເຄື່ອງ [illegible] [illegible] ໃສ່ ຄົກ ໃຫຍ່ [illegible] ຄົນ [illegible] [illegible] ໃບ ຜັກ ຫົວ [illegible] [illegible] ຈະເບິ່ງເຫັນ [illegible] [illegible] ເອົາ [illegible] [illegible] [illegible] 10 ນາທີ [illegible] [illegible] [illegible] [illegible] [illegible] [illegible]

Mawk Dok Khae **Recipe 55**

STEAMED STUFFED KHAE FLOWERS

Ingredients

10 *khae* flowers (see drawing below)—remove their stamens and wash them
1 piece of pork, including a little fat, the size of a hand, minced
1 spoonful (1 tbsp) of sticky-rice flour (see page 22)
7 (small) shallots } these two ingredients to be pounded together finely
1 dried chilli pepper, soaked in water until soft } these two ingredients to be pounded together finely
chopped spring onion leaves
salt, fish sauce and ground black pepper

Method

Put the pounded and minced ingredients into a large bowl, mix them thoroughly and sprinkle with salt and fish sauce. Then add the chopped spring onion leaves and ground black pepper. Taste and check the saltiness. Stuff the mixture into the *khae* flowers, and wrap them in pieces of banana leaf, making two packages. Secure the packages with bamboo or coconut stem pins and steam them in a steamer (see page 16). When cooked, open the packages, transfer the contents to a platter and serve.

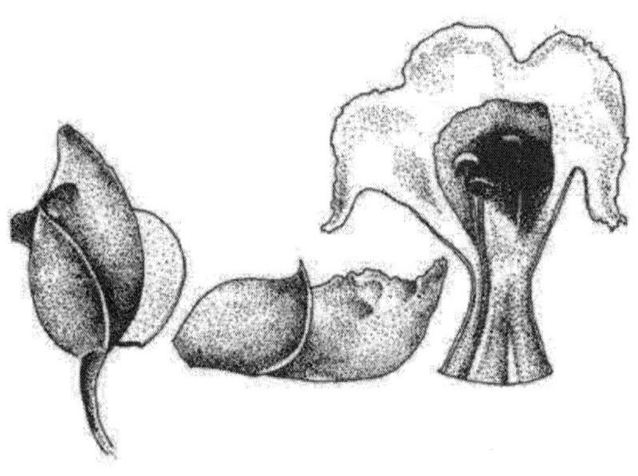

Khae flowers, MARKHAMIA STIPULATA

໕໖ ມອກປາເຂັ້ນ

ເຄື່ອງປະສົມ — ເຊັ້ນເຄັມ ສອງກ້ອນ ເນື້ອໝູ ເອົາມາ
ຕັ້ງ ຕົ້ມ ຂອງກາເລືອດໃສ່ ຕາກ ບ່ອນ ແລ້ວໃຫ້ດີ
ຫົວຊີ້ນ ຫຼື ບໍ່ ທານ ດອກ ເຂັ້ມ ຂອງ ເຄື່ອງເອົາ
ໄປລ້າງ ນໍ້າໃຫ້ສະອາດ ແລ້ວໃສ່ ຂູດ ນມ ...
ມັນ ໜຶ່ງ ຕ່ອນ — ຜັກໃບ ກາ ... ເຂົ້າ ໜຽວ
ແຊ່ ນໍ້າ ເບື່ອ ແລ້ວ ... ມາ ຕໍາ
ໃຫ້ ລະອຽດ ...
ໃສ່ ຫຍ້າ ນໍ້າ ... ຫົວ ຈະ ເອົາ
ແປ້ງ ສາລີ ໃສ່ ຕາງ ກໍ ໄດ້
ຫົວ ຜັກ ບົວ ໃສ່ ຫົວ — ໝາກ ຖົ່ວ ໃສ່ ພຸ່ມ ນໍ້າ ເປັນ
ແລ້ວ ໜຶ່ງ ບ່ວງ ເອົາ ທໍາ ປະສົມ ກັນ ໃຫ້ ແຫຼກ ລະ
ອຽດ ເກືອ — ນໍ້າ ປາ — ຜັກ ທ້ອງ ປູ ນໍ້າ ຕອນ

ວິທີ ເຮັດ — ໃຫ້ ເອົາ ເຄື່ອງ ຜັກ ແລະ ເຄື່ອງ ທໍາ ປະສົມ ກັນ ໃສ່
ຖ້ວຍ ແມ່ ... ໃຫຍ່ ຄົນ ເຂົ້າ ກັນ ໃຫ້ ທົ່ວ -
ແລ້ວ ຈຶ່ງ ເອົາ ເນີ້ງ ... ນໍ້າ ປາ ລົງ ... ໄປ
ຊີມ ເບິ່ງ ... ແລ້ວ ແລະ ເບິ່ງ ... ໃສ່
ໃບ ... ໃສ່ ... ໃຫ້ ທົ່ວ ... ຈຶ່ງ ເອົາ
ຕາງ ... ເປັນ ... ໃສ່ ...
ໃຫ້ ... ... ເອົາ ... ... ໄວ້

ໜຶ່ງ ... ແລ້ວ ... ໃຫ້ ... ເພື່ອ ... ໃຫ້
ມື້ ... //

Mawk Hed Kaen **Recipe 56**

MUSHROOMS STEAMED IN BANANA LEAF PACKETS

Ingredients

2 soupbowlfuls (i.e. individual Chinese soupbowls, holding one pint each) of *hed kaen* (a kind of mushroom, see page 44)—cut off their roots, then put the mushrooms in a mortar and use the pestle to dislodge the soil from them, after which wash them

minced pork, including a little fat

2 soupspoonfuls of sticky-rice flour, (see page 22)—or substitute cornflour

7 (small) shallots } these two ingredients to be pounded together

1 dried chilli pepper soaked in water until soft }

salt and fish sauce

chopped spring onion leaves

Method

Mix thoroughly the minced and pounded ingredients in a small bowl. Then add the mushrooms, salt and fish sauce and mix thoroughly together. Taste and check the saltiness.

Put the prepared mixture in a wrapping of pieces of banana leaf and secure the packages with bamboo or coconut-stem pins. Steam in a steamer (page 16). When cooked, transfer them to a platter and serve.

An individual Chinese soupbowl

໕໒ ຫໍ່ສົ້ມໂນວກນາວ

ເຄື່ອງປະສົມ — ເນາະເນັ້ອ ຊີ້ນທ້າວມ່ຽງ ໝາກໄມ້ ໃຫ້ສຸກ ແລ້ວ ອອກມາ ຟັກທອງ ອອກໃຫ້ມາລາໆ ນ້ຳໃຫ້ສະອາດ ຫົວຜັກ ບົ່ວ ຫົວກະທຽມ ຜັກຫອມ ສົດໆ ຫົວ ມາກໃນ ໃຫ້ສຸກ ແລ້ວ ອອກ ເພາະຕາມ ອອກ ໃຫ້ງາມ ໃສ່ ຊີ້ນໝູ ອີ່ເປີ່ ຜັກໃຫ້ ແຫຼກເກົ້າມ່ຽງ ໄປ ເກີດ- ໜັງປາ- ນ້ຳປາ ນາວ ສອງ ມ່ຽງ- ຜັກ ຕອນ ລຸຍ ຕົ້ນ

ວິທີເຮັດ — ໃຫ້ເອົາຊີ້ນ ທີ່ຜັກໄວ້ ມາປັ່ນ ກໍ່ມຽງ ນາງ ແລ້ວ ໝັ້ນ ເສັ້ນ ຕັດໃນ ມາໄວ້ ພ້ອມ ຕອນ ນາ ປາ ໄວ້ ນໍ້າ ເປັນ ຕົ້ນ ໃສ່ ສັກ ຢູ່ ລົງ ຕັກ ແລ້ວ ຕອນ ນຳ ຜັກ ນັ້ນ ມາ ຕຳໃຫ້ ລະອຽດ ແລ້ວ ຕັກ ອອກ ແລ້ວ ນຳ ມາ ເໜັ້ຽ ມາກ ມາ ຕຳ ໃຫ້ ລະອຽດ ແລ້ວ ຈຶ່ງ ເອົາ ຜັກ ບົ່ວ ມາ ຜັກ ຫອມ ມາ ຕຳ ເຂົ້າ ກັນ ຈົນ ແຫຼກ ລະອຽດ ແລ້ວ ໝູ ຕຳ ໃສ່ ມາ ກັນ ຈົນ ໃສ່ ເຄາະ ເປື້ອງ ເລີມ ຈາງ ຊົ່ວ ຍາ ກໍ ຕັ້ງ ນໍ້າ ປາ ລົງ ປົນ ນໍ້າ ໝາກ ນາວ ໃສ່ ແປ ເນື້ອ ທາງ ລ່ວ ຂື້ນ ກໍ ຕັ້ງ ນໍ້າ ປາ ນາງ ໂຕ ແຕ່ ປາ ໄດ້ ຂຶ້ນ ແລ້ວ ຕັດ ໄວ້ ກູ້ ຢູ່ ມັນ ຜັກ ຫອມ ລຸຍ ໃສ່ ເທິງ ນໍ້າ ນັ້ນ ຕໍ່ ດ່ຽວ ໃຫ້ ຢູ່ ທາງ ນຶ່ງ ນັ້ນ ນອນ ນາງ ./.

ໝາຍເຫດ — ຫໍ່ສົ້ມໄວ້ ຢູ່ ທາງ ນຶ່ງ ນັ້ນ ນອນ ນາງ ນີ້ ນາງໆ ການ ນໍ້າ ຈະ ແລ້ວ ຢູ່ ມູນ ໄວ້ ແທນ ຊີ້ນ ໝູ ກໍ່ ໄດ້ ໄດ້ ເລືອກ ກັນ ແຕ່ ເສັ້ນ ເພາະ ສຸກ ງ່າຍ ເປັນ ຕ່ອນ ນາ ສາ ກ່ອນ ໄປ

Mawk Khai Pa **Recipe 57**

FISH EGGS STEAMED IN BANANA LEAF PACKETS

Ingredients

1 soupbowl of fish eggs (any kind)—add some water and beat them until they have swollen up well
1 piece of fish (any kind), minced
1 piece of three-layer pork, the size of three fingers, minced
7 (small) shallots
1 dried chilli pepper, soaked in water until soft
} these two ingredients to be pounded finely to make the *kheuang hom*
salt and fish sauce
chopped spring onion leaves
ground black pepper

Method

Put the *kheuang hom*, the minced fish and the minced pork in a large bowl or a small mixing bowl. Sprinkle with salt and fish sauce. Mix together thoroughly, then add the swollen fish eggs, the chopped spring onion leaves and the ground black pepper. Mix all together again thoroughly. Taste and check the saltiness. Wrap the mixture in pieces of banana leaf, making three packages, and secure them with bamboo or coconut-stem pins. Steam the packages in a steamer (page 16). When they are cooked, unwrap the packages, transfer the contents to a platter and serve.

48 ໝົກປາແດກ

ເຄື່ອງປະສົມ —

ປາແດກ ເລືອກເອົາແຕ່ຕອນງາມ ສາມກ້ອນ
ລ້າງ [illegible] ເອົາເກັດອອກໃຫ້ໝົດ ຜັກໃສ່ເຂົ້າໝົກ
ໃບສາມຊຸມ ໃບກ້ຽງຫອມ ເຂົ້າໜ້າ [illegible] ຜັກໃສ່ເຂົ້າໝົກ
ຜັກທຽມ ແລະ ຕົ້ນຫອມ ຜັກຫອມ ແລະ ຂີງ [illegible]
(ສີໄຄ ໝາກເພັດ ຫົວຜັກທຽມ ຄັດ ໝາກ [illegible]
[illegible] ໝົດ ແລະ [illegible] ຕາມທີ່ໃຫ້ [illegible]
ຈົນແຫຼກ) ໃບຜັກຫອມ - ໝາກເຜັດ [illegible]

ວິທີເຮັດ — ເມື່ອ [illegible] ເກືອ ຫຼາຍ [illegible] ຈຶ່ງເອົາ [illegible]
ຜັກ ແລະ [illegible] ຕາມ [illegible]
[illegible] ຫົວ ຜັກທຽມ ແລະ ຜັກຫອມ ແລະ
ໝາກເຜັດ [illegible] ຜັກທຽມ [illegible] ແລະ [illegible]
[illegible] ໃສ່ປາແດກ [illegible]
[illegible]
[illegible] ສຸກ [illegible]
[illegible] ໃຫ້ [illegible] ຫານ ./.
(ໝາຍເຫດ - ໝົກປາແດກນີ້ [illegible] ໃຫ້ [illegible]
[illegible] ແລະ ໝາກ [illegible]
[illegible] ຈຶ່ງແຊບດີ)

Mawk Padek

Recipe 48B

STEAMED FISH FROM THE PADEK POT

Ingredients

3 pieces of fish from the *padek* pot (see page 23), washed to get rid of the rice husks, and minced
1 piece of three-layer pork (see page 26), the size of a hand, minced
5 (small) heads of garlic peeled and the cloves peeled also
10 (small) shallots, peeled
2 stalks of lemon grass (chopped)
7 (small) shallots
2 dried chilli peppers, soaked in water until soft
(these three ingredients to be pounded together)
spring onion leaves, chopped
10 small chilli peppers

Method

After preparing the above ingredients, mix the pounded and minced ones in a bowl. Add the whole peeled shallots, the peeled garlic cloves, the chopped spring onion leaves and the chilli peppers. Taste and check the saltiness. If it is not salty enough, squeeze out some *padek* liquid on to it.

Wrap the mixture in pieces of banana leaf and secure the packages, of which you should make two, with bamboo or coconut-stem pins. Steam them in a steamer (see page 16). When they are cooked, open them, transfer the contents to a platter and serve.

Note

It is nice to serve this *Mawk Padek* with various vegetables which have been blanched in boiling water, young cucumbers, fried moist pork skin and boiled round eggplants.

49 ມອກໝາກ[illegible]

ເຄື່ອງປະສົມ — ໝາກ[illegible] ຊີ້ນອ່ອນ ເອົາມາ
ເຈາະຫົວ [illegible] [illegible]
[illegible] ໃຫ້ [illegible] ແລ້ວ [illegible]
ທີ່ [illegible] ໄປ [illegible] ຫົວ [illegible] ໃສ່
[illegible] ເຂົ້າ [illegible] ເຂົ້າ ກັບ [illegible] ໃສ່
[illegible] ໃສ່ [illegible] - [illegible]
[illegible] ແກ່ ປາ

ວິທີ ເຮັດ — ໃຫ້ເອົາ [illegible] ແລະ [illegible] ໃສ່ [illegible]
[illegible] ມາ [illegible] [illegible] ໃສ່ [illegible]
[illegible] ໃຫ້ ຫົວ [illegible] ແລ້ວ
[illegible] ແລະ [illegible] [illegible] ແຕ່ [illegible]
[illegible] ໃຫ້ ຫົວ ເອົາ ໝາກ [illegible] ທີ່
[illegible] ອອກ ມາ [illegible]
[illegible] ໝາກ [illegible] [illegible]
[illegible] ແລ້ວ ໃຫ້ ເອົາ [illegible] ແລ້ວ [illegible]
[illegible] ເອົາ [illegible] ໃສ່ [illegible]
[illegible] ມາ ໃສ່ [illegible] ໃຫ້ [illegible]

50 ມອກໄຂ່[illegible]

ເຄື່ອງປະສົມ — ໄຂ່ [illegible] [illegible] ແລະ ໃສ່ ເອົາ [illegible]
ແລະ 2 [illegible] ໃຫ້ [illegible]
[illegible] ໃຫ້ [illegible] ໄຂ່ ໄກ່ ຫຼື ໄຂ່ [illegible]
[illegible] ໃຫ້ [illegible] [illegible]
ໃຫ້ [illegible] [illegible] ແກ່ ປາ ໃບ ຜັກ
[illegible]

ວິທີ ເຮັດ — ໃຫ້ເອົາ [illegible] - [illegible] ໃສ່ ໄກ່
[illegible] ແລະ [illegible] ມາ [illegible]
[illegible] ແກ່ ປາ [illegible] ແລ້ວ ເອົາ ໄຂ່ [illegible]
[illegible] ແລ້ວ [illegible] ແລະ [illegible]
[illegible] [illegible] ໃຫ້ ຜັກ [illegible]
ໃສ່ [illegible] ແລ້ວ ແກ່ ໄປ [illegible]
[illegible] ເປັນ [illegible] ໃສ່ [illegible]
[illegible] ແລ້ວ [illegible] ມາ ໃສ່
ໃສ່ [illegible] ໃຫ້ [illegible]

Mawk Mak Phet **Recipe 49B**

STEAMED STUFFED FRESH CHILLI PEPPERS

Ingredients

10 large fresh chilli peppers, to be cut lengthwise but without completing the cut, then cored and seeded and soaked in water
1 piece of pork, including some fat, the size of a hand, minced
7 (small) shallots, finely pounded
2 soupspoonfuls of sticky rice, soaked and then pounded to make rice flour
chopped spring onion leaves
ground black pepper, salt and fish sauce

Method

Mix thoroughly in a bowl the pounded and minced ingredients. Add salt, fish sauce and ground black pepper. Taste and check the saltiness. Sprinkle the chopped spring onion leaves on to the mixture and mix them in.

Next, stuff the opened fresh chilli peppers with the prepared mixture and wrap them up in pieces of banana leaf, making two packages. Steam these in a steamer (see page 16). When cooked, open the packages, transfer the contents to a platter and serve.

Mawk Khai Mod **Recipe 50B**

ANTS' EGGS STEAMED IN BANANA LEAVES

Ingredients

1 cup of ants' eggs (the eggs of the red ant, known in Laos as *mod som*, the 'sour ant')
minced pork, including some fat, a quantity the size of a betel nut
2 hen's or duck's eggs
3 (small) shallots, pounded
ground black pepper, salt and fish sauce
chopped spring onion leaves

Method

Mix together the minced pork, the pounded shallots and the hen's or duck's eggs. Sprinkle with salt and fish sauce. Add the ants' eggs after washing them clean. Taste and check the saltiness. Then add the ground black pepper and the chopped spring onion leaves and mix thoroughly.

Wrap the mixture in pieces of banana leaf, making two packages, and secure these with bamboo or coconut-stem pins. Steam them in a steamer (page 16). When cooked, open the packages and transfer the contents to a platter and serve.

51. ຄະນ່ອງປາສະງົ້ວ

ເຄື່ອງປະສົມ — ເນື້ອພ້ອມທ້ອງປາສະງົ້ວ ແລະ ຣາກຫຍ້າ ເທື່ອງນີ້ປາກໍໄດ້ ຫຍ້າໃຫ້ເປັນຕ່ອນໃຫຍ່ ລ້າງນ້ຳໃຫ້ສະອາດ ຄັ້ນ

ເຄື່ອງພັກໃສ່ . ສີໄຄ 2 ຫົວ - ໝາກເຜັດສົດ 3 ໜ່ວຍ - ຫົວພັກບົ່ວ 5 ຫົວ ຂ່າແຫ້ງ 1 ຕ່ອນ ຂອງ 4 ຢ່າງ ນີ້ເອົາໃສ່ກາບໃຫ້ສຸກ ເກືອ - ນ້ຳປາ - ພັກຊີ ປີ້ງຫອມ . ໃບພັກບົ່ວ ໃບເລັກນ້ອຍ . ໃບຫອມ

ວິທີເຮັດ — ໃຫ້ເອົາເຄື່ອງ ຄົວລົງໃສ່ຄົກ ເກືອ - ນ້ຳປາ ພັກຊີ ໃສ່ຄົກ ໃຫ້ຕຳ ເອົາປາທີ່ທຳສະອາດໃສ່ ລົງຄົກ ໃຫ້ມີນ້ຳ ຕຳພໍແຫລກ ແລະ ເອົາ ໃບພັກບົ່ວ ໃສ່ຄົກ ໃດຫົວ ຈົ່ງເອົາໃບຫອມ ມາຮ່ວມ ກໍ່ຂອງໃຫ້ເອົາໃບຕອງ ຫຍ້າ ມາຫໍ່ເປັນ ຫໍ່ນ້ອຍ ນຶ່ງໃສ່ໄຟ ຫລືປີ້ງໃສ່ໄຟຖ່ານ ເອົາ ອອກມາ ໃສ່ຖ້ວຍ ຍົກໄປໃຫ້ກິນ %

ໝາຍເຫດ — ເຮັດຄະນ່ອງປານີ້ ຖ້າບໍ່ມີໃບ ໃຫ້ເອົາໃບຕອງ ຕໍ່ໃສ່ກໍໄດ້ ແຕ່ພັກໃຫ້ດີ ລາວເຮົາ ໃສ່ກັບ ເຂົ້າໜຽວ ຖ້າເປັນປາ ສົດ ໃຫ້ສົມ ໃຫ້ເປັນແຕ່ດີ ເອົາໃຈໃສ່ ຮູ້ບໍ ສ່ວນຄະນ່ອງປານີ້ ຈະໄດ້ຫາປາ ເອົາ ໃສ່ ປາທີ່ມີ ກ້າງຫລາຍ ເພາະວ່າ ນ້ຳຕາ ເຈົ້າ ມີຫລາຍ ຖ້າວ່າ ຈະເຮັດໃຫ້ ດີກິນ ເຮົາ ຕ້ອງ ຕຳໃຫ້ ແຫລກ %

Kanab Pa Sa Ngoua **Recipe 51B**

SHEATFISH GRILLED IN BANANA LEAF PACKETS

Ingredients

the belly part of a *pa sa ngoua* (a sheatfish, see drawing on page 119, cut into large pieces and salted

2 stalks of lemon grass
3 fresh chilli peppers
5 (small) shallots
a piece of crisp-fried pork skin (*khiep moo*)
} these four ingredients to be pounded together finely

salt and fish sauce
3 sprigs of dill, chopped
chopped spring onions
1 leaf of *toon* (*bai toon*, see page 38)

Method

Mix together in a mixing bowl the pounded ingredients with salt and fish sauce. Add the pieces of fish and mix some more. Taste and check the saltiness. Then add the chopped spring onions, mix some more and wrap the mixture up in the toon leaf. Overwrap it in some pieces of banana leaf and use a bamboo holder (page 18) for grilling it. When it is cooked, place it on a platter to serve.

Note

If *khiep moo* is not available, you can substitute minced pork, which should include some fat. However, it will not taste as good.

If the fish is *pa koum*, let it 'go bad' a little—this will give it a very good flavour unless it doesn't suit your taste.*

To make this fish *kanab* one can use any kind of fish that doesn't have too many bones, which would make it very difficult to eat unless it appealed to your taste. The ingredients and method are the same, whatever fish you use.

* Editors' Note. We think that Phia Sing is saying that for a *kanab* the fish need not be fresh because of all the herbs put in. Thanks to them the cooked fish would not have a bad smell. However, apart from this, many Lao people would agree that slightly bad fish has more flavour than fresh fish, but it must be only slightly bad. The reference to *pa koum* as an alternative fish for this recipe is the only mention of it by Phia Sing. This fish is THYNNICTHYS THYNNOIDES (see Davidson, *Fish and Fish Dishes of Laos*, page 40).

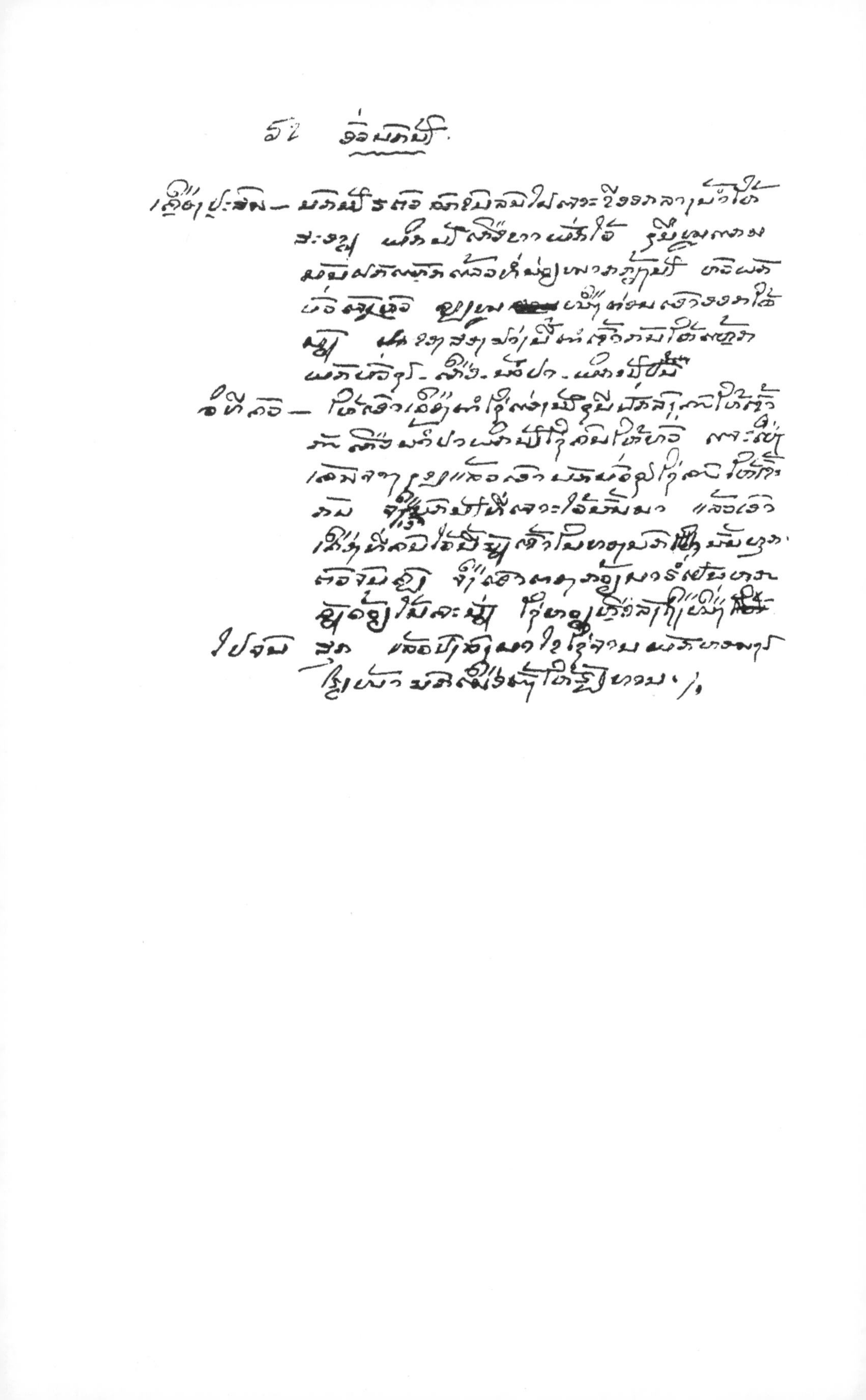

໕໒ ອໍ່ມກາຍ

ເຄື່ອງປະສົມ — [illegible]

ວິທີເຮັດ — [illegible]

ໄປຈັນ [illegible]

Ua Nok Noi **Recipe 52B**

STUFFED SMALL BIRDS

Ingredients

5 small birds (*nok noi*, a Lao term which means any small birds)—pluck, singe, wash and gut them, then sprinkle salt and ground black pepper on them
minced pork, including some fat, a quantity the size of a small tangerine (3 tbsp)
7 (small) shallots } these two ingredients to
1 piece of crisp-fried pork skin } be pounded together
4 to 5 whole spring onions, chopped
salt, fish sauce, ground black pepper
(chopped coriander, all apart from the roots)

Method

Put the pounded ingredients and the minced pork in a bowl and mix them; then add salt, fish sauce and ground black pepper and mix again, thoroughly. Taste and check the saltiness, then add the chopped spring onion. Mix this with the other ingredients.

Stuff the mixture into the cleaned birds, wrap them in pieces of banana leaf and secure the packages with bamboo or coconut-stem pins. Steam them in a steamer (see page 16). When they are cooked, take them out of their wrapping of leaves and place them on a platter. Garnish with chopped coriander and serve.

59 ຫົວສີໂຄ

ເຄື່ອງປະສົມ — ເອົາຈຸ່ມ ໝາກນາວ ເຫົ້າ ຜ່າມືທີ່ເຜົາໃຫ້ແຫຼກ ພັດ
ໄວ້ ຊີໂຄ ຫົວໃຫຍ່ ສົ້ມຫົວ ມາລົງ ເທົ່າລອມໆ

ນໍ່ສຸກດີເລືອດ ລ້າງນ້ຳໃຫ້ສະອາດ ຕຸ້ມເອົາເທົ່າຕາກ
ນ້ຳຮ້ອນຂື້ນ ຈຸ່ມເອົາເຫຼົ້າມາ ຖູ່ມ ທີ່ອີດເຫັດ
ລາງໃຫ້ເປັນເສັ້ນສ່ຽງໆ ແລ້ວນໍໃຫ້ຂຽງອອກຈາກ
ລານໃຊ້ຄາມໄວ້ ຫົວພັດຫໍ່ອບ້າວ ຫົວຕ່ຳໃຫ້ແຫ້ງ
ໃສ່ໄວ້ ສາມມ່ຽງ ເພື່ອ-ນໍ້າປາ-ແປ້ງສາລີ ບີ້ ນ້ອງ
ພິກມໍ່ປ່ນ- ໃບພັກທ້ອງໃຫ້ແຫຼມເລືອດ ນໍ້າ

ວິທີ ຄື — ໃຫ້ເອົາໝາກພ້າ ພັກຫົວຕໍາປະສົມເຂົ້າກັນ ເພື່ອ
ໃຫ້ນໍ້າປາຣົດ ພິກມໍ່ປ່ນ ໃຊ້ຄົນເຂົ້າກັນ ແລະ
ເບີ່ງເລື່ອຍໆຕາມຄວມ ໃບພັກທ້ອງໃຊ້ຄົນໃຫ້ທົ່ວ
ຈຶ່ງຫົວສີໂຄທີ່ຊຸ່ມໄວ້ນັ້ນມາ ແລ້ວໃຫ້ເອົາປູນ
ທີ່ຄົນໃຊ້ເລື່ອຍທີ່ຍິ້ນເຂົ້າທັ້ງລາງ ຫົວສີໂຄ ແປງ
ໃຫ້ງາມຈົນໝົດ ແລ້ວເອົາຕາກຕາດມາວາງລົງເປັນ
ຕະຫຼຸ ບໍ່ໃຫ້ໃຟສົດ ແລ້ວເອົາອອກມາໃຫ້ຄົນໄວ້
ໃຫ້ເຢັນ ເວີໃຊ້ໄດ້ ມາໃຫ້ ໃຈກູ່ ທີ່ເຫຼົ້າຂັ້ນ
ແລະເພື່ອ ຍົກໄປ ຂວາງຂັ້ນ ຕຸ້ມນຳພລໃຊ້
ນໍ້າມັນຮອນ ແລ້ວໃຫ້ເອົາສີໂຄລົງໃສ່ທີ່ລະໜ້ອຍ
ຈົນສຸກເຫຼືອງ ແລ້ວເອົາຖ້ວຍໃສ່ຈານ ເພື່ອທ່າງ
ໃຫ້ສວຍງາມ /.

Ua Sikhai **Recipe 53B**

STUFFED LEMON GRASS STALKS

Ingredients

1 piece of pork the size of a hand, minced

10 large stalks of lemon grass—place them in hot charcoal and ashes, then wash them and cut off the leaves at a point about 10 cm from the base of the stalk, after which use a needle to open out the strands of each stalk (as shown in the drawing), but without letting the cuts reach either its base or the cut top end, which must remain intact

5 (small) shallots, pounded

3 hen's eggs

salt and fish sauce

1 spoonful (1 tbsp) of cornflour

ground black pepper

a small amount of finely chopped spring onion leaves

Method

Mix together the minced pork and the pounded shallots. Add salt and fish sauce and a sprinkling of ground black pepper. Mix thoroughly, taste and check the saltiness. Then add the chopped spring onion leaves and mix these in too.

Open out the slit centre part of each lemon grass stalk and stuff it with the minced pork mixture. Smooth the minced pork mixture so that it looks nice (i.e. smooth down any bits which project from the slits).

Wrap the stuffed lemon grass stalks in batches in pieces of banana leaf as you would when making a *kanab* (see page 18). Grill them until they are cooked, then open the banana-leaf containers and let the contents cool.

Beat the eggs with salt. Heat some fat in a wok. Dip the stuffed lemon grass stalks in the beaten egg, then fry them in the hot fat. Lay them out nicely on a platter and serve.

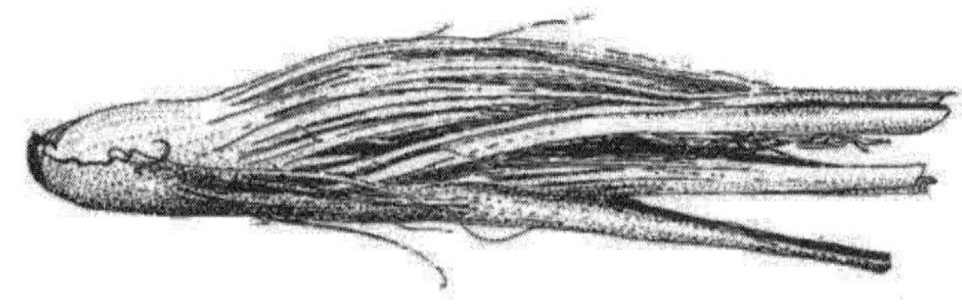

໖໔ ອິ່ວບໍ່ໃສ່

ເລື່ອງປະສົມ — ບໍ່ໃຊ່ຫຼືບໍ່ໃສ່ເຖິງກໍໄດ້ ແຕ່ໂຕເລື່ອງ

ເຈົ້າບໍ່ເຫັນບໍ່ປະສົມຄວນທີ່ຕ້ອງຊູ້ຕາລອງ ເຕົາບໍ່
ມາປະກາດແລະຊູ້ເອົາແຕ່ບອ່ນອອ່ນແປງງາ ອ້ອມ
ໃຫ້ງານກິນບ່າໃຫ້ໃຫຍ່ຫຼາຍ ເຈົ້າເວັນມາຮຽນກາງ
ຈຳເສັບຈົນເກືອນເກົ່າໃອ້ ທອນເກັບເອົາຊູ້ເກືອຕາ
ໃຫ້ແຫ້ກ ຊຸບໍ່ແມແກມນົມທີ່ຜ່ານມີອີ່ມັກໂຕລຸກ
ໃຊ່ສອງພອ່ງ - ເຄື່ອ - ນ້ຳປາ - ແປງສາລີ - ເນີກາຍປີ
ໃນເກັບເອົາ - ນ້ຳນົມເນ -

ຈຸດທີ່ຄວນ — ໂຕເຈົ້າຊຸບໍ່ມັກ ເກັບເອົາເກົ່າ ເກົ່າມໍປີບໍ່ແປງສາ
ລີເຫຼືອບອ່ນເກົ່າ ນາງອອນກິນໃຊ້ຕາງ ຄົນໂຕເອີ
ກິນເລື້ອ ນ້ຳປາເກັບເອົາໃຊ້ຄົນໃຫ້ເກືອ ແລະຊື້
ເຄີມຈາງຕາມາງຮູ ~~[illegible]~~ ຈຶ່ງເອົາຊູ້ເຂົ້າ
ໃນໃຈຄອງບໍ່ໃມ່ຈົບໃຊ້ ຣ໌ຊູ້ຕາງກາງຊູ້ເຫຼືອ
ກະບ່ອງ ຊື່ຫຼືຍາງໃຜຈົນສາ ເຈົ້າຂອບມາໃຊ້ປະໃອ້
ໃຫ້ໃສ່ ສິ່ງເປົ່າຍາງຂົບຕາງບໍ່ມັນບົມໃຊ້ ຫຼື
ໃຊ້ໃຊ້ຫຼູແປງສາຣີເລື້ອໃຈດີໂຕເຕົ້າກັບ ຈຶ່ງເອົາບໍ່ໃສ່
ທີ່ງອົບໃອ້ຊູ້ ໃຊ່ຈົບໃຫ້ງານເກົ່າເຫຼືອງອອ່ນຈົນຫຼີ
ບໍ່ ເຈົ້າຊູນໃຊ້ຈານບົກເລື້ອຕົ້ງໂຕຊູ້ຫາຍ ໚

Ua No Mai **Recipe 54B**

STUFFED BAMBOO SHOOTS

Ingredients

5 bamboo shoots, which may be *no mai lai* (GIANTOCHLOA NIGROCILIATA) or *no mai bong* (BAMBUSA TULDA)—choose small ones, boil them until they lose their (bitter) taste, then cut off all the hard outer layer and cut the trimmed shoots into sections 8 cm long—after this use a needle (as in recipe 53B) to make slits in them lengthwise, but leaving the ends of each section intact
7 (small) shallots, pounded
1 piece of pork, including some fat, the size of the palm of a hand, minced
2 eggs
salt and fish sauce
flour (about 2 tbsp)
ground black pepper
chopped spring onion leaves
pork fat

Method

Mix together in a large bowl the minced pork, the pounded shallots, ground black pepper and 1 tablespoonful of the flour. Mix all this thoroughly. Add salt, fish sauce and some of the chopped spring onions. Mix again, taste to check the saltiness, and add more of the chopped spring onion.

Stuff the mixture into the slit-open bamboo shoots and wrap these in pieces of banana leaf as you would in making a *kanab* (see page 18). Use a bamboo holder (see page 18) to grill the packages until they are cooked, then open up the banana leaf coverings and leave the contents to cool.

Heat some pork fat in a wok. Beat the eggs in a bowl with salt and some flour mixed in. Dip the cooked bamboo shoots in the egg mixture and fry them in the hot fat until they are nice and golden. Place them on a platter to serve.

55 ເລາງນໍ້າໄວ້ປາບາງ

ເຄື່ອງປະສົມ — ນໍ້າໃສ່ໃນໝໍ້ ຕົ້ມໃຫ້ເດືອດ ນໍ້າໜ້ອຍ ເອົາ ໝາກນໍ້າໃສ່ ໃຫ້ເປັນຕອນ ນໍ້ານັ້ນ ສົມຄວນ ພ້ອມເຕັ້ມ ເລາງລາງ ມາກ ເຫັດໃສ່ ໃນປາບາງ ພໍໃຫ້ ລ້າງ ມາກໃຫ້ສະອາດ ພ້ອມທັງ ຕົ້ມ ເຫລະ ນີ້ ໃສ່ ນ້ຳທ່າ ສອງ ໂຕ ແດ້ວ ເມື່ອ ນີ້ ປາບາງ ນີ້ ແກງ ສຸກ ແລ້ວ ທີ່ ຕາ ຕົ້ມ ສາ ຕາມ ໃຫ້ສຸກ ເພື່ອ ໃສ່ ນໍ້າ ໃສ່ ເອົາ ລີບ ຂາ ແກງ ເພື່ອ ສອງ ບ່ອນ ມາກ ມີ ຫົວ ເຜັດ ບົວ ຕາ ຫາ ຫົວ ບອກ ປາ ເລີ່ມ ເພັດ ຂາງ ໄຟ ໃຫ້ ໃນ ສອງ ຕອນ ມາ ສຸກ ເປັນ ຕອນ ນໍ້າ ໝາກ ແຂງ ໃຫ້ ດູ ບ່ອນ ໃບ ເຜັດ ບົວ - ໃບ ຫົວ - ສີ - ມາກ ສີ ໃສ ເພັດ ໃນ ລ້າງ ມາກ ໃຫ້ ສະອາດ ເຫັນ ຫົວ

ວິທີຄົວ — ໃຫ້ ເອົາ ມາກ ປາບາງ ຖູ ເອົາ ໄວ້ ໃນ ເລາງ ຍັງ ຂັ້ນ ຂ້າງ ໃນ ທຸງ ເອົາ ນໍ້າ ໃສ່ ບ້ານ ປາ ເສົາ ເພື່ອ ຫົວ ເຜັດ ບົວ ທ່າ ສີ ໃຫ້ ໃສ່ ລົງ ໃນ ເພື່ອ ໂຮງ ສຸກ ຜ່າ ເຫັນ ຕົ້ນ ໃນ ນໍ້າ ສຸກ ແລ້ວ ມາກ ປາ ໃສ່ ໝາກ ແຂງ ໃຫ້ ລົງ ສຸກ ຜ່າ ຕາມ ຫ່ອມ ໃສ່ ບ່ອນ ສາ ຊີມ ເບິ່ງ ເຄັມ ຈາງ ເອົາ ເຜົ່າ ພໍ ດີ ພາກ ບົວ ອີ ຕາ ໂຮງ ປ່າ ລົງ ຕາ ໃສ່ ຖ້ວຍ ຍົກ ເພື່ອ ຕັ້ງ ໃຫ້ ຮັບ ທານ

ໝາຍເຫດ- ເລາງ ນໍ້າ ໃສ່ ນີ້ ກໍ ຄວນ ໃສ່ ຊີ້ນ ງົວ ເພາະ ພາ ໃຫ້ ດີ ທົ່ວ ຫາ ຕາ ນໍ້າ ມີ ໝັ້ນ ປາ ໃຫ້ ເອົາ ໝາກ ຄວາມ ເພັດ ຫຼື ຊີ້ນ ຄວາມ ເພັດ ໆ ກໍ ໄດ້ ສ່ວນ ເຂົາ ເປືອງ ໝູ ເຂົ້າ ໝັ້ນ ແລ້ວ ຂາງ ໃນ ມາ ໝູ ໃສ່ ກໍ ໄດ້ ຄື ກັນ

Keng No Mai Sai Yanang **Recipe 55B**

SOUP MADE WITH BAMBOO SHOOTS AND YANANG LEAVES

Ingredients

a bamboo shoot, boiled until it loses its (bitter) taste—if it is a large shoot, cut it into smaller parts of the right size for soup and wash

40 yanang leaves (see page 37), washed and then put into 2 metal jugfuls (2 pints) of water and rubbed until they are all broken up—the liquid is then strained through a fine white cloth (or through a strainer) and left in a pot

2 soupspoonfuls of sticky-rice flour (see page 22)

5 (small) shallots, pounded

2 pieces of the dried skin of a *pa leum* (a large catfish—page 24), grilled until 'puffy' and then cut into smaller pieces

20 small eggplants (see page 33)

chopped spring onion leaves

sweet basil leaves

salt and fish sauce

1 stalk of lemon grass, placed in glowing charcoal embers and ashes and then washed

Method

Put the juices obtained from the yanang leaves in a pot to boil. Add the pieces of bamboo shoot, the dried fish skin, the sticky-rice flour, the pounded shallots, the lemon grass and salt. Put the lid on the pot and leave it to come back to the boil. Then add the fish sauce and eggplants, cover again and leave to boil again. When it is done, taste and check the saltiness.

Garnish with the chopped spring onion leaves and the sweet basil leaves and put in a (large) bowl to serve.

Note

One should not put fresh meat in *Keng No Mai* (Bamboo soup), because it will then have an animal odour.

If dried fish skin is not available, dried water-buffalo skin or dried water-buffalo meat can be substituted.

As for the sticky-rice flour, one may use kneaded cooked sticky rice instead.

56 ໜໍ່ນອນນາງ

ເຄື່ອງປະສົມ – ໜໍ່ໄມ້ຕາມ້ຽງ ຄົ້ລອງ ລຶ້ງນໍ່ ເອົາມາປອກເປືອກອອກ
ຫຼຸດອັນແກ່ນ ເຫຼືອໄວ້ ເອົາອີໄວ້ແຕ່ແກ່ນ ອ່ອນລ່ຽມ
ຈຶ່ງເອົາເຂົ້າມາ ຊຸ່ມໃຫ້ເປັນເສັ້ນຄ່ຽງໆ ແຕ່ໄວ້
ໃນປ່ານາງຫາດສູ້ເປົ່າລ່າງນຳໃຫ້ສະອາດ ຄັ້ນເອົາ
ມາຕັ້ມເອົາຊຸ້ງນຳສະອາດ ເນື້ອໄກ່ເສືອໃຫຍ່ ຄົ້ນ
ໄປຈົນນຳອຸ່ນດີແລ້ວ ຈຶ່ງຕາງຕຸ້ມເສົ້າແລນໃຫ້ມູ
ເປື່ອຍແຕ່ໄວ້ ຫົວພັກບົ່ວສານຫົວ ສີໄຄເກືອຫົວ
ຜັກຊີ – ມາປ່າ – ໃບພິກບົວສີໃຫ້ຄ່ອງ

ວິທີເຮັດ – ໃຫ້ເອົານໍ້າມາປາມາໆ ຄູ່ອົກໃຈ່ທັ້ງຫາງໄພ ບໍ່ໃສ່
ຫົວພັກບົ່ວສີໄຄ ແລະ ຜັກຊີໃຈລາໄປ ເມື່ອແລ້ວໄປສູກ
ແລ້ວນຳໃຈ່ ອຸ້ມເຫຼົ້າ ເຕັມຈາງໆຕາມຂຸ່ຍ ປຸງລາຕາ
ໃຈ່ຈານພັກຫົວ ຊີໃຫຍ່ປາວ ເສີງຕາງໃຫ້ຊຶມທານ

ໝາຍເຫດ – ບໍ່ນອນນາງ ມີຕາຕຸ້ງກັນ ລູກແລ້ວ
ສົມມາກັບນາງຄານກາວ ແລະ ປີ້ງຈູມີ ເອງອອນນູນ
ກູ່ຈະເອົາໄປເຮັດຄູ່ກັບອາຫານ ລາວຈານແລ້ວ
ກໍ່ໃຊ້ປົນອາຫານ ເພື່ອຊູເນື້ອ ນາງອາຫານລາວເຮົາ
ມູໄດ້ວ່າ ໃນອາຫານສາມປະເທດນີ້ຮອມກັນ

No Non Nang **Recipe 56B**

BAMBOO SHOOTS COOKED IN YANANG JUICE

Ingredients

10 bamboo shoots of the kind called *no lai* (GIANTOCHLOA NIGROCILIATA) boiled until they lose their (bitter) taste—then cut off the hard parts and wash the trimmed shoots, after which use a needle to separate each into thin strands (as in recipe 53B)

60 yanang leaves (see page 37), washed and squeezed in a large metal jugful (1 pint) of water until the water is a good dark colour, after which it should be strained through a light cotton cloth or through a strainer).

3 (small) shallots

1 stalk of lemon grass

salt and fish sauce

finely chopped spring onion leaves

Method

Put the yanang juice in a pot on the fire. Add the bamboo shoots, the shallots, the lemon grass and salt. Leave to boil slowly until cooked; then add some fish sauce, taste and check the saltiness.

Dish up on a platter. Garnish with the finely chopped spring onion leaves and serve.

Note

No Non Nang is served with *Jaew Som Nam Mak Nao* (see the next recipe) and *Sin Ngon Moo* (grilled neck of pig). It is typical of Lao cookery to serve these three things together.

57 ໝົກໄຂ່ປາ (ນິຍົມທຸກບ່ອນ)

ເຄື່ອງປະສົມ — ໃຫ້ເອົາໄຂ່ປາໃຫຍ່ໆ ຄູ່ໜຶ່ງ ແລ້ວຕີ ມາຕີໃສ່ ນ້ຳປາແດກ ໃສ່ໄຂ່ໄກ່ ຫຼືເປັດ ຫຼືໜ່ານ (ຈະເປັນໄຂ່ປາ ອັນໃດກໍໄດ້), ຊີ້ນປາໃຫຍ່ ຕຳໃຫ້ແຫຼກ ມາປົນ ເຂົ້າສານ ມື້ ຜັກໃສ່ແຫຼກ ຫົວຜັກ ຫົວສີໄຄ — ຫອມແດງ ພິກ ນ້ຳປາ ເກືອ ໜ້ອຍໜຶ່ງ ຂ່າ ສົ້ມ ປາ ... ເຂົ້າສານ ໃຫ້ແຫຼກ ເປັນ ເຄື່ອງຫອມ ຜັກ — ນ້ຳປາ — ໃບຜັກ ບົວ ໃບມັກ ...

ວິທີເຮັດ — ຈົ່ງເອົາເຄື່ອງທັງໝົດ ແລະປາ ມາປົນເຂົ້າກັນ ໃສ່ ... ໃຫ້ ... ເອົາ ... ນາທີ ປາຍອນ ... ເຂົ້າກັນດີແລ້ວ ຈຶ່ງເອົາໃສ່ປາ ທີ່ຕີໄວ້ ... ລົງ ໃບຜັກບົວ ... ແລ້ວ ... ແລະ ... ຈາກ ... ໃຫ້ ... ມາລົງໃນ ... ປະມານ ... ລະນັ້ນ ... ໄດ້ ... ປາ ... ໃຫ້ ...

Jaew Som Mak Nao **Recipe 57B**

LIME SAUCE

Ingredients

5 fresh chilli peppers—place them in the hot embers and ashes of charcoal, then peel off the skin and wash them
5 (small) shallots
2 (small) heads of garlic, to be treated like the chilli peppers above
minced pork, a quantity the size of a hen's egg (2 tbsp)
salt and fish sauce
3 limes
2 coriander plants, chopped (without the roots)

Method

Make the minced pork into a ball.

Put a small pot on the fire with the meat and some water in it, just enough to cover the meat. Add fish sauce and leave to boil. When the meat is cooked, remove it and pound it finely. Then pound the cooked chilli peppers. When they are finely pounded, add the prepared shallots and garlic and pound all together. Add the pounded pork mixture to the broth. Taste and check the saltiness. If it is not salty enough, add some fish sauce. Squeeze the limes into it. If the mixture starts to become too thick, add the juice of the yanang leaves (from the dish described in recipe 56B). Put it in a small bowl, garnish it with the chopped coriander and serve it with *No Non Nang* (recipe 56B).

Note

Some people like to put into this *Jaew Som*, which is cooked to serve with *No Non Nang*, crisp-fried pork skin instead of the meat itself. This is acceptable, but the taste is spoiled; it then tastes more like a *Jaew Mak Kawk* (a sauce made with *mak kawk*—see page 30—treated like the chilli peppers in the recipe above).

58 [illegible] ປາແດກ

[illegible] — ປາແດກ [illegible]

[illegible]

[illegible] — [illegible]

[illegible]

Phan Kieo Padek **Recipe 58**

PADEK SAUCE FOR RICE VERMICELLI

Ingredients

1 beaker (½ pint) of *padek*, already boiled and strained
minced pork, a quantity the size of a duck's egg
1 piece of fish, four fingers wide—this and the minced pork should be cooked together in the *padek*—when they are cooked, take them off the fire, remove the bones from the fish and pound it finely together with the pork (reserving the *padek*)
4 stalks of lemon grass, finely chopped
10 (small) shallots, chopped } both these ingredients to be
10 (small) heads of garlic, chopped } fried until golden-brown
4 rice cakes (see page 22), finely pounded with the fried chopped shallots and garlic
2 pieces of crisp-fried pork skin
1 *na* (½ kilo) of rice vermicelli, cut into pieces 3 cm long
2 round eggplants, sliced
10 lettuce leaves
3 spring onions, chopped
2 sprigs of coriander, chopped
young *phak kadone* leaves (these are forest leaves, see page 36), washed
1 small jugful (4 tbsp) pork fat

Method

Put the pork fat in a wok and set it on a low fire. Add the chopped lemon grass, but do not allow it to turn golden. (Before this happens) take it out; and pour the fat out of the wok and reserve it. Now put the *padek* in the wok, over a reduced heat. Add the pounded pork and fish, and mix them thoroughly. Add also the fried lemon grass and the prepared mixture of pounded rice cakes, shallots and garlic, and stir thoroughly. The mixture should be neither too liquid nor too thick. Next, add the chopped spring onions. Taste, and check the saltiness. Transfer the contents of the wok to a platter and garnish with chopped coriander.

Arrange the *kadone* leaves and the lettuce leaves around the edge of another platter, put the rice vermicelli in the middle, and dispose the pieces of crisp-fried pork skin and the slices of eggplant around the rice vermicelli. Serve all this accompanied by the other platter containing the *kieo padek* (i.e. the prepared *padek* mixture).

Editors' Note. The way to eat this dish is to use the *kadone* and lettuce leaves to make little packages of the rice vermicelli with its accompaniments. The word *phan* in the recipe title indicates this manner of eating. The word *kieo* indicates slow simmering.

59 ຫ່ອມຕົ້ນບານ

ເຄື່ອງປະສົມ — ຕົ້ນເຂ ເຫຼົ້າ ຕົ້ນ ເອົາ ມາ [illegible] ຂົມ ເພາະ ເລືອດ ລາງ
ມກ ເທື່ອ ລະ ວັນ ແມ່ກ ພໍ່ ປ່ວນ ແລະ ກາງແລ້ວ ຢູ່ ຕົກ ຫົວ
ແມ່ກ ຫຼາຍ ເທົ່າ ຫົວ ເພາະ ກາງ ອອກ ທ່າ ສາມ ແປ່ນ
ແມ່ກ ທາ ອອກ [illegible] ເອົາ ໃນ ສາມ ຄັ້ງ ແມ່ກ ພໍ່ ລາງ
ແມ່ [illegible] ຮອກ ຖືກ ຈີ່ ຕົ້ນ ລາງ ມກ ໃຫ້ ລະ ວັນ ຂອງ [illegible]
ໃຫ້ ແລ້ວ ທາ ຫົວ ຕົ້ນ ເພາະ ກາງ [illegible] ແຕ່ ແປ່ນ
ອອກ ແລ້ວ ເຫຼົ້າ [illegible] ແລ້ວ ກາ [illegible] - ເຄື່ອ - ມກ ປາ
ແມ່ກ ເປີ ປ່ອນ ແມ່ກ ທາ ອອກ ຖື ແລ້ວ ທ່າວ ຕອງ [illegible]
ແລ້ວ ເຫຼົ້າ ໃນ [illegible] ຄັ້ງ ເອົາ ມກ ກາ ໃຫ້ ເລື່ອງ ແກ້ວ
ມກ ສ່ວນ ມກ ປຽງ ເຫຼົ້າ [illegible] ທັກ ລາງ ເຖິງ

ວິທີເຮັດ — ໃຫ້ເອົາ ມກ ກະທຳ ປຽງ ມັນ ໃຫ້ ແມ່ກ ຂື້ນ
ຄາງ ໄຟ ເອົາ ຕົ້ນ ບານ ເພາະ ລ່າງ ເຄື່ອ. ແມ່ກ ທາ ອອກ ເຄື່ອງ
ແມ່ກ ພໍ່ ທີ່ ຂຽ ເຄື່ອ [illegible] ທ່າວ ຄັ້ງ ໃປ ຈົບ [illegible] ເອົາ
ມກ ປາ [illegible] ຕອງ ແມ່ກ ພໍ່ ເພາະ ທາງ ເພາະ ແລ້ວ ທ່ອ ລື້ນ
ເຄື່ອ ສີ່ ຮ່ວນ ໃປ ຈົບ ຕົ້ນ ບານ ເປື້ອນ [illegible] ແລ້ວ ຈີ່ [illegible]
ກະທຳ ມກ ກາ [illegible] ໃປ ແມ່ ແຕກ ສາບ ຖືກ ເຫຼົ້າ ແອນ
ຈາກ ຕາມ [illegible] ເປັນ ລາງ ມາ ກາ ຕົ້ນ ບານ [illegible] ທາງ ລົບ
ຖືກ ແລ້ວ ລູກ ອອກ [illegible] ເປັນ ຕອນ [illegible]
ຈີ່ ຕົ້ນ [illegible] ເອົາ ທ່ອ ທາ ອອກ ເທົ່າ ອ່ອນ ແລ້ວ ເທ
ມກ ເຄື່ອ ຂອງ [illegible] ຕົ້ນ ບານ ແມ່ ແມ່ກ ທາ ອອກ
ຖືກ ເຫຼົ້າ ມກ [illegible] ໃຫ້ [illegible] ທາງ [illegible] ລ່ອງ
ສົມ [illegible] ມກ ຈົບ ./.

60- ແມ່ນບານປີ

ເຄື່ອງປະສົມ — ບານ ປີ ປື້ນ ເຫຼົ້າ ຕ່ອນ ເອົາ ມາ [illegible] ຕ່ອນ ເປື່ອຍ
[illegible] ທາງ ມາ ໃຫ້ ຄຸ ມາ ແມ່ກ ໃຫ້ ແມ່ກ ພໍ່ ຫົວ ປ່ອນ ມກ ໃຫ້
ສຸກ ແລະ ກາງ ໃຫ້ [illegible] ຫົວ ແມ່ກ ຫຼາຍ ມກ ສກ ແລ້ວ
ເພາະ ກາງ ອອກ ສາມ ທາງ ຂາງ ສອງ ເທົ່າ ປີ ຄ່ຳ ໃຫ້ ສຸກ
ແມ່ກ ໃຫ້ ບານ ວາ ທ່ອ ດື່ມ [illegible] ແກ້ວ ຕາ ລະ [illegible]
ເຫຼົ້າ ທອງ ມກ [illegible] ງາ ຂື້ນ ສຸກ ຫາ ລະ [illegible] ເທື່ອ
ມກ [illegible] ມກ ຕາມ ບານ ເຫຼົ້າ [illegible]

ສະຫຼຸບສັນຍາ ຕົ້ນ - ເຫຼົ້າ ເອົາ ຄ່ຳ ໃບ ລາງ ມກ
ແມ່ກ ມກ ຂື້ນ " ຕົ້ນ ອອກ " "
" ອ້ວນ ສາ ເຫຼົ້າ ກຳ ມື - ເຫຼົ້າ ເອົາ ແຕ່ ໃບ ແລະ ສ່ວນ ອອນ
ລາງ ມກ

Om Teen Moo **Recipe 59**

PIG'S TROTTER BOILED (IN COCONUT MILK)

Ingredients
1 pig's trotter
15 (small) shallots, peeled
5 (small) heads of garlic, the cloves separated and peeled
3 slices of galingale
3 sprigs of coriander, the leaves only
4 straight-bulbed spring onions—cut off the roots, wash the spring onions and tie them into a loose knot
1 small rice-bowl (approximately a handful) of shelled peanuts
salt, fish sauce and ground black pepper
2 sprigs of coriander, chopped
half a mature coconut, the meat grated to produce two extractions of coconut milk, the first to be half a glass beakerful (¼ pint), the second to fill a large soup bowl (1¼ to 1½ pints)

Method
Put the second extraction of coconut milk in a pot on the fire. Add the pig's trotter, the galingale, salt, coriander leaves and the knotted spring onions. Cover and leave to come to the boil. Then add fish sauce, the shallots, the garlic and the peanuts. Leave the pot on the fire until the trotter is well cooked, and the liquid is reduced.

Next, add the first extraction of coconut milk. When the cream has separated, taste and check the saltiness, and take the pot off the fire. Pick out the trotter, remove the bones and cut the meat into nice large pieces. Place them in the middle of a platter. Strain out the other cooked ingredients from the pot and place them round the edge of the plate, then pour the strained liquid over the pieces of trotter, just enough to cover them. Garnish with ground black pepper and the two chopped sprigs of coriander. Serve with *Jaew Som* or *Nam Jeem* (page 48).

Phan Moo Pin **Recipe 60**

ROAST PORK WITH RICE VERMICELLI AND VEGETABLES

Ingredients
1 piece of spit-roasted pork, cut into small pieces
10 (small) shallots } these ingredients to be seared in a charcoal
3 (small) heads of garlic } fire, peeled and pounded finely together
1 soupspoonful of roast peanuts, shelled and ground
1 small jugful (¾ pint) of pork broth
2 lettuces, washed
10 watercress plants, with the roots cut off
1 bunch of mint—only the leaves and young buds to be used

" ສະ■ຫ່າວ ຊູ່ທັນ - ເຖິງເຂົ້າແຕ່ສອນອອນ ລ່າງນໍ້າ
" ຊີ້ທ່ອງເຂົ້າແຕ່ໃບໜີ້ທໍາມືອ - ລ່າງນໍ້າ
" ຫົວລາງເລີ່ຍເທົ່າຕາມີ້ເຖິງຕອນ ນາງສອງຊາວ - ລ່າງນໍ້າ
" ທອນເຖິງເຂົ້າແຕ່ສ່ວນອອນສູງຕາມ - ລ່າງນໍ້າ
ໝາກດີເພື່ອໜີ້ນຫຼຸ້ງສັງເຂດ - ລ່າງນໍ້າ
ກ່ຽວອ່ອນໜີ້ນ້ອງປອດເປີ້ນ່າເຜົາສາກຕຸ້ງກອນນາ ລ່າງນໍ້າ
ໝາກກະເຊີງເກືອ■ໃຫຍ່ ສັກສາມ່ຽງກະ ກໍານມອງກາ
ໝາກແແກສ່ອນຊູ່ໜີ້ນຫຼຸ້ງ ປູ່ເປັນຕາອອນມີລ່າງນໍ້າ
ໝາກກາທ່ວງດັນຂົວລອນເກືອ ເດິ່ງເພື່ອນນໍ້າ
ເຂົາປົ່ນໜີ້ນໝາກ ຊູ່ເປັນຕາອອນນາວ ສ່ວນຂຸດ
ໝາກລາວພຸ່ງຫລານ ຊື່ມ່ຽງປີ້ຂວນຊື່
ນໍ້າປາຍ່າງດີ ນໍ້າຕາມຊຽງ ໝາກບອງນໍ້າຊູ
ພາສາທອນໜີ້ນຕາມເຕີກ ແຕ່ໃບ ຟັກໂຫ້ຫນັກ

ວັດທີ່ຕ່ອງ— ພາສາທອນຊູ່ສົງຫາ ພັກມີປົ່ນ
ໃຫ້ເຂົາເກືອງທໍາມາກອນຕາມ ນາກີ້ຕາມຊູ່
ຊີ້ຖືງໃຫຍ່ ຄົນໃຫຍ່ເຂົ້າກັນ ເກີ້ມ ນໍ້າປາໃຊ້ກະ
ສົ່ງແທນລາວ ໃຫ້ແກ່ສາກນໃອ້ ພາສາທອນພັກ
ຊື່ເກົ່າໃຫ້ທ່ອງ ຕາໄຊ້ຖືງ ມີພາສາທອນຊູ່ເພື່ອ
ມີປົ່ນ

ໂຊງທັ້ງພາສາໃອ້ ໃຫ້ເຂົາຈານໃຫຍ່ມາ ກອງສູງເສົາ ໃຫ້ພາສາສະອາດງາມ ອ່ອນລອມຈວນ ແລ້ວເຂົ້າປົ່ນລາງ ລັງທ້າງທາງຊູ່ໃຫ້ງາມ ຕີ້ມຈວນໜີ້ນ ຈ້າງແລ້ວນະ ດາພາສາດູ ເປັນປ່າງ ງູນການຕາມຈວນ ແລ້ວ ເດີ່ນຕຸ້ງແລະ ຊອງລາງທາງໃຫ້ເປັນຢ່າງ ພໍ່ໃຫ້ສູງ ງາມເກົ່າຊູ່ທານ ສ່ວນນາທີ່ຖຸ້ງໃຊ້ມີກໍໃຫ້ແລ້ວ ພາສາທອນໂຊງທ້າວ ເພື່ອຖົງເຕີມວ່າສູງງາມຊູ່ຖ່ອນ ຕໍ່ລອງ ກໍໃຫ້ນັກເພື່ອຕາໃຫ້ຊູ່ທານ ພອ້ມກັນ ທັ້ງ ຊີ້ຈານ

ນາງສາດາ— ພາສາທານປີນີ້ ຊື່ນາມີທໍາໄດ້ເພາະເພື່ອ ໝື້ນອ່ອນ ແລະຊີ້ທໍາທານດີຕໍ່ລາວນາໃຫຍ່ ຊູ່ບໍ່ມີປີ້ຕໍ່ສາກສາຊູ່ທານ ແລ້ວພໍ້ນ ທ້ອງນາສວນຊື່ມາລ້ຽງເຂົ້າ ແຕ່ຕ້ອງ ໃຫ້ໃນກແລະ ພໍ່ທໍາຊື່ໄດ້ສືບການ

10 stalks of *phak sa-ao* (page 37)—the leaves and young buds only
1 bunch of sweet basil leaves, washed
5 spring onions, cut into pieces 2 cm long and washed
10 coriander plants—take only the young parts and wash them
1 star-fruit (*mak feuang*, page 30), chopped and washed
1 young banana of the kind called *kuay tanee* (page 31), peeled, divided into two lengthways, chopped into thin pieces and washed
2 large tomatoes, the cores removed, sliced
1 cucumber, sliced thinly and washed
1 glass beakerful (½ pint) of roasted peanuts
1 *na* (½ kilo) of rice vermicelli, cut into pieces 3 cm long
10 small fresh chilli peppers, cores removed
fish sauce
1 soupspoonful white sugar
1 sprig of coriander, the leaves only, finely chopped
2 sprigs of coriander, leaves and stems, chopped
ground black pepper

Method

Mix the pounded ingredients and the broth in a big bowl. Add fish sauce and check the taste—it must taste salty. Add the chopped coriander leaves and mix thoroughly. Then put the mixture into small bowls and garnish each with ground black pepper and chopped coriander

Place the lettuce leaves on a large platter and put the rice vermicelli in the middle. You should arrange two platters thus. On another (third) platter arrange the various vegetables, with the leaves on the outside and the chopped vegetables in the middle, to create a pleasing effect. Place the sliced pork on another (fourth) platter and garnish it with chopped coriander. When all four platters are beautifully arranged, serve them.

Note

Phan Moo Pin is not as good as (the same dish made with) *moo noi* (piglet), because a piglet's skin is much softer and its aroma much more pleasing.

If it is impossible to get either *moo pin* or *moo noi*, then pork belly, which is three-layered, can be substituted. In this case, toast the pork, allowing it to cook slowly. It should be puffy and crunchy.

Editors' Note. The list of ingredients is confusing here. What Phia Sing refers to as the 'vegetables' in his instructions run from the lettuces to the peanuts, inclusive. The use of the fresh chilli peppers is not stated. It would be usual to pound them with the shallots and garlic listed earlier.

໖໔.- ຈຸ່ມສົ້ມຜັກກາດ

ເຄື່ອງປະສົມ— ປາຄາວເນື້ອດີສົດມາ ເຖາະເກັດ ເຈາະຂີ້ອອກ
ລ້າງແນ່ໃຫ້ສະອາດ ຜັກບົ່ວລາງແລ້ວໃສ່ຊອງ ຕົ້ນໜໍ່ ໝາກຫົວ
ປາຫາ ເກືອ ນ້ຳປາ ໃສ່ ອີກ ຜັກກາດ ເກືອ ກ່ຽວ ກະແຍມ
ຜັກບົ່ວລາງແລ້ວ ສ່ວນຕົ້ນ ຢູ່ໃຫ້ສະອາດ ຢູ່ໝາກຂ້າງ ຢູ່ໃຫ້
ແຫ່ງ ຜັກຫຼາຍ ຜັກວຽນ ຢູ່ໃຫ້ແລ່ງ ສ່ຽງຫົວ ຜັກຫອມ
ຢູ່ສ່ວນສ່ວນ ແນວກາລັງຂອງເນື້ອ ນ້ຳ ຢູ່ໃຫ້ແລ້ວ
ໃຫ້ຜັກກາດ ກ້ານຂາວ ຊື່ ໃບ ລ້າງແນ່ໃຫ້ສະອາດ ເອົາປະ
ເນື້ອປາ ຫຼາຍ ສາມຈອກ ແນວກາລີວ ແລ້ວສຽງ ແນ່ຢູ່
ຢູ່ສອງ ນາວແນວ ດີ ຈອກ ລ້າງແນ່ໃຫ້ສະອາດ. ນ້ຳຫອມ ໃບ
ເນື້ອ ກູ້ ນ້ຳປາ

ວິທີຄື— ໃຫ້ເອົາປາ ທີ່ ລ້ຽງ ໄວ້ນັ້ນ ປີ້ງ ໃຫ້ສຸກ ແລ້ວເອົາ
ອອກມາ ໃສ່ໄວ້ ໃສ່ຈານ ສ່ວນສົ້ມຜັກ ກໍໃຫ້ເອົາເຄື່ອງ
ຫອມທີ່ ຢູ່ໄວ້ນັ້ນ ປະສົມເຂົ້າກັບ ລົມ ຕຳ ຫົວ ຢູ່ໃສ່ຈານ
ຜັກ ຫອມ ໄວ້ ໃຫ້ ເອົາໃບຜັກກາດ ທີ່ ລ້າງສະອາດ
ແລ້ວ ລຽນ ຈັດ ແຕ່ງ ຈານ ເອົາປົ່ນ ໃຫ້ ໃສ່ ກາງ ເອົາ
ໝາກ ເຂືອ ຢູ່ ວາງ ອ້ອມ ເຂົ້າປົ່ນ ຢູ່ໃນ ຈານ ນ້ຳ ຫອມ ຢູ່
ໃຫ້ ເອົາ ນ້ຳປາ ໃສ່ ຈຸ່ມ ເນື້ອ ເຄີ່ງ ຈອກ ແລ້ວ ຕັ້ງ ໃສ່ ເທິງ
ໃຫ້ ເປັນ ເນື້ອ ແລ້ວ ກໍ ຈຸ່ມ ປຣຸງ ຜັກ ຫອມ ໄວ້ ແລ້ວ ນ້ຳ ພິ
ຕັ້ງ ໃຫ້ ຮູ້ ອາຫານ ແຊບ ສົມ ກັບ ທີ່ ສຸດ

ໝາຍເຫດ— ປາຢູ່ຈະເອົາມາ ເຮັດ ຈຸ່ມສົ້ມຜັກນີ້
ບໍ່ ໄດ້ ແນ່ ລ້າງ ແຕ່ ປີ່ ສະ ອາດ ກໍ ແຊບ ໃຫ້ ດີ ກວ່າ ແຕ່ ກິນ
ຮູ້ ເລາະ ເນື້ອ ແຫຼວ ກັບ ປາ ຄາວ ດຽວ ສະ ນັ້ນ ຈຸ່ມສົ້ມຜັກ
ມີ ຈຳ ເອົາ ປາ ແກງ ເປັນ ຫຼັກ ຖ້າ ບໍ່ ມີ ຈະ ເອົາ ປາ ອື່ນ
ໃດ ກໍ ໄດ້ ຕາມ ./.

Jum Som Phak Kad **Recipe 61**

PICKLED GREENS, LAO STYLE

Ingredients

1 *pa keng* (a barb, see page 24), washed and gutted
2 straight-bulbed spring onions—crush the heads and then stuff them into the fish, which should also be salted and then placed in a bamboo holder (see page 18), ready for grilling
1 medium-size bowl (¾ pint) of *som phak kad* (pickled 'greens' of the cabbage family—see page 35)
3 (more) straight-bulbed spring onions, finely chopped
1 piece of ginger, finely chopped
2 (small) heads of garlic—place them in the hot embers of a charcoal fire, but do not let them cook as much as is usual in other recipes—then chop them finely
3 sprigs of coriander, finely chopped
1 fresh red chilli pepper, finely chopped
10 lettuces, washed
1 *na* (½ kilo) of rice vermicelli, cut into pieces of 3 cm
2 round eggplants, cut into slices 1 cm thick and washed
1 small bowl (½ pint) of beef stock
fish sauce

Method

Grill the fish in its bamboo holder and set it aside on a platter.

Mix together thoroughly the pickled greens and the finely chopped ingredients (except for the coriander). Put this mixture on a platter and garnish it with chopped coriander.

Arrange the washed lettuces around the sides of a third platter and put the rice vermicelli in the centre. Place the slices of eggplant around the rice vermicelli.

Add the fish sauce to the beef broth and taste it. It should be quite salty. Put it in a small bowl, garnish it with chopped coriander and serve it together with the other prepared platters.

Note

Any fish could be used for making this dish but all others taste very different from the *pa keng*. *Jum Som Phak* should, therefore, be made with *pa keng* if possible. Should *pa keng* not be available, other fish may be used.

໖໒- ໝົກໄຂ່

ເຄື່ອງປະສົມ— ໄຂ່ໄກ່ຫຼືໄຂ່ເປັດ ສາມໜ່ວຍ ຊີ້ນໝູເນື້ອອ່ອນເທົ່າ ຟອງໄຂ່ ຜັກໃບຫອມຕູ້ກ ເມັດພິກໄທປົ່ນ ຫົວກະທຽມ ເພາະ ກຸ້ງແຫ້ງກໍາໂຕສໍານານ ໃບເຜັກບົວໃບເນື້ອກັນ ໃບເຜົາ ຕອງຊຸ້ມຫຍໍ້ ເກືອ ນ້ຳປ່ອນ-ເສັ້ນ-ນ້ຳປາ ນ້ຳມັນ

ວິທີເຮັດ— ເອົາໄຂ່ຫຼາຍໜ່ວຍໃສ່ຖ້ວຍ ແລ້ວເຮັດໃຫ້ເປັນເນື້ອດຽວ ກັນ ແລ້ວຈຶ່ງເອົາເນື້ອຫມູຂີ້ມ້ຽງໃສ່ ນ້ຳມັນໜ້ອຍໜຶ່ງ ເພື່ອບໍ່ໃຫ້ເນື້ອຕິດໃສ່ກັນເປັນກ້ອນ ບໍ່ດັ່ງນັ້ນ ຈະເອົາອອກບໍ່ໄດ້ເລີຍ ຈຶ່ງຈັກເອົາຜັກຫອມທໍ່ກັນແລ້ວໃສ່ ລົງໃສ່ພາຊະນະ ແລ້ວເອົາໄຂ່ທີ່ຕີແລ້ວນັ້ນເທລົງໃສ່ ໃນຖ້ວຍນັ້ນ ແລ້ວຈຶ່ງຈັກເອົາຕ່ອນໃບເຜົາວາງໃສ່ໃຫ້ ຈຶ່ງເອົາໄຂ່ທີ່ຈີບໃສ່ວາງເທິງຊີ້ນ ໂຮຍດ້ວຍເມັດ ແລ້ວປິດຝາໃຫ້ແໜ້ນ ກົດໃຫ້ຕິດໃສ່ກັນ ທີ່ເອົາເນື້ອເຂົ້າ ປົນກັນ-ເກືອ-ເສັ້ນ-ນ້ຳປາ-ເຄື່ອງປອງໃສ່ຮວມກັນ ລົງໃສ່ໃນ ແລະເນື້ອເຄັງຈາງພໍສົມຄວນ ຫໍ່ດ້ວຍໃບຕອງ ໃສ່ໝໍ້ແໜ້ນເນື້ອທັງໝົດ ເອົາໄປໜຶ້ງເຈື່ອນນັ້ນ ແລ້ວ ໃສ່ໄຂ່ບາງໆ ແລ້ວຮາໃຫ້ພາວອອກໆລູນຫາໃຫ້ສຸກ ໝົກໄຂ່ ຈຶ່ງເອົາໃສ່ຕອງຫໍ່ເອົາອອກມາລວງໆນາດໄປໃສ່ ໃສ່ຈານ ນີ້ລະໝົກໄຂ່ລູກໃຫ້ງາມເຄັກທາງໝາກເຜັດ ໃສ່ເສັ້ນໃຫ້ງາມ ./.

Phan Khai **Recipe 62**

EGG ROLLS

Ingredients
3 hen's or duck's eggs
1 piece of pork, the size of a hand, minced
6 (small) shallots, peeled and finely pounded
the chopped leaves of 1 spring onion
the chopped leaves of 2 sprigs of coriander
ground black pepper, salt and fish sauce
pork fat

Method
Break the eggs into a bowl, sprinkle salt on them and beat them.

Put a wok on the fire and add a little of the pork fat (just enough to grease it). When the wok is hot, pour into it some (about a fifth) of the beaten egg, making sure that it sets in a circular shape. Once it is cooked, take it out and place it on top of a piece of banana leaf which has been torn to the same size, and place a similar piece of banana leaf on top of the cooked egg. (Put a little more pork fat in the wok.) Make another round of cooked egg and put it on top of the first one (i.e. above the second round of banana leaf). Repeat until all the egg mixture has been cooked (and all the rounds of cooked egg are separated by banana leaf).

Mix together the minced pork, the pounded shallots, ground black pepper, salt, fish sauce and chopped spring onion leaves. Taste and check the saltiness.

Take one round of fried egg with the banana leaf still under it, and spread out thinly some of the minced pork mixture over it. Then make it into a roll. Do this with all the fried rounds of egg in turn. Then wrap them in pieces of banana leaf and steam them. When they are cooked (i.e. when the filling is cooked), dispose them on a platter, garnish them with chopped coriander and serve them.

63- ເຈົ້າປົ່ນຈີນ [illegible]

ເລື່ອງປະສົມ — ເຈົ້າປົ່ນຈີນຕົ້ນມາຕັ້ງ [illegible] ຈາກ
[illegible] ລ່າງ
[illegible]
ແມ່ແລະ [illegible] [illegible] ແລະ [illegible] ບໍ່ມີ [illegible]
[illegible] ໄດ້ [illegible]
[illegible]
ໄດ້ [illegible]
[illegible] ປາ — [illegible] — [illegible]
[illegible]

ວິທີລ້ອ — [illegible]
ສອງ [illegible]
[illegible]
[illegible]
[illegible] ແລະ [illegible]
[illegible]
[illegible] ເຈົ້າປົ່ນຈີນ [illegible]
[illegible]
[illegible] ສາວ [illegible]
[illegible]
[illegible]

[illegible] — [illegible] — [illegible]
[illegible]

[illegible] — [illegible] ວ່າ
ຂອງເຈົ້າປົ່ນຈີນ [illegible] ວ່າ ຄືເຈົ້າປົ່ນ
[illegible]
[illegible] ວ່າ ຄືເຈົ້າປົ່ນ

Khao Poon Chin Pad Haeng **Recipe 63**

FRIED CHINESE VERMICELLI

Ingredients

1 plateful of Chinese vermicelli, already boiled
1 piece of pork, including some fat, the size of four fingers, washed and sliced into pieces 3 by 1.5 cm, then rubbed with salt and ground black pepper
1 (small) head of garlic—separate the cloves and crush them
2 eggs—mix one and fry it into a thin layer, which you then roll up and slice thinly
5 straight-bulbed spring onions—cut off (and discard) the roots, cut off the green leaves, then crush and chop the bulbs
1 fresh red chilli pepper, sliced into long thin strips
salt, fish sauce and ground black pepper
chopped spring onion leaves
chopped coriander leaves
(2 soupspoonfuls of) pork fat
(2 ladlefuls of meat broth)

Method

Put the wok on the fire. Add the two soupspoonfuls of pork fat. When it is hot, put in the crushed spring onion bulbs and fry them until they smell good. Then add the sliced pork and fish sauce. Fry until the liquid is reduced, then add 2 ladlefuls of the meat broth. Taste. It must be quite salty. Then put in the prepared vermicelli and continue frying until this too gives off a good smell. Break in the second egg and keep stirring until it is cooked. Taste, and check the saltiness.

Now take the wok off the fire and add the chopped spring onion leaves and the strips of red chilli pepper. Transfer the contents of the wok to a platter and garnish with ground black pepper, the sliced fried egg and chopped coriander leaves. Serve with young cucumbers.

Note

Usually people call this dish *Khoua Khao Poon Chin*; but this is wrong, because there is no *kheuang tam* (pounded ingredients mixed together). If there were pounded ingredients then we could call it *Khoua Khao Poon* (*Chin*).

64- ແຈ່ວຫອຍ

ເຄື່ອງປະສົມ — ຫອຍຈາ ສົມ ແທ້ໆ ຊື່ນ້ຳອ່ງ ຕໍ່ຂວງ ໄຟ ໃຫ້ໝໍ້ໂປ່ວ
ໃຫ້ສຸກ ຫຼື ໃສ່ ໃນໄຟຄົ່ວ ແລ້ວມາຍ່ອຍໃສ່ ໃຫ້ລະອຽດ ເອົາ
ໝາກເຜັດ ຫົວຫອມ ບົ່ວ ທຽມ ຈີ່ ໝາກເຂືອ ແລະ
ຂີງ ໃຫ້ສຸກ ແລ້ວປອກເປືອກ ແລ້ວ ເອົາ ມາ ລາງ
ແລ້ວ ໃຫ້ ສະອາດ ຕຳ ໃຫ້ ລະອຽດ ປະສົມ
ຍ່ອຍ ໃສ່ ... ລະອຽດ ເກືອ- ນ້ຳປາ- ຜັກຫອມ
ບົ່ວ- ໝາກນາວ ... ເຂົ້າ ... ໃສ່ ... ເອົາ ຊີ່
ມາ ... ລະອຽດ ແລ້ວ ... ເປັນ ... ຕົ້ມ ...
ນ້ຳ ເຄື່ອງ ໃສ່

ວິທີ ເຮັດ — ໃຫ້ ເອົາ ຫອຍຈາ ... ປັ່ນ- ຜັກບົ່ວ- ຜັກຫອມ-
ລາວ ... ໃສ່ ... ລວມ ... ...
... ...
... ...

... ...
... ...
... ...
... ... %/-

Jaew Bong **Recipe 64**

BONG SAUCE*

Ingredients

10 dried red chilli peppers, to be grilled slowly until brittle (but do not let them burn and turn black) and then pounded finely

5 (small) shallots } these ingredients to be seared in a charcoal

5 (small) heads of garlic } fire, then washed and pounded finely

2 slices of galingale, finely pounded

salt and fish sauce

chopped coriander leaves

½ a strip (see page 25) of dried water-buffalo skin, grilled until done, then scraped smooth, cut into thin small slices and soaked in salt water

Method

Pound together, until they are thoroughly mixed, all the previously pounded ingredients. Sprinkle salt on them and add a little water. Mix, and add the pieces of water-buffalo skin. Taste and check the saltiness. If the mixture is too thick, add some boiled water, still warm.

Put the mixture on a platter and garnish it with chopped coriander leaves. Serve it with *Jee Sin Lod* (grilled dried beef—take a long, thin piece of dried beef, say, a foot long and as thick as a finger; cook it by putting it directly into a charcoal fire; then remove it, rub off the blackened parts, beat it to make it tender and cut it up as you wish).

* Editors' Note. *Bong* means pickled. This sauce is not, literally, a pickle; but it keeps for a very long time, as pickles do, and that seems to be why it has this name

65- ໄຂ່ຕົ້ມໜ້າສົ້ມ

ເຄື່ອງປະສົມ— ໄຂ່ໄກ່ດິບສິບໜ່ວຍ- ພິກທ່ອນລາງໆເລັກ ສາມເມັດ ຫົວຜັກ
ກາດໃບ ດອກ ຫຼາຍໂຫ້ ແຕງກວາໃຫ້ແກ່ໃບ້ ຜັກຫອມ
ຊຸບ (ຖ້າມີຜັກບົ່ວທັງໃບກໍ່ດີ) ໝາກເຂືອເທດ
ຂອງສົ້ມໆໜຶ່ງກະ
ບ່ວງນ້ອຍ- ນໍ້າຕານຊາຍໜຶ່ງບ່ວງ- ພິກ ນ້ອຍໜຶ່ງ- ເກືອ- ນໍ້າປາ
ວິທີເຮັດ— ໃຫ້ເອົາ ນໍ້າໃສ່ໝໍ້ ຂຶ້ນ ຕັ້ງໄຟຕົ້ມພໍເດືອດ
ພໍເດືອດ ຕອກໄຂ່ໃສ່ ຄ່ອຍໆ ຢ່າໃຫ້ແຕກ
ເມື່ອພໍສຸກ ຊ້ອນເອົາຂຶ້ນວາງໃສ່ຖ້ວຍ ຕອກມາ
ລຽນໃສ່ຈານ ແລ້ວ ເອົາເນື້ອໄຂ່ອອກມາ
ໃສ່ຈານ ໃຫ້ຜັກໃວ້ ຈຶ່ງເອົາ ນໍ້າສົ້ມ ທ່າ
ຫຼີ ບັ້ງ ຂຶ້ນ ລົງ ນໍ້າ ສົ້ມ ໃສ່ໝໍ້ ຕົ້ມ ເອົາ
ຫົວຜັກບົ່ວ ລົງ ຈື່ມ ໃສ່ ນໍ້າຫອມ ໝາກເຂືອເທດ
ສີໃສ. ໝາກເຜັດ ປົ່ນ ເຄັມ ແລ້ວ ໃສ່ ນໍ້າ ໃສ່ ຫອມ ດີ
ແລ້ວ ຈຶ່ງ ເອົາ ນໍ້າ ຕົ້ມ ຂຶ້ນ ຄາວ ນໍ້າປາ ໃສ່ ຄົນໄປ
ພໍແຫຼວ ເລີກ ນໍ້າ ຂຶ້ນ ເດືອດ ເຄັມ ຈາງ ພໍດີ ແລ້ວ ລົງ ພັກ
ຫອມ ຊຸບ ຄົນ ໃຫ້ ທົ່ວ ເມື່ອ ແລ້ວ ໃຫ້ ເອົາ ໄຂ່ ທີ່ ຕົ້ມ
ໄວ້ ລຽນ ໃສ່ ຈານ ຈຶ່ງ ເອົາ ນໍ້າ ສົ້ມ ທີ່ ແປງ ໄວ້ ມີ ຮອຍ
ໜ້າ ໄຂ່ ຕົ້ມ ແລ້ວ ໃສ່ ຜັກ ຫອມ ໂຮຍ ໜ້າ ພິກ ເສີ່ງ
ໜ້າ ໃຫ້ ສວຍ ງາມ %-

Khai Tom Na Som **Recipe 65**

'SOUR' POACHED EGGS

Ingredients
6 hen's eggs
(1 soupspoonful pork fat)
3 straight-bulbed spring onions—cut off the roots and the leaves, crush the bulbs and chop them finely
chopped coriander leaves
(if you had a large onion, it would be better)*
1 small can of tomato paste
1 (small) bowl of meat broth
salt, fish sauce and ground black pepper
(ground dried red chilli pepper)

Method
Boil some water in a pot. Crack one of the eggs, open it and slip the egg into the boiling water without letting the yolk break. When it is cooked use a perforated ladle to take it out. Put it on a plate. Repeat until all the eggs are cooked.

Heat 1 soupspoonful of pork fat in a wok. Fry the onion (it is not clear what kind of onion is meant here—see editors' note below) until it gives off a good aroma. Add the tomato paste, salt and ground red chilli pepper. Keep stirring the mixture until a good aroma is again given off, then add the meat broth and fish sauce. Stir until the mixture becomes fairly liquid. Taste, and check the saltiness.

Take the wok off the fire and add the chopped coriander leaves. Mix thoroughly.

Arrange the cooked eggs (which are in fact poached eggs, but there is no Lao word for poach) on a platter and cover them with the sauce. Garnish with ground black pepper and chopped coriander leaves, and serve.

* Editors' Note. This comment, one of the few which Phia Sing himself placed in brackets, seems to be in the wrong position, since it presumably relates to the spring onions and does not mean that a large onion would ideally be used in addition to the other ingredients. The ambiguous reference to 'onion' in the instructions supports this view.

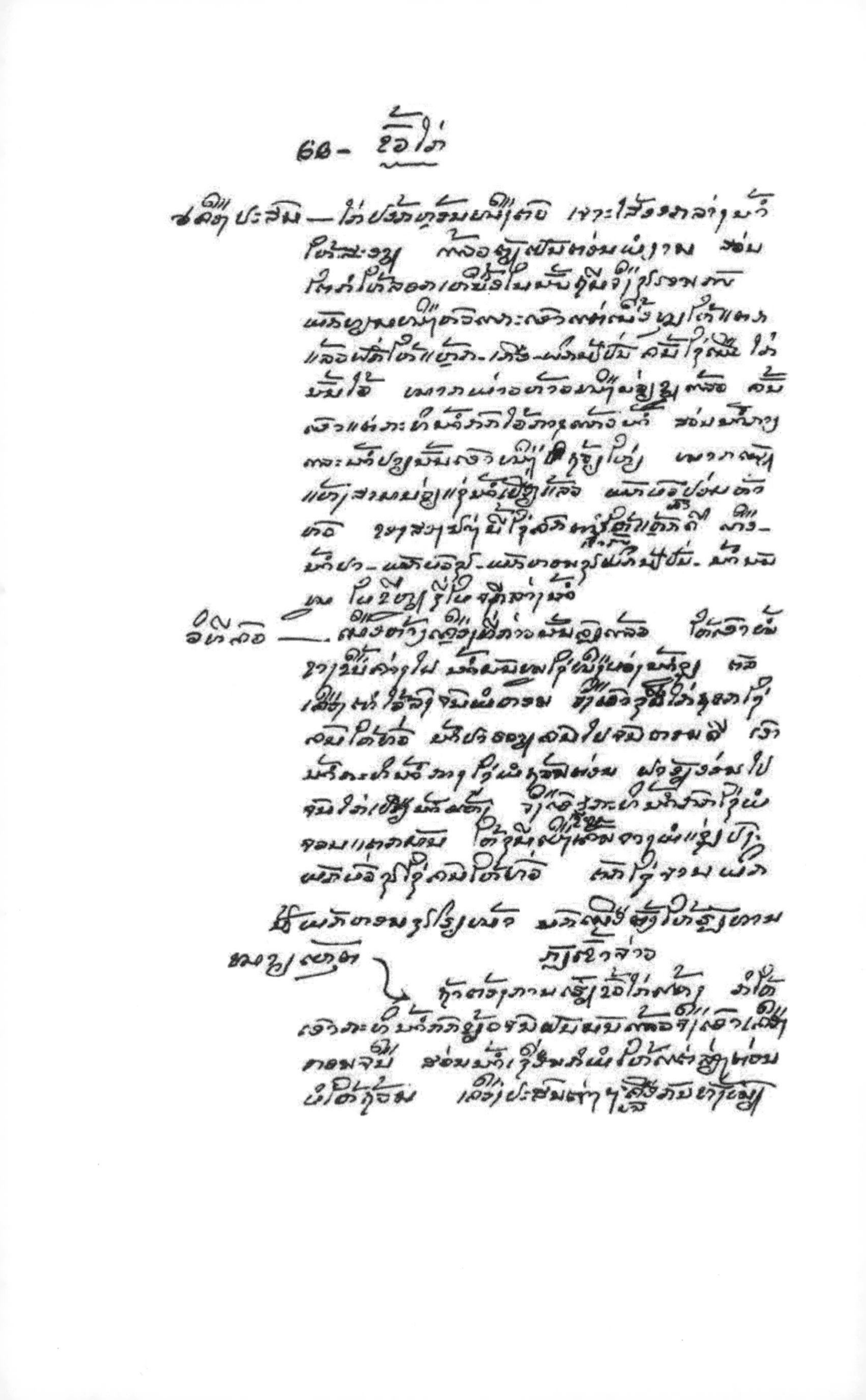

໖໘- ຂໍ້ໄກ່

ຂໍ້ຄິດປະສົມ — [illegible]

[illegible]

ອີກເລື່ອງ — [illegible]

[illegible]

[illegible]

[illegible]

Khoua Kai **Recipe 66**

FRIED CHICKEN

Ingredients

1 chicken, washed and gutted and cut into medium size pieces—wash also its gizzard and slice it finely

1 (small) head of garlic—separate and peel the cloves, crush them and chop them finely

salt } to be rubbed into the
ground black pepper } pieces of chicken

1 mature coconut—grate the meat and make three extractions of coconut milk —half a litre of the first and a large soupbowlful (i.e. just over half a litre) of the other two combined

3 dried red chilli peppers, soaked in water until soft } these two ingredients to be
5 (small) shallots } pounded finely together

salt and fish sauce
chopped spring onion leaves
chopped coriander leaves
ground black pepper
pork fat
4 Kaffir lime leaves, to be torn apart and washed

Method

After preparing all the ingredients, heat a soupspoonful of pork fat in a wok. Add the pounded ingredients and fry them until they give off a good aroma. Then put in the chicken pieces, mix and stir, add the fish sauce, and keep stirring until a good aroma is again given off. Now add the second and third extractions of coconut milk, but only enough to cover the chicken pieces. Put a lid over the wok and leave it until the chicken pieces are tender. At this point add the Kaffir lime leaves and the first extraction of coconut milk. When it has come to the boil, and the cream begins to separate, taste and check the saltiness. Take the wok off the fire, add the chopped spring onion leaves and stir thoroughly. Transfer the contents of the pot to a platter and garnish the dish with chopped coriander and ground black pepper. Serve it with plain rice.

Note

If you would like to make *Khoua Kai Haeng* (the drier version—do not put in the second and third extractions of coconut milk, to cover the chicken pieces, but simply) heat the first extraction of coconut milk until the cream separates and then add the pounded ingredients. This liquid should be enough to keep the chicken moist. Apart from this, the ingredients and method are the same.

67 - ເພື່ອຍິງອີ ຊາວສວນ

ເຄີຍປະສົມ — ໂທ້ລອດຄູ້ນ້ອງ ເພື່ອທ່ອນທໍ່ ຜ່ານເມືອງລ່າງ ພໍໄດ້ໂທລະສັບ
ພາວລົມເປັນຕ້ອນ ບໍ່ມີ ນາງສາວນາງຄຳ ກ່ອນ ເພື່ອຊາຍ ນາງ
ເພື່ອຊາຍ ຄົນລາວ ພໍກ່ອນບໍ່ໄດ້ ພໍກໍ ຫຼາຍຫຼາຍ ເລື່ອ
ໄດ້ໄກ ສອງ ບໍ່ຫຼາຍ ຈຶ່ງ ເປັນແພ່ນແລ້ວ ຮູ້ ກ່ອນ ເພື່ອ ຊາຍ ນາງ
ສອງຄູ່ ພໍສະເລີລາວ ເລີ່ ຮູ້ຫວັງ ຫຼາຍໄດ້ຫຼາຍໃນໃຈ ລ່າງ
ນ້ຳຫຼາຍ ຕານີ ອອດ ຕໍ່ເລົ່າ ໝູ່ ແມ່ ນຳ ພາກ ຫຼາຍ ເປັນ ລອນ
ຕ່ອນ ພາວກາ ແຕ່ ລ່ອນ ທໍາ ຕໍ່ ບໍ່ຫຼາຍ ບໍ່ເຄີ ເບື້ອງ ວາລາ ສ້າງ
ວີ້ ແລ້ວ ລົມ ລວງ ຂອງ ໂດຍ ທາງ ໃຈ ເພາະ ເພື່ອ ນາງ
ເຊື້ອເຄືອ ໃຫຍ່ ສູງ ສາວ ລາວ ນ້ອຍ ຫຼາຍ ຕ້ອງ ຄູ່ ລືມ ສາວ ໃຫ້ ເພາະ
ແກ່ນ ຖືມື ~~[illegible]~~ ລາງ ເພື່ອ ຊູ ໂລກ ນາງ ພາວ ເພື່ອ ຄູ່ ຊາຍ
ພໍກ ຊູ ນາງ ລື ສາວ ຕາມ ເພາະ ຫຼາຍ ແກ່ ຄູ່ ມື ຫຼາຍ ຫມື
ຈ່າງ ນ້ຳ ຫຼາຍ ຕ່ອນ ນາງ ລາວ ຄູ່ ຊາຍ ເຫຼົ່າ ສະບາຍ ຫຼາຍ ຄືນ
ສ່ວນ ນ້ຳ ແລ້ວ ສື ເປັນ ຕ່ວນ ເພື່ອ ສຳ ເມື່ອ

ທາງ ລາວ ຫຼາຍ ສາວ ເຫຼືອ ເບື້ອງ ນາກ [redacted] ຫຼາຍ ໃນ ອາລາ
ຈີ່ ຫຼາຍ ທາງ ຊູ ທີ່ ນາງ ເປັນ ຕ່ອນ ວີ່ ຄູ່ ນ — ເດີ —
ນ້ຳ ປາ — ພໍກ ນໍ້າ ປີ — ໃນ ພໍກ ຕາມ ທັງ ຫມື ເດີ ເອົາ
ແກ່ ໃນ ລູກ ນ້ອຍ ໃນ ພໍກ ນ້ອງ ສອງ ຫົນ ຫຼາຍ ນາງ ສາວ
ຄູ່ ຊາຍ ນ້ຳ ລົມ ເປັນ ບໍ່ ໄດ້ ຫຼາຍ ແລ້ວ ສອງ ບໍ່ ຫຼາຍ ເອົາ
ພາຍ ອ່ອນ ລ່າງ ນ້ຳ ປ່ອຍ ນາງ ສາວ ຄູ່ ຊາຍ ພໍກ ນ້ອງ ຕົວ

ອໍ່ ທີ່ ລືວ — ປ່ອນ ສາວ ຄູ່ ຕົວ ຫຼາຍ ໂທ ພາລາ - ມື ນ້ອຍ ຫຼາຍ ເມື່ອ ສາ ນ ຫົວ
ໂດຍ ລາວ ນ້ຳ ທາງ ຂື້ນ ທຸ່ງ ໃນ ນ້ຳ ນ ເພ ໃຫ້ ຮູ້
ເພື່ອ ຄູ່ ພໍກ ບໍ່ ຫຼາຍ ລື ນໍ້າ ຫອມ ລື ວີ່ ໃຫ້ ລົມ
ໃນ ນ້ຳ ປາ ຮອງ ລົມ ເປັນ ນ້ຳ ເພ ທໍ້ ລະ ຫອມ ສີ
ຕ້ອງ ຈີ່ ເຊົາ ກາ ຫຼາຍ ນໍ້າ ໃນ ເຫຼົ່າ ໂດຍ ນໍ້າ ຫຼາຍ ຫຼວງ
ເລີກ ນໍ້າ ນໍ້າ ຫົວ ພໍກ ສາ ຈີ່ ເສີຍ ພໍ່ ເມືອງ ຫຼວງ ນໍ້າ ໄດ້
ແກ່ ລົມ ຈາ ໃຈ ຮູ້ — ໃນ ພໍກ ເພື່ອ ພໍກ ຫອມ ເດີ
ເພື່ອ ເລີກ ເລົ່າ ນ ນໍ້າ ສາ ຂອງ ຊູ ນໍ້າ ເປົ້າ ເລີ່ມ ຈາງ
ນໍ້າ ແລ້ວ ພາລະ ມື ນ້ຳ ນໍ້າ ຫຼາຍ ຕາ ຕາ ລີ ລວນ
ພໍກ ນໍ້າ ພໍກ ຫອມ ເອົາ ໃຈ ຫົວ ນ້ຳ ເພື່ອ ທັງ
ເທົ່າ ຫຼາຍ ທານ ເຫຼົ່າ ສ່ຳ ລາງ ວັນ

Pad Sin Ngua Sao Souan **Recipe 67**

FRIED BEEF, COUNTRY STYLE

Ingredients

1 piece of beef the size of a hand, washed and sliced into small pieces of 3 by 1.5 cm, and with salt rubbed into them
black peppercorns, crushed
1 (small) head of garlic, the cloves separated and crushed
2 hen's eggs, beaten and cooked as a thin omelette and cut into pieces 1 by 2 cm
4 straight-bulbed spring onions—cut off the bulbs close to the leaves, wash them, trim off the roots, then beat the bulbs just enough to break them, and cut each into three parts
half a young cucumber, peeled, cut into four lengthways and thinly sliced
3 large ripe tomatoes—slice off the tops and discard them, then divide the tomatoes into halves, remove the seeds, wash the tomato halves and slice them into pieces 1 cm thick
3 stalks of celery—remove the old and withered stems, cut off the roots and wash the remainder, then cut them into sections 3 cm long
1 handful of jelly mushrooms (see page 44), washed and torn into pieces of medium size
3 carrots—scrape off the skin and chop off the tops, then cut each into half lengthways and dice them
salt, fish sauce and ground black pepper
5 sprigs of coriander—pick off only the leaves and young tender stems
2 spring onions, washed and cut into sections of 3 cm
pork fat (1 ladleful)
2 cooked bamboo shoots—cut off the tender parts only, wash them and cut them into pieces 3 cm long
3 (small) shallots, (peeled and) crushed
3 potatoes, peeled, sliced and fried
(broth)

Method

Heat 1 ladleful of fresh pork fat in a wok. Put in the crushed shallots and fry them until they give off a good aroma. Put in the slices of beef and add fish sauce. Keep stirring until the liquid is reduced and smells good. Then add the carrots, the bamboo shoots, the mushrooms and a little of the broth. When these are cooked, put in the remaining ingredients except for the fried potatoes, the sliced omelette, the spring onion leaves and the coriander leaves. When they are cooked and the liquid is enough to cover the vegetables (i.e. has reduced to the point where it just covers them), taste and check the saltiness.

Dish up on a platter and garnish with ground black pepper and with the fried potatoes, the pieces of omelette, the chopped spring onion leaves and the chopped coriander leaves. Serve when it is all still hot.

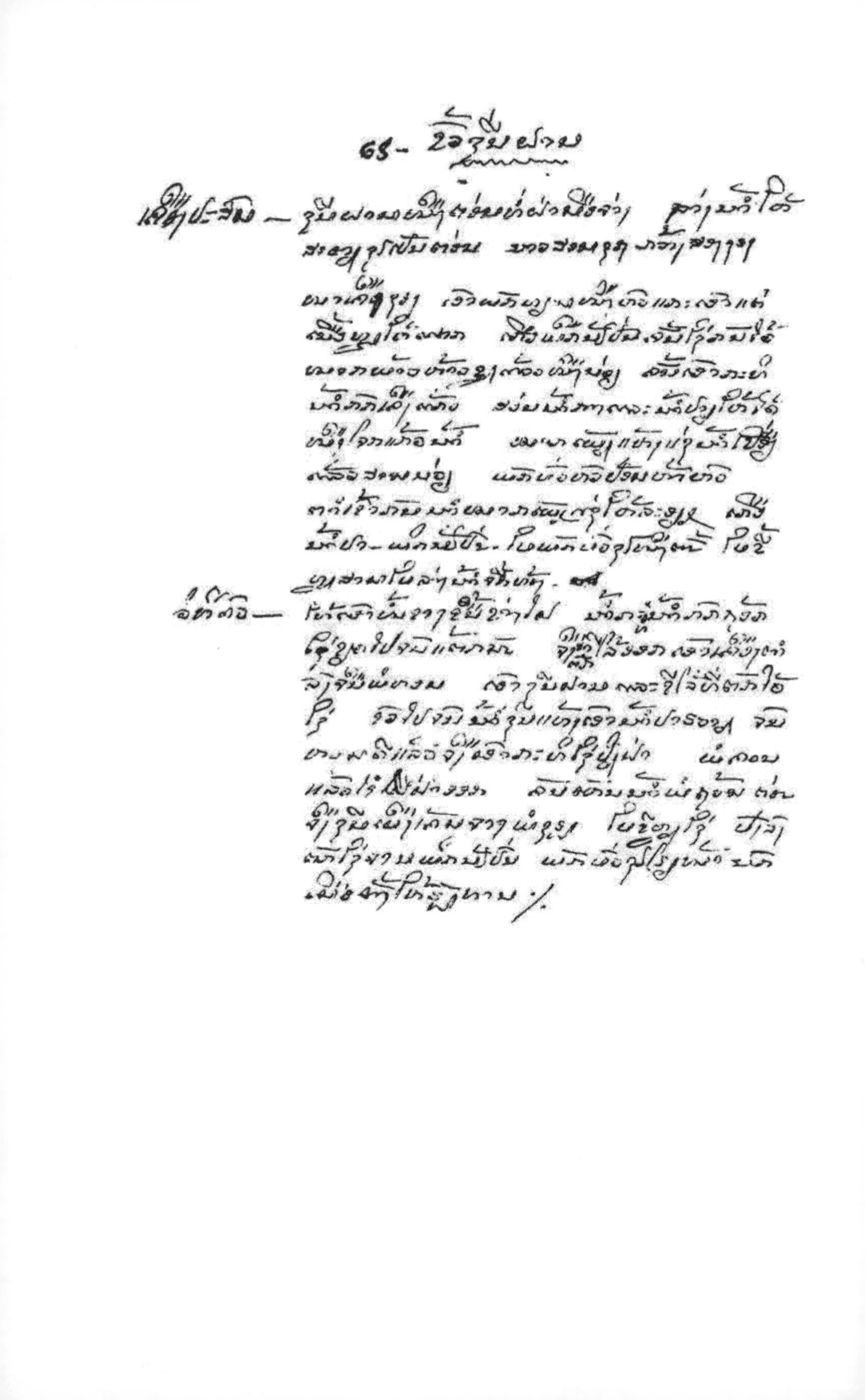

໖໕ - ຂ້ອງຈີ້ນຟານ

ເຄື່ອງປະສົມ — [illegible]

ວິທີເຮັດ — [illegible]

Khoua Sin Fahn **Recipe 68**

FRIED DEER MEAT

Ingredients

1 piece of deer meat (see page 27), the size of the palm of a hand, washed and sliced into pieces 3 by 2.5 cm
1 (small) head of garlic—remove the skin and crush the cloves
salt and ground black pepper
} these ingredients to be mixed together

1 fully ripe coconut—grate the meat and make half a glass beakerful ($\frac{1}{4}$ pint) of the first extraction of coconut milk, and one glass beakerful ($\frac{1}{2}$ pint) of the second and third extractions combined

3 dried red chilli peppers, soaked in water until soft
5 (small) shallots
} these two ingredients to be pounded together finely

leaves of 1 spring onion, chopped
3 Kaffir lime leaves, washed and torn in half

Method

Heat the first extraction of coconut milk in a wok until the cream separates. Spoon out the thick part (which has sunk to the bottom, and reserve it in a bowl for later use). Add the pounded ingredients to the remaining (thin part of the) coconut milk in the wok and leave them until they give off a good aroma. Then put in the pieces of deer meat and the thick liquid which was removed earlier. Continue to cook until the liquid is reduced; then add fish sauce. When a good aroma again arises add the second and third extractions of coconut milk and put a lid on the pot. Leave it for a little (about 5 minutes), then remove the lid. The liquid should be covering the meat. Taste, and check the saltiness. Add the Kaffir lime leaves.

Dish up on a platter, garnish with ground black pepper and the chopped spring onion, and serve.

໖໕- ແກງຈືດໄກ່

ເຄື່ອງປຣະສົມ — ໄກ່ປະຫັດ ຫຼາຍແລ້ວ ໜຶ່ງໂຕ ເອົາພ່າ ຖອດກະ
ໃສ້ ລ້າງເອົາ ຕີນ ປຼູ ແຕ້ມ ຈາມູ ຈາກ ປີກ ອອກ ລ້າງ ແລ້ວ
ໂຫ ສະອາດໄວ້ ຜັກຫອມ ສຽງເລີ້ງ ສວນ ຫັ່ນ ລ້າງ ແລ້ວ
ຊອຍເຂົ້າເຖົ້າ ໃບ ແລະ ຫົວ ຜັກບົ່ວ ສາມ ຕົ້ນ ລ້າງ
ແກ່ ເອົາ ຕັດ ຍາວໄວ້ ຜັກຫອມ ຕະໄຄ້ ໜຶ່ງໂຕ
ແລະ ວຸ້ນ ຂອງ ຫລາຍ ນ້ຳ ປູ ລອງ ນອວ ໂຫ ແກງ ໆ
ຜັກສຽງ ຕົ້ນປັ່ນ ແລະ ໜຶ່ງ ກໍ່ ພື້ນ ຜັກຫຼາຍ ແລະ
ຫຼາຍ ສ່ວນ ສອງ ໂຕ ເກືອ - ນ້ຳປາ - ຜັກປັ່ນ - ຜົງແກ
ບົວ ຈູ

ວິທີ ເຮັດ —— ໂຕ ເອົາ ນ້ຳ ສະອາດ ໃສ່ ໝໍ້ ຕາງ ໃສ່ ກະຊຽງ ຕາງ
ຂຶ້ນ ເຕົາໄຟ ເອົາໄກ່ - ຜັກ ຫົວ - ຜັກ ຫອມ ທີ່ ຊອຍ
ໄວ້ ແລະ ເຄື່ອງ ອື່ນໆ ຕົ້ມ ຈົນ ໄປ ຈົນ ໄກ່ ເປື່ອຍ
ດີ ແລ້ວ ຈຶ່ງ ປຸງ ລົງ ໃສ່ ອອກ ສ່ວນ ນ້ຳ ໄວ້
ຕາມ ເອົາ ກະດູກ ຕ່າງໆ ຖິ້ມ ແລ້ວ ຕຳ ຕົ້ມ ນ້ຳ
ແກງ ຖົ່ວ ໃສ່ ຜັກ ຂີ້ ຫອມ ຕໍ່ ໄປ ຕົວ ຜັກ ໃສ່ ປັ່ນ
ຫົວ ຜັກ ຫອມ ຈູ ສະຫຼຸບ ແລະ ໃຫ້ ສຸກ ດີ ໄປ ຈົນ ເຫັນ
ຜັກ ຫອມ ສຸກ ຈຶ່ງ ຕັກ ໃສ່ ຖ້ວຍ ໄວ້ ໃຫ້ ພົ້ນ ຜົງ ຣົ້ນ;
ໂຕ ຈູ ນີ້ ເປັນ ເຄື່ອງ ສົມ ແລ້ວ ປຸງ ລົງ ຕັກ ໃສ່ ຖ້ວຍ
ແລ້ວ ໃສ່ ຜັກ ຫອມ ໃຫ້ ງາມ ຍົກ ເອົາ ຕັ້ງ ໃຫ້ ຍົງ
ທານ ./.

Keng Jeeg Kai **Recipe 69**

SHREDDED CHICKEN SOUP

Ingredients

1 chicken, washed and gutted
3 straight-bulbed spring onions, washed and each tied into a loose knot
3 coriander plants, washed and tied together with a thin strip of bamboo
1 large onion—remove the outer skin and chop finely
1 handful of (small) peeled shallots
3 (small) heads of garlic—separate the cloves and peel them
salt, fish sauce and ground black pepper
chopped spring onion leaves

Method

Heat 2 soupbowlfuls ($1\frac{1}{2}$ pints) of water in a pot. Put in the chicken, the loosely knotted spring onions and salt. Cover and boil until the chicken is cooked and tender. Then take the pot off the fire, remove the cooked chicken and strain the broth to produce a clear soup. Put this back in the pot and bring it to the boil. Add the chopped onion, the peeled shallots and garlic and boil until the shallots are cooked. Shred the chicken breast and put it in the soup. Taste and check the saltiness. Remove the pot from the fire, transfer the soup to a serving bowl, garnish it with ground black pepper and the chopped spring onion leaves and serve.

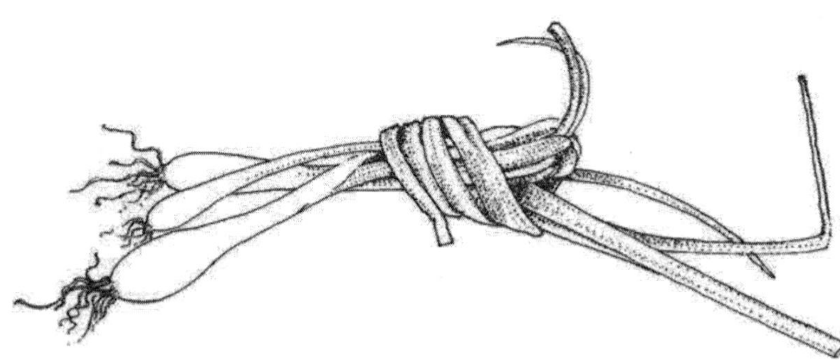

This drawing of spring onions knotted together shows the ordinary kind, not the straight-bulbed ones mentioned in the recipe above.

໒໐ - ຂົ້ວໄກ່ໃສ່ເຂົ້າປຸ້ນຈີນ

ເຄື່ອງປະສົມ — ໄກ່ປອກໜັງອອກເໝີ້ຍທ່ອນ ເອົາມາຈັກໃສ່ຂອງກ
ລ້າງນ້ຳໃຫ້ສະອາດ ຈຶ່ງຕັດເປັນຕ່ອນໃຫຍ່ພໍສົມ
ຄວນ ຄັ້ນແລ້ວເອົາໝາກເຜັດແລະຜັກບົ່ວແຫຼມໃຫ້ແຫຼກ
ກໍ່ ໝາກພ້າວ ຫົວໜຶ່ງ ເຄືອ ໝາກນາວ ຄັ້ນ
ເອົາ ແກງປະທີ ນ້ຳມັນພາງ ເກືອນ້ຳ, ສ່ວນນ້ຳພາງນ້ຳ
ປາຈຸເອງ ສອງຊ້ອນກິນ ຜັກບົ່ວໃບ ໃຫຍ່ ໝີ່ຫົວ
ປອກກ່ຽນ ນາມສາ ຊອກຄູ່ ຫົວ ຂອງ ໝາກເຜັດ
ແຫ້ງ ເປັນ ເກືອ ສາມ ບ່ວງ ຜັກບົ່ວ ຫົວ ປ່ອນ
ບ້ານ ຫົວ ຂອງ ສອງ ຢ່າງນີ້ ຕຳ ໃສ່ກັນ ໃຫ້ລະອຽດ
ໃຫ້ຂົ້ວ ສານ ໃສ່ ໃຈ ຫ່ອງ ຜັກ ບົ່ວ ຊອຍ ໜຶ່ງ ຫົວ ເຖິງ
ນ້ຳປາ ຜັກ ນ້ຳມັນ ນ້ຳສົ້ມ ເຂົ້າປຸ້ນຈີນ ໜຶ່ງ ກຳ ແລ່ນ
ວິທີທຳ — ໃຫ້ຂົ້ວ ຊາງ ນີ້ ຢ່າງ ໃສ່ ຜັກ ນ້ຳ ມັນ ໃສ່ ໝໍ້ ປ່ອງ ພໍ ຮ້ອນ
ເອົາ ເຄື່ອງ ປະສົມ ທັງໝົດ ໃສ່ ລົງ ໄປ ທັນ ທີ ເອົາ ໄກ່ ແລະ ຫົວ ຜັກ
ທີ່ ໃຫຍ່ ໃສ່ ນ້ຳ ປາ ຮ້ອນ ຂົ້ວ ໃຫ້ ຈົນ ນ້ຳ ຊື່ມ ເຂົ້າ ແລະ ຫອມ ນັບ ແລ້ວ
ຈຶ່ງ ເອົາ ປະທີ ນ້ຳ ພາງ ສອງ ຈອກ ນັ້ນ ໃສ່ ເມື່ອ ໄກ່ ສຸກ ແລະ ເປື່ອຍ
ພໍ ໃສ່ ໄດ້ ແລ້ວ ກໍ ໃຫ້ ເອົາ ປະທີ ນ້ຳ ພາງ ~~ເສັ້ນ~~ ທີ່ ເຫຼືອ ນັ້ນ
ແລະ ເຂົ້າປຸ້ນ ຈີນ ໃສ່ ເຫັນ ວ່າ ຄວນ ຈະ ແຫ້ງ ກິນ ແລ້ວ
ຈຶ່ງ ຍົກ ລົງ ເພື່ອ ເລີກ ຈາກ ຕາ ໄຟ ປຸງ ແຕ່ງ ຈານ ເລີດ
ປົນ ຜັກ ທີ່ ລຽບ ໃສ່ ໜ້າ ພໍ ເຫັນ ດີ ແລ້ວ ໃຫ້ ຮັບ ປະທານ

Khoua Kai Sai Khao Poon Chin **Recipe 70**

FRIED CHICKEN WITH CHINESE VERMICELLI

Ingredients

1 chicken, washed, gutted and cut into fairly large pieces, which are to be rubbed with salt and ground black pepper and crushed garlic
1 fully ripe coconut—grate the meat and make ½ glass beakerful (¼ pint) of the first extraction of coconut milk, and 1 glass beakerful (½ pint) each of the second and third extractions
1 large onion, peeled and chopped
3 dried red chilli peppers, soaked in water until soft } these two ingredients to be pounded finely together
5 (small) shallots }
3 Kaffir lime leaves, washed and torn in half
1 spring onion, chopped
salt, fish sauce and ground black pepper
1 spoonful pork fat
1 handful of Chinese vermicelli, soaked in water

Method

Heat 1 spoonful of pork fat in a wok. Fry the pounded ingredients in this until they give off a good aroma. Add the chicken, the onion, the Kaffir lime leaves and fish sauce, and continue frying until the liquid is reduced and again gives off a good aroma.

Now add the two glass beakers of the second and third extractions of coconut milk. When the chicken is cooked and tender, add the first extraction and the (drained) vermicelli. When the cream starts to separate, taste, and check the saltiness.

Dish up on a platter, garnish with the chopped spring onion and serve.

໑໔ - ເອາະປາແດກ

ເຄື່ອງປະສົມ — ປາແດກດີ ເອົາຕ່ອນງື່ມເນື້ອຍ່ອນ ມີໄຄ ເນົ່າ ຫົວ
ຫອມໃຫ້ແກ້ມາ ຫຼາຍສອງສາມຕ່ອນ ຄ່າສາມຝ່າຍ
ຂອງ ໝາກເຜັດ ຫົວບົ່ວ ເກົ່າຫົວ ໝາກໃຫຍ່ສົມຄວນສາງ
ມາ ໝາກຫຼາຍ ສອງເມັດ ໝາກເອ່ຍ ສູງ ຄອງເຄື່ອງ
ຕາງລ່າງມາ ນອກາເນື່ອດີ ມີກົ ຝີ່ນ່ອງ ໝາກໃຫຍ່ສົງ
ແກ້ວແລະ ກາງຕາວ ເຂົ້າສານ ຂອງກ ລ່າງມາ ໝາກເອົາໃບ
ຊາໂຫກລຸ່ງ

ວິທີເຮັດ — ຈຶ່ງເອົາປັ້ນມົ້ນ ມ້ຽງໃສ່ ເອົາຕ່ອນປາແດກ - ຄ່າຝ່າຍ
ມີໄຄ ໃສ່ ໃຫ້ຂີ້ໄປ ຈົມປາແດກ ມາອຸ່ມດີ ແຕ່ຢ່າໃຫ້
ໃຫມ້ ຈຶ່ງເອົາມາ ຢ່າງ ໃສ່ ທາງ ເຄື່ອງ ມີເປີ ໃຫ້ ກະທົງ ຫຼື
ລັງ ເອົາ ກາກ ໄປ ຫຼື ກັນ ລ່າງ ປັ້ນ ໃຫ້ ສະອາດ ທີ່ເອົາ
ມາ ປາແດກ ທີ່ ຕາງ ແລ້ວ ສາງ ໝາກ ເຜັດ ທີ່ ໃປ ເອົາ ໝາກ
ເມື່ອ ໝາກ ຫຼາຍ ທີ່ ໝອກ ອາເປັນ ໃສ່ ງື່ມ ເຖິງ ເຄິ່ງ ຈາງ ແຕ່ ໃຫ້
ເຄິ່ງ ໃວ້ ເລັກ ນ້ອຍ ເມື່ອ ໝາກ ໃສ່ ຢູ່ ແລ້ວ ຍົກ ລົງ ໃສ່
ນ້ອຍ ເອົາ ມາ ເຮັດ ຊື່ ເພາະ — ຜັກ ຢູ່ ແລ້ວ ນຸ່ມ
ໃສ່ ຕາມ - ແນວ ກາ ເຂົ້າ ຕາມ - ໝາກ ແຕງ - ບົ່ວ ຕ່ອມ -
ເຂົ້າ ແຕງ ອ່ອນ - ມີ ໄຄ ອອນ -

ໝາຍເຫດ — ເອາະປາແດກນີ້ ຄອບ ມີ ເຄື່ອງ ຊູ ໃຫ້ ຄົງ
ເປັນ ຈີ່ ຈະ ແຊບ ດີ ກູ ເອົາ ແຕ່ ເອາະປາແດກ
ເອົ້າ ແລ້ວ ນຳ ຄອບ ມາ ໃຫ້ ຊຸງ ທານ ./

Or Padek **Recipe 71**

PADEK STEW

Ingredients

1 piece of fish from the *padek* pot (see page 23)
1 stalk of lemon grass, crushed and cut into three parts
3 slices of galingale
5 (small) shallots—sear them in a charcoal fire, then remove and wash them
2 (small) heads of garlic—treat them like the shallots, but peel them before washing them
10 small chilli peppers—treat them likewise, but remove the black burned skin and the stems before washing them
chopped spring onion leaves

Method

Put a small pot on the fire and place in it the piece of fish from the *padek* pot, the galingale and the lemon grass. Keep stirring until the *padek* fish gives off a good smell. Take care that it does not burn.

Next, add half a glass beakerful ($\frac{1}{4}$ pint) of water and boil until the bones separate from the fish. Remove the pot from the fire and strain the contents. Then wash the pot, return the strained and clear *padek* liquid to it and bring back to the boil. Put in the shallots, garlic and chilli peppers. Taste; it should be quite salty.

Transfer the contents of the pot to a small rice-bowl and garnish with the chopped spring onion leaves.

Serve with moist fried pork skin, boiled (i.e. hard-boiled) eggs, boiled round eggplants, dill, young banana 'flower' (page 32), young cucumbers and young lemon grass.

Note

This *Or Padek* should have the right amount and varieties of vegetables served with it. There shouldn't be just the *Or Padek* alone.

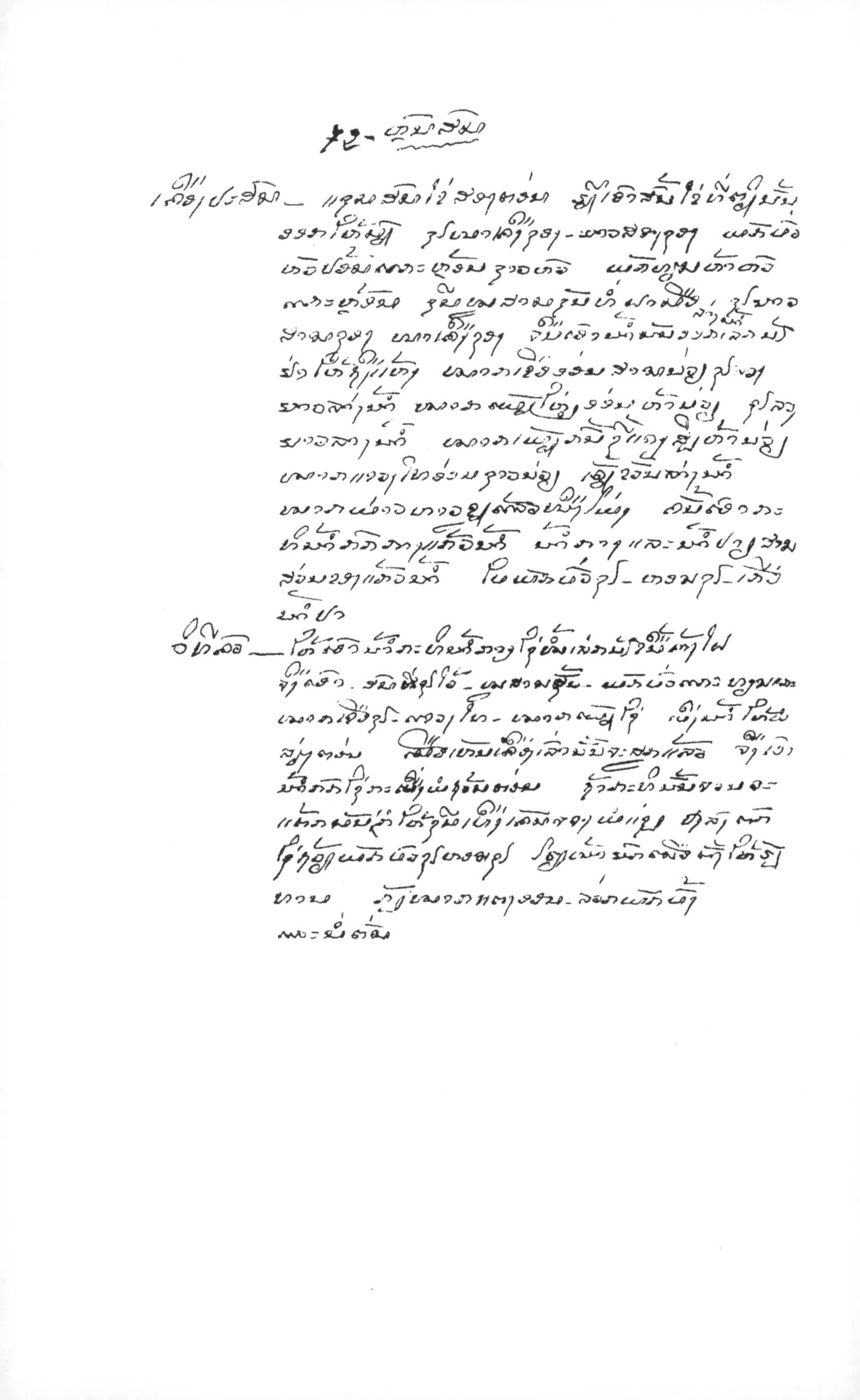

72- [illegible]

ເຄື່ອງປະສົມ — ແຈ່ວສົ້ມ [illegible] ໃສ່ [illegible]
[illegible]

ວິທີເຮັດ — ໃຫ້ເອົາ [illegible]
[illegible]

Loen Som **Recipe 72**

PICKLED FISH-ROE MEMBRANE, COOKED WITH VEGETABLES

Ingredients

2 pieces* of *san som khai* (the membrane, already emptied, cut up and pickled, which had enclosed the roe of a large fish)—cut them into bits measuring 1 by 0.5 cm
20 (small) shallots, peeled
5 (small) heads of garlic—separate the cloves and peel them
1 piece of three-layered pork, the size of a hand, sliced into pieces measuring 3 by 0.5 cm and fried a little to remove some of the fat, but without letting the meat become too dry
3 young round eggplants, sliced lengthways
5 young large chilli peppers, sliced lengthways and washed
15 fresh red chilli peppers
20 small 'Thai' eggplants (see page 33)—remove the stems and wash them
half a fully ripe coconut—the meat grated to produce ½ glass beakerful (¼ pint) of the first extraction of coconut milk and ¾ glass beakerful (⅜ pint) of the second and third extractions combined
chopped spring onion leaves
chopped coriander leaves
salt and fish sauce

Method

Put a little of the (combined) second-and-third extractions of coconut milk in a pot on the fire and add the sliced fish roe membrane, the pork, shallots, garlic, young eggplants, 'Thai' eggplants and (both kinds of) chilli pepper. Make sure that the liquid is just enough to cover all this. When these ingredients are cooked, add the first extraction of coconut milk, so that the ingredients are once more just covered with liquid. When the coconut cream starts to separate, taste and check the saltiness. Then take the pot from the fire, transfer the contents to a serving-bowl and garnish with ground black pepper and chopped spring onion and coriander leaves.

Serve with young cucumbers, *phak bong* (see page 36) which has been blanched, and cooked bamboo shoots.

* Editors' Note. The membrane enclosing the roe of a really large catfish would itself be very large, perhaps over 18 in long, and would be cut up into 'pieces' about the size of the palm of a hand before being pickled.

13 – ສ້າງບັ້ງ

ເຄື່ອງປະສົມ – [illegible]

(ໃບພັກບົ່ງ [illegible]) [illegible]

ວິທີເຮັດ – [illegible]

ໝາຍເຫດ – [illegible]

Sa Hoi Pang **Recipe 73**

WATER-SNAILS LAO STYLE

Ingredients

25 *hoi pang* (a kind of water-snail, see page 25)—cut off the tips of their shells so that you can remove them from their shells, discard the inedible parts and cut the remainder of each animal into three bits, which are to be salted and mixed with the juice of 2 limes

1 small rice-bowl of freshwater shrimps (*koung*, see page 25), to be cooked with salt, after which remove their heads and tails

boiled pork, a piece the size of three fingers, shredded

boiled pork fat, a piece the size of three fingers, cut into cubes of 3 cm and rubbed with salt and lime juice

1 handful of bean sprouts—blanch them in boiling water and cut off their roots

1 handful of finely chopped young banana 'flower' (page 32)

5 spring onions, the bulbs only, sliced lengthways and soaked in water

3 fresh red chilli peppers, sliced lengthways, cored, seeded and soaked in water

5 sprigs of coriander, washed

1 (small) head of garlic, sliced across

(fish sauce)

(more limes)

Method

Blanch the pieces of water-snail and the shredded boiled pork, which have both been salted and soaked in lime juice, to harden them. Wash them in cold water and shake them free of the water. Then put all the prepared ingredients together in a large bowl, add fish sauce, mix thoroughly, taste, and check the saltiness. Squeeze some more lime juice over the mixture, transfer it to a platter, and serve it.

Note

If salt-water crabs are available, add them to the mixture; if not, you may substitute some canned crabmeat. The same applies to the shrimps. When we are making *Sa Hoi*, we usually use fresh shrimps and small crabs which have been opened, have had their legs cut off and have been fried until they give off a fragrant aroma. Because the dish does not look nice when arranged after being prepared in this way, it is now more popular to use salt-water crabs or canned crabmeat.

๗๔ – ພູມີປາສະງົ້ວ

ເຄື່ອງປະສົມ — ປາສະງົ້ວ ໜຶ່ງສອງໂຕ ຫົວຜັກບົ່ວ ມີ [illegible] ຫົວກະທຽມ ລ້າງແລ້ວ
ໃຫ້ສະອາດ ແລ້ວເອົາຫົວໃສ່ [illegible] ສອງຖ້ວຍ [illegible] ຫົວ
(ແລ້ວເອົາຫົວປ່ຽນ ຫົວ - [illegible] ສອງ ສາມ ປ່ຽງ ມີ [illegible]
[illegible] ໃຫ້ແຫ້ງ ລະອຽດ) ກະລີ - ໝາກເຜັດ [illegible] ໝາກ
[illegible] ໝາກ [illegible] ພໍສົມຄວນ
[illegible] ແລ້ວຫ່ຽ ແລ້ວ [illegible]
[illegible] ແລ້ວ [illegible]
[illegible] ໝາກ [illegible] ພໍສົມຄວນ

ວິທີເຮັດ — [illegible] ເກືອ. ແລ້ວ
[illegible] ແລ້ວ [illegible]
[illegible] ແລ້ວ [illegible] ເອົາ
[illegible] ໃສ່ [illegible] ແລ້ວ [illegible]
[illegible] ເຄື່ອງ [illegible] ໄປ
[illegible] ສົມ [illegible]
[illegible] ໃສ່ [illegible] ໄປ [illegible]
[illegible] ແລ້ວ [illegible] ໄປ [illegible]
ກະປາ [illegible] ແລ່ [illegible]
[illegible] ແລ້ວ [illegible] ໃສ່ [illegible]
[illegible] ເຂົ້າຈ້າວ

Kalee Pa Sa Ngoua **Recipe 74**

SHEATFISH CURRY

Ingredients

5 pieces of *pa sa ngoua* (a sheatfish, see drawing on page 119), cut into bits about the size of a finger and washed
2 large onions, peeled and sliced across (and chopped)
6 (small) shallots } these two ingredients to be
1 piece of ginger } pounded together finely
curry (powder, about 3 soupspoonfuls)
1 can of tomato paste (of which only 1 tbsp is needed)
ground dried red chilli peppers
1 fully ripe coconut—grate the meat and make three extractions of coconut milk, $\frac{1}{2}$ glass beakerful ($\frac{1}{4}$ pint) of the first and $1\frac{1}{2}$ glass beakers ($\frac{3}{4}$ pint) of the second and third combined
2 sprigs of coriander—pick off the leaves only
1 chopped spring onion
10 potatoes, washed and peeled
3 fresh red chilli peppers
(broth from the soup-pot)
(fish sauce)

Method

Put the second and third extractions of coconut milk in a pot on the fire. Add salt, (some of the) coriander leaves and the chopped onions.

Put a pan on another fire and heat the first extraction of coconut milk in it until the cream separates. Add the pounded ingredients and fry them until a good aroma is given off. Then add 3 soupspoonfuls of curry (powder), and when it too gives off a good aroma add 1 tablespoonful of tomato paste. Stir and add some broth until the mixture is fairly liquid.

Now add the contents of the pan to the ingredients in the pot, and put in also the potatoes. When all this comes to the boil, add the pieces of fish, the whole chilli peppers, (the ground dried red chilli pepper, the remaining) coriander leaves and fish sauce. When the fish and potatoes are cooked, taste, and check the saltiness.

Dish up on a platter or in a bowl, garnish with chopped spring onion and serve with ordinary rice.

25 – ອໍ່ຕີນຄວາຍ

ເຄື່ອງປະສົມ — ຕີນ ຫຼື ໜັງຄວາຍ ໜຶ່ງຕີນ ຫົວສີໄຄ ໝາກເຂືອ ເອົາມາຫຼາຍໆໜ່ວຍ
ແລະ ເລືອກເອົາ ຈະໃສ່ກອງແຕ່ ຂອງເຈົ້າຈະກິນ ເລື້ອງ
ລາງນ້ຳໃຫ້ສະອາດ ທາເກືອ ແລ້ວຍ່າງໄວ້ (ໝາກເຂືອ ເປັນ
ທຸກນ້ຳໃຫ້ເປື່ອຍ ແລ້ວເອົາຫົວປອມທາ ຕຳເຂົ້າກັນໃຫ້
ໃຫ້ລະອຽດ) ຊູບເພງ ສາມຕ່ອນ ເພາະຕ້ອງຍ່າງ ຂອງ
ຕຳໃຫ້ແຫຼກ ແລ້ວເອົາຫົວປອມ ເພາະໝາກຊີ ແລ້ວ
ທຸກ ເພາະ ບຸກອຍ ສາມຫົວ ແລ້ວເອົາຫົວໃບຫອມ ຄັດມາ
ຈອງໃຫ້ແຫຼກ ໝາກເຂືອ ລົບ ຈົ່ງ ນີ້ໃຫ້ຫຼາຍ ເນື້ອກໍ່ນີ້
ແລ້ວຫາອມ ສູບ ສອງຕົ້ນ ໝາກພ່ອງເກືອບ ແລ້ວທາ ເນື້ອ
ຄັນ ເອົາ ແຕ່ນ້ຳ ກິນ ຕາມ ແຕ່ ຈະໄດ້ ຈົ່ງ ເອົານ້ຳ ໃສ່ ຄັນ
ເອົານ້ຳ ລາງ ເນື້ອ ແກງ ນ້ຳ ເກືອ- ນ້ຳປາ- ແລ້ວໃສ່
ນ້ຳ ຫມາກ ໃສ່

ວິທີເຮັດ — ໃຫ້ເອົາເຄື່ອງທີ່ຫາໄດ້ມາ ລວມກັນໄວ້ ແຕ່ງໄວ້ ແລ້ວ
ປີ້ງ ເອົາ ນ້ຳປາ ໃສ່ ລົມ ໃຫ້ທົ່ວ ເພາະ ເນື້ອ ເຄີມ ຈາກ ນ້ຳ ແກ່
ຈຶ່ງເອົາມາ ຫຼັງ ຕົ້ນ ຕີນ ຄວາຍ ທີ່ ກອງ ຕາ ໃສ່ ໃຫ້ ເຕັມ ແລ້ວ
ເອົາ ໃສ່ ໝໍ້ ປາກ ຕົ້ນ ໃຫ້ ແກ່ ໃຫ້ ເອົາ ຫົວ ສີໄຄ ໃສ່
ລາງ ໃສ່ ນ້ຳ ໜັງ ຄວາຍ ໃສ່ ເນື້ອ ແລ້ວ ນ້ຳ ຮ່ວມ ເອົາ ຕົ້ນ ຄວາຍ
ມາ ແລ້ວ ໃສ່ ແລ້ວ ມາ ຢ່າ ໃຫ້ ໄຟ ຮ້ອນ ຫຼາຍ ເມື່ອ ເຫັນ
ຕີນ ຄວາຍ ເນື່ອ ເປື່ອຍ ດີ ແລ້ວ ກໍ ໃຫ້ ປຸງ ລົດ ອາດ ນ້ຳ ກິນ ອອກ ໃຫ້ ເຫຼືອ
ແລ້ວ ໃສ່ ຕັ້ງ ໃສ່ ນ້ຳ ຄວາຍ ເນື້ອ ຄວາຍ ຮູ້ ສຸກ ແລ້ວ ຄ່ອຍ ໃສ່ ຈອບ
ຫົວ ຄວາຍ ເນື້ອ ໃຫ້ ນ້ຳ ເລັກນ້ອຍ ປຸງ ລົດ ແລ້ວ ຕົ້ນ ຄວາຍ ຈາກ
ຊູ ໃສ່ ຂອງ ລົມ ໃສ່ ຈອມ ແຍ່ ນ້ຳ ເລື່ອນ ໃຫ້ ແຊ່
ແລ້ວ ເອົາ ຂອງ ຕົ້ມ ຄວາຍ ແລ້ວ ທາ ອົມ ຊູ ແລ້ວ ກັບ ເຂົ້າ
ເນື້ອ ປີ້ງ ເນື້ອ ສົ້ມ ໃຫ້ ຮັບ ປະທານ

Ua Teen Moo Hum **Recipe 75**

SLOW-COOKED STUFFED PIG'S TROTTER

Ingredients

1 pig's trotter (use a hind trotter)—scrape off the hair, cut off the nails and carefully pull out the bones down to the nail ends, wash thoroughly and rub with salt and ground black pepper

red chilli peppers, soaked in water until soft
5 (small) shallots
} these two ingredients to be pounded finely together

3 pieces of crisp-fried pork skin—pound finely, after removing the fat

1 handful of (small) shallots, peeled

3 (small) heads of garlic, the cloves separated and peeled

half an onion, sliced thinly crossways and chopped

1 handful of roasted peanuts

2 sprigs of coriander, chopped

half a fully ripe coconut—grate the meat and make as much as you can of the first extraction of coconut milk and 1 glass beakerful (½ pint) of the second

salt, fish sauce and ground black pepper

fresh pork fat (1 tbsp)

Method

Put together in a small bowl all the prepared ingredients (from the red chilli peppers down to the peanuts). Sprinkle over them some ground black pepper, salt and fish sauce, and mix thoroughly. Taste, using the tip of your finger, and check the saltiness. Then stuff the mixture into the trotter and use a thread to sew up the openings.

Put a pot on the fire and put the spoonful of pork fat into it. When the fat is hot, add the stuffed trotter. Keep turning it, and make sure that the fire is not too hot. When the trotter becomes golden-yellow, take the pot off the fire. Pour out all the liquid fat and return the pot to the fire with the coconut milk (both extractions) and the trotter in it. Cover, and cook slowly until the trotter is cooked and tender, and has given out a small amount of liquid.

Remove the trotter, slice it across and arrange it on a platter. Pour the liquid from the pot as a sauce over the slices. Garnish with the chopped coriander and ground black pepper, and serve.

26 – ຫຍ້າຂີ້ເໝີ້ງ

ເລື່ອງປະສົມ — ຫຍ້າປະສົມຫຼາຍເໝີ້ງຫົວ ງົວຄວາຍບໍ່ຄ່ອຍໃຫ້ກິນ ເພາະ
ກິນແລ້ວຈະເມົາ ໃສ່ນ້ຳໃນທ້ອງໃຫ້ເປັນ ຫຍ້າກໍ່ເປັນຕົ້ນ
ລົ້ມແກ່ໃຫ້ສະອາດ ແລ້ວເອົາມາຕາກໃຫ້ແຫ້ງ ແລະ
ໃສ່ໝໍ້ໄວ້ ໃຫ້ເອົາຜ້າຂາວບາງປົກປິດໄວ້ ແລ້ວ
ແກ່ໃຫ້ສະອາດຈຶ່ງປັ້ນໃສ່ຫ່ວຍຕ່າງໆ ສ່ວນຫຍ້າມັນ
ຈະບໍ່ໃຫ້ແຫ້ງຕາຍໄດ້ (ເພາະວ່າຫຍ້າແຫ້ງແລ້ວກໍ່ເປື່ອຍແລວ
ບໍ່ເອົາແກ່ນຊື່ນຫຍ້າ ແລ້ວທົ່ວສອງເທື່ອ ຫົວທົ່ວ ແກ່ໃຈກໍ
ແກ້ທ້ອງປັ້ນເພາະຫຼາຍ ເໝີ້ງຄາວນີ້ – ແລ້ວຫຼາຍ
ເພາະຫຼາຍ ~~ເໝີ້ງ~~ ຫົວທົ່ວ ໝາກກາບວັດນີ້ ເພາະ
ຫຼາຍ ເໝີ້ງກຳນີ້ ເຊັ່ນຫາງນາງໃຫ້ເປັນຊື່ມູນປົ້ງ
ຊື່ດັ່ງກ່າວ ຫຍ້າເໝາ ~~ຂ~~ ມູນເຊື້ອສອງບາງຫຍ້າຕາໃຫ້ແຫ້ງ
ຊື່ຕ່ອນ ໝາກແກ່ວຫົວງູແລ້ວຫາງເໝີ້ງ ຄັນເອົາແກ່
ກະທົວສອງໆ ບໍ່ໃຊ້ແກ່ ໃບແກ້ຫາງນຸ່ມສອງທົ້ວ ໃບແກ້
ທົ່ວງູເໝີ້ງຕາມີ ແລ້ວ – ແກ່ປາແກ້ນີ້ປ່ນ ຊື່ມູນແກ້ເທົ່າໃຫ້

ວິທີແກ້ — ໃຫ້ເອົາຕົ້ນເຖົາ. ເລື່ອງປັ້ນ – ເຄື່ອງເພາະ ຮອນກິນໄດ້ແຮງ
ແກ້ກະທຽມ ແລ້ວ ແກ້ປາຮອງ ຄັນໃຫ້ເອົາກິນ ເພາະເຫັ້ງ
ເຄັມຈາງບໍ່ແຊງ ຊື່ເອົາຫຍ້າເຂົ້າໃນທ້ອງຫຍ້າໃຫ້ແກ ແລ້ວ
ຫຍ້າເໝີ້ງກິນ (ໃບແກ້ຫົວງູໃຊ້ກິນໃຫ້ແດງ)
ໃຫ້ຫຍ້າກິນແຈ່ງ ໃຈງູໃຫຍ່ບໍ່ສົມເຫຼືອ
ເພື່ອບໍ່ໃຫ້ເຊື້ອແກ່ ຈຶ່ງເອົາໃບເໝີ້ງດູແລ ຊື່ເຊື້ອ
ໝູງູຫາງງູອາມໃນນາກໍໄດ້ ບໍ່ເຫັນເປື່ອຍດີແລ້ວປົວ
~~ດ~~ ຕາກເຫຼືອອອກມາສົ້ນປັບຮັງເປັນຂາໃຫ້ອ່ວມ
ເອົາວາງລູນອ້ອມຈານກ່ອນ ຈຶ່ງເອົາເລື່ອງປໃນ
ຫລັງເສັ້ງວາງລົງກາງ ແລ້ວໃຫ້ງູກິນເຊື້ອບໍ່ ຫຍ້າຕາກນັ້ນ
ແຫງເທົ່າແຊ່ ເອົາຮອງເຄື່ອງວິວຫຍ້າໃຫ້ໝູ ແລ້ວນີ້
ແກ້ເກອນກຸໄປງູແລ້ວ ນາເເລື້ອຕັ້ງເຕັ້ງກາງ

ໝາຍເຫດ — ວິວເຫຼືອເໝີ້ງນີ້ ຄອນຫຼາຍເຫຼືອງຮອງໆ ຈຶ່ງແຊ່
ດີ ງູຕັ້ງການຮັກສາເຂັ້ນ ຕັ້ງໃຈເຂັ້ມແຂງ
ກ່ອນ ບໍ່ດັ່ງນັ້ນແລ້ວເຫຼືອຈະມາບໍ່ແກ້ຮັກສາ

Ped Ua Nung **Recipe 76**

STEAMED STUFFED DUCK

Ingredients

1 duck, gutted—make a hole through the tail to remove the giblets, cut off the neck and feet, wash the duck and rub it with salt and ground black pepper; split open the gizzard, and, having removed and discarded its inner lining, wash it and slice it thinly; chop the liver finely

4 red chilli peppers, cored and soaked in water until soft
5 straight-bulbed spring onions, heads only
} these two ingredients to be pounded together finely

1 handful of shallots, peeled
5 (small) heads of garlic, the cloves separated and peeled
1 handful of shelled peanuts
4 fragrance mushrooms (page 00), cut into small squares
4 pieces of crisp-fried pork skin—scrape off all the fat and pound the skin finely
half a fully ripe coconut—grate the meat and make an extraction of coconut milk without adding any water
2 sprigs of coriander, the leaves only, chopped
1 spring onion, the leaves only, chopped
salt, fish sauce and ground black pepper
minced pork, a quantity the size of a hen's egg

Method

Mix together in a big bowl the pounded ingredients, the (sliced, chopped and) minced ingredients (except for the coriander) and the peeled ingredients. Add the extraction of coconut milk, salt and fish sauce. Mix it thoroughly, taste, and check the saltiness. Add the chopped spring onion leaves and mix again. Stuff the mixture into the duck's stomach until it is full and sew up the skin at the bottom.

Place the stuffed duck in a bowl of suitable size, so that when it is cooked the liquid from it will not be lost. Then cook it by steaming it in a steaming pan or in an aluminium steamer. When it is cooked and tender, take it out and separate it into different parts such as the breasts and legs and arrange these around the rim of a platter. Put the stuffing in the middle. Taste the liquid remaining in the bowl, to check its flavour, use it as a sauce to pour over the stuffing. Garnish with ground black pepper and chopped coriander, and serve.

Note

Ua Ped Nung should be served hot. If you wish to serve it cold, you must put it in the refrigerator beforehand, since otherwise the duck meat will be tough and unpleasant to eat.

๓๒ - ພັນທຸຍິ່ງຜ່ານ

ເຄື່ອງປະສົມ — ຮາກວາດຳ ຮາກສົ້ມປ່ອຍ ປູງລວງຂວາງ. ໝາກສົງ
ຮຸງ. ກ້ວາງແມ່ງຮຸງ ເອົາປົນໃສ່ໃຫ້ໃສ່ຕົ້ມນອນເທົ່າ
ທ່ອນ ເອົາໝາກຫຼວງໃຫ້ເຖິງປາກທ້າງມື - ລ້າງ.
ໝາກມີທາງໃຈ (ໝາກເຫົ່າ ຫົວປົງ ໝາກໂສ້ ຫົວ
ໝາກຫຼວງ ໝາກ ສາມ ຫົວ) ຂອງສອງປ່ຽນມີໜ່າະເອົາ
ເທົ່າເມື່ອແກ່ 1 ງ ກາມໃຫ້ລະລູງ ງາຂອງແກ່ລະລູງ
ນຶ່ງບ່ອງ ໝາກທາວຄືນຈື່ແກ່ລະລູງ ໝາກບ່ອງ
ກ້ຽງຕ້ອງແກ່ລະລູງ ສາມຕົວ ມາໃສ່ຮູບໃນໜ້າກູ
ໝາກສົມເຫັດທາງປົນ ໝາກດາຍນໍ້າເຫຼືອໃຫ້ສົມ
ໝາກດາຍສຸງສົງຕົວ ໝາກຂາຍມາເຫຼືອເອົາເທົ່າໃນ
ຮອງສົ່ງຕົວ ສະຫຼຸບເອົາແກ່ໃນຫົວນັ້ນ ໝາກມາ
ເຫຼືອເອົາມາບ່ອນ ຮອງຕົ້ນ ກາລະເກົ່າເຫຼືອເອົາແກ່ໃນ
ລູງນຶ່ງເມື່ອກາໍໃຫ້ໃຫຍ່ ໝາກໃຫຍ່ມີໃຫ້ລ້າງມາໃສ່ສົມ
ບ່ອນ ໝາກບໍ່ລຽງເຄື່ອງຕົວ ຫຼືເອົາຫົວສົ່ງຮູ້ແກ່ມາ
ໃສ່ ຂ່ອນໃນກໍ່ຫຼືເປັນຕ່ອນບາວໃຫ້ສົມ ໝາກຫຼາຍບ່ອງ
ໜ່າະເປັນງືນຕາວຫົວ ໝາກທາວຄືນຂັ້ນມີໃຫ້ຫຼາຍເນື້ອ
ສົມເມື່ອ ໝາກໜ້ອນກູລ່ອງມາໃສ່ບ່ອງ ໝາກໃສ່ໃສ່
ໃຫ້ຮູລວງບາວໃສ່ເອົາແດ່ນສົງບ່ອງ ໝາກຕາແກ່ຕອນປົນ
ເປື້ອນໝາກຫຼືບາວສາມຮູ ແລ້ວຮູລ່ອງບາວໃຫ້ບາງ
ກ້ຽງຂື້ນ ໝາກໃສ່ໃນໝາກຫຼືທາງ ຮູລວງບາວເປັນຕ່ອນບາງ

ໝາກໃຊ້ເລື່ອຕາງຈາງຜັກ. ໝາກບໍ່ຕາໃຫ້ຮູລວງຕາງຫັກ
ໝາກກາເພງກິນຮູ້ແຕງສູງຫົວບ່ອງ. ມາມີມີໃສ່ແກ່ແລ້ວ

ວິທີເຮັດ — ເກົງ. ມາປາ. ໝາກມີບໍ່. ເຂົ້າປ່ນບາງບາກຫຼືເປັນບ່ອນ
ເມື່ອໃດຕ້ອງເກີງໃສ່ຖົງແລ້ວ ໃຫ້ເອົາສະລູບມອ້ນຈານ
ໃຫຍ່ ເທື່ອເອົາໝາກທີ່ເຫຼືອໃວ້ນັ້ນ ວາງລົງເທິງກາງໃຫ້
ເປັນຈຸ້ ຕັ້ງຈານນຶ່ງໃຫ້ເອົາເຂົ້າປູນໃສ່ທັງກາງ ເອົາ

Phan Sin Fahn **Recipe 77**

'WRAPPED' DEER MEAT

Ingredients

5 pieces of deer meat (page 27), taken either from the leg or the sirloin—slice them across into slices of about 2 by 8 cm and beat the pieces gently with a pestle in order to soften them, after which rub into them 5 crushed cloves of garlic, salt and ground black pepper

7 (small) shallots } peel the shallots and the garlic cloves
3 (small) heads of garlic } and pound them together finely

1 spoonful of ground sesame seeds

1 spoonful of ground roasted peanuts

3 dried shrimps, pounded

1 sprig of coriander, chopped finely (for the 'dip')

2 sprigs of coriander, chopped roughly (to serve as garnish)

10 sprigs of coriander—pick off only the young tender shoots and leaves
5 lettuces—separate the leaves
20 sprigs of watercress—pick off the tender shoots only
1 large bunch of *kan kam* (a variety of mint with darkish leaves—page 46)—pick off only the tender young shoots and leaves
} wash all these vegetables and reserve them apart to go on the first platter

7 straight-bulbed spring onions—cut each bulb into four lengthways and put these to soak in water, then cut the leaves into long pieces (about 5 cm in length)

5 heads of pickled garlic—separate them into their cloves

1 handful of roasted peanuts, rubbed together to rid them of their skins

2 star-fruit (*mak feuang*—see page 30), sliced thinly and washed

2 tomatoes, sliced vertically and seeded

1 cucumber, peeled, cut into sections 3 cm long, and each section sliced thinly lengthways

1 unripe banana, peeled, cut into half crossways, and each half sliced thinly lengthways

1 can tomato paste } for the sauce
1 onion, sliced and finely chopped } for the sauce

15 small red chilli peppers (pounded, for use in the 'dip')

butter

sugar

(meat broth)

salt, fish sauce and ground black pepper

1 *na* (½ kilo, see page 22) of rice vermicelli, cut into suitable pieces (it is usual to divide each bundle into four)

Method

When the above ingredients have been prepared, arrange the lettuce leaves, and the other three vegetables (reserved with them) on a platter. Arrange the rice

ເຄື່ອງເພາະພາະເຕີມຊູປໃສ່ຕ່າງໆ ລາງ ອ່ອນເຈົ້າປັ້ນໃສ້
ຜັກສະເໜີ້ດ ຮີບຄີ່ໃດໃສ່ແມ່ ເປີ້ງບັນເຫຼັ່ງ ໃຫ້ງາມ
ເອົາຄີ່ນປອງ ໂຕະ ຜ້າຂາວ ປົກໄວ້ ຈັ່ງເອົາຫົວຜັກ
ບົວເທົ່າ ຊາເທົ່າ - ໝາກກະຫຼ່ຳດີນເທົ່າ - ກະທຽມເທົ່າ ຜັກ
ຫອມເປົ້າ. ມາຈອມເຂົ້າກັນໃສ່ກູ້ງ ເກືອ - ນ້ຳ
ປາແດກ ໝາກເພັດເປັ່ຍປາ - ນ້ຳຕານກຸ້ນໃສ່ດ້ວຍໃຫ້ເຂົ້າກັນ ເພາະເປັນ
ແດດຈາງໆ ແຕ່ນ້ຳໃຫ້ຂຸ່ນຫຼາຍ
ຜັກໃສ່ກູ້ງ ເປັນຜັກຍຸບໃຫຍ່ ໝາກ ນ້ຳຕັ້ງໄວ້
ໃຫ້ເອົາຜັກໃສ່ໃນຂັນຊີ້ນຂ້າງໃນ ພໍ່ເດັ່ນ ເອົາແຜ່ນປອ
ຕັດໃຫຍ່ລົງປົ້ນ ໝາກກາເຂືອເສື້ອສາບ່ອງໃສ່ລົມໃບຈົມ
ຫອມ ຈັ່ງເອົານ້ຳຊີ້ນໃສ່ຜັກໂຕ້ແຫຼວຫຼາຍປົ່ງໄວ້
ກອງໃຫ້ເອົາຍ່ອນຂີ້ຂ້າງໃນເພາະກາງບ່ອງ ພໍ່ເດັ່ນຮ້ອນ
ເປັນຄວນຈຶ່ງເອົາຂຶ້ນພານລົງລາງ ໃຫ້ສາແຕມແມ່
ສາຍແກ້ວ ສ່ວນຫັກກາງໃຫ້ແດງນີ້ ປັ້ນໃສ່ກອງ
ມາດູເປັນເທົ່າລູກໃຈງາມ ເອົາໝາກເຂືອເສື້ອທຳເປັ
ໃສ່ມັນ ຮ້ອນໆ ຮອງແກ້ວ ແກ້ວຫອມປົ່ນກົ່ນ
ປັ່ນໃສ່ແກ້ວ. ນກີເສືອຕຸ່ງໃຫ້ລົງທານ

ໝາຍເຫດ — ເພັນຊູນຜານ ຫອຊູນຈຶ່ງຈັກໃຫ້ສີ່ວັນ
ສ່ວນແປ່ງເຂົ້າໜຽວຊູນນ້ຳຮ້ອນຄາລອ ນາແກ້ວ
ນັ້ນເປັນອາຫານພາກເຈາ ສ່ວນຊາວລາວເຮົາ
ແຕ່ກ່ອນບໍ່ເອົາ ຊູບນີ້ເຄື່ອງຄຶດພະແກດຕ່າງ
ປະເທດເຂົ້າມາຫຼາຍ ຈຶ່ງສະເໜີກໍາການ້ຳມື້
ເໝືອໃຫ້ເປັນລະບຽບ ເພາະສະເໜີເນົ່າຮູ້ທານ
ໄດ້ດີ ສະນັ້ນ ຈຶ່ງຮູ້ແປງທານກາງລະສະໃໝ ແກ້ວ
ໃຫ້ເຫດຈະສົມໃນການຮູ້ທານ ສ່ວນຊູນນັ້ນ
ຄວນ [struck] ຫຼັງໃຫ້ເຫຼືອກ່ອນ ບໍ່ຕ້ອງຊູບເພາະ
ການຮູ້ທານໄດ້ສະໃໝມີແລ້ວ ຈຶ່ງນ້ຳຈຳ
ເປັນຊູ [struck] ຕ່ອນນີ້ ຈະມີການສະເໜີເສັງຂຶ້ນທັງ
ອີກ

vermicelli in the middle of another platter, and place around them the various peeled and chopped vegetables. (i.e. the seven ingredients from the straight-bulbed spring onions to the unripe banana). Arrange these so that they are separate from each other. Place the platters on a table and cover them with a thin white cloth.

Mix together in a bowl the pounded shallots (and garlic), the ground sesame seeds, peanuts and shrimps, the finely chopped coriander, some salt, the dried red chilli pepper and the sugar, with a sprinkling of fish sauce and some meat broth. Dip the tip of your finger into the mixture and taste it, to check the saltiness. Make sure that the mixture is not too thick. Put it in a small bowl and garnish it with (1 sprig of roughly) chopped coriander. This constitutes the 'dip'.

Put some butter in a small cooking pot, and put the pot on the fire. When it is hot, fry the chopped onion in it. Add 2 spoonfuls of the canned tomato paste, and stir until a good aroma is given off. Then add some more of the meat broth, but without letting the mixture become too runny. Remove the pot from the fire. (This constitutes the sauce to be poured over the deer meat).

Now put another pot on the fire, and in it half a spoonful of butter. When the pot is hot and the butter is smoking, add the pieces of deer meat. Leave them, (turning them as necessary), until they are well done on both sides (*sook haem*, meaning well done and crispy and crunchy), but with the inside still red (i.e. rare). Then take the pot off the fire and slice the meat into bite-size pieces.

Arrange the pieces of deer on a platter. Use the tomato mixture as a sauce to pour over the meat. Garnish it with (the second sprig of roughly) chopped coriander and ground black pepper, and serve. (The way of eating this dish is to wrap a piece of meat, with sauce, in a leaf or leaves from the first platter. It is this wrapping which accounts for 'wrapped' in the title of the recipe. Each wrapped piece of meat is dunked in the 'dip' before being eaten.)

Note

You can make *Phan Sin Ngoua* (i.e. with beef instead of deer meat) in just the same way as *Phan Sin Fahn*.

The (alternative) method of parboiling the raw meat, before wrapping it in leaves, is Chinese. The traditional Lao way of preparing this dish is by first grilling the meat (as opposed to the frying described above). But, since cooking utensils and certain vegetables from foreign countries have been imported, cooking can be done with greater convenience and in a better organised and hygienic way; the science of cooking and feeding people has developed with the passage of time.

As for the fried meat, one should make large pieces, because the modern way of eating provides us with the necessary conveniences such as individual cutlery.

໔໘- ມຸ່ມບອນ

ເຄື່ອງປະສົມ – ບອນບາວານ ສອງສາມກໍ້ ລອກເປືອກອອກໃຫ້ໝົດ ຊອຍ ແລ້ວໃສ່ໝໍ້ຕົ້ມຈົນເປື່ອຍ ບີບນ້ຳອອກໃຫ້ແຫ້ງໄວ້ ບົ່ວແດງ ກະທຽມ ເຜົາ ຂີງ ໝາກເຜັດແຫ້ງ ຕ່ອນ (ເນື້ອ ປາ ໄກ່ ເປັດ ແລ້ວແຕ່ ຫາໄດ້) ຂາ ຕະໄຄ້ ໃບມ່ວງ ຫອມແປ້ນ ສີ່ ຫ້າ ແລະ ນ້ຳປາ ກະປິ. ຜັກຫອມ ຫົວສີ່ - ໃບສີ່ປາ - ມີຜັກຍັງ

ວິທີເຮັດ – ໃຫ້ເອົາຜັກບົ່ວ ໃສ່ໝໍ້ ຂົ້ວກັບນ້ຳມັນ ໃຫ້ຫອມ ຕາມເຄີຍ ແລ້ວໃສ່ ຊີ້ນລົງ ຂົ້ວ ແລ້ວໃສ່ນ້ຳ ຕົ້ມ ຈົນສຸກ ແລ້ວຈຶ່ງໃສ່ບອນລົງ ທີ່ເອົາບອນລົງໃສ່ ໃຫ້ໃສ່ ຈົນ ເຄື່ອງ ແກງ ໃສ່ແລ້ວ ຫອມ ຫລືຜັກ ຈຶ່ງໃສ່ ໃບຜັກ ແລ້ວ ຄົນໃຫ້ທົ່ວ ປຸງລົດຊາດໃຫ້ພໍ ແລ້ວ ຍົກລົງ ໃສ່ຖ້ວຍ ຫຼືໃຫ້ຮ້ອນໆ

Nian Bon

Recipe 78

A 'MASH' OF BON

Ingredients

2 handfuls of *bon* (see page 38)—peel off the skin (which pulls off easily once one end is cut), put the *bon* in a steamer (see page 16) and steam until well cooked, then take it out and pound it finely (so that it turns into a purée)

1 piece of pork, the size of four fingers, including some fat, chopped finely

1 dried red chilli pepper, soaked in water until soft
4 straight-bulbed spring onions, the bulbs only
} these two ingredients to be pounded together finely to constitute the *kheuang tam*

5 (small) shallots, sliced across and fried until golden-yellow

chopped spring onion leaves

chopped coriander leaves

salt and fish sauce

pork fat

Method

Put some pork fat in a wok and put the wok on the fire. Put in the *kheuang tam* and fry until fragrant. Then add the chopped pork and sprinkle some salt and fish sauce over the mixture. Continue frying until it gives off a good aroma. Then add the *bon*, and go on cooking, in order to reduce the liquid, until the mixture thickens. Taste, and check the saltiness.

Now add the fried shallots and the chopped spring onion leaves. Stir until thoroughly mixed. Take the pot off the fire and arrange the contents on a serving platter. Garnish with the chopped coriander leaves, and serve.

໒໙- ຂນົມ[illegible]

ເຄື່ອງປະສົມ— ຊີ້ນໝູ [illegible] ທ່ອງ ກໍໄດ້ ມັກໄດ້ [illegible] ໝາກພ້າວ ໃຊ້ [illegible] ເກືອ - ນ້ຳປາ [illegible] ຈຶ່ງ [illegible] ມາ [illegible] ໄດ້ສະໜູ [illegible] ແລ້ວ [illegible] ແລ້ວ [illegible] ຫ່ອງ - [illegible] ແຕ່ [illegible] ຫ້ອງ ແລ້ວ [illegible] ຂນົມ [illegible] ສາມດູງ [illegible] ເຂົ້າ [illegible] ແປ້ງ [illegible] ຫ່ໍ [illegible] ສາມ [illegible] ແລ້ວ [illegible] ແຕ່ [illegible] ນ້ຳ [illegible] ແຕ່ [illegible] ສາມ [illegible] ແຕ່ [illegible] ໃສ່ [illegible] - ໃສ່ [illegible] ນ້ຳປາ - ນ້ຳຕານ [illegible] ສາມ [illegible] ໃສ່ສະໜູ [illegible]

ວິທີເຮັດ— ໃສ່ເກືອ - ເຂົ້າຂົ້ວ - [illegible] - ໝາກ[illegible] - [illegible] ໃຫ້ [illegible] ເຂົ້າ [illegible] ສະໜູ [illegible] - [illegible] - [illegible] ແລ້ວ [illegible] ໃສ່ [illegible] ສະໜູ [illegible] ແລ້ວ [illegible] ແລ້ວ [illegible] ສະໜູ [illegible] ນ້ຳ [illegible] ສະໜູ ແລ້ວ [illegible] ແລ້ວ [illegible] ໃຫ້ [illegible] ແລ້ວ [illegible]

Moo Naem

Recipe 79

A MIXED PORK DISH

Ingredients

½ kilo lean pork, minced finely and seared in a hot pan without fat until it gives off a good aroma and has dried out—then pound it
1½ glass beakerfuls (¾ pint) of rice which has been toasted until brown in a hot dry pan, pounded and sifted
½ glass beakerful (¼ pint) ground galingale—use the soft parts of the rhizomes only and sift after grinding
1 piece of pork fat, about the size of a hand, boiled, sliced into pieces measuring about 3 cm, salted and dipped in hot water
(some pork skin, cooked and sliced)
half a pig's heart, boiled and sliced into squares of 3 cm
5 spring onions, cut along their length—bulbs and green parts adjoining the bulbs only, not the leaves
5 heads of pickled garlic—separate and peel the cloves and slice them lengthways
3 fresh red chilli peppers, cored and seeded, cut lengthways and soaked in water
1 bowl of meat broth
chopped spring onion leaves
chopped coriander leaves
salt and fish sauce
sugar
1 piece of pig's tripe about the size of three fingers, sliced into squares of 3 cm
3 lettuces
(1 lime)

Method

Put the ground rice, the ground galingale and the pounded minced pork into a bowl. Mix until the ingredients are well blended. Sprinkle some fish sauce into the meat broth and add it to the mixture. Add also the pork skin, the pork fat, the pig's heart and tripe. Taste, and check the saltiness. If you like your food sweet, add sugar.

Next, add the slices of spring onion and the chopped spring onion leaves, the chopped coriander leaves and the chopped chilli peppers. Grate some lime peel on to the mixture and blend it thoroughly together. When all has been added, arrange the washed lettuce leaves on the platter and dispose the pork mixture in the centre. Then serve.

໔໐- ລ່ຽງຈຸ່ມສາມເຄື່ອງ

ເຄື່ອງປະສົມ — ຈຸ່ມເລື້ອງລາວອີ່ງໃຊ້ ບໍ່ໄດ້ກໍໃຊ້ ແລະເອັນ ທໍ່ຜັກບົ່ງ ລ້າງເຂົ້າໃຫ້ສະອາດ ເອົາໃສ່ຖ້ວຍຜັກໃຫ້ແຫ້ງ ໆ ໄວ້ (ພວກເຄື່ອງຄົວທີ່ຈ່ອມເອົາໃສ່ໃຫ້ເປັນ ຈານເປັນຄ່ຳທາງໜ້າ ພວກຜັກແຕ່ງທາງໃຫ້ສີ ສົ້ມໜ້າ ຜັກບົ່ວທັງເປັນຜັກສະຫຼາກ ແລະຜັກຂອງ ຊີທ້ອງ -ຜັກຫອມຜັກສະຫຼາກ ແລະຜັກແກ່ຂອງ ສະຫຼາທ້ອງ ສ່ວນສາຍພັກ) ຂອງຫົວບູກມີໃຊ້ຄ່ຳ ເອົາກັບໃຫ້ແຫ້ງກ່ອນໃຫ້ເສັ້ນແກ່ນ (ຊີ້ນຄາຍ ຫົວໃຊ້ລອງ - ແກ່ນລອງ ເອົາໄດ້ຫົວຈຸ່ມ)

ຂອງສາມຢ່າງນີ້ເອົາຕັ້ງເມັດຫຼາຍ ສຸກແລ້ວ ພັກຂອງກາມກຽງເປັນຕ່ອນນ້ອຍ ຜັກຫອມ ສາມເວລາປະສົມຂາງຈືນເນື້ອທີ່ຈ່ອນຄາກຂອງ ຜັກບົ່ວ ສາມເວລາປະສົມຂາງຈືນນ້ຳເກືອ ຂອນຜັກຂອງ ສີໃສ່ບໍ່ ເວລາປະສົມຂາງນ້ຳທາງກາຄາກຂອງ ຂອງເປົ້າຈືນນີ້ບໍ່ເກົ່າ ໃຫ້ມີ ຈະພາໄດ້ກິນຍາຫານໃປ ນ້ຳສົ້ມຈຸ່ມນ້ຳກູ້ງ ນ້ຳສະປາແລ້ວທີ່ກູ້ງ ເອົາຂອບປົນເກືອຊີ້ງເອົາມາ ຈ່ອມໆ ສາມບ່ອງນ້ຳຖູ້ໃຫ້ພວກມັນປູແລ້ງ ໆ ຜັກຫອມ ຈຸ່ມ ເມື່ອຈຶ່ງຈຸ່ມໃຫ້ແລ້ວສອງໃປ

ວິທີເຮັດ — ເມື່ອຕັ້ງເຄື່ອງນັ້ນໃຫ້ລຽງແລ້ວ ຈຶ່ງເອົາຈຸ່ມລ່ຽງເຄື່ອງ ຫົວຄໍໃຊ້ໃສ່ນ້ຳ ຄາໃຫ້ເຂົ້າກັນດີ ໆ ສົ່ງເອົາ ນ້ຳປາແລ້ວໃສ່ເກືອສະນີ້ ລົມໃຫ້ແກ່ເຂົ້າກັນຈົນຂົ້ນ ເອົານ້ຳສາງລອງສົ່ງລົມໃປ ເອົາຂອງໃສ່ຖ້ວຍນ້ຳ ໂຫຕັ້ງນ້ຳຊາກນ້ຳ ເລືອງປູ-ເລືອງຈີນໃສ່ຈຸ່ມ ເປັນເລົາລາວຂົ້ນແຫ້ງຕາມຈຸ່ມ ຈຶ່ງເອົາໃສ່ໃຫ້ ເລກັບ ເອົາຕາມໃຊ້ຄົນໃຫ້ໃສ່ ຕາມສົງສານ ເລືອງໃສ່ປູຜັກຫອມ ໃຊ້ເອົາຂອງຜັກເມື່ອຕັ້ງໃຫ້ສຸກ

Lap Sin Song Kheuang **Recipe 80**

WATER-BUFFALO MEAT SALAD

Ingredients

1 piece of dark (blackish) water-buffalo meat, about the size of a hand, washed and chopped finely on a chopping board

<table>
<tr><td>6 young bitter eggplants (see page 33), seared in the fire until the skin is burned
2 dried red chilli peppers, grilled on the fire until crisp
4 (small) shallots, placed in the embers of a charcoal fire until almost cooked, then removed and peeled
2 (small) heads of garlic, treated like the shallots, with the cloves peeled
2 slices of galingale</td><td>pound these ingredients together into a smooth paste until it is no longer possible to distinguish any of them in the mixture</td></tr>
<tr><td>water-buffalo liver
water-buffalo heart
water-buffalo spleen</td><td>a quantity equivalent to four fingers of each, boiled in broth from the stock-pot until cooked, then sliced into small pieces</td></tr>
<tr><td>3 (small) heads of garlic, sliced across and fried until golden-yellow, then taken out of the pan
3 spring onions, bulbs only, sliced across and fried until golden-yellow, then taken out of the pan
1 stalk lemon grass, chopped finely, fried until it gives off a good aroma, then taken out of the pan</td><td>these fried ingredients must not burn, or the general flavour of the dish will be spoiled</td></tr>
</table>

1 bowl of meat broth
1 bowl of *or padek* (see recipe 15)
3 soupspoonfuls of ground *khao khoua* (rice which has been toasted until brown in a hot dry pan and then pounded), sifted in order to achieve the finest texture, like that of flour
finely chopped spring onion leaves
finely chopped coriander leaves
2 finely chopped Kaffir lime leaves

Method

After preparing the ingredients, pound together the chopped meat and the five ingredients which have already been pounded. Add the *or padek* while you do so, a little at a time. Stir until you have a well blended and thick mixture. Then add meat broth, a little at a time, stirring constantly, and the ground rice (*khao khoua*). If the mixture is too thick, add more meat broth.

Next, add the ingredients which have been (sliced or) chopped and then fried. Taste, and check the saltiness. Then add some of the sliced liver, heart and spleen and the fragrant ingredients (*kheuang hom*, i.e. presumably the chopped spring onion leaves and chopped Kaffir lime leaves, the only ingredients otherwise unaccounted for).

Transfer the mixture to a platter and garnish with the rest of the sliced liver, heart and spleen and with the chopped coriander leaves. Then serve it.

ບາງຫາດ — ການເຮັດລ່ຽງຈົນມີ ກໍ່ເປັນຄວາມດ່ວນດ້ວຍ
ບໍ່ຄວນຈະເຊື່ອ ເພາະວະນາຍາໂທເຈົ້າເທົ່າ ລ່ຽງຈົນມີ
ແຕ່ເດີມທີ່ບໍ່ມີຄວາມແຫ້ງບໍ່ ຫຼາຍປີມາແລ້ວ ເພາະເປັນ
ຂອງເກົ່າມາແຕ່ນານໃຫຍ່ ກໍ່ຈະຢູ່ ຈະໃຊ້ທຳໄດ້ [illegible]
ມາຍາມາລາໄປປີ່ໃດ ຕ້ອງມີແຕ່ [illegible] . [illegible].
ໃນຂະນະເດືອນນ່ວນ ໃນເວລານັ້ນລາວ ເອົາແລ້ວ
ເວລານັ້ນກັບມີ ສ່ວນແຫ່ງຄວາມໃຈສາງ ດ້ວຍຄວາມ
ເສີ້ຍແຊ ຕ່າງໆ ການສາງ ການຄົນລ່ຽງ ກໍ່ບໍ່ມີ
ປາແດກ ກໍ່ເອົາໃຈມັກປາແດກ

Note

In making this meat *lap*, one should not use light-coloured (pale pinkish) water-buffalo meat, because this could cause stomach-aches.

Originally, dried water-buffalo skin was also added, but it is not common to add this now, because it is too hard. However, if it appeals to a person's taste, it may be added. Also, the dish could be even better if thick tripe were added (after being scraped, boiled and sliced).

This dish should be served with:

bai khom kadao (an edible leaf, illustrated below)—only the young leaves;

bai mak deed (a plant bearing small dark green fruits in clusters, of which both the fruits and leaves are eaten at Luang Prabang), the leaves only, blanched in boiling water (to reduce the bitter taste);

khae flowers (see recipe 55), grilled; and

small fresh chilli peppers.

(As for a soup to accompany the *lap*) one should serve *Keng Om Duk Luad*. (Phia Sing does not give a recipe for this. The name means literally 'soup, slow-cooking, bones, blood'). This is better (for the purpose) than any other soup.

In making this *lap*, use fish sauce instead of the *or padek* if you do not like the latter.

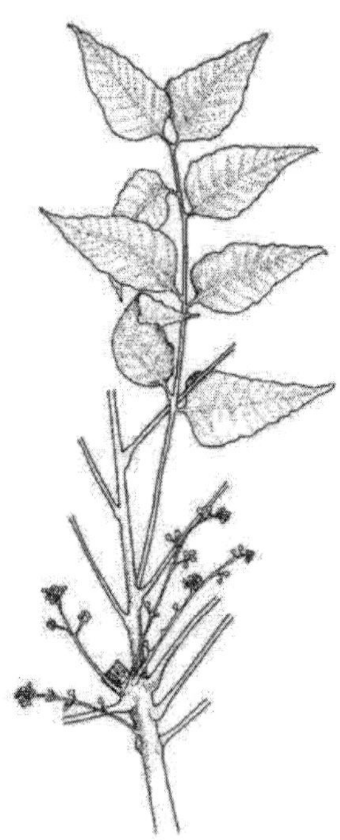

Bai khom kadao, the edible leaf referred to above and mentioned on page 37.

໘໔- ຂ້າເຫົາ

໑ ຄຸນປະໂຫຍດ— ເຫົາເປັນປັນຫາໃຫຍ່ຢູ່ລາວ ພວກເດັກນ້ອຍມັກອອກ
ໄປຫຼິ້ນນຳສັດ ແລ້ວ ເປັນພວກອອກໄປຫາຫຍ້າໃຫ້ກິນ
ຢູ່ນອກບ້ານເປັນເວລາດົນ ບໍ່ໄດ້ອາບນ້ຳ ຂໍໃຫ້ແກ້ໄຂ
ໂດຍການສາຍນ້ຳໃຫ້ແກ່ເຂົາ ພວກເຂົາຈະບໍ່ໄດ້
ແຕ່ງ ສານເຄມີຂ້າເຫົາ ພວກເຂົາເຫັນວ່າ ຈະໃຫ້ແກ່ຍ
ເປັນນ້ຳ ຕົ້ນໝາກຂີ້ຫູດ ໃບໜາດ ສານຕົວ
ໝາກຫຸ່ງ ໝາກຣາງ ໃຫ້ແກ່ຍ ນ້ຳຕົ້ມ ພວກເຂົາສາມາດ
ໃຫ້ແກ່ຍ ເຂົ້າແຕ່ ມື້ເປັນນ້ຳ ຄົນທີ່ເປັນຫວັດ
ສາມາດຕົ້ມລ້າງຫົວໃຫ້ສະອາດ ໝາກ ຫາຍ
ໃບ- ໝາກປາ- ນ້ຳສົ້ມ ໃບໝາກຂີ້ຫູດໃຫ້ກ່ຽວ

໒ ວິທີເຮັດ— ໃຫ້ເອົານ້ຳຕົ້ມໃຫ້ ກິນ ແລະ ແລ້ວເອົາລົງ
ລ້າງ ເອົາໄປໃຫ້ ຍາ ຕົ້ມ- ນ້ຳປາໃສ່ ແລ້ວເອົາ
ເທົ່າທີ່ລ້າງມາໃຫ້ມັນ ຢູ່ ລົງໄປ ຫລືໝາກ
ຂີ້ຫູດ- ໝາກຖົ່ວ ພວກເຂົາເອີ້ນ ຖົ່ວ- ງາ ປັ່ນລົງ
ໃສ່ ຖ້າ ໃຫ້ເອົານ້ຳ ຕົ້ມ ຢູ່ ຫົວ ເຖິງ
ຈາກນັ້ນ ໝາກຂີ້ຫູດ ລົງ ຫາໃສ່ ຫົວ ໝາກ
ໂຮງໝໍ ນຳໄປໃຊ້ ຫາຍ

ຂໍ້ລະວັງ— ຫ້າມເອົານ້ຳ ຫາຍ- ພວກເຂົາ
ຂີ້- ລາຍ ເຂົ້າ- ໃຫຍ່- ໝາກ- ປີ
ຜົມ ພຽງ ຕົ້ມ ແຕ່ ດີ

Sa Thao **Recipe 81**

ALGAE MIXED WITH OTHER INGREDIENTS

Ingredients

1 fistful* of *thao* (a dark green kind of algae, see page 25)—wash, pick out any foreign matter and squeeze out the water

minced pork, a quantity the size of a duck's egg; 3 soupspoonfuls of sesame seeds } parched in a hot pan without fat and then pounded finely

1 round eggplant

3 spring onion bulbs

1 (small) head of garlic, placed in the embers of a charcoal fire until almost cooked (and then peeled); 1 fresh red chilli pepper, seeded } finely chopped

1 handful of small shrimps (*koung foi*, a very small freshwater species)—pick off heads and tails, and wash

chopped coriander leaves

salt and fish sauce

1 bowl of meat broth

chopped spring onion leaves

Method

Put a small amount of the meat broth in a bowl and the pounded minced pork, to produce a fairly liquid mixture. Sprinkle it with salt and fish sauce. Chop the washed *thao* so that it is not all stuck together, and stir it into the mixture. Add also the chopped spring onion bulbs, garlic and eggplant, the shrimps and the pounded sesame seeds. If the mixture is too thick, put in some more meat broth. Taste, and check the saltiness. Add the chopped spring onion leaves. Dish up on a platter, garnish with the chopped coriander and serve.

Note

Sa Thao must be served with *mak kheng khom* (a very small variety of eggplant which may be red in colour and has a bitter taste—see page 33); *man neng phao* (grilled *man neng* flowers, see page 32); rice cakes (page 22); puffy pork or water-buffalo skin; grilled pork meat; and mangoes (in their immature, very small state).

* Editors' Note. A *pan* (translated as fistful) refers to something which may be a paste or of sticky consistency, e.g. sticky rice or a sticky mass of ripe tamarind flesh from which one needs to squeeze out the water and bitter taste, the amount being the capacity of a man's hand loosely closed.

ສ໑– ຂອງມາຕົ້ນເກມໂຈ່ທັ່ນຫັກ

ຫລັກປະຫັນ — ຕົ້ນເກມເຫຼົ່ານີ້ ລົມໃນແລ້ວນຸ່ງຫົ່ມໃຫ້ສຽງເພາະເຂົ້າມາ ລ່າງນັກໂທດສະໝຸດ ທັ່ນໃຫ້ຫັກຕາມຫູແລ້ວ ຈູໃຜບໍຕ່ານ ລາວເຫຼົ່ານັ້ນ ທົວແຫັກທ່ອງເພາະເຫຼົ່ານັ້ນ ແຫັກຫຼາຍ ເພາະເຫຼົ່ານັ້ນ ທອງກາທອງຄືນ ເພາະເຫຼົ່ານັ້ນ ຕ່າງ ສາມສ່ວນ ເຊັ່ນ– ນັກປາບແຫັກທ່ອງຈູ ແຫັກທາງມາ ແຫັກບໍ່ເປັນ

ຈຸດທີ່ຄື — ເມື່ອເຄົ້າເຂົ້າໄດ້ລ້ຽງເສືອ ກໍໄດ້ເອົາເນື້ອທາງຂົ້ນສິງ ໃນ ນັກໂທດສອງຕອນເອົາເກືອແລະຄ່າໃຊ້ ນັ້ນ ນັກສູ້ຈາກເອົາຕົ້ນເກມສົງ ແຕ່ເພີ່ມເຕີມເອົາໄປເພາະນໍ້າ ໃນຕ່າງໆ ~~[illegible]~~ ຈູ້ຫຼາແລ້ວກໍເລີ່ມນັກປາກຽເລີກນໍ້າ ຂອງມາໃປຈົນຕົ້ນເກມ ~~[illegible]~~ ເຊິ່ງຂອງ ຕາມຂອງມາວ່າ ເປັນຕ່ອນທັ່ງງານ ໂດຍຈາກແຫັກນັ້ນແຫັກການນຳ ໂຮງແຮມ ສ່ວນນັກເພາະກໍໄດ້ຕາມນັກນັ້ນຖືນ

ເຫຼົ່ານັ້ນຈຽງສາຂາທີ່ສະຫຼຸບ ແລ້ວຕາກໂກຼບ ທາງທົ່ວນໍ້າໃນແລະແຫັກເມື່ອທາຄືນ ແຫັກນີ້ໃນແຫັກ ທ່ວໂຮງນໍ້າ– ຍົກເຫັນທ່າໂຫ້ຮູ້ຄວາມເລືອກຕົວລົງຮ້ອນ ໆ ກົງຕ່ອງສົມ

ທອງຖິ່ນ — ຂອງມາຕົ້ນບາກນີ້ ແຕ່ກ່ອນນອກໂຈ່ກະທົ່ ແຫ່ງຂາງພະເຈົ້າມາກໂຮງຮູ້ການເຫັນ ນັ້ນນັກນັ້ນ ທາງເຂົ້າໃນ ເພາະວ່າຕົ້ນເກມຈະເປັນ ກໍ ກາຍຂອງທາງຫຼຽງເມື່ອນັ້ນແລ້ວ ນັກກະທົ່ຈາກຫຼາ ເປັນນັກສົມບົນຕົ້ນເກມກໍເອງ ນັ້ນນັ້ນຂອງການໃນເກົ່າ ກູ້ທາງຈາກເມືອງນັກນັ້ນເທົ່າໃນຄູ່ທາງນຳໃຊ້ມາ ກູ້ຄົວຊຸ່ມແລະ ບໍ່ໃນລອງຕາກມາຂອງມາເຫັນເກມ ຈະຊາວກາວ

Om Teen Moo Sai No Hok **Recipe 82**

PIG'S TROTTER WITH BAMBOO SHOOTS

Ingredients

1 pig's trotter—singe it over a flame, scrape off all the hair, remove the nails and wash it
1 bamboo shoot (*mai pai hok*, page 41), boiled until it loses its taste, then cut into bite-size pieces
1 handful of peeled shallots
1 handful of peeled garlic (cloves)
1 handful of shelled peanuts
3 slices of young galingale
salt, fish sauce and ground black pepper
chopped spring onion leaves
chopped coriander leaves

Method

After preparing all the ingredients, put a pot on the fire. Put a considerable amount of water in it and add salt and the slices of galingale. When the water comes to the boil, put in the pig's trotter, the shallots, garlic, peanuts and sliced bamboo shoot. When the water comes back to the boil, sprinkle in some fish sauce and let it go on boiling until the trotter is tender. Then take the trotter out and cut it into pieces of medium size. Arrange these on a platter and garnish with ground black pepper and chopped coriander leaves

As for the soup, spoon out the fat or strain it through a clean white thin cloth and put the remaining broth in a soupbowl with the bamboo shoots, shallots, and peanuts (etcetera). Garnish with ground black pepper and the chopped spring onion leaves. Serve it while still hot, with *Jaew Som* (see page 48).

Note

When *No hok* was made in former times it was common to add an extraction of coconut milk, but when I experimented (with this method) I found that there was too much fat. The reason is that it takes a long time for the trotter to become tender, and by that time the cream of the coconut extraction would have separated and the trotter itself would also have given out a lot of fat. The surface of the soup in the bowl would therefore be full of fat, and would not look appetising and pleasant.

If this dish is prepared for guests, the pieces of bamboo shoot should be arranged around the pieces of pig's trotter. This will make it more beautiful.

໔໓ - ຕົ້ນຜັກກະລໍ່າປີ

ເຄື່ອງປະສົມ — ຕົ້ນປີນເນື້ອເຄື່ອງ ລົບໃບເພື່ອເລາະເລື່ອງອອກ ສ່ວນທີ່ເຫຼືອ
ສະອາດໃຫ້ ຜັກບົ່ວຫົວປົ່ນເລາະເນື້ອສຳ ຜັກບົ່ວຫົວ
ໃຫຍ່ຈືນລອງເນາອເນື້ອເຫຼືອ ຜັກຊູບເລາະເນື້ອສຳ
ຜັກທັ່ງລຽງເລື່ອງສາມຕົ້ນລ່ວງມາຍູ່ໃຫ້ ຜັກຫອມ
ສາມຕົ້ນມີຫູກັນລ່ວງມາ ກະລໍ່າປີນ້ຳຫົວເນົ່າ
ຊີລ່ວງມາ ໃບຜັກບົ່ວໄປ ໃບຜັກຫອມໄປ
ຜັກມີປົ່ນ ເກືອ - ມາກປົກ ຫົວຜັກເພີ້ກປ່ວກ
ເປື່ອນເນົ່າຊີລ່ວງມາ

ວິທີເຮັດ — ໃຫ້ເອົາມາກໍ່ໃສ່ເນັ້ນແກງອີ່ນໃນ ເກືອ - ເກົວ ຜັກຕ່າງໆ ໃສ່
ນຳເນັ້ນພູ້ໃຫ້ຕົ້ນປີນມາປົກໃສ່ເລັກນ້ອຍ ຜັກບົ່ວ
ຫົວຫອມລົງອອກມາໃປປັ້ນ ຈນຕົ້ນປີນເປື່ອຍອ່ອນ ຈຶ່ງ
ເອົາຕົ້ນປີນອອກມາຕົບຕ່ອນເນື້ອງາໃຫ້ງາມ ຊຸບ
ປີຫົວຜັກສາກອອກມາ ອ່ອນຕົ້ນປີນ ເນື້ອນີ້ຜັກ
ຫອມໃສ່ໜ້າ ສ່ວນນ້ຳໃຫ້ຈືນເນື້ອເຄົາມາຈາກນ້ຳ
ແຊ່ ຫົວໃສ່ໃສ່ແກງຜັກບົ່ວໃສ່ໜ້າ ຮັກ
ເອົາຕົ້ງໃຫ້ຮ້ອນກາຍ ກັບເຂົ້າສົ້ມ

Teen Moo Om Kalampi **Recipe 83**

PIG'S TROTTER WITH CABBAGE

Ingredients

1 pig's trotter—singe it over a flame, then scrape off all the hair, remove the nails and wash it
1 handful of peeled shallots
1 large onion, sliced vertically
1 handful of peeled garlic (cloves)
3 straight-bulbed spring onions, washed and tied into a loose knot
3 sprigs of coriander, washed and tied together
1 head of cabbage, quartered and washed
chopped spring onion leaves
chopped coriander leaves
salt, fish sauce and ground black pepper
(1) Chinese radish (page 42), cut into four sections and washed

Method

Put some water in a pot and put the pot on the fire, adding salt and the various 'head vegetables' (presumably meaning the shallots, garlic, cabbage and Chinese radish). When the water comes to the boil, put in the trotter and a sprinkling of fish sauce as well as the spring onions and onion. Leave it to go on boiling until the trotter is well cooked and tender. Then take it out, slice the meat into large pieces and arrange them on a platter. Dispose the cabbage and other vegetables around the meat, and garnish with ground black pepper and some of the spring onion leaves.

As for the liquid left in the pot, taste it to check the saltiness, pour it into a soup bowl and garnish it with the rest of the chopped spring onion. Serve with *Jaew Som* (see page 48).

໘໔ – ໄກ່ໜຶ້ງໝາກກາເຂືອເຄື່ອງ

ເຄື່ອງປະສົມ – ໄກ່ປອກກະດູກອອກແລ້ວໜຶ່ງໂຕ ພ້ອມທັງຈັກໄສ້ອອກໝົດ ແລະ ປິ້ງເອົາມັນປົງກົ້ນກີ້ນ ລ້າງນ້ຳໃຫ້ສະອາດ ຈັກສົ່ງ ຂາຂອງກະດູກເປັນຂາໄລະຊີ້ຕ່ອນ ສ່ວນຊີ້ນຜ່າຕາໃສ່ກໍໃຫ້ ຕັດເປັນສາມຕ່ອນ ຄັ້ນໝາກພ້າວຫຍ້ ແລະ ເສື້ອໝາກ ນຳໃຊ້ ໝາກເຜັດຫົວໃຫຍ່ເໝົ້ງເມັດ ຫຼືລາບຍາວ (ໝາກເຜັດຫົວປ້ອມແກະເມັດອອກ ໝາກເຜັດລາບເນື້ອກົ້ງ) ຂອງສອງເມັດ ນ້ຳຊີ້ນໄກ່ ມັນໝົມ ນຳເຖີ້ງຂອງ ໝາກເຜັດ ລາບເລີຍເທົ່າທ້ອງກີອາເນົ້າຫຼາໃຫ້ແຕ່ຕັດເປັນຕ່ອນ ນັ້ນ ນ້ຳມັນໝູ ໝາກກາເຂືອເຄື່ອງເນື້ອງຽງນັ້ນ ເກືອ - ນ້ຳປາ - ໃບໝາກຫອມນ້ອຍ ພັກສີປັ່ນ

ວິທີເຮັດ – ໃຫ້ເອົາເອັນຂາງອັນຕາງໄຟ ນ້ຳມັນໝູໝາໃຊ້ເນື້ອ ແຕ່ງນ້ຳງົວ ເອົາຫົວໝາກເຜັດຫຼາ ໃສ່ລົງຈີ່ ຈີ່ນໍ່ ນ້ຳຫອມເອົາຕ່ອນໃຫ້ຫອມໄວ້ ໝາກເຜັດບາວໃຫຍ່ກົ້ງ ເອົານ້ຳປາຮອງຈີບ ນ້ຳໄກ່ຕ່າງ ຈຶ່ງເອົາຍັດໝາກກາເຂືອເຄື່ອງໃສ່ແລ້ວ ໃຫ້ເອົາກັນນ້ຳຫອມ ກໍເອົານ້ຳຕົ້ມຈົນຮວງ ນຳລົງຕ່ອນ ໝາກເຜັດຈີ່ນ ໝາກເຜັດລາບຈີ່ນລົງ ຄົນຮ່ວມໄປ ຈົນໄກ່ສຸກຈົນເຫຼືອງເຄັມຈາງນໍ້າແຫ້ງ ແລ້ວໃຫ້ຈານ ໝາກສີປັ່ນ ຫອມນ້ອຍໃສ່ເທິງ ນ້ຳ ເສີບຕັ້ງໄດ້ຮັບປະທານ

Kai Pad Mak Kheua Khua Dong **Recipe 84**

FRIED CHICKEN WITH TOMATO SAUCE

Ingredients

1 chicken, washed and gutted and divided into two—then cut each leg into four parts and each breast into three parts, and rub crushed garlic, salt and ground black pepper into all the parts
1 large onion, sliced vertically
(1 handful of peeled shallots
1 handful of peeled garlic cloves)* } fry these two ingredients in fat until they are pale yellow
5 straight-bulbed spring onions, crushed and cut into small pieces
(1½ to 2 soupspoonfuls) pork fat
1 small can of tomato paste
salt, fish sauce and ground black pepper
chopped coriander leaves

Method

Heat a soupspoonful of pork fat in a wok. Fry the crushed spring onion in it. When it gives off a good aroma, put in the chicken pieces and the sliced onion and sprinkle fish sauce over them. Leave the mixture to cook until the liquid is reduced, and then add the tomato paste. Stir until a good aroma is given off, then add just enough meat broth to cover the chicken. Add the shallots and garlic. Let it all continue to boil until the chicken is cooked. Taste, and check the saltiness. Then dish up on a platter, garnish with ground black pepper and chopped coriander leaves and serve.

* Editors' Note. The brackets are Phia Sing's. He used such brackets very rarely and the reason for their presence here is not clear.

໕໒.໑ ໄກ່ຜູ້ສົ້ມ [illegible]

ເຄື່ອງປະສົມ — ໄກ່ [illegible] ຜ່າທ້ອງ [illegible]
[illegible]
ສະອາດ [illegible] ເປັນ [illegible]
[illegible] ສ່ວນ [illegible]
[illegible]
[illegible]
[illegible]
[illegible]
[illegible]

[illegible]
[illegible]
[illegible]
[illegible]
[illegible]

ວິທີເຮັດ — [illegible]
[illegible]
[illegible]
[illegible]
[illegible]
[illegible]
[illegible]
[illegible]
[illegible]

Kai Pad Som Mak Kheua Khua Sod **Recipe 85**

FRIED CHICKEN WITH FRESH TOMATOES

Ingredients

1 chicken—wash it, gut it and cut off the feet; cut each leg into four parts and each breast into three; break and cut to divide the wings at the joints; tear off (and discard) the inside lining of the gizzard, then wash and slice the gizzard and the liver—then put all the pieces together and rub into them crushed garlic, salt and ground black pepper
5 (small) shallots, peeled and crushed
10 straight-bulbed spring onions—wash them, after stripping off any withered leaves, then cut off the bulbs, making the cuts as close as possible to the point at which the green part divides into the leaves—crush the bulbs on the chopping-board, cut off the green parts attached to them and reserve these separately*
1 large onion, sliced vertically
3 ripe tomatoes, sliced vertically and seeded
1 spring onion, the leaves only, cut into long sections
3 sprigs of coriander—pick off only the leaves and young shoots
salt, fish sauce and ground black pepper
pork fat (1 tbsp)

Method

Heat a spoonful of pork fat in a wok. When it is hot, put in the shallots, fry them until they give off a fragrant aroma, then add the chicken pieces, stir, and sprinkle salt and fish sauce over them. Add the sliced onion and continue cooking until the chicken begins to dry out and gives off a good aroma. Then add the crushed spring onion bulbs and a little meat broth, just enough to keep the chicken moist. Add also the sliced tomatoes. When the dish is almost cooked, taste, and check the saltiness. Then add the spring onion leaves, take the wok off the fire, transfer its contents to a platter, garnish with coriander leaves and ground black pepper, and serve.

* Editors' Note. The reserved green parts of the 10 spring onions are not mentioned in the instructions. Phia Sing may have intended them to be kept for use in a soup, or he may simply have forgotten to add them to the present dish, e.g. when the sliced tomatoes are put in.

96 - ວິທີເຮັດແໜມຫົວຜັກບົ່ວ

ເຄື່ອງປະສົມ — ຊີ້ນໝູເນື້ອສ່ວນທີ່ເປັນມັນ ລ້າງໃຫ້ສະອາດ ເອົາມາຊອຍເປັນຕ່ອນ ຂະໜາດສາມາດ. ກະທຽມເຫຼືອງ ເພາະ ທ່ອນໆ ເນື້ອຊີ້ນເປັນຕ່ອນງາມໃຫ້ຮຽບຮ້ອຍ ເຄື່ອງ ເກືອ - ພິກໄທປົ່ນ ພິກຂີ້ໜູແຫ້ງໃສ່ - ຫົວຜັກບົ່ວດອງ ປອກແລະຊອຍ ປົ່ນເປັນເຂົ້າຈ່ອມເປັນກ້ອນໃຫຍ່

ຜັກຫອມແລະເຂົ້າໜົມປັ້ນຈີ່ ເຫຼົ້າສົມ ໃຫ້ກະ ຜັດແກ ບົ່ວດອງໃຫຍ່ຊອຍບາງ ເນື້ອດອງ ພັກບົ່ວ ລາງເຂົ້າສຸກ ຂູດໃຫ້ຍັງໃຍຍູ່ເລືອຈາງ ທ່ານທີ່ສົ້ມ ສອນມີໃບຍູ່ອ່ອນ ໃນທັດຫົວຊຽວບໍ່ ພິກຫອມເຄື່ອງເອົາແຕ່ໃບຊາ ສາມແກ ທາຫານ່ອນເທົາ ເຄື່ອງທ່ອນ ເຂົ້າແຕ່ ນ້ຳປາ ຜັກປາ - ພິກປັ່ນ ນ້ຳຫມັນ

ວິທີເຮັດ — ໃຫ້ເອົານ້ຳມັນໝູໃສ່ໃນ ຂຶ້ນໄຟ ພໍນ້ຳ ມັນຮ້ອນເອົາຫົວຜັກບົ່ວລົງ ເຂົ້າ ຈຶ່ງໃສ່ກະທຽມ ຊີ້ນໝູ ຂົ້ວໄປ ນ້ຳປາ ຈົນ ຊີ້ນແຫ້ງ ແລະ ຫອມດີແລ້ວ ຈຶ່ງເອົາ ຜັກບົ່ວ ຫົວໃຫຍ່ ໃສ່ ນ້ຳ ທຳ ເມື່ອສຸກ ຕ່ອນ ຈຶ່ງ ຊອຍເປັນເສັ້ນ ຕາມ ໃສ່ ຜັກ ໃສ່ ສາ ຕັກໃສ່ຈານ ພິກ ຜັກຫອມ ໂຮຍໜ້າ ແລ້ວ ນຳໄປຕັ້ງໂຕະຮັບປະທານ

Sin Moo Pad Houa Phak Boua **Recipe 86**

FRIED PORK WITH ONION

Ingredients

1 piece of pork, about the size of a hand, sliced into pieces measuring 3 by 1.5 cm—make sure that you cut it into pieces which look nice—then rub salt ground black pepper and crushed garlic into them
1 large handful of peeled shallots } these two ingredients to
1 handful of peeled garlic cloves } be fried until pale golden
1 large onion, sliced vertically
10 straight-bulbed spring onions—cut off the bulbs as far up towards the leaves as possible, then divide what you have cut off into the bulbs themselves and the adjacent green parts, and reserve both of these separately
3 (more) spring onions, leaves only, chopped
3 sprigs of coriander—pick off the leaves only
half a fully ripe coconut—grate the meat and make only one extraction of coconut milk
salt, fish sauce and ground black pepper
pork fat (1 spoonful)

Method

Put a spoonful of pork fat in a wok and put the wok on the fire. When the fat is hot, fry in it the bulbs of the (10) spring onions and the pieces of pork. Continue frying and sprinkle fish sauce on it. When the pieces of pork are beginning the dry out and are giving off a good aroma, add the onion, together with enough coconut milk to cover the meat.

When the meat is cooked, taste, and check the saltiness. Add the spring onion leaves, dish up on a platter, garnish with ground black pepper and coriander leaves, and serve.

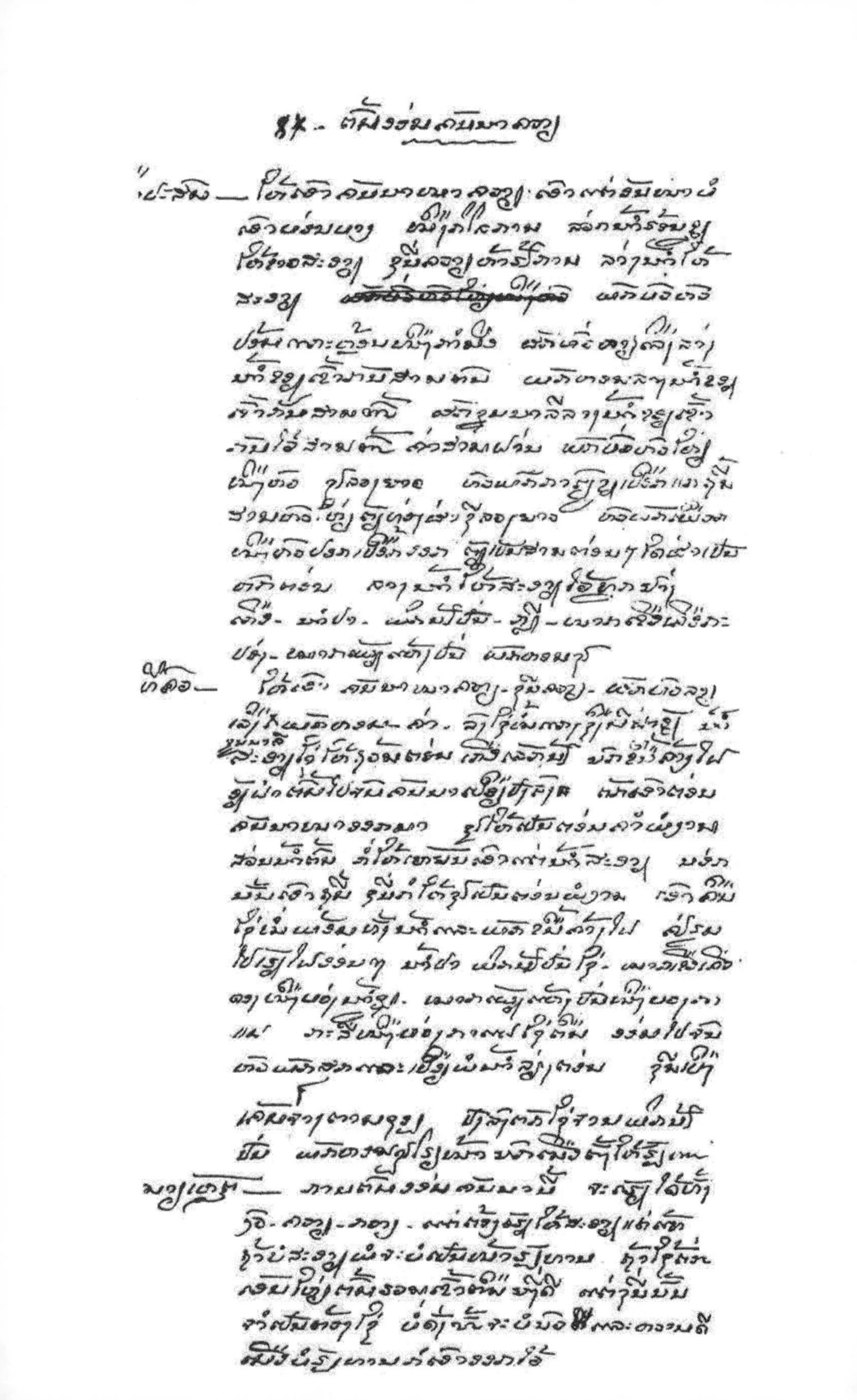

໘໗ - ຕົ້ນອ່ອນ[illegible]

ປະສົມ — ໃຫ້ເອົາ [illegible]

[illegible]

ວິທີທຳ — ໃຫ້ເອົາ [illegible]

[illegible]

ໝາຍເຫດ — [illegible]

[illegible]

Tom Om Kanna Kuai **Recipe 87**

SLOW-COOKED WATER-BUFFALO TRIPE

Ingredients

1 kilo thick water-buffalo tripe—not including any thin tripe—blanch in boiling water and scrape until white and clean
500 grams water-buffalo meat, washed
1 handful peeled shallots
3 spring onions, washed and each tied into a loose knot
3 sprigs of coriander, washed and tied together
3 stalks of celery, washed and tied together
3 slices galingale
1 large onion, sliced vertically
3 large carrots—scrape off the hard outer skins, cut each carrot across into two halves, and then cut each half into quarters lengthways
1 Chinese radish—peel and cut across into three, then cut each of the three sections into six parts lengthways, and wash all the pieces
salt, fish sauce and ground black pepper
curry (powder, 1 coffeespoonful)
canned tomato paste (1 soupspoonful)
ground dried chilli pepper (1 coffeespoonful)
chopped coriander

Method

Put the tripe, the meat, the spring onions, the celery, the coriander and the galingale into a pot with a lid, and add enough clean water to cover these ingredients. Sprinkle a little salt over them and put the pot on the fire. Cover, and leave to boil until the tripe is tender. Then remove the pot from the fire, take out the tripe and cut it into bite-size pieces.

As for the soup, pour (into the container, slowly,) the contents of the pot, so that you keep only the clear broth and throw away the rest, (except for the meat). Cut the meat into suitable slices and return it to the pot along with the soup and vegetables. Simmer over a low fire. Then sprinkle with fish sauce, ground black pepper, the soupspoonful of canned tomato paste, the ground dried chilli pepper and the curry (powder). Cook slowly until the vegetables are cooked and tender and the liquid has been reduced to an amount just sufficient to keep the meat from drying out. Taste, and check the saltiness. Take the pot from the fire, dish up on a platter, garnish with chopped coriander and serve.

Note

Tom Om Kanna may be made with the tripes of cow, water-buffalo or deer; but one must clean them very thoroughly or else the dish will not look appetising. If large tendons of the animal could be included in the boiled ingredients, it would be even better.

We have to put in the meat, otherwise the flavour of the dish would not be exactly right. If a person does not like the meat, he can put it aside.

໔໔- ໄກ່ຕົ້ມຫົວພັກກາດສົ້ມ

ເຄື່ອງປະສົມ — ໄກ່ປ່ອຍຕົວອ້ວນເນື້ອ ໑ ຕົວ ເອົາທ້ອງ ເອົາໄສ້ອອກ ລ້າງນ້ຳໃຫ້ສະອາດ ຫົວພາກກາດສົ້ມ ປີ້ນອອກ ເທົ່າ ເທົ່າ ລ້າງນ້ຳສົ້ມ ໑ ຖ້ວຍ ຕົ້ນຜັກບົ່ວ ປອກເປືອກ ເທົ່າ ໒ ລ້າງ ນ້ຳ ສອງຖ້ວຍ ຫົວຂີງ ປອກເປືອກ ເທົ່າ ໂຕ ລ້າງນ້ຳ ສອງຖ້ວຍ ກະລຳປີ ຊອຍ ໝາກພ້າວ ອອກ ລ້າງນ້ຳ ໃຫ້ສະອາດ ກະລຳປີ ຫົວ ເທົ່າ ໒ ລ້າງນ້ຳ ຜັກຊີ ນ້ຳປາ ລ້າງນ້ຳສະອາດ ຜັກຫອມ ເທົ່າ ເມືອ ເນື້ອ ໑ ຕົວ ຜັກບົ່ວ ເຂົ້າ ຊອຍ ລ້າງນ້ຳ ຂີ້ເກືອ ເທົ່າ ໂຕ ຜັກຫອມ ຊອຍ ລ້າງນ້ຳ ສາມຕົ້ນ ເກືອ - ນ້ຳປາ - ພິກໄທປົ່ນ ໃສ່ພໍສົມຄວນ ໃສ່ ພໍສົມຄວນ

ວິທີເຮັດ — ໃຫ້ເອົານ້ຳສະອາດ ໃສ່ໝໍ້ ປະມານ ເຄິ່ງໝໍ້ ຕັ້ງໄຟ ໃຫ້ຟົດ ແລ້ວ ຈຶ່ງເອົາໄກ່ ແລະ ຫົວພັກກາດສົ້ມ ລົງໃສ່ ຕົ້ມໄວ້ ພໍຕົວ ເນື້ອເຄິ່ງສຸກ ຈຶ່ງເອົາເຄື່ອງ ໃສ່ ພໍສົມຄວນ ທຸກຢ່າງ ໃສ່ ຈົນໄກ່ ແລະ ຫົວພັກກາດສົ້ມ ສຸກດີ ຈຶ່ງຍົກລົງ ຈາກເຕົາໄຟ ໃສ່ ຖ້ວຍ ໃຫ້ ໄກ່ ຂອງ ເປັນຕ່ອນ ຈານ ລົງ ຖ້ວຍ ແລະ ຈຶ່ງເອົາ ຫົວພັກກາດ ໃສ່ ຕ່ອມ ພັກຫອມ ຊອຍ ໃສ່ ສ່ວນເນື້ອ ກັບ ໄກ່ ຈຶ່ງ ແຕ່ງ ພັກບົ່ວ ພັກຫອມ ໃສ່ ເປັນ ນຳກັນ ຕັ້ງ ໄວ້ ກິນ ແຊ່ ສົ້ມ

Kai Tom Houa Phak Sao Souan **Recipe 88**

BOILED CHICKEN, COUNTRY STYLE

Ingredients

1 chicken, washed and gutted
10 carrots, washed and halved
2 Chinese radishes, peeled, quartered and washed
2 kohlrabi (the turnip-shaped part at the bottom of the stem), peeled, quartered and washed
10 flowerlets of cauliflowers
½ a small cauliflower, quartered and washed
2 stalks of celery—cut off the roots and wash
1 large onion, quartered
4 straight-bulbed spring onions } cut off the roots
3 sprigs of coriander } and wash
salt, fish sauce and ground black pepper
chopped spring onion leaves
chopped coriander leaves

Method

Put approximately 1 large soupbowl (1¼ to 1½ pints) of water in a pot with a little salt, then put the pot on the fire. When the water comes to the boil, put in the chicken and the vegetables (i.e. the carrots, Chinese radishes, kohlrabi, cauliflower, celery and onion) and cover the pot. When the vegetables have started to shrink down, sprinkle some fish sauce into the pot, then cover it again and leave it until the chicken and vegetables are well cooked. Taste, and check the saltiness.

Next, take the pot off the fire, remove the chicken, cut it into suitable pieces and arrange these in the middle of a platter. Dispose the various vegetables around the chicken pieces. Garnish the chicken pieces with ground black pepper and chopped coriander leaves. Put the soup in a soup bowl and garnish it with black pepper and the chopped spring onion leaves. Serve with *Jaew Som* (see page 48)

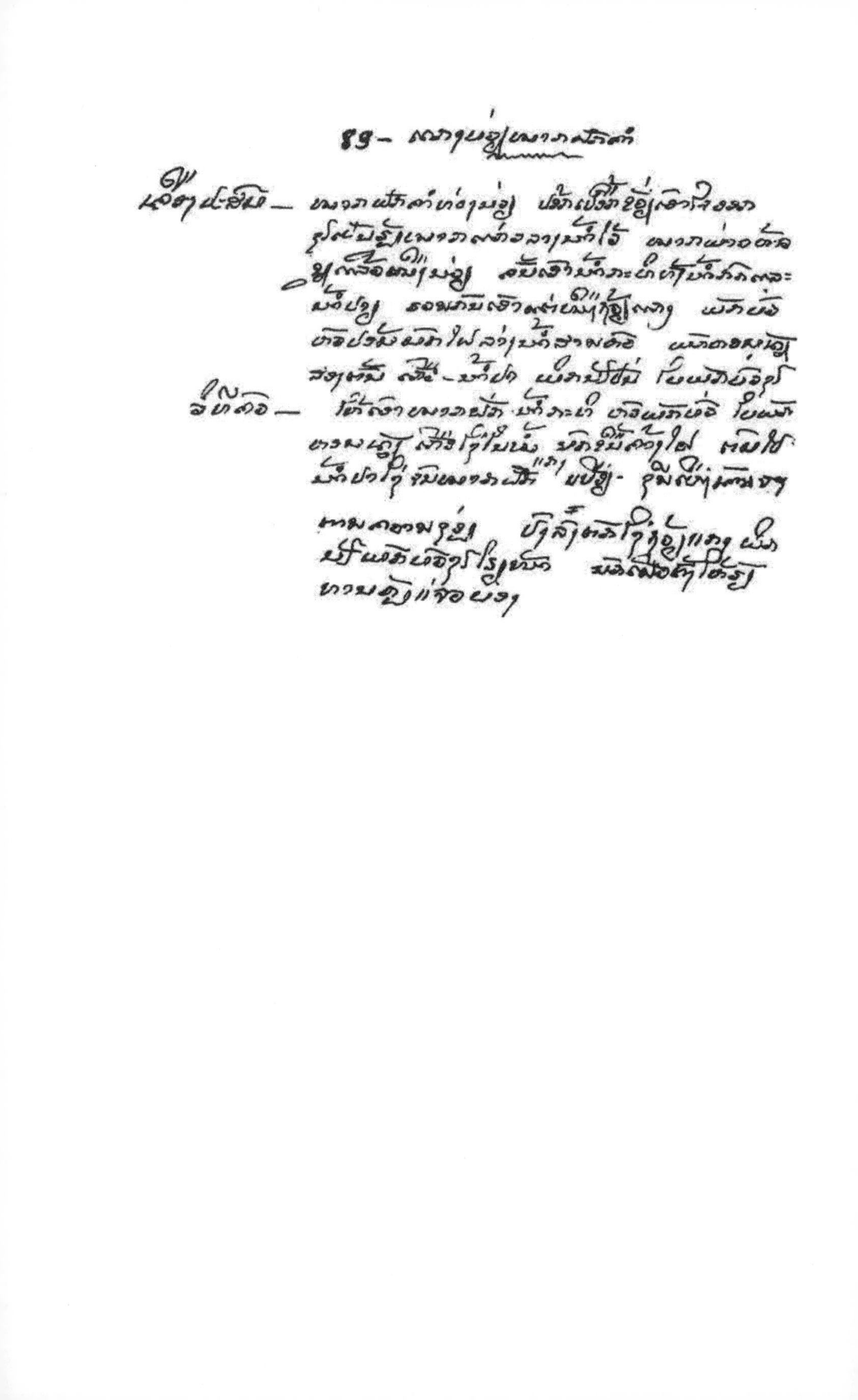

໔໑ – ເລື່ອງ [illegible]

ເນື້ອ[illegible] — [illegible]

ຂໍ້[illegible] — [illegible]

Keng Bouad Mak Fak Kham **Recipe 89**

PUMPKIN AND COCONUT MILK SOUP

Ingredients

half a pumpkin—peel it, take out the seeds and the soft centre, cut it into bite-size pieces and wash them

1 fully ripe coconut—grate the meat and make one soupbowl of the first and second extractions of coconut milk combined

3 (small) shallots, cooked in the embers of a charcoal fire and then washed

2 sprigs of coriander—pick only the leaves and the tender parts of the stems

salt, fish sauce and ground black pepper

chopped spring onion leaves

Method

Put the sliced pumpkin, the two extractions of coconut milk, the shallots, the picked coriander and a sprinkling of salt into a pot. Then put the pot on the fire and let it come to the boil. Sprinkle some fish sauce over it and leave it to cook until the pumpkin is tender. Taste, and check the saltiness, then take the pot from the fire. Transfer the soup to a (large) soup bowl, garnish it with ground black pepper and chopped spring onion, and serve it with *Jaew Bong* (see recipe 64).

A pumpkin, *mak fak kam*, (?) HODGSONIA MACROCARPA.

໑໐ - [illegible]

[illegible] — [illegible]

[illegible]

[illegible]

[illegible]

[illegible] — [illegible]

[illegible]

[illegible]

[illegible]

[illegible]

[illegible] — [illegible]

[illegible]

[illegible]

[illegible]

[illegible]

[illegible]

[illegible]

[illegible]

[illegible]

[illegible]

[illegible]

Hum Ped Sai Hed Saed **Recipe 90**

SLOW-COOKED DUCK WITH ORANGE MUSHROOMS

1 duck, washed and gutted—cut off the two legs and two breasts; discard the intestines, but keep the liver, gizzard and heart; remove and discard the inner lining of the gizzard; wash the gizzard thoroughly; cut the legs and breasts into two parts each; cut the neck into large pieces—rub salt and ground black pepper into all parts
1 large soupbowl of orange mushrooms (see page 44)—cut off the bottoms of the stems and wash in warm water
1 handful of peeled shallots
1 large onion, sliced vertically
5 straight-bulbed spring onions—cut off the roots, wash, cut off and crush the bulbs and divide them into halves
3 sprigs of coriander—pick off only the leaves and the tender parts of the stems
salt, fish sauce and ground black pepper
chopped spring onion leaves
chopped coriander leaves
pork fat (2 ladlefuls)

Method
Put the two ladlefuls of pork fat in a wok and put the wok on the fire. When the fat is hot, fry in it the pieces of duck, a few at a time, until the skin turns light golden. Remove the pieces from the wok before the blood exudes from the meat. When all the pieces of duck have been fried, put them in a pot which has a cover. Add the mushrooms, the shallots, the sliced onion, (the crushed spring onion bulbs) and the picked coriander. Sprinkle some salt and some water into the pot, then put it on the fire and let it cook over a medium heat. Sprinkle some fish sauce over it, and leave it to cook until the meat is tender. Taste, and check the saltiness. The liquid should be just enough almost to cover the meat.

Now mix in the chopped spring onion leaves, dish up on a platter, garnish with ground black pepper and chopped coriander leaves, and serve with *Jaew Som* (see page 48).

໑໔- ຂົວເຣື່ອງທີ່ນ

ເຄື່ອງປະສົມ — ຊີ້ນເນລະກາຍເນັ້ນເນື້ອຕ່ອນເທົ່າຟ້າມື ລ່ວງ ມັກໄດ້ຂະ-
ຫນາ ຊູປສົ້ມຕ່ອນ ມັງເນັ້ງງາມ ເສົາເພິກພັດລຶອ ເຜັດ
ນຸ້ມມາ ບຸ້ງເນີ້ງ ຫົວ ຄົ້ນໃຈ້ ຊູບັ່ງໂລ້ ເຣັ່ງແສ້ງ ເນົ້າກອງ
ດິກໂດງໂຕ່ງ ຕຸ້ງຕົ້ນລ່າງ ມັກອຸ່ນໂຕ້ສະຂາງ
ເນອກ ພາະ ຫົວອຸ ເກືອ ເນື້ອນອູ່ ຄົ້ນເສົາກະທິ
ເນື້ອງ ໃສກແກ້ວ ມັກ (ເນາກ ເນ້ຍໃຈ ເທົ່າງ ເຫລາະ ເຕົ່າ ບອນ
ແຈ່ມ ເປື້ອງ ແສ້ ສາມ ມ່ອຍ ເພັກ ເນື້ອ ຕົວ ປອມ ເກົາເຫື່ອ)
ຊອງ ສອງ ເນື້ອງ ມີ້ ຄຳ ໄຈ້ ກັນ ໂຕ້ລະ ອັ້ງ ເອົ້ນ ຈ່າ ເຄື້ອ ຕອມ
ພິກາມ ປ່ຽນ- ເລື່ອ- ມັກປາ- ເພັກ ເນ້ອກ- ມັກ ສົ້ມ ບູເນ
ເພັກ ດອມ ນຸ.

ວິທີເຮັດ — ເອົາມັກ ສົ້ມ ໄຈ້ ເນັ້ງ ຂາງ ເນື້ອ ພອງ ວັ້ນ ຂ່າງ ໃສ່ ຈັ່ງເອົາ
ເຄື່ອງ ເກາະ ອນ ໄຈ້ ຂ້ອ ໄປ ຈັ່ນ ເກາະ ນ ຊູບັ່ງ ເນາລົງ ມັກປາ
ຣອງ ເນັ້ງ ຊູບັ່ງ ລາງ ເທື່ອ ຈັ່ງ ເອົາ ເຣັ່ງແສ້ງ ໄຈ້ ລົ້ນ
ໄຫ້ ສ້ອງ ມັກ ຈັ່ງ ເສົາກະທິ ໄຈ້ ເນັ້ງ ກອມ ຕ່ອນ
ເສື້ອ ເຣັ່ງ ສຸກ ເກືອ ຈັ່ງ ຊູ້ນ ເນື່ອງ ເກາະ ນ ພາງ ຕາມ ກູ່
ເພັກ ບ້ອງ ໄຈ້ ລົ້ນ ໂຕ້ ຫົວ ດຽວ ຈາງ ພິກ
ມັ້ນ ເພັກ ບາອມ ກູ ໃສ່ ເນົ້າ ຂນ ເສ້ອງ ຕ້ງ ໄດ້ ຮູ້ ເການ

Khoua Hed Saed **Recipe 91**

FRIED ORANGE MUSHROOMS

Ingredients

1 piece of pork, about the size of a hand, washed, sliced into suitable pieces and rubbed with salt, ground black pepper and crushed garlic
1 large soupbowl of orange mushrooms (see page 44)—cut off the bottoms of the stems and wash in warm water
1 fully ripe coconut—grate the meat and make one beakerful ($\frac{1}{2}$ pint) of coconut milk extraction
3 dried red chilli peppers, seeded and soaked in water until soft } these two ingredients to be pounded finely to constitute the
5 (small) shallots (peeled) } the *kheuang hom*
salt, fish sauce and ground black pepper
chopped spring onion
chopped coriander
pork fat (1 ladleful)

Method

Put the ladleful of pork fat in a wok and put the wok on the fire. Fry the *kheuang hom* in it until it gives off a good aroma, then add the pork and a sprinkling of fish sauce. When the pieces of pork begin to stiffen, add the mushrooms. Continue to cook, stirring, until the liquid has dried up, then add just enough of the coconut milk to cover the meat. When the mushrooms are cooked, taste, and check the saltiness. Add the chopped spring onion and stir thoroughly. Then dish up on a platter, garnish with the chopped coriander and ground black pepper, and serve.

໙໑ - [illegible] ຫົວໜັກ-ງວງຊ້ອນ

ເຊື້ອປະສົມ — ຫົວໜັກກາງຮຽງ ມູເປືອກລາງແມ່ ຊຶ່ງເປັນພັນຊື່ລູ່ມ
ໝື່ນກູ່ຊຽງມີ ຫົວໜັກເມືອກປ້ອມເປືອກລາງແມ່
ຊຶ່ງເປັນພັນຊື່ລູ່ມ ໝື່ນກູ່ຊຽງມີ ພັນພໍ່ຢູ່ປາກເປືອກລາງ
ແມ່ ຊຶ່ງເປັນພັນຊື່ລູ່ມ ໝື່ນກູ່ຊຽງມີ ລູກປີທອງ ຍູ່ເປັນຕອງ
ລາງແມ່ ໝື່ນກູ່ຊຽງມີ ໝາກຫົວລີ ຊົ່ວເວລາ ທົ່ງເຂດ
[illegible] ທາງລຳຊື່ເມືອ ໝື່ນກູ່ຊຽງມີ ຫົວໜັກທັງສູງທີ່ກ່າວນີ້
ໄດ້ຕາມໄວ້ແລ້ວຈົນເສີດ ເມື່ອຈາກເອົາ ອອກປາງແມ່ເກີດ
ປະໄວ້ເຂົ້າແກ່ແມ່ ຊຶ່ງເປັນພັນໄດ້ແທ້ກາກໍ່ໃຫ້ຢູ່ ຕົ້ນ
ໄຈ່ແມ່ປາ ສາກເກີດເລີ່ມ ຈາກການລາກໍໄດ້ລະອຽດ
ກ່ຽວກັບ ທາງຕົວລາງແມ່ໄດ້ສະຫຼຸບ ຊຶ່ງແມ່ພັນພ
ພໍ່ພັນກໍ່ໄດ້ສະຫຼຸບ ໝາກຫົວລີ ຂອງນີ້ ໝື່ນ ອອກຈົບ
ຂາວ ລາກໍໄດ້ສະຫຼຸບ [illegible] ປ່ອງແມ່ວ່າ ງາວຈົ່ງລາກໍລະ
ອຽດເສັງ ປ່ອງແມ່ວ່າ (ຫົວໜັກເມືອງ [illegible] ທາກົວ
ເພາະຫຼາຍແນວ ສາມທາງ ໝາກຕົ້ນຢູ່ ເທົ່າປີນີ້ ຂາງ ປອງ
ລາວເລີຍ) [illegible] ສາມ [illegible] ເວລາ ໄດ້ແກ່ [illegible] ເອີ້ນ
[illegible] ພັກທາງ [illegible] ໄດ້ແຍ່ໆ ຕົວຕົ້ນ
ໂຍພັກ [illegible] ໃຫ້ [illegible] ແມ້ຕົ້ນ ພັກ [illegible] ແລ້ວ
ແມ່ປາ ໃຫ້ [illegible] ເອົາ [illegible] ສ່ວນການ [illegible]

໑໙ ຂໍ້ດີ — ໃຫ້ເອົາ [illegible] ທີ່ [illegible] ໄວ້ເອີ້ນ ໃຫ້ [illegible] ເອົາແມ່ [illegible]
[illegible] ໃຫ້ [illegible] ໄດ້ [illegible] ເອົາ [illegible]
[illegible] ແມ່ [illegible] ສ່ວນ [illegible] ໄດ້ [illegible]
[illegible] ໃຫ້ [illegible] ໄດ້ [illegible] ແມ່ [illegible]
[illegible] ເຂົ້າ [illegible] ໄດ້ [illegible] ລະອຽ
[illegible] ໄດ້ [illegible] ເອົາ [illegible] ແມ່
[illegible] ໄດ້ເຂົ້າ [illegible] ເອົາ [illegible] ຫົວໜັກ [illegible]
[illegible] ໄດ້ [illegible] ເອົາແມ່ [illegible] ປະ [illegible]
[illegible] ໄດ້ [illegible] ຈາກ [illegible] ໄດ້ [illegible]
[illegible] ແມ່ [illegible] ເຂົ້າໃໝ່

ເໝາະສົມ — [illegible] ຫົວໜັກງວງຊ້ອນນີ້ [illegible] ໄດ້ [illegible]
[illegible] - ແມ່ [illegible] - ໄດ້ [illegible] - [illegible] - ເຂົ້າໃໝ່ ຈະມີ
[illegible] ໄດ້ [illegible] ແຕ່ເຂົ້າໃໝ່ [illegible]
[illegible] ຈະໄດ້ [illegible] ໃຫ້

Soop Houa Phak Sao Souan **Recipe 92**

MIXED COOKED VEGETABLES, COUNTRY STYLE

Ingredients

1 small rice-bowl of carrots, scraped, washed and diced 1 small rice-bowl of Chinese radishes, scraped, washed and diced 1 small rice-bowl of potatoes, scraped, washed and diced 1 small rice-bowl of cauliflower flowerets, washed 1 small rice-bowl of mange-tout French beans—string them and cut them into pieces the length of the joint of a finger	boil these vegetables with a pinch of salt until cooked, then rinse them with cold water and drain them

minced pork, a quantity the size of a duck's egg, boiled with a little fish sauce and then pounded finely
6 dried shrimps, washed and fried in pork fat until crisp, then pounded finely
3 soupspoonfuls of (shelled) peanuts, toasted in a hot, dry pan and then rubbed together so that their skins come off
2 soupspoonfuls of sesame seeds, toasted by stirring them over a medium heat in a (dry) pan, and then pounded finely

6 (small) shallots which have been cooked in the embers of a charcoal fire 3 (small) heads of garlic, also cooked in the embers of a charcoal fire ½ coffeespoonful of ground dried chilli pepper	these three ingredients to be pounded together finely to constitute the *kheuang hom mok*

5 sprigs of coriander, finely chopped
1 spring onion, the leaves only, finely chopped
salt, fish sauce and ground black pepper
4 hard-boiled duck's eggs—separate the yolks and chop up the whites
(meat broth)

Method

Put the *kheuang hom mok* in a big bowl, add a small amount of meat broth and stir until they are mixed. Add, together, the other pounded ingredients, with salt and fish sauce. Pound the yolks of the duck's eggs and mix them in also. Taste and check the saltiness—the mixture should be quite salty. (Make sure also that) it is not too runny. Sprinkle in the chopped onion, the chopped coriander and some ground black pepper, and mix thoroughly.

Put the boiled vegetables in a mixing bowl, together with the chopped whites of the duck's eggs. Pour the first mixture over the vegetables and mix thoroughly. Dish up on a platter and serve, accompanied by grilled pork and rice cakes.

Note

The accompaniments for *Soop Houa Phak Sao Souan* should be grilled pork (as mentioned above, and such as could be bought ready prepared in a Lao market), or fried chicken or grilled fish, and rice cakes. It may be served with one or more of these, but the rice cakes must not be omitted.

93 - ແກງສົ້ມໄກ່ປ່າ

ເຄື່ອງປະສົມ — ໄກ່ປ່າກະທ້ອນຂະໜາດເນື້ອຫົວ ແກ່ງທາງຈັກເຄົາໃສ່ຂອງ
ສົ້ມພັກ ເອົາໂຕສະອາດສົ້ມພັກເກືອ ຖົ່ວເຂົາມະກາຖົ່ວ
ເຂົ້າໜຽວຕອນແນ່ງາມ ສີໄກ່ ສົ້ມພັກຖົ່ວປ່ຽງກີ່

ເນື້ອຫົວຫຼາໂຫາແຕງ ແກ່ນເຂືອສາມເສົາສາມຫົວ
ຖົ່ວຮາກກຸ້ມລ່ວງນໍ້າ ຫຼາຫົວອີ່ຫ້າແທກ ຂີ່ຫຼີໃສ່ກັບເອົ້
ສົ້ມປອນເນື້ອໝູ່ ເຄື່ອງ ພັກປາ ແກ່ນເຂືອ

ວິທີເຮັດ — ໂຕເອົາມາໃຊ່ທໍ່ມເຄື່ອງເນື້ອກູ່ຫຼາງແກງໃຫ້ ຂຶ້ນເຄື່ອງ
ໃຟເພາະແກ່ນເຂືອຂີ່ ສີໄກ່ຫຼາເຄືອໃຊ້ ໂຫາພັກໃຫ້
ແລ້ວຈຶ່ງເອົາຕ່ອນໄກ່ລົງໄປ ພັກປາຮອງສູ່ຜ່າ
ຈົນໄກ່ສຸກດີ ຈຶ່ງເອົາຫຼາໃສ່ໃຊ່ສົ້ມປອນຈົນມາໄດ້
ຊີ້ວດາວໃຫ້ເອົາຂອກ ຊຸ່ມເນື້ອສົ້ມແກມຊວງດາວມ
ມາກິ ຕັກໃສ່ກອງເຄື່ອງແກ່ນເຂືອໄໃຫ້ເນົ້າ
ນອກເນື້ອຕໍ່ໃຫ້ຮູ້ຫາງນ ຂີ່ລົງໄກ່

ໝາຍເຫດ — ແກງສົ້ມໄກ່ນີ້ - ນາງທ່ານກໍຍັງ ໝາກດາ
ໝາກອອນ - ບໍ່ໃຊ່ - ບໍ່ເຫຼ - ໝາກດາເຂືອສົ້ມ - ກາໍປີ
ເລືອກນີ້ ຖົ່ວເຂົ້າກໍເຄື່ອງມາມັດເກືອ ສົ້ມສົ້ມປອນ
ບໍ່ໄດ້ເພາະສົ້ມມັນວ່າອາຫານສົ້ມ

Keng Som Kai Pa **Recipe 93**

SOUR WILD CHICKEN SOUP

Ingredients

1 (wild) chicken, washed and gutted and cut into suitable pieces
1 stalk of lemon grass—wash it, cut off the leaves and crush the main stalk only
3 straight-bulbed spring onions—cut off the roots, wash them and tie them into a loose knot
1 bunch of *som pon* (the leaves mentioned on page 36)
salt and fish sauce
chopped spring onion

Method

Put 1 large soupbowl (1¼ to 1½ pints) of water in a pot on the fire. Put in the knotted spring onions, the crushed stalk of lemon grass, and salt. When the water comes to the boil, add the pieces of chicken and sprinkle some fish sauce over them. Cover the pot and leave it cooking until the chicken is well done.

Next, dip the *som pon* into the soup, in a *padek* strainer (see page 17) and leave it in the soup for a short time (two or three minutes). Then remove the *som pon*, taste, and check the saltiness and sourness—the dish should be quite sour.

Transfer the contents of the pot to a (serving) bowl, garnish it with chopped spring onion and serve it with *Lap Kai* (Chicken *lap*, recipe 41).

Note

With *Keng Som Kai* young jackfruit (page 31) are sometimes served, as are pickled bamboo shoots, either finely chopped or in larger pieces; also fresh tomatoes and cabbage. As for making the dish sour, nothing can match *som pon*, which has just the right flavour.

໓໔ - ເຈົ້າປ່ອຍນົກຍູງ

ເລື່ອງປະສົມ — ຍູງທີ່ລັກຈັບມາຂາຍທົ່ວເມືອງນັ້ນຄື ພໍ່ຄ້າທີ່ຢູ່ຈັກໂກະ
ເມືອງໃນຂອກໃກ້ໃຫ້ຫຼາຍແລ້ວລ່າມນົກ ແຫກສອງໂຕສົ່ງມາ
ຂອກ ມາຍູງເປັນສັດຕອນຕາມສໍ່ຄູ ພາກເຈົ້າເກົ້າໃຫຍ່
ລໍາເກົ້າພໍ່ກາຍ ຫາລະພັກພໍ່ລາງເພື່ອເກົ້າຫາວ ຍູງຮ່າກ
ຂອກລາງນົກຫຼາຍຍູງກັບໃຈ້ ພະກິສ້າມແຕ້ມລາງນົກ ຕາມ
ມຸ້ງຫ້ອມກັບໃຈ້ ຫາລະພັກພໍ່ລາງເຄິ່ງລ່າງນົກໄປ
ທັ້ງໃນແລະຕົວໂຕ້ເຫຼົ່າ ຊື່ຫາວ ໃນພັກຫາວມາໄສ້ສາມສົ້ນ
ມໍໃນໃສ່ຄໍມຸ້ງທີ່ເພື່ອເອົາຄ່າບ່ອນຂອນ ຈາກໃຫ້ເຫຼົ່າ
ກູ້ມໍ່ ພາກາຮ່າລ່າງນົກຫຼາຍໂຕເລັ້ນເຫຼົ່ານັ້ກປີ ກະລໍາປີ
ຂອມຊູໃຫ້ແລ້ວເສຍໄປ ເຈົ້າປ່ອນເທົ່າໜ້າ ພາກາຍູງ
ແຕ່ງຊູໃຫ້ແລ້ວສົ່ງນູ້ ນົກຕາຍ ລີ້ວ-ນ້ຳປາ

ຂໍ້ຄິດ — ໃຫ້ເອົານົກສະຂອງໄກ່ເພັ້ນໜາງ ສອງຄູ່ເພາະໄກ່ເຄົ້າ
ໃໝ່ ຈົ່ງເອົາເກີ້ - ແລະຄ່າ ພັກພໍ່ຂອງ ບາຍມ ຊູ້ໄກ່
ສະນັ້ນໃປຈັບຍູງ ຈົ່ງເອົາຍູງທີ່ເຫຼືອສະຂອງແລ້ວນັ້ນ
ໄດ້ ແລ້ວທັ້ງນົກປ່ອຍລາງໃປຍູງເປົ່າໄດ້ ~~ຈມ~~
ຈັບຍູງເປັນສູ່ເອົານົກມົນຄູ່ນັ້ນ ຄຸນຮູບໃນຂ່ອນກູໃຍ
ຊູ້ມີເປັນເດັມຈຸກເລືອງເຄົາມໍ່ຈັກ ຊູນົກໃຈ້ກ - ພາກາຍູງ ຂອງຂອມເອົາ
ກັບ ຍູງໄກ່ຄູ່ເພາະນິນຄອນ ເຈົ້າເຈົ້າປ່ອຍວາງເຄົາ
ຫາ່ງເພົ້າ ຕັກຊູນັ້ນເປັນຂອງກາມາຈັກຂປັນຕ່ອນນີ້ປີງ
ພ້ອງເຈົ້າປ່ອຍ ພັກພໍ່ຊູຫາຂອງຊູໃຫ້ຍູງໜ້າ ພາກນົກ
ຕັ້ນຍູງນັ້ນຂອງ ນັກເພື່ອຕັ້ງໃຫ້ຍູງຫາວ
ສ່ອນພາຂອງກາຍູງຊູນັ້ນເກື້ອາລະນິເພື່ອລາງໃຈ້ໃຫ້
ແລ້ວຄ່າຊູ່ເຫຼົ່າ ແລະນົກເພາ ທີ່ຈິຫາວາມ

ບົດສະຫຼຸບ — ເຈົ້າປ່ອຍນົກຍູງນີ້ ຮູ້ພາວແກ່ງຍາງເພາະ
ຍູງຫາຂອມດີ ຈະເອົາໄກ່ຍູງກໍໃດສິກັບ ແຕ່ນົກ
ເພາະຕ່ອນຕ້ອງໃຫ້ສົມຄັກ

Khao Poon Nam Ped **Recipe 94**

RICE VERMICELLI WITH DUCK

Ingredients

1 duck, plucked and cut open in order to gut it and remove the giblets—cut each leg into two and each breast into two—keep all the bones (not used in this recipe, but perhaps reserved for making duck soup)
5 slices of galingale
5 straight-bulbed spring onions—cut off the roots, wash them and tie them into loose knots
3 sprigs of coriander, washed and tied together
4 straight-bulbed spring onions—wash them and chop finely both the bulbs and the leaves
3 sprigs of coriander—chop the leaves only
4 bamboo shoots, of the kind called *no mai lai* (see page 41)—boil them until they lose their taste, then take the tender parts only and cut them up
1 piece (perhaps a quarter) of an unripe papaya, washed and grated into small strips
2 young cabbage leaves, cut into thin strips
5 *na* (2½ kilos, see page 22) of rice vermicelli
2 fresh red chilli peppers, finely chopped
sugar
salt and fish sauce

Method

Put a large soupbowlful (1¼ to 1½ pints) of clean water into a pot and put the pot on the fire. Sprinkle salt into it and add the galingale, the knotted spring onions and the bunch of coriander. When the water comes to the boil, put in the pieces of duck and a sprinkling of fish sauce. Cover, and leave until the pieces of duck are cooked; but keep spooning out the fat which collects on the surface of the water. The cooking of the duck should be done over a low heat. Taste, and check the saltiness.

Mix together the cut up bamboo shoots, the cabbage and the papaya. Put a suitable amount of this mixture in a bowl, and on top of this put some of the rice vermicelli. Then take the pieces of duck out of their pot, cut them up and shred the meat and place the shredded meat on top of the rice vermicelli. Garnish with chopped spring onion and chopped coriander leaves, pour some of the soup from the pot over everything and serve.

Put the chopped chilli peppers and the sugar in small plates, separately, so that people can use them to make the dish 'hotter' or sweeter, as they wish.

Note

This *Khao Poon Nam Ped* is very tasty and has a very fine aroma. Chicken can be cooked instead of duck, in the same way, but the quantity of liquid should be proportionate to the quantity of meat (i.e. less liquid for a chicken, which is smaller than a duck).

95 - ແກງອ່ອມຝານ

ເຄື່ອງປະສົມ — ໃຫ້ເອົາກະດູກກ້ານຄໍຝານ ສາມຂໍ້ ລ້າງນ້ຳ
ໃຫ້ສະອາດແລ້ວຟັກເປັນທ່ອນ ມີໄສ້ຝານຫົວລ້າງນ້ຳ
ໃຫ້ສະອາດ ໝາກເຜັດລາບ ສາມເມັດ ຫົວສິງໄຄ
ໃບຫອມ ໃບແມງລັກ ຫົວຫອມ ໝາກເຂືອ
ໃບຫຍ້າ ເຂົ້າ ຜັກຊີ ນ້ຳປາ ເກືອ
ມີນ້ຳ ໃຫ້ສະອາດ ຜັກຫອມ ລ້າງນ້ຳ

ວິທີເຮັດ — ໃຫ້ເອົານ້ຳໃສ່ໝໍ້ ຕົ້ມກະດູກ ສັກຄູ່ ມີໃສ່ ຜັກຫົວ
ເຂົ້າ ໃສ່ ຜັກຫອມ ຕົ້ມ ແລ້ວໃສ່ ນ້ຳປາ ເອົາຊີ້ນຝານ
ໃສ່ ນ້ຳປາ ຕົ້ມ ໃສ່ຊີ້ນ
ແກງ ນ້ຳສົ້ມ ໂດຍ ຜັກຊີ ໃສ່ ຄື
ຊາວ ນາທີ ເອົາ ລົງ ແກງ ຈະ
ແຕ່ງ ໃສ່ ເກືອ ໃຫ້ ເປັນ ຕ່ອນ ໃສ່
ແກງ ເກືອ ໃສ່ ໃບ ຜັກ ຫອມ
ຜັກ ໃຫ້ ກິນ ລ້ຽງ ຝານ

ໝາຍເຫດ — ແກງອ່ອມຊີ້ນຝານນີ້ຈະລືມໃສ່ ເອົາ
ແຕ່ ເຄື່ອງ ສະອາດ ເປັນ ຈະເອົາ ໃສ່ ຫົວ ໝາກ
ນີ້ ຜັກ ກິນ ໄດ້ ເປັນ

Keng Om Fahn **Recipe 95**

VENISON SOUP

Ingredients

3 sections (vertebrae) of the neck, including the meat, of a small deer (see page 27), washed and cut into suitable pieces
1 stalk of lemon grass, washed and crushed
3 spring onions, washed and each tied into a loose knot
5 leaves of *phak i leut* (salad leaves, see page 35), washed and cut up (e.g. into three parts)
chopped spring onion leaves
ground black pepper, salt and fish sauce
rice (sticky or ordinary, about 1 tbsp), washed thoroughly (with your hands, rubbing the grains together)
2 sprigs of coriander, washed and tied together

Method

Put 2 soupbowlfuls (1½ pints) of water in a pot and add the crushed lemon grass, the knotted spring onions, the washed rice, the sprigs of coriander and some salt. When the water boils (the pot having been put on the fire), add the pieces of deer meat and sprinkle some fish sauce on top. Let it go on cooking over a low fire until the meat is tender and the liquid has reduced. Add the *phak i leut* leaves. Taste, and check the saltiness. Take out the pieces of deer neck and separate the bones from the meat; then return the pieces of meat to the pot. (If some of the pieces are large, cut them into smaller bite-size pieces.)

Transfer the soup to a large bowl and garnish it with the chopped spring onion leaves. Serve it with *Lap Sin Fahn* (Venison *lap*—see recipes 25 and 41 for the method of making a *lap*).

Note

There are various ways of cooking *Keng Om Duk Fahn*, depending on the ingredients which are available. Bamboo shoots, *mak noi* (a kind of ridged gourd—see page 42), cabbage, (*phak kad*—see page 35) and ginger which has been cooked by placing it in the embers of a charcoal fire, after which it is to be washed and crushed, are all ingredients which could be added (at the beginning of the cooking).

໑໖- [illegible]

ເຄື່ອງປະສົມ — [illegible]

ວິທີໃຊ້ — [illegible]

໑໗- [illegible]

ເຄື່ອງປະສົມ — [illegible]

[illegible]

Pad Hed Khao **Recipe 96**

FRIED WHITE MUSHROOMS

Ingredients

1 piece of pork, including some fat, the size of a hand—wash it, cut it into oblong pieces and rub them with salt, ground black pepper and crushed garlic
1 soupbowlful of young white mushrooms (*hed khao*, see page 43)—cut off the bottoms of the stalks and wash them—if they are large tear them into smaller pieces of uniform size
2 duck's or hen's eggs
6 (small) shallots, peeled and crushed
3 spring onions—chop the bulbs and the leaves
chopped coriander
salt, fish sauce and ground black pepper
(2 soupspoonfuls of) pork fat
(meat broth)

Method

Put a wok on the fire and put the 2 soupspoonfuls of pork fat in it. When the fat is hot, fry the crushed shallots in it. When these give off a good aroma, add the pieces of pork. Continue frying until the liquid is reduced, then sprinkle in some fish sauce. When the pieces of pork stiffen and are cooked, add some of the broth, just enough to keep the meat moist. Then add the mushrooms and fry them until they are cooked. Next, break the eggs into the mixture in the wok, stirring to mix them in thoroughly. Taste, and check the saltiness. Sprinkle in the chopped spring onion bulbs and some of the chopped spring onion leaves.

Dish up on a platter, garnish with the chopped coriander and ground black pepper, and serve.

Khao Poon Nam Jaew **Recipe 97**

RICE VERMICELLI WITH A PIQUANT SAUCE

Ingredients

1 bunch (as sold in Lao markets) of pig's lungs
1 pig's head, skinned, split open, and scraped clean so that it loses its animal smell—then wash it to get rid of any trace of the smell
1 piece of three-layer pork, the size of a hand, scraped clean of the hair and washed thoroughly
1 piece of three-layer pork, about the size of three fingers, washed and finely minced
1 piece of fish, about the size of four fingers
6 pieces of (dried) pig's blood, each measuring about three fingers by one
5 slices of galingale

ຫົວລາງ ນາຍຂຸນ ຄົນໃດ ແມ່ກອງ ເພື່ອ ຫົວ ໂຕ້ງ ເຜົ່າ ຈິ່ງລາງ
ນາຍແກ້ ຫົວ ແມ່ກອງ ທາວນ ຜູ້ຜູ້ ຄົນລ່າງ ນາຍສາມ ເຫັນ
ເຂົາປ່ນ ຈຶ່ງ ບໍ່ມາ ລາວ - ນາຍປາ - ໝາວ ກາຜູ້ ປັນ
ໝາກາວ ເມີ ແລ້ວສົ່ງຂຶ້ນ ບໍ່ໄປໄດ້ ການລ່າງ ນາຍທາງ ຫົວ
ແມ່ກອງ ເອົາ ຕຳແໜ່ງ ບໍ່ໄດ້ ແຫ່ງ ເມືອງ ໃນນາ
ບໍ່ໄປໄດ້ ແລ້ວ ສົ່ງໃນ ແມ່ກອງ ລາງ ເລີຍ ລ່າງ ນາຍໄປໄດ້
ມື້ນັ້ນ ໃນ ແລະ ຫົວ ຕົວຕົນ ບໍ່ໃນ ຕົນ ເມືອງ
ຈຶ່ງໄປໄດ້ ແລ້ວ ເພື່ອ ສົ່ງ ເອົາ ໃຫຍ່

ຂໍ້ທີ [illegible] — ໂຫດ ເອົາ ນາຍ ໄດ້ ສົ່ງ ຄູ່ ຕົວ ທາງ ຂຶ້ນ ຂ່າງ ໃນ
ເມືອງ ເອົາ ເຊື້ອ ເລົ່າ ແມ່ກອງ ຫົວ ຂຸນ ແມ່ກອງ ຫົວ ໂຕ້ງ
ແມ່ກອງ ທາວນ ໃດ ໄດ້ ນາຍ ເມືອງ ເອົາ ຫົວ ເມືອງ ແລະ
ຫົວ ປັນ ສອງ ສົ່ງ ໄປ ຈຶ່ງ ນາຍ ເຫັນ ເມືອງ ໄດ້
ເອົາ ປາ ແລະ ນາຍ ບໍ່ໄດ້ ບໍ່ ປາ ໄດ້ ຫາ ອອກ ໄວ້
ຫົວ ໄປ ຈັບ ຫົວ ຂຸນ ຈະ ອອກ ໃຫ້ ຈັບ ຕົວ ມາ ນາ ທັງ
ໝົດ ເມືອງ ເອົາ ຄາງ ທີ່ ເອົາ ຕົນ ແລະ ກອງ
ແມ່ກອງ ຕ່າງໆ ອອກ ໄປ ເອົາ ສ່ວນ ເມືອງ ໄດ້ ສ່ວນ ນຳ
ໂດຍ ມີ ຜູ້ ອອກ ໝູ່ ໄດ້ ຈຶ່ງ ເອົາ ນາຍ ເຈົ້າ ປັນ ທີ່ ຄາງ
ເມືອງ ຕົນ ຈຶ່ງ ສົ່ງ ໄປ ນາ ຂຶ້ນ ຕ່າງ ໃນ [illegible] ແມ່ກອງ
ຜູ້ ເມືອງ ກໍ ເອົາ ແມ່ ເຊື້ອ ລ່າງ ນາຍ ໃດ ຈຶ່ງ ຕ່ອນ ຜູ້ ຫາ
ປັນ ໃນ ເມືອງ ຄາວ ເມືອງ ກໍ ໄດ້ ອອກ ມາ ໃດ ຮູ່ນ ໃຫ້ ວ່າ
ໆ ກໍ ໃຊ້ ສ່ວນ ລາງ ກໍ ຈະ ເອົາ ຂຶ້ນ ມາ ໄປ ຕ່ອນ ນັ້ນ ງາມ
ເຜົ່າ ຫົວ ປັນ ແລະ ສອງ ຂຸນ ນັ້ນ ຈະ ໄປ ເປັນ ຕ່ອນ ນີ້ ໃດ
ຕ່ອນ ໂຕ້ງ ເອົາ ເຜົ່າ ຈຶ່ງ ເມືອງ ເອົາ ໝູ່ ສາມ ຂຸນ ທີ່ ແມ່ກ
ໄດ້ ນັ້ນ ໃດ ປາ ກໍ ໄດ້ ໃຫ້ ກອງ ຈັບ ຜູ້ ເອົາ ຈາ ບ້ານ ທີ່ ເຈົ້າ ເຜົ່າ
ເທົ່າ ນາຍ ເຈົ້າ ປັນ ຈຶ່ງ ເມືອງ ແຄມ ຈາກ ສາມ ຊຸມ ຈຶ່ງ ເອົາ
ສົ່ງ ປັນ ລາວ ຜູ້ ເປັນ ຕອນ ໃດ ຫາ ໃຫຍ່ ເອົາ ສົ່ງ ທີ່ ໄປ
ໄດ້ ນັ້ນ ນາງ ລາວ ສຸ່ມ ອອກ ເຈົ້າ ປັນ ຕ່າງໆ ໄດ້ ງາມ
ແລະ ເຜົ່າ ກາ ຜູ້ ທີ່ ກໍ ເອົາ ໃດ ຫາ ນາ ບໍ່ ໃດ ນາຍ ເມືອງ ຕໍ່
ໄດ້ ຍີ່ ຫາກ

3 straight-bulbed spring onions, washed and each tied into a loose knot
1 onion, washed, (peeled) and quartered
3 sprigs of coriander, washed and tied together
4 *na* (2 kilos, see page 22) of rice vermicelli
salt and fish sauce
pounded dried chilli pepper
2 quarters of an unripe papaya, grated into thin strips
half a banana 'flower' (see page 32), thinly sliced
water spinach (*phak bong*, see page 36), the stems only, chopped into suitable pieces
2 cabbage leaves, chopped thinly
5 straight-bulbed spring onions—wash them and chop both the bulbs and the leaves
1 large handful of bamboo shoots which have been boiled until they have lost their taste and then finely chopped

Method
Put 3 large soupbowlfuls (about 4 pints) of water in a pot on the fire. Sprinkle some salt in, and add the sliced galingale, the knotted spring onions, the onion and the coriander. When the water comes to the boil, add the pig's head and lungs and the (whole piece of) three-layer pork.

When the water comes back to the boil, add the fish and a sprinkling of fish sauce. When the fish is cooked, spoon it out and let the mixture continue to boil until the pig's head is sufficiently done for the bones to separate from the meat. Then spoon out the pig's head and use a strainer (like a *padek* strainer—see page 17—but larger) to strain out the small bits of bone and fragments of cooked vegetable. Wash the pot, making sure that no little bits of bone are left in it, and then pour back into it the clear soup. Put the pot back on the fire. When the soup comes to the boil, add the pieces of pig's blood, previously washed. When the pieces of blood come up to the surface, spoon them out and reserve them on a plate. Leave the pot of soup over a low fire.

Separate the meat (of the pig's head) from the bone, and cut the meat into suitable pieces. As for the lungs and the three-layer pork, cut them into large or small pieces as you prefer. (Return all these to the pot, and) add the minced three-layer pork also.

Remove all the bones from the fish and use (the bottom of) a ladle to mash the fish meat and put it too into the soup. Taste, and check the saltiness.

Cut the rice vermicelli into large pieces and arrange them on a large platter. Arrange the chopped vegetables, separately, around the vermicelli. Put the pounded dried chilli pepper on a small side-plate. Serve. (You may serve the blood separately, or else add it to the soup just before serving. It must not be cooked.)

໑໔ - ຕົ້ນຖົ່ວງອກ

ເຄື່ອງປະສົມ — ໃຫ້ເອົາຖົ່ວ ດອງ ເມັດໃຫຍ່ ໃຫ້ມີເປັນ ສອງ ທ່ອນຫົວ
ມ່ວງສີ້ ວ່າງນຳ ໃຫ້ສະອາດ ຄັນແລ້ວ ກໍເອົາຍັງໃປ
ໃຫ້ເຕັ້ນ ທັງເນື້ອ ແລະ ເຄື່ອງງາມ ຄ່ວຕາ ພ້ອມ
ຜັກຫອມ ຕອງໃຫຍ່ ຢູ່ລອງ ນອກ ເໝົ້າ ຫອ ຜັກຫອມ ລາງເຄື່ອງ

ຖົ່ວລອງ ຂອງ ໃຫ້ ຄລຸ່ມ ແລ້ວແຕ່ ຕອງ ສູງ ກິນ ຖີ້ ຫອ
ຜັກຫອມ ນຳ ສຽງ ຖົ່ວ ທັງ ຂອງ ສົ່ງ ຫອ ໝາກ ເພັດ
ເຜັດ ຖົ່ວ ທັງ ຂອງ ສົ່ງ ນຸ່ງ ໃນ ພັກ ຂອງ ສຸ ພິດ ມີ
ປົນ ເກືອ ນ້ຳປາ ໝາກ ນາວ ສົ່ງ ນຸ່ງ ໃນ ຂີ້ ໝູ
ຖົ່ວ ໃຫ້ ຄລຸ່ມ ເສັງ ໃປ

ວິທີເຮັດ — ໃຫ້ເອົາຖົ່ວ ແລະ ຖ້ວ ຜັກ ຫອມ ຫອ ແລ້ວ ນຳ ສະອາດ ໃຈ
ນຳ ກອງ ລົງ ທ່ອນ ຖົ່ວ ຍັງ ຂີ້ ຂ່າງ ໃນ ນຳ ຜູ້ ເພື່ອ ຈະ ເອົາ
ນຳ ຢາ ລອງ ພໍ ຄອນ ແລ້ວ ຄ້ານ ໃປ ຈົນ ນຳ ເຕັ້ນ ຖົ່ວ
ເຫຼືອງ ຈຶ່ງ ຫັກ ເອົາ ຖົ່ວ ອອກ ມາ ຖູ ໃຫ້ ເປັນ ທ່ອນ ນາງ
ໆ ວາງ ແລະ ນອກ ໃຫ້ ມີ ງາມ ສ້ອມ ທ່ອນ ຄ້ຳ ມັ້ນ ໃຫ້
ຫັກ ຖົ່ວ ຈຶ່ງ ເອົາ ຖົ່ວ ທີ່ ມີ ມັນ ຄົນ ໃຈ ນັ້ນ ເຄື່ອງ ນຳ
ນຳ ລຸງ ທ່ອນ ວາງ ນຳ ຄົນ ທາງ ຖູ ມື ແລ້ວ ນໍ ນ້ຳ
ເຄື່ອງປຸງລົດ ຄົນ ໃຫ້ ທອດ ທັ່ງ ໃຈ ງາມ ພັກ ມີ ພັກ ບາງ ຫາ ໃຫ້ ແລ້ວ ຍັງ ເສັງ ຕັ້ງ ໃຫ້
ມີ ງາມ. ຊັບ ໝາກ ວາ ເລງ ສ່ວນ

Seum Sin Kuai **Recipe 98**

SLICED WATER-BUFFALO MEAT STEW

Ingredients

2 pieces of water-buffalo meat, each the size of a hand, with the tendons removed—wash them, rub salt into them and toast them over the fire until the outside is golden
5 slices of galingale
1 large onion, sliced vertically
4 straight-bulbed spring onions—chop the bulbs and adjacent green parts only (not the leaves)
2 (small) heads of garlic—place them in the embers of a charcoal fire until they are partly cooked but not well done, then remove them, take off the charred outer skin, and chop them vertically
2 fresh red chilli peppers, chopped crossways
chopped coriander leaves
salt, fish sauce and ground black pepper
2 limes
2 Kaffir lime leaves, finely chopped

Method

Put into a pot the meat, the galingale, the onion, a sprinkling of salt and enough water to cover the meat. Put the pot on the fire. When the water boils, sprinkle in some fish sauce and let it go on boiling until the water is reduced and the meat tender.

Take out the meat and slice it thinly. Spoon out and throw away the galingale. Return the sliced meat to the pot. (At this stage) the amount of water should be just sufficient to keep the meat moist. Taste, and check the saltiness. Stir in the chopped ingredients (and the juice of the two limes).

Put the soup in a large bowl, garnish it with ground black pepper and the chopped coriander leaves, and serve it with young cucumbers.

[illegible]

[illegible] — [illegible]
[illegible]
[illegible]
[illegible]
[illegible]
[illegible]

[illegible] — [illegible]
[illegible]
[illegible]
[illegible]
[illegible]
[illegible]

Pad Som Phak **Recipe 99**

FRIED PICKLED CABBAGE

Ingredients

1 medium-sized bowl (capacity about ¾ pint) of *som phak kad Meo* (pickled cabbage, see page 35), with the excess liquid squeezed out of it
1 piece of three-layer pork, the size of a hand, scraped, washed and sliced into suitable thin slices which are then rubbed with salt, ground black pepper and crushed garlic
4 spring onions—crush the bulbs and cut them into long sections, but only the bulbs and adjacent green parts, not the leaves
chopped spring onion leaves
chopped coriander
salt and fish sauce
pork fat (1 small ladleful)

Method

Put a wok on the fire with the small ladleful of pork fat in it. When the fat is hot, fry the sections of crushed spring onion in it. When these give off a good aroma, add the three-layer pork. Keep frying until this turns golden, then sprinkle some fish sauce on it and add just enough water to keep the meat moist. Next, add the pickled cabbage. Taste, and check the saltiness. Stir in the chopped spring onion leaves, arrange on a platter, garnish with chopped coriander, and serve.

໑໐໐ - ເອາະປີ່

ເສັ້ງປະສົມ — [illegible]

[illegible]

ອໍທາລິວ — [illegible]

[illegible]

Or Khai

Recipe 100

DUCK EGG 'STEW'

Ingredients

4 duck's eggs

10 (small) shallots, cooked in the embers of a charcoal fire, then peeled
3 (small) heads of garlic, similarly treated
2 chilli peppers, similarly treated, and then shredded
} these three ingredients constitute the *kheuang mok*

water-buffalo meat, washed and chopped—a quantity the size of a duck's egg

3 slices of galingale

chopped coriander

salt, fish sauce and ground black pepper

Method

Put half of a section of a finger (i.e. about 1 cm) of water in a small pot, with the galingale and a sprinkling of salt. Put the pot on the fire. When the water comes to the boil, sprinkle some fish sauce over it and add the minced meat. Mash the meat with a spoon to separate it into little bits. Taste, and check the saltiness. Then add the *kheuang mok* and break the eggs, one at a time, into the pot. Do not let the water boil too vigorously, or the eggs will fall apart and the dish will not look appetising. The yolks of the eggs should be two thirds cooked.

Arrange on a platter, garnish with ground black pepper and chopped coriander and serve.

108 – ໄຂ່ຈືນໝາກສົ້ມ

ເຄື່ອງປະສົມ — ໄຂ່ໄກ່ ໜາກແດ່ງ ຈີ່ນເຄື່ອງສະໝູນລະອຽດປ່າໃຫ້ແຫຼວ
ແລ້ວກໍ ໝື່ນເນີ່ ໃຕ້ກໍໃຫ້ເນີ້ຍ ສຸກຊ້ວງປັກແຂບໄວ້
ແລ້ວເອົາປີ້ນເນື້ອເທິງລົງ ຍໍເປັນໄຂ່ຊຸກຍັງກໍໃຫ້ຕັດ
ອອກລຽນໄຂ່ຈານໄວ້ ຈັບຂຽງໃຊ້
ຊີ້ນໝູ ແກງເນົ່າ ໃຫ້ຕອກ ທໍ່ ແຊ່ງ ໄຂ່ຕົ້ມໃຫຍ່ ເອົາໄປຈ່ອໄວ້
ນໍ້າປາໃຫ້ສຸກ ແລ້ວເອົາ ອອກມາ ລາງໃຫ້ສະອາດ ຄືນເອົາໄປຕົ້ມ
ຈົນໃຫ້ ອ່ອນ ຈຶ່ງ ຍົກ ອອກມາ ໄວ້
ແກ່ ເຄື່ອງ ໃຫຍ່ ທ່າງ ຕາຍ ຄ່ອງ ຂາງ ເອົາມາຊອຍ
ໃຫ້ເປັນຊີ້ນ ນ້ອຍໆ ຈີ້ນ ກໍ ແຜ່ນ ເນີ່ ເທິງ ຈອບ ເຕັກ ອອກ
ໄວ້ ໝາກເຂືອ ໃຫຍ່ ເນື້ອ ແດ່ງ ລອກ ເອົາ ເປືອກ ອອກ
ໝັກ ເກືອ ຈຶ່ງ ເອົາ ຊີ້ນ ເປື່ອຍ ເອົາ ໃຫ້
ເປັນຊີ້ນນ້ອຍໆ ຄືກັນ ໝາກເຂືອ ສຸກ ເອົາ ໝາກ ຊີ້ນ
ມາ ປົນ ເນື້ອ ໃຫ້ ເປັນຊີ້ນ ຄືກັນ ແກ່ ແຜ່ນ
ຫອມ - ຜັກ - ນໍ້າປາ ແລ້ວ ຄົນ ໃຫ້ ເຂົ້າ ກັນ
ວິທີເຮັດ — ໃຫ້ ເອົາ ໝໍ້ ຕັ້ງ ໄຟ ເອົາ ນໍ້າມັນ ໃສ່
ໝາກເຂືອ ໃສ່ ລົງ ຈືນ ລອງ ຈົນ ໄດ້ ກັນ
ສົມ ໃຫ້ ທ່ວງ ຈີ່ນ ແລ້ວ ຈຶ່ງ ຕັກ ແຫຼວ ເອົາ
ໄຂ່ ໃສ່ ຈານ ໄວ້ ແກ່ ໃສ່ ຫອມ ຜັກ ໃຫ້ ງາມ
ແລ້ວ ຈຶ່ງ ໃສ່ ຫອມ

Khai Jeun Na Som **Recipe 101**

FRIED EGGS WITH A SOUR MIXTURE ON TOP

Ingredients

6 hen's eggs—fry them one at a time, taking care that the yolks do not break, and if possible turn them over to cover the yolks, always keeping them intact; once the yolks are nearly cooked, take them out and arrange them on a platter

1 piece of lean pork, minced, a quantity equivalent to a duck's egg—cook it in a pot or pan, without any oil or fat, over a low fire until it gives off a good smell, then take it out

half an onion, sliced first crossways and then vertically, and fried in pork fat until light golden

1 tomato, plunged into hot water for a minute, then peeled, after which dice the flesh, including the centre part but not the seeds

1 section or wedge of a ripe star-fruit (see page 30), peeled and diced

salt, fish sauce and ground black pepper

chopped coriander

2 straight-bulbed spring onions—chop the bulbs only, finely

Method

Mix together the cooked pork, fried onion and chopped spring onion bulbs with the diced tomato and star-fruit. (Add salt and fish sauce.) Taste, and check the saltiness. Then arrange the mixture on top of the fried eggs, garnish with ground black pepper and chopped coriander and serve.

໑໐໒ - ງູ່ຂຽວ

ເກີດປະສົມ — ໃຫ້ໄກ່ຕົວແມ່ສຸກເຕັມທີ່ກ່ອນ ໃຫ້ຜູ້ລ້ຽງສາມເດືອນ (ຫລືເພາະຫຼາຍເມັດໃຫ້ສຸກ ເພາະເຈົ້າເທົ່າເນື້ອສຸກເລີ ເພາະ ເລີຫລືປະເມີນເມັດໃນໃຫ້ສຸກ ເພາະເຈົ້າເທົ່າເນື້ອທົ່ວເລີ) ງູ່ບ່ມເຄັ່ງມີກໍໃຫ້ແທ້ໆ ເທົ່າໃຫ້ໄກ່ ຂໍໃຫ້ສຸກຈົນທາມ ~~[illegible]~~ເຈົ້າຂອງກາມາຫາໃຫ້ເຫຼືອ ສົມໃຫ້ປາເບິ່ງ ໃນເມັດຕາມສຸ ເກີດນຳປາ - ນຳເຄີຍເລ ເມື່ອນໍປີນ

ວິທີລ້ຽງ — ໃຫ້ເອົາໃຫ້ໄກ່ສຸກມາປະເພີ້ນເນີກາງເກ ເຫລືອເຜົາສອງເທື່ອ ແລ ອອກເປັນສິ່ງໃນ ເພາະເຈົ້າມອບອອກຫລາຍໄວ້ ຈົນຜູ້ໃຫ້ ຈຶ່ງເອົາມອບໃຫ້ຫົວ~~[illegible]~~ຜູ້ລ້ຽງໃຫ້ເຕີບເຕີມ ຕາມ ງູ່ບໍ່ຕາຍ ສົມໃຫ້ເຫຼືອເຄິ່ງ ນອກ~~[illegible]~~ເຈົ້າກິນ ງູ່ເຂັ້ມແຂງ ກູ້ຂາງທີ່ເພາະປາຍໃຫ້ແຫ່ງ ~~ເຫລືອ~~ ~~ໃຫ້[illegible]ຜູ້ໃຫ້ໃນວາກນີ້ເມ່ງາມ~~ ເພາະນໍປີນ ໃນເມັດທາງສຸໃຫ້ຄົນໃຫ້ທ້ອງ ຫລືເຈົ້າມາຜູ້ໃຫ້ໃນ ທ່ານໃຫ້ໃຫ້ເມ່ງາມ ຈົນຜູ້ທ່ານໃຫ້ທີ່~~[illegible]~~ເພາະອອກ ໄວ້ ຈຶ່ງເຈົ້າເຫັນຂາງເຄິ່ງໃນນຳເມັດເມໃຫ້ ຫລືຈຶ່ງ ຜູ້ໃຫ້ລ້ຽງໃຫ້ຖືກໃຫ້ເຈົ້າກິນ ເພາະເກືອນຮ້ອນກໍໃຫ້ ເຈົ້າໃຫ້ທີ່ອອໃຫ້ນັ້ນຢູ່ໃຫ້ລ້ຽງ ຈົນໃຫ້ເຫຼືອງ ອ່ອນຕາກແດດ ~~[illegible]~~ ຈົນເຫຼືອງໃຫ້ຫົວອໍໃຫ້ນັ້ນ ຫລືເຈົ້າລຸ້ມໃຫ້ງາມ ເພື່ອເມື່ອ ເວລາສຸ ໃຫ້ເມາະນົກເລີ້ມໃຫ້ຮູ້ທາງ

Khai Khouam **Recipe 102**

UPSIDE-DOWN EGGS

Ingredients
10 boiled (i.e. hard-boiled) hen's eggs
3 duck's eggs
2 (small) heads of garlic } cooked in the embers of a charcoal fire and
5 (small) shallots } then peeled to constitute the *kheuang hom*
minced lean pork, a quantity equivalent to a hen's egg to be cooked in a dry pot or pan until it gives off a good aroma
pa beuk 'caviar'*
chopped coriander leaves
salt, fish sauce and ground black pepper
pork fat

Method
Shell the hard-boiled hen's eggs and cut them in halves. Remove the yolks carefully and pound them together with the *kheuang hom*, the pork and the 'caviar' in a mortar. Taste. If the taste is not strong enough, add a little fish sauce. Then add ground black pepper and (some of) the chopped coriander leaves. Mix thoroughly and stuff the mixture into the whites of the eggs.

Put a wok on the fire, with some pork fat in it. Break the duck's eggs into a bowl and beat them. When the fat is hot, dip the stuffed hen's eggs in the beaten duck's eggs and fry them until they are pale golden. Arrange them on a platter, garnish with ground black pepper and (the rest of) the chopped coriander and serve.

* Editors' Note. The *pa beuk* is PANGASIANODON GIGAS, the giant catfish of the Mekong, which has become very rare in the last decade or two. There is a traditional way of preparing its eggs, to make 'Laotian caviar', at Luang Prabang (which would be what Phia Sing meant) and a slightly different technique used at Ban Houei Sai. Other cured fish roe, e.g. that of the *pa va*, may be substituted—the general effect will be similar, although the exact flavour cannot be duplicated.

103 – ປາສະງົວຈີ່ນໍ້າສົ້ມ

ເຄື່ອງປະສົມ — ປາສະງົວໜຶ່ງເປັນຂະໜາດພໍຫ່ອນມືໜຶ່ງ ກ້ອງເລົາ
ຫານຫົວປາເປັນ ລ້າງນໍ້າຫາລາງນີ້ເສົາໃນນໍ້າ ເຄື່ອງໃຊ້
ທາກາຕ່ອນ ໝາກເລັ່ນ ເກືອ ຊູ່ອ ໜໍ່ໄມ້ ຮູບເສັ້ນ
ແກມມັນ ລ່າງບໍ່ ໝາກໂຫ້ ແຄູກ ທາໄຂ່ ເສັ້ນ ຜັກບົ່ວ
ຫົວໃຫຍ່ ທາງ ຫົວປລອງ ນາວ ຜັກບົ່ວດາວ ປຣັ້ນສາມ
ຫົວ ຖາງໂຕ ແຕກ ໃບຜັກ ບົ່ວປ ໂຕແລ່ງ ຕາມກາ
ຜັກຊີ ເບີ່ນ ລູກຈີ່ - ນໍ້າປາ - ນໍ້າມັນໝູ

ວິທີເຮັດ — ໃຫ້ລ້າງ ບາ່ນຊາງ ລອກເປື່ອ ນໍ້າມັນ ມູນ ໃຊ່ຫນັ້ງແຫ່ງ ແປຣ້ນ
ໃຫ້ລ້າງ ຫົວ ຜັກບົ່ວ ລາງຈີ່ນ ນາງມ ກ້ອນ ຄືດາວ ງນີລາງ ນໍ້າ
ປາຣາ ອະປາ ປີ່ ຕັ້ງ ນໍ້າ ບໍ່ເນື້ອ ອາ ກ້ອ ເດືອດ
ຜັກບົ່ວ ຫົວ ໃຫຍ່ ໝາກເລັ່ນ ແລ້ວ ລົງ ໂຈ້ ໃຫ້ ສຸກ ວໍ ໄປ ຈີ່ນ
ຫອມ ເສົາ ນໍ້າ ຄາງ ຣາງ ໂຕ ພໍ ຂົ້ນ ງນີ ເຊັ່ງ ເສັ້ນ
ຈາງ ແປ ແຊງ ໃບຜັກບົ່ວ ຜັກຊີ ໃສ່ ລົງ ໂຕ ຫົວ
ປາລົງ ຈຶ່ງ ເສົາ ປາ ຕື່ມ ຊູບ ໃສ່ຈານ ເວລາ ນໍ້າ ເດືອດ
ຣາງ ເນົ້າ ຜັກຊີ ຫາງ ມຸມ ໂຮງ ປາ ເມື່ອ ເຫັນ ໂຕ ຮຸ້
ຫອມ

Pa Sa Ngoua Jeun Na Som **Recipe 103**

FRIED SHEATFISH WITH A SOUR SAUCE

Ingredients

6 pieces of *pa sa ngoua* (see the drawing on page 119), about as thick as a finger and the width according to the size of the fish, washed in water, salted, fried until golden (and reserved)
1 small can of tomato paste
pork meat, to include a bit of fat, washed and finely minced, quantity equivalent to a duck's egg
half an onion, cut into slices vertically
3 spring onions, the bulbs to be crushed and the leaves finely chopped
fresh chopped coriander
ground black pepper, salt and fish sauce
(a spoonful of) pork fat
(broth)

Method

Put a frying-pan on the fire and put a spoonful of pork fat in it. When it is hot, put in the crushed spring onion bulbs. Then add the prepared pork meat and a little fish sauce. When this is cooked and of a golden colour, add the slices of onion and the whole contents of the can of tomato paste and cook the mixture until it is fragrant. Add a bit of broth to make the paste less sticky. Taste and check the saltiness. Then add the chopped spring onion leaves and some of the ground black pepper. When they are well mixed in, take the pan off the fire.

Arrange the prepared pieces of fish on a platter, then pour the mixture from the pan on top of them. Garnish with the coriander and the rest of the ground black pepper over it, and serve.

104 - ໝົກໄຂ່ປາ

ເຄື່ອງປະສົມ — ໂຕເລືອກໄຂ່ປາ ມາລາຍເນື້ອກຸ້ງ [illegible] ທີ່ໃຫຍ່ ເນື້ອໃຫ້ເລືອກ [illegible] ໃຂ່ [illegible] ຈຶ່ງປາຍ [illegible] ບໍ່ມີກ້າງ [illegible] ເກືອ [illegible] (ໝາກ [illegible]) [illegible]

ວິທີເຮັດ — [illegible] ເອົາປາ [illegible] ມາຮອມກັນ [illegible] ໄຂ່ປາ [illegible] ແລະ [illegible] ເອົາ [illegible] ໄປ [illegible]

ໝາຍເຫດ — [illegible] ໄຂ່ປາ [illegible] ໄຂ່ປາ

105 - [illegible] ສົ້ມໄຂ່

ເຄື່ອງປະສົມ — ສົ້ມໄຂ່ປາ ເນື້ອກຸ້ງ [illegible] ເນື້ອຕ່ອນ [illegible] ເອົາມາໃສ່ [illegible] (ເອີ້ນວ່າ [illegible]) ປາ [illegible] ເນື້ອຕ່ອນ [illegible] ເນື້ອກຸ້ງ [illegible]

Mawk Khai Pa **Recipe 104**

FISH EGGS STEAMED IN BANANA LEAF

Ingredients

1 soupbowl of fish eggs—add water and beat them until they have swollen up well
1 piece of *pa gnon* (a catfish, see page 71), minced, a quantity the size of a duck's egg
1 piece of three-layer pork, minced, a quantity the size of a hen's egg
1 dried red chilli pepper, seeded and soaked in water until soft
5 (small, peeled) shallots
} these two ingredients to be pounded finely together to form the *kheuang hom*, and left in the mortar
chopped spring onion leaves
salt, fish sauce and ground black pepper
some pieces of banana leaf

Method

Put the minced fish and pork into the mortar which contains the *kheuang hom* and mix them together. Then transfer the mixture into the bowl containing the fish eggs, add salt and fish sauce (and black pepper) and mix thoroughly. Taste, and check the saltiness. Next, wrap the mixture in the pieces of banana leaf and secure the package(s)* with bamboo or coconut-stem pins. Steam the packages in a steamer. When they are cooked, open them, transfer the contents to a platter, and serve.

Note

Usually *Mawk Khai Pa* should have chilli pepper and pork fat in it, to help ensure that the fish eggs remain moist and do not become hard. If these additions are not to your taste, omit them; but in that case you will not be following the correct method of making *Mawk Khai Pa*.

* Editors' Note. Phia Sing does not make clear whether there is one package or several. Guided by recipe 57, we think there are three.

Miang Som Khai **Recipe 105**

'CAVIAR' MIXTURE

Ingredients

1 small bowl of 'caviar' (salted fish roe, e.g. of the *pa va*, page 125)
1 piece of lean pork, the size of four fingers, minced and mixed with 3 (small, peeled and pounded) shallots, salt and ground black pepper—when all this is a sticky mass, cook it in a dry pan until done and golden—the result is known as *moo paen* (pork sheet or leaf)
1 piece of fish, free of bones, the size of four fingers—wash it and cut it into pieces about the size of one finger, rub these with salt and ground black pepper and fry them until well done and golden

ເຫຼົ່າທັງສອງກາຍເປັນຂໍ້ໂຕ້ແຍ້ງ ພໍອີ່ນແກ່ນອື່ນລົງເລີ່ມ
ທາງດ້ານຂອງຍາດກຸ່ມກຳ ພວກເຫຼົ່າເຄື່ອງສາມມັນ
ຜູ້ເປັນສະມາຊິກ ຂອງຍາດກຸ່ມກຳມະກຳ
ຊຸດນີ້ຈະໄດ້ຕົກລົງເລີ່ມຕົ້ນເກັບຂອງສາມຊ້ຽງ ໃນພາກ
ເໜືອຜູ້ນຳຂອງຄະນະສາມານຕົນ ພວກທາງທີມເຫຼົ່າ
ເຂົາແຕ່ໃນພາກສະໜາມຕໍ່ຕ້ານ ທາງດິນຂອງພວກເຫຼົ່ານຳ
ພາກເໜືອບາງພາກສະເຂົາໝົດເນື່ອງຈາກທາງ ສີໂຄດໄດ້
ແລະໆເຫຼົ່ານີ້ ເຈົ້າປົ່ນທ່ອງທ່າງ ຜູ້ເປັນຕົ້ນບາງຄົນ
ງົ່ນນີ້ ໃນຕອນກາງຄືນ ກຳມະການນຳທີ່ມານັ້ນຈ່າງເຂດ
ທີ່ຜູ້ສາມານຸ່ມ

ຈົດໝາຍ — ເນື່ອງທາງພາກຕ່າງໆ ຢູ່ກຸ່ມກຳລັງ ຈຶ່ງໄດ້ໃຊ້ໃຫ້ຜູ້
ທີ່ຜູ້ຄົນໄດ້ເຂົ້າກັນ ເອົາຕອນທີ່ຕ່ານເກົ່າມື້
ມາແລ້ວປະໄດ້ຟັງມັນ ແລ້ວທັກເນັ້ນຂາງຈີ່ນສ້າງ
ໃນ ເຂົາເສົາມູນກຳມະພາບເຫຼົ່າກັນເປັນຜູ້ນຸ່ມ ຈຶ່ງ
ເອົາຕອນທີ່ຈັກໂອ້ນມື້ ລູກໃສ່ລວງກາຂອງໄປຂວາງມ
ໄດ້ເປັນຕາງແຕ ຫລືອເຂົາໃຫ້ຂ່ອນໆ ເປື້ອອ່ານຂມາ
ໃຊ້ຕອນທີ່ຈັກໂອ້ນັ້ນ ເອົາຕ່ອນໂພ່ມາປົດຊູຊັ້ນ
ກັນ ຈີ່ນີ້ໃຊ້ມາໃຈໃນຕອນນັ້ນໂປ້ນ ເຫຼືອຊອນໆກັນ
ບໍ່ໄປຈັບຜູ້ໃຊ້ ຈຶ່ງທັກເອົາສົມໃຈ ພໍ່ສົມຄວນ ມາຕໍ
ຮູ້ສີໂລທີ່ຈຸໂອ້ນັ້ນໄດ້ເຫົາກັນ ຫລືອໂຕ້ນທີ່ນັກໃຊ້
ທີ່ຈັບໂອ້ນັ້ນທັງໃນຕອນມາປົດໃຊ້ຈອນ ຫລຸງເຂົາ
ມາແຕ່ມປາຈີ່ນພາະເລືອນາຄົມຕ່າງໆ ເຈົ້າຢູ່ມສົມໃຈໃຈ
ໄດ້ພໍ່ດີ ຜູ້ສົນເຈົ້າຮໍ່ເປັນລູກໂທ້ງວາມ ພັກ
ອອກຈາກຕອນລູກໃຈຈອນ ເມື່ອຕັ້ງໄດ້ຮູ້ເທ
ທອງຢູ່ໂຕ — ເຫຼົ້ງສິ້ນໃຈນີ້ ຖ້າທາກາບໍ່ມີໃຊ້ຜູ້ຢູ່ໃນໃກ່ຫລືອ
ຈະໃຈ້ໃນສະລູແທນກໍ່ໃຊ້ ແຕ່ທາງກາຈະພາໂຕ້ເສັ້ງຮູ້ໃນ
ກລູເປັນເຫຼຸປາແກງ ເອັ່ນໃອ້ຫລ່າຈາວເປັນຫລ່ຫລ່າ

1 bowl of shrimps (page 25)—pick off heads and tails, mix them with salt and cook them in a dry pan

6 spring onions, the bulbs only, thinly sliced lengthways and soaked in cold water
3 red chilli peppers, halved, sliced lengthways and seeded
3 rhizomes of ginger, very finely chopped and with the juices squeezed out
3 spring onions—take the leaves only and cut them into lengths about as long as the section of a finger
5 sprigs of coriander—pick only the leaves and tender parts of the stems
1 handful of roasted peanuts
5 heads of pickled garlic (the cloves only, peeled)

} these ingredients to be mixed together to constitute the *kheuang hom*

1 stalk of lemon grass, finely chopped
½ *na* (¼ kilo, see page 22) of rice vermicelli, cut into pieces as long as the section of a finger
banana leaves, torn into 12 pieces, each the size of an outspread hand
pork fat
3 duck's eggs

Method
After preparing the ingredients, break the eggs into a bowl and mix them. Take a piece of banana leaf, (reduce it to) the size of four fingers and make (many small) tears in one end of it, so as to create a fringe.

Put a wok on the fire and use a cloth to smear it with pork fat, just enough to grease it. Dip the fringed piece of banana leaf in the beaten egg, fringe end down, and then move it to and fro, from one side of the wok to the other, to create a net-like web of cooked egg. Use a pliable stick to lift the web out of the wok and on to a piece of banana leaf. Then place another piece of banana leaf on top of it. Fry another web of egg, put this on top of the upper banana leaf, cover it in turn and continue thus until all the egg has been used.

Mix together the 'caviar' and the chopped lemon grass. Take the fried webs of eggs, one at a time, each on its piece of banana leaf, and transfer them to a platter. Top each with a little of the thinly sliced pork, the fish, the *kheuang hom*, the rice vermicelli and the 'caviar' mixture. Fold up the two ends of the egg webs, and then the sides, to make a nice shape (i.e. a sort of rectangular package). Lift this off the piece of banana leaf and arrange on a serving-platter. (Continue doing this until all the egg webs have been made into such packages. Discard the pieces of banana leaf as you work.) Serve.

Note
This *Miang Som Khai*, if you haven't got any duck's eggs or hen's eggs, can be prepared with salad leaves instead of egg webs. But the flavour will then be more like that of *Miang Padek* than of *Miang Som Khai*.

106 – ນຳໂຕ່ງ

ເຄື່ອງປະສົມ — ໄກ່ທາອູ່ງ ເໝົ້າຕອງ ເຂົາຄ່າງ ຮູ້ນີ້ອີງ ນາງຈັກໂຕ້ເປັນຄົງ
ຮູ້ນີ້ບູນ ຄາກນອນມັນ ຕົນສຸກຄ້ອງ ທຳຮູ້ນີ້ ຈະກີໂຕ້ເປັນຄົງ
ທາວໃຈບູນຕັ້ນ ຫາກຄ້ອງ ທ່າງນອູ່ງ ຊີໂຕ້ເປັນກີ່ສູ່ນ
ບໍ່ແຕ່ນ ເໝົ້າຄ່ນ ຊູ ນາງ ສງາ ຈີນີ້ ໂຕ້ເປັນກີ່ສູ່ນ ເນື້ອ
ປອເໝີກ ຕອງ ນຳຈັນ ອ່ອນ ຈະກີໂຕ້ເປັນຄົງ ເໝົ້າຕອງ
ປລອງ ທາງ ກະປູງ ໃຈ້ກ່າງ ຈະກີໂຕ້ເປັນຄົງ

1. ມັນສະຫຼຸບ ປອກ ເປືອກ ອອກ ປລອງ ນາງ ໂຕ້ເປັນ ກີ່ສູ່ນ ເນື້ອ
ຈະມີ ນຳ ມັນ ເນ ເນັ່ງ ເຫຼົ້າ ອ່ອນ ຕົວຕົວ
ໃຈ ຫຼູ ນັ່ນ ປອກ ເປືອກ ປລອງ ນາງ ສ່ວນ ນອູ່ງ
ໃຈ ຫຼູ ອີ ບໍ່ເປັນ ຄ່ນ ຫຼູ ນາງ ສງາ ຈີນີ້ ຢູ່ເປັນ ກີ່ສູ່ນ.
2. ເພາະກາ ຕອງ ອ່ອນ ຈະກີ ເຂົາ ຄ່າງ ເນື້ອ ສງາ ນອູ່ງ
3. ເພາະກາ ທ່ອນ ບໍ່ ຫຼູ ຕົ້ນ ລອກ ນຳ ຮອນ ສ່ວນ ຄ້ອງ ເໝົ້າ ກີ່ສູ່ ນະເພີ້.

Yam Yai **Recipe 106**

A 'GRAND' YAM (mixed dish)

Ingredients

1 fried chicken breast, finely shredded
a piece of boiled pork, including some fat, about the size of 4 fingers, shredded
half a boiled pig's heart, cut into cubes
1 *yo* (a piece of pork meat, minced, mixed with flour, salt and ground black pepper, all pounded finely together, flattened into a layer about 0.5 cm thick and steamed), cut into small squares measuring about 2 sections of a finger (say, 5 cm)
1 dried squid, soaked in water until tender and then finely shredded
half a can of crabmeat—discard all fragments of shell and shred the meat finely
5 potatoes, peeled and diced, then fried in pork fat until light golden in colour
3 boiled (i.e. hard-boiled) duck's eggs, shelled and sliced lengthways
2 duck's eggs (beaten and) fried, then cut into strips about 2 sections of a finger (say, 5 cm) long and sliced across into square pieces
2 young cucumbers—take the flesh only (i.e. peel them and discard the centre part with its seeds), cut this into sections and slice the sections very thinly
(*At this point Phia Sing's recipe breaks off, as explained on page 9. Mrs Nouane Sy Sakulku, from Luang Prabang, has kindly completed it as shown below, reconstructing the rest from her own experience*)
1 medium-sized bowl of bean sprouts—blanch them in hot water, then cut off their roots
3 yard-long beans }
5 tender young shoots of water spinach (*phak bong*, see page 36) } blanched and cut into pieces
3 round eggplants—take the flesh only and chop it finely
1 tomato, thinly sliced
1 coriander plant, stems and leaves only finely chopped
5 shoots of mint, finely chopped
2 spring onions, the leaves only, finely chopped
1 tablespoon of roasted sesame seed or peanut, finely pounded
1 head of garlic }
3 shallots } to be placed in a charcoal fire until cooked, then peeled and finely pounded
pork broth
1 lime, the juice only
salt and fish sauce (or *padek* liquid)

Method

Put all the vegetables (potatoes, cucumber, bean sprouts, yard-long beans, water spinach, eggplants and tomato) in a large serving-bowl. Sprinkle them with salt and mix them thoroughly. Add the flesh ingredients (from chicken breast down to crabmeat inclusive). Sprinkle with fish sauce (or *padek* liquid), the lime juice, the pounded ingredients and the pork broth, and mix thoroughly again. Taste and check the saltiness. Add the chopped coriander, spring onion and mint, mix everything again, then transfer it all to a platter, garnish it with the sliced duck eggs and the strips of omelette, and serve.

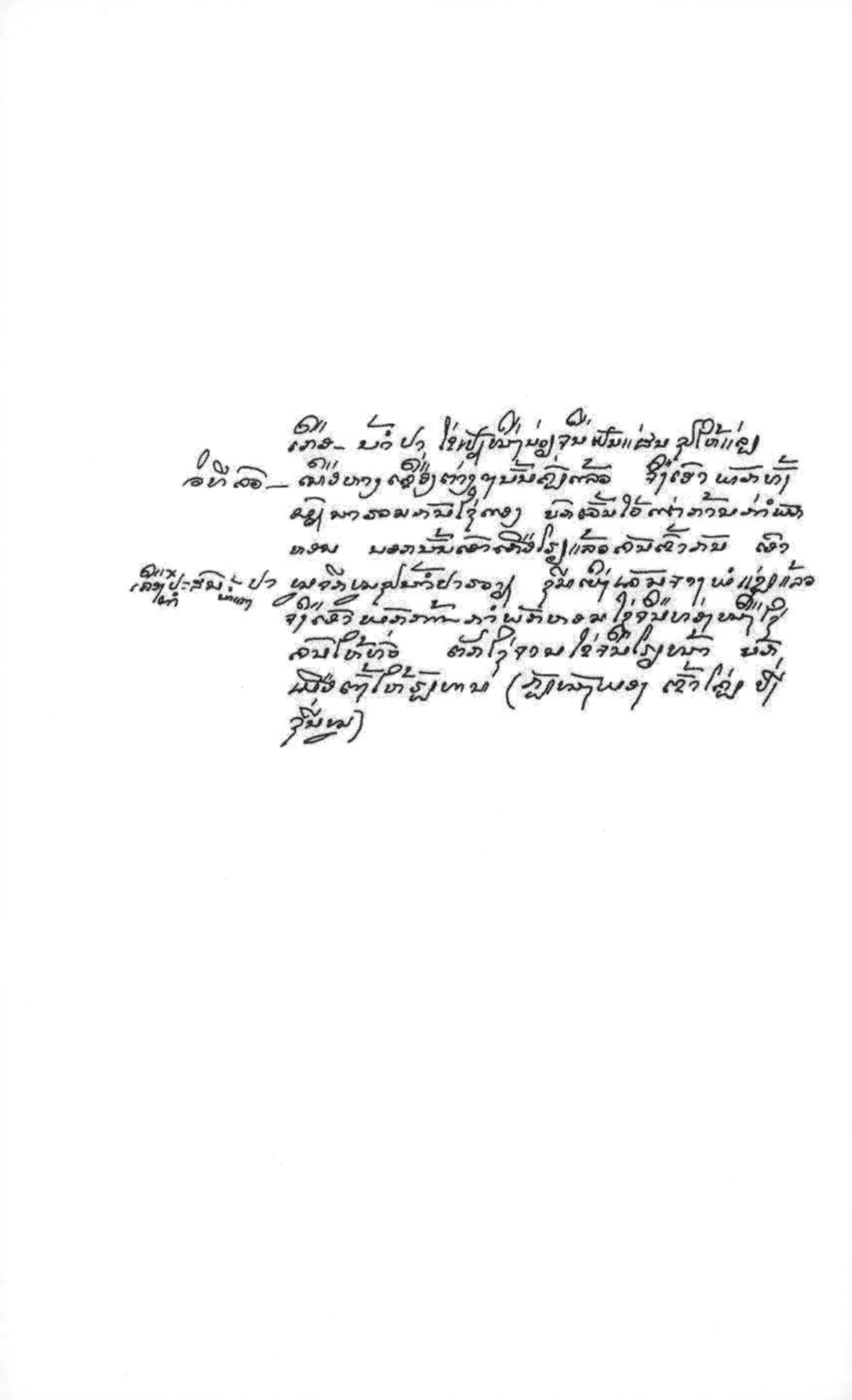

[illegible] — [illegible] ปา [illegible]

[illegible] — [illegible]

[illegible]

[illegible] แล้ว [illegible]

[illegible] ปา [illegible] แล้ว

[illegible]

[illegible]

[illegible] ([illegible])

Yam Noi

Recipe 107

A LESS ELABORATE YAM (mixed dish)

Ingredients

1 piece of fish } cooked and shredded
1 piece of pork }
1 piece of three-layer pork, cooked and sliced thinly
1 hen's egg, made into an omelette and sliced thinly
4 yard-long beans (page 40) } blanched
5 tender young shoots of *phak bong* } and cut
(water spinach, page 36) } into pieces
half a Chinese cabbage }
1 cucumber, the flesh only } all thinly sliced
3 round eggplants, the flesh only }
1 coriander plant, stems and leaves only, finely chopped
5 shoots of mint, finely chopped
1 tablespoon of roasted sesame seeds or peanuts, pounded
1 (small) head garlic } placed in a charcoal fire until cooked, then
2 (small) shallots } peeled and pounded to become the *kheuang tam*

(*The above, including the recipe title, is a reconstruction by Mrs Nouane Sy Sakulku—see recipe 106—of what preceded the surviving last half of Phia Sing's recipe 107, which follows below.*)

salt and fish sauce
1 duck's egg, made into an omelette and thinly sliced

Method

After preparing the above ingredients, put all the vegetables together in a large bowl, except for the mint and coriander. Sprinkle on some salt, and squeeze them while mixing them thoroughly together.

Mix the pounded ingredients (*kheuang tam*) with some broth. Add the shredded fish and pork, and the sliced three-layer pork, and a sprinkling of fish sauce. Taste, and check the saltiness. Then add the mint and coriander and the sliced hen's egg omelette. Mix thoroughly and transfer the mixture to a serving-platter.

Garnish the dish with the sliced duck's egg omelette, and serve it with crisp-fried pork skin, rice cakes and roast pork (such as could be bought, ready prepared, in Lao markets).

108- ນໍ່ໄກ່ຕົ້ມ

ເຄື່ອງປະສົມ — ໄກ່ທີ່ລ້ຽງບໍ່ປາກ ຫຼາຍ ເຄື່ອງໃນຫົວ ປັ້ນໃຫ້ງາມ
ຂອງກາໂຕກໍລອກ ເນັ້ງຕຳນະ ພະຍາຍາມ, ລ້າງນ້ຳໃຫ້ສະອາດ
ໝາກເຜັດ ແລ້ວເອົາເສັ້ນຫົວພາກບ່ອນ ໃຫ້ຮວມກັນໄວ້ເນື້ອ
ຕົ້ມ ນ້ຳໃສ່ ຫົວຫອມ [illegible] ໄກ່ ເອົາ
ບາງ [illegible] ແຕ່ງ ຂອງ [illegible] ປາ ເນື້ອ [illegible] ແກ່ນ ກະທຽມ ຫົວຫອມ
[illegible] ເກືອ ໃຫ້ ລວມ [illegible] ຂອງ [illegible]
ໄປລ້າງ ນ້ຳ ເອົາ [illegible] ບໍ່ ເອົາ ໃສ່ ກະທຽມ ຫົວໜຶ່ງ
[illegible] ໃສ່ [illegible] ກະທຽມ ສອງຫົວ
[illegible] ໃສ່ ບໍ່ ເອົາ [illegible] ສອງໜ່ວຍ
[illegible] ສອງ ຫົວຫອມ
[illegible] ສອງ ຫົວ
[illegible] ສາມ ຕົ້ນ
ເກືອ — ນ້ຳປາ — ພິກໄທ — [illegible] —

ວິທີເຮັດ — ໃຫ້ [illegible] ເອົາ ໄກ່ ຕົ້ມ [illegible] ໃສ່ [illegible] ເປັນ ຕົ້ນ
ກະທຽມ [illegible] ໃສ່ [illegible] ໃຫ້ ຈືດ ເອົາ
[illegible] ໃສ່ [illegible] ເກືອ [illegible]
[illegible] ໃຫ້ [illegible] ເປັນ [illegible] ໃຫຍ່ [illegible] ສອງ [illegible]
[illegible] ເອົາ ເກືອ [illegible] ນ້ຳ [illegible]
[illegible] ໃສ່ [illegible] ນ້ຳ [illegible]
ໄກ່ [illegible] ໃຫ້ [illegible] ເປັນ [illegible]
[illegible] ໃສ່ [illegible] ແລ້ວ [illegible]
[illegible] ໃຫ້ [illegible] ແລ້ວ [illegible]

Yam Kai Tom **Recipe 108**

BOILED CHICKEN YAM (mixture)

Ingredients

1 chicken, plucked—split open its underside and pull out the intestines; remove and cut open the gizzard, and strip it of its lining; wash the chicken and the gizzard thoroughly, and put them with some salt and (peeled) shallots in a pot, with water to cover the chicken (but no more), and boil until the chicken is tender

(1) young cucumber, peeled and quartered lengthways—then cut the pieces into slices of suitable size

2 large, ripe tomatoes, dipped in hot water (for a minute), peeled, halved and sliced lengthways, discarding the centre part and the seeds

2 straight-bulbed spring onions, chopped—both the bulbs and the leaves

2 large fresh red chilli peppers, cut across into halves, sliced lengthways, cored and soaked in water

5 (small) shallots
2 (small) heads of garlic } these two ingredients to be almost, not completely, cooked by placing them in the embers of a charcoal fire, and then (peeled and) sliced across

3 sprigs of coriander, chopped

salt, fish sauce and ground black pepper

a lime

Method

Take the boiled chicken out of its pot and transfer it to a large bowl. Tear off the breasts and legs and remove all the meat from the carcase. Break the legs and the wings at their joints. Tear the breasts into suitable large pieces, and do the same with the legs and the wings. Then add the sliced or chopped ingredients (*kheuang soi*), except for the spring onions and coriander, to the bowl (of chicken). Sprinkle them with salt and add some of the chicken broth, just enough to keep the mixture moist. Then sprinkle it with fish sauce (and the juice of the lime). Mix thoroughly, taste, and check the saltiness. Sprinkle ground black pepper and the chopped spring onion leaves on top, arrange on a platter and garnish with the chopped coriander.

109 – ຢາບຳລຸງເລືອດລົມ

ຈຸດປະສົງ — [illegible] ເລືອດ [illegible] ບໍ່ [illegible]
ເອົາ [illegible] ໄດ້ [illegible] ໃຫ້ແກ່ [illegible] ເອົາ [illegible] ເຊາະ [illegible]
[illegible] ໂດຍ [illegible] ໄດ້ [illegible] ໄດ້ [illegible]
[illegible] ໃຫ້ [illegible] ຈື່ [illegible] ໄດ້
ສະດວກ [illegible] ໄດ້ [illegible] ໄດ້
[illegible] ບໍ່ [illegible] ໄດ້ [illegible]
[illegible] ໄດ້ [illegible] ບໍ່ [illegible] ໄດ້ [illegible]
[illegible] ແລະ [illegible] ໄດ້ [illegible]

(ໝາກ [illegible] ໃບ [illegible] ໄດ້ [illegible]
[illegible] ໃບ [illegible] ໄດ້ [illegible]
[illegible] ໃບໄດ້ [illegible] ສອງ [illegible]
[illegible] ໄດ້ [illegible] ເປັນ [illegible])
[illegible] ສອງບາດ — [illegible]
[illegible] ສອງ [illegible]
[illegible] ສອງບາດ — [illegible]
[illegible] — [illegible]
[illegible]
[illegible] ສອງບາດ — [illegible]
[illegible] — [illegible]

ວິທີເຮັດ — [illegible] ໄດ້ [illegible] ໃສ່ [illegible]
[illegible]
[illegible] ໃຫ້ [illegible] ສະ [illegible]
[illegible] — [illegible] — [illegible] —
[illegible] ໃຫ້ [illegible]

ບາງຂໍ້ໃຈ [illegible] ໃຫ້ [illegible]
[illegible] ໄດ້ [illegible]
[illegible] ໄດ້ [illegible] ([illegible]
[illegible])

Yam Mak Kheua Khuen **Recipe 109**

A BITTER EGGPLANT YAM (mixture)

Ingredients

10 bitter round eggplants (*mak kheua khuen*, page 33)—choose only the fresh, crunchy ones, put them in a large bowl and use your hands to separate their cores and seeds and to break what is left into small pieces, then soak these pieces in water with (a little) lime (the powder, not the fruit), drain them and wash them thoroughly—finally, discard the cores (but keep the seeds), or else the taste will be too bitter*

minced lean pork, a quantity the size of a duck's egg—form it into a round (like a thin hamburger) and boil it in just sufficient water to cover it

1 dried red chilli pepper, grilled until crisp

4 (small) shallots } cook until done by placing them
2 (small) heads of garlic } in the embers of a charcoal fire

the above three ingredients to be pounded together finely to form the kheuang hom

3 straight-bulbed spring onions, chopped

2 stalks of lemon grass, chopped

2 leaves of a ginger plant, chopped

3 sprigs of coriander, chopped

sesame seeds, roasted in a dry pan and ground

2 (small) heads of garlic cooked until almost done in the embers of a charcoal fire, then (peeled and) sliced across

salt and fish sauce

(meat broth)

Method

Put the boiled minced pork in a mortar and pound it finely. Then pound and stir into it the *kheuang hom*. Add meat broth, just enough to produce a thick mixture. Add this to the bowl in which the eggplants have been processed, and mix in the chopped lemon grass and spring onions and the sliced garlic. Sprinkle with salt, fish sauce and the ground sesame seeds. Taste, and check the saltiness. Then mix in, thoroughly, the chopped ginger leaves and half the chopped coriander.

Arrange on a platter, garnish with the remaining coriander, and serve with fried fish, rice cakes and (slices of) roast pork.

* Editors' Note. It would be more practical to discard the cores (which are more bitter than the seeds) at an earlier stage, and this may be what Phia Sing intended.

110 – ຢາຜັກພໍ່ເຖົ້າ

ເຄື່ອງປະສົມ— ຜັກກາດ ຕົ້ນລ້ຽງເອົາແຕ່ໜ່ວຍລ່າງມາ - ໜັກກຳມື
ຜັກກາດຂາວ ປີ້ລ້ຽງເອົາແຕ່ໜ່ວຍລ່າງມາ— ໜັກກຳມື
ຜັກສົ້ມລີ່ ລ້ຽງເອົາແຕ່ໃບອ່ອນເພາະໜ່ວຍລ່າງມາ— ໜັກກຳ
ຜັກຢານາງອ່ອນ ລ້ຽງເອົາແຕ່ໜ່ວຍລ່າງມາ - ໜັກກຳມື
ໝາກແປ້ງອ່ອນ ລ້ຽງເອົາລ້ຽງກ້ານ ຫຍ້າເກົ່າລ່າງມາ- ຊັ່ງຜັກ
ໝາກຫາດ ຂາວ ລ້ຽງ ຂາວ ຕົ້ນ ໃບ ລ່າງມາ - ຫົວຜັກ
" ປີກລຽງມາຈາວ ເພາະກ້ຽງ ແກ່ກູມີ ເອົາຈີ້- ໜັກບ່ຽງ
ໜ່ວຍເຫຼືອງ ເອົາໂກສິກ ຫຼຽເປັນອ່ອນ ເມື່ອລ່າງມາໃຊ້- ສາມບ່ຽງ
ໝາກເສື່ອເຫລົ້າ ບ່ອນ ເອົາຂູ ລ່າງມາ — ຫົວບ່ຽງ
ໝາກແຄວ ໃບ ຢູ່ ເອົາແຕ່ບ່ຽງ — ສາມຜົວ
ບໍ່ໃສ່ໄລ ຕາມ ຫຼຽ ເຄືອ ສາໂທ ລ່າງມາ— ໜັກບໍ່
ເຮັງສະບູນ ຫຼຽ ຕົ້ນ ລ່າງມາ ໄຕ ລ່ຽງ — ໜັກກຳມື
ໝາກຜັກປົມ ລ່າງມາ — ໜັກກຳມື
ເຫຼັງ ຈອງອ່ອນ ຫຼຽ ຕົ້ນ ລ່າງມາ ຊູປ ເປັນ ຕອນ ໃບ- ໜັກກຳມື
ຂອງຕ່າງໆ ທີ່ກ່າວມານີ້ ໂຕ ເອົາ ໄວ້ ທາງ ເທື່ອ ຈົນ ສຸກ ນັກເລີບ
ແຕ່ ໜ່ວຍ ທາງ
ປອບປີ ໃສ່ ກ້າງ ບອ່ງ ໂຕ ລາ — ໜັກຕ່ອນ ເທົ່າ ງີ ເມື່ອ ,
(ໝາກ ... ໜ່ວຍ ຈາງໂຕ ສົ່ງ ໜັກບ່ຽງ ຜັກບົວ
ທົວ ປອມ ມາ ໃບ ທາງ ທົວ- ຜັກ ... ສົງທົວ
ຈາກສາມ ເມື່ອ ... ຕາ ເອົາ ກັນ ເອີບ ຕາ ເຫດ ຕອນ)

ຕົວ ຜັກບົວ ລຽງ ເລີ້ງ ຊູປ ... ຈາງ ໂຕ ລູ- ສາມຕົວ
ໃບ ຜັກບົວ ຊູປ ໂຕ ແລ້ວ — ໜັກໜັ້ນ
" " ຕອນ ຊູປ — ສິບ ໜັ້ນ
ງາ ຂາວ ຕາ ໂຕ ... — ຊີ່ ແອ່ງ
ເກືອ- ໝາກປາ
ວິທີຕົວ— ໂຕ ເອົາ ຜັກ ນັ້ນ ທັງ ... ເພາະ ໜ່ວຍ ທາງ ຮວມ ກັນ ໃຈ
... ເອົາ ເກືອ ໃສ່ ມາ ປາ ... ມື້ ... ບ່ອນ ໂຕ ເອົາ
ກັນ [illegible] ... ຜັກ ບົວ ຊູປ ໄວ້ ງາມ ... ...
... — ຕາມ ໃຈ ຊູ [illegible] ໃບ ຜັກບົວ ຊູປ ໄວ້ ... ລົງ ຈາຍ
ນັກ ... ໂຕ ... ທາງ (ນັກ ເອົາ ໃຊ້ ໜັກ ...
ປີ ... ... ປອບ ປີ)

Soop Phak Po Kha **Recipe 110**

MIXED COOKED VEGETABLES, MERCHANTS' STYLE

Ingredients

1 bunch of *phak kan tan* (an edible leaf, page 37), the tender shoots only
1 bunch of *phak kaab pi* (an edible leaf, page 37), the tender shoots only
1 bunch of *phak tam ling* (an edible leaf, page 37), the young leaves and tender stems only
1 bunch of young spinach, the tender shoots only
10 young *mak paep* (sword bean, page 40)—string the pods
6 yard-long beans (page 40), cut into pieces as long as the section of a finger (say, 3 cm)
all the above ingredients to be washed
1 *nam wah* (banana 'flower', page 32)—discard the old petals and cut the 'flower' into four quarters
3 young stalks of rattan—burn them in the fire until done, peel off the hard outside, cut the inner part into small pieces and wash them
5 sweet young round eggplants (page 33), quartered and washed
3 bunches of *mak kheng Thai* (a tiny eggplant, page 33), stems removed
1 shoot of *no mai lai* (a kind of bamboo, page 41), boiled until it loses its (bitter) taste and then chopped finely with a knife
1 handful of jelly mushrooms (page 43)—cut off the bottoms, chop finely and wash
1 handful of *mak phak poom* (Chinese radish pods, page 42), washed
1 bunch of young white mushrooms—cut off the bottoms and wash
put all the above ingredients except the rattan in a steamer and steam them until they are done
1 piece of grilled fish, about the size of four fingers, rid of all bones and then prodded with a pestle until separated into flakes

5 (small) shallots, cooked in the embers of a charcoal fire 1 dried red chilli pepper, grilled until crisp 2 (small) heads of garlic, cooked in the embers of a charcoal fire	these three ingredients to be pounded together to constitute the *kheuang hom*

3 straight-bulbed spring onions, the bulbs only, finely chopped
1 spring onion, the leaves only, finely chopped
2 sprigs of coriander, the leaves only, chopped
4 spoonfuls of roasted sesame seeds, finely ground
salt and fish sauce

Method

Put all the steamed vegetables and the prepared rattan in a large bowl (together with the *kheuang hom*). Sprinkle salt and fish sauce over them. Mix thoroughly and add the fish and ground sesame seeds. Taste, and check the saltiness. Then put in the chopped spring onion leaves (and bulbs), arrange on a platter, (garnish with coriander) and serve.

The accompaniments should be rice cakes, crisp-fried pork skin and (slices of) roast pork, or fish.

໑໘໘ — ອູ່ສົ້ມໄກ່

ເຄື່ອງປະສົມ — ໄກ່ປ່ອງກ້ຳນຸ່ມ ໜຶ່ງໂຕ ເພາະເພິ່ນໃຊ້ຂອງເຈົ້າແຜ່ນດິນໂດ ທີ່ເຂົ້າໄດ້ເລົ່າເຖິງໜຶ່ງຕົວມາກະພາຍະກຸ່ມ ລ່າງ ແກ້ໂດສະອາດ ເອົາຊີ້ແຫ່ງຊອດໃຫ້ແຫ້ງດີ ໃສ່ ເສັ້ນຫົວ ຜັກບົ່ວດີ ນຳໄປສັກໃສ່ ໄຟເລັ່ນ ໄປຈົນໃສ່ເຫຼືອງ

ໝາກນາວ ... ສີ່ງອອກ — ສາມໜ່ວຍ

ຫົວຜັກບົ່ວຫົວ ... — ສີ່ຫົວ

ຜັກຫອມ ... — ສອງຫົວ

... ສາວສາມ ... ເປັນເຄື່ອງ ...

ໝາກນາວ — ສອງໜ່ວຍ

ຜັກເຜັດ ... ລະໃບ — ໜຶ່ງຫົວ

ຜັກຫອມຊູ — ສອງຕົ້ນ

ເກືອ - ນ້ຳປາ - ແປ້ງນົວ - ໃບ ... ສອງໃບ

ວິທີເຮັດ — ໂຕ ... ເອົາໄກ່ ... ອອກ ... ທ່ອນ ... ຍາ ອອກມາ ... ສ່ວນ ... ແລ້ວ ... ໃຫ້ ... ສຸກ ... ຈຶ່ງ ... ເອົາ ... ລ່າງ ... ໃສ່ ... ໃສ່ ... ... ໂຕ ... ນ້ຳ ... ໃຫ້ ...

ສຸກ ທານ

Soop Som Kai **Recipe 111**

A SOUR CHICKEN DISH

Ingredients

1 chicken, gutted, but with the liver and gizzard retained—the gizzard to be split open and its inner lining pulled off before it is washed; then put the chicken, with liver and gizzard, in a pot, with water to cover, but only just, a little salt and some (peeled) shallots; put the pot on the fire and leave it until the chicken is tender

3 chilli peppers, cooked in the embers of a charcoal fire, then peeled	these three ingredients to be pounded together finely to constitute the *kheuang hom*
4 (small) shallots, similarly treated	
2 (small) heads of garlic, similarly treated	

2 limes

1 straight-bulbed spring onion—chop both the bulb and the leaves

2 sprigs of coriander, finely chopped

salt, fish sauce and ground black pepper

2 Kaffir lime leaves, chopped

Method

Take the boiled chicken out of the pot and transfer it to a large bowl. Tear the breasts and the legs into large pieces, separating the legs and wings at the joints. As for the carcase, choose only bits with meat on them. Discard the bones. Add the *kheuang hom* and some chicken broth, just enough to come half way up from the bottom of the bowl to the top of the chicken pieces. Sprinkle the chopped spring onion, (the Kaffir lime leaves) and fish sauce over the mixture and squeeze lime juice on to it. Taste, and check the saltiness. Arrange on a platter, garnish with ground black pepper and chopped coriander, and serve.

119- ໝົກໜໍ່ປາຂອນ

ເຄື່ອງປະສົມ — ປາຂອນທັງຕົວ ເອົາມາໃສ່ໃຫ້ຖ້ວນຕົວເປັນເທື່ອນ
ທ່ອນໆ ຖູເກັດຖູເກືອ ລ້າງນໍ້າໃຫ້ສະອາດ
ໃບມາກອຶ່ງຊຶ່ງມາກສົ້ມແລ້ວປີ້ງ — ສາມໜ່ວຍ
(ໃບມາກເຜັດ ... ມາກໄມ້ສຸກແລ້ວປອກ — ສາມໜ່ວຍ
ຜັກບົ່ວຫົວ ປອກມາກໃສ່ສາກຕໍາ — ຫ້າຫົວ
ບອນ ມາກໃສ່ສາກໄວ້ — ສອງຫົວ
ໃບ ... ຕໍາໃຫ້ມຸ່ນແລ້ວ ... ໃສ່ເຄື່ອງຕາມ
ໃບຜັກບົ່ວ - ໃບມາກຫອມ

ເກືອ - ນໍ້າປາ - ນອກສາຫາດ

ວິທີເຮັດ — ໃຫ້ເອົານໍ້າໃສ່ເຄື່ອງໃສ່ແຕ່ງໃຫ້ເຂົ້າໃຈ ...
ຜູ້ເກືອຈຶ່ງເອົາປາ ... ນໍ້າປາ ... ໃບປາ ...
ຈຶ່ງຕັກ ... ໃສ່ ... ເອົາເຂົ້າໄປ ...
... ເອົາໃບ ... ໄວ້ ... ຕາມ ...
... ໃຫ້ໃສ່ ...
... ໃຫ້ກິນ
(... ໃບ ... ຂອບ)

Tom Jaew Pa Ngon **Recipe 112**

PIQUANT SOUP OF CATFISH

Ingredients

6 *pa gnon* (the kind of catfish illustrated on page 71)—gut them, cut off their heads and tails and wash them

3 fresh chilli peppers 3 sweet young round eggplants 5 (small) shallots 2 (small) heads of garlic	these four ingredients to be cooked in the embers of a charcoal fire and then peeled and pounded together, to constitute the *kheuang hom*

chopped spring onion leaves
chopped coriander leaves
salt and fish sauce
a lime

Method

Put a little water in a pot and put the pot on the fire. Sprinkle some salt on the water. When it comes to the boil, add the fish and sprinkle some fish sauce over them. Leave the fish until they are cooked, then transfer them to a serving-dish.

Put the *kheuang hom* into the water which was used for boiling the fish. Taste, and check the saltiness. Squeeze lime juice over it, then use it as a sauce to pour over the fish. Use all of it for this purpose.

Garnish the dish with the chopped coriander and (spring onion leaves, and) serve with young cucumbers.

The round eggplants shown here are of the white variety (see page 33).

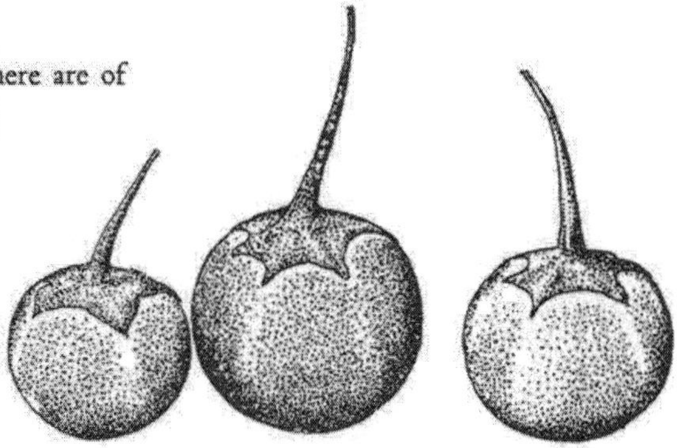

113 - ຢ່ຳປາເລີ້ມ

ເຄື່ອງປະສົມ — ງູມິ່ງ ຢ່ຳປາເລີ້ມ ຂນົບ ຂ່າ ນ່ຳເຟີ້ນ ສ່ວນນ້ຳ ໂຕ້ນະ
ມາງ, [illegible] ໃສ່ ໃນ ຫ່ວນ ເມື່ອ [illegible] ເອົາ ນ້ຳ ໃສ່ ພໍ ກ່ວມ
ສ່ວນ ເຖີ່ງ ນ້ຳ ປາ ໃສ່ ໂຕ້ ຄາມ ເອົາ ຕົ້ມ ໃປ ຈົນ ປາ ສຸກ
ທີ່ ບັງ ໄດ້
(ບວກ ກັບ ເຄື່ອງ ຫອມ ອ່ອນ ຜັກ ໃປ ໃສ່ ສຸກ ປອາ ເບື້ອງ ອອກ ຕົ້ມ
ຜັກ ເຜັດ ທາວ ປອມ ຜັກ ໃປ ໂຕ້ ສຸກ — ຂີ່ ທາວ
" ຫຼາຍ ຜັກ ໃປ ໂຕ້ ສຸກ — ສົ້ມ ທາວ
ບວກ ກັບ ເຄື່ອງ ຊຶ່ງ ທີ່ ໃປ ໂຕ້ ສຸກ ເຜັດ ກຽມ ຍາກ ຍາກ - ສາມ ນ່ອງ
ຂອງ ຊີ່ ເພີ່ມ ນີ້ ໂຕ້ ສາກ ເອົາ ກັນ ເປັນ ເຄື່ອງ ຫອມ
ຜັກ ບໍ່ ສຸກ ເອົາ ງູ ໂຕ້ ແລ້ງ ທັງ ທາວ ແລະ ເປີ ຂນົບ ສົ້ມ
ຜັກ ຫອມ ງູ ຂນົບ ຕົ້ມ - ຊີ່ ຫຼາງ - ສົ້ມ ເປີ

ລາບີ - ນ້ຳ ປາ

ວິທີເຮັດ — ໂຕ້ ຜັກ ເອົາ ເຄື່ອງ ປາ ຄາມ ເກັ້ງ ສຸກ ໃຊ້ ລາບ ລື່ ງາ ຫອມ ລະກໍ
ໂຕ້ ເຂົ້າ ກັນ ຈົນ ແຫຼກ ທີ່ ເອົາ ນ້ຳ ຕົ້ມ ປາ ນັ້ນ ໃສ່
ລົງ ໂຕ້ ເຂົ້າ ກັນ ຈົນ ຂຸ້ນ ເອົາ ຜັກ ບໍ່ ເກັ່ງ ຕົ້ນ ລະ
ໃບ ຂີ້ ຫຼາງ ໃສ່ ຢ່າ ໃຫ້ ຂຸ້ນ ຫຼາຍ ເພາະ ລົດ ຊາດ ຫຼາຍ ລອມ
ກະ ເລີ່ມ ໂຕ້ ນັ້ນ ງາມ ງູມ ເລີ່ມ ເຄື່ອງ ຍໍ ແຫ້ງ ເອົາ ໃສ່
ຈານ ຜັກ ຫອມ ງູ ໃບ ປ້ອງ ນັກ ທີ່ ນີ້ ໂຕ້ ຮູ້ ທານ
(ໃນ ເພາະ ສົ້ມ - ບວກ ກັບ ແຫ່ງ ອ່ອນ ເພາະ ຜັກ ຮູ້ ຕ່າງໆ)

Pon Pa Leum **Recipe 113**

A DISH OF POUNDED CATFISH

Ingredients

1 piece of *pa leum* (a large catfish, see drawing below), free of bones, the size of a hand—wash it, slice it thinly, put it in a pot with water barely covering it, sprinkle it with salt and fish sauce (it should be quite salty), boil it until cooked, then take the pot from the fire

6 sweet young round eggplants 4 (small) shallots 2 (small) heads of garlic 3 fresh chilli peppers	these four ingredients to be cooked in the embers of a charcoal fire, then peeled and pounded together to constitute the *kheuang hom*

1 straight-bulbed spring onion—chop both the bulb and the leaves finely
1 sprig of coriander, chopped
2 Kaffir lime leaves, chopped
salt and fish sauce

Method

Combine the boiled fish with the *kheuang hom* in a mortar and pound together finely. Then add the water in which the fish was cooked and stir until the mixture is thick (i.e. like a thick soup). Add the spring onion and chopped Kaffir lime leaves. Do not let the mixture become either too thick or too runny. Taste, and check the saltiness.

Arrange the mixture on a platter, garnish it with the chopped coriander and serve it with *Keng Som* (a sour soup—see, for example, recipes 18 and 29), young cucumbers and other vegetables which are suitable accompaniments.

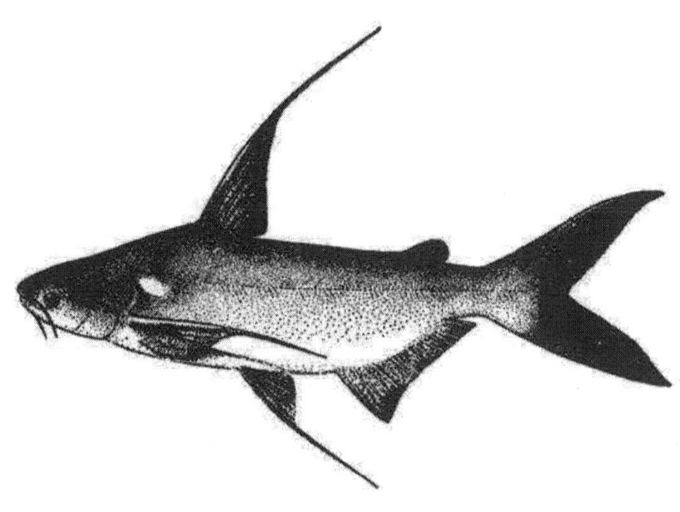

Pa leum, PANGASIUS SANITWONGSEI, a large catfish.

114 - ຈ່ອມປາເຄັມ

ເຄື່ອງປະສົມ — ຊີ້ນ ຍີ່ ປາເຄັມແຫ້ງ ຕ່ອນ ທີ່ຜ່າມື້ ລ້າງນໍ້າ
ໃຫ້ສະອາດ ຊອຍເປັນຕ່ອນນ້ອຍໆ ໃສ່ໝໍ້ ນໍ້າໃສ່
ຖ້ວມຕ່ອນ ເສີບນໍ້າປາໃສ່ໃຫ້ນານ ໄດ້ແລ້ວໄປຈີ່ນປາສຸກ
ຈຶ່ງເອົາໄດ້

(ໝາກອາກາດ ໝາກເຜັດ ຂາ ໃບໂຫລະພາ — ສາມໜ່ວຍ
ໝາກເຂືອ ຫອມແດງ ໃບໂຫລະພາ ຫອມ — ຫົກໜ່ວຍ
ຜັກບົ່ວ ຕົ້ນ ປອມ ໃບໂຫລະພາ — ຊີ້ ຫົວ
ຜັກຫອມ ໃບໂຫລະພາ — ສອງຫົວ)
ຈາກນັ້ນຈຶ່ງເອົາໄປໂຂລກໃຫ້ລະອຽດ ຈົນແຫຼກດີ ເອີ່ນວ່າເຄື່ອງຂອງ
ຜັກບົ່ວ ລວງ ເສັ້ນ ຊອຍ ນາວ . ສາມຕົ້ນ
ໃບຜັກ ຊອຍໃຫ້ແຫຼກ . ໜຶ່ງຫົວ

ຜັກຫອມຊອຍ — ໜຶ່ງຫົວ
ເກືອ - ນໍ້າປາ - ນໍ້າຕານຊາຍ ໃສ່ພໍສົມຄວນ - ຊອງໃບ

ວິທີເຮັດ — ເອົາຜັກທັງໝົດປານັ້ນ ໃສ່ໃນຄົກໂຂລກ
ນັ້ນ ເສີຍ ໃຫ້ຈົນເຂົ້າກັນດີ ຈຶ່ງເອົານໍ້າປາ
ໃສ່ ໃຫ້ເປັນໂຕເຂົ້າກັນຈົນຂຸ້ນ . ຈຶ່ງເອົາໄຟສອງ
ໃສ່ຈານ ຈັກຊົ່ວ ແລ້ວໃຫ້ເອົານໍ້າສົ້ມ , ໃສ່
ຂອງເຄື່ອງ ຊອຍໃສ່ ເອົາໃສ່ຜັກບົ່ວ ຊອຍ
ຈີ່ ແລ້ວ ຈຶ່ງເອົາ ໄປ ປາເຄັມ ທີ່
ໄວ້ນັ້ນ ມາລົງຈີ່ມ ໄປຈົນຂຸ້ນດີ ຈຶ່ງເອົາ
ໃສ່ແລ້ວ ໃສ່ຜັກບົ່ວ ຫອມຜັກບົ່ວ
ຊົ່ວໃສ່ໃຫ້ ລົມໃຫ້ ແລ້ວ ຫອມຜັກບົ່ວ
ແລະຜັກຫອມຊອຍໃສ່ແລ້ວ ນໍາເອົາໄປໃຫ້ກິນ
(ກິນກັບໝາກແຕງ ຮື ຜັກສົດຕ່າງໆ ກໍໄດ້)

Khoua Gnu Pa Leum **Recipe 114**

A DISH OF POUNDED FRIED CATFISH

Ingredients

1 piece of *pa leum* (a large catfish—see previous recipe), about the size of a hand, deboned, washed and sliced into thin pieces, which are to be boiled in just enough water to cover, with salt and fish sauce—the liquid should be quite salty

3 dried red chilli peppers 6 sweet young round eggplants 4 (small) shallots 2 (small) heads garlic	these four ingredients to be put in the embers of a charcoal fire, then peeled and pounded together to form the *kheuang hom*

3 straight-bulbed spring onions, the bulbs only, chopped
the leaves of 1 spring onion, finely chopped
1 sprig of coriander, chopped
salt and fish sauce
pork fat
2 Kaffir lime leaves, finely chopped

Method

Take out the boiled slices of fish and pound them together with the *kheuang hom* until they are well mixed. Add the liquid in which the fish was cooked and mix well until you have a thick mixture (like a thick soup). Taste, and check the saltiness.

Put the pork fat in a pan and put the pan on the fire. Fry the chopped spring onion bulbs until they turn golden; then take them out, leaving the fat in the pan. Now put the fish mixture into the pan and fry it, stirring well. Taste again, and check the saltiness.

Add the chopped Kaffir lime leaves and half of the fried spring onion bulbs, with the chopped spring onion leaves, to the mixture. Mix thoroughly. Transfer to a platter, garnish with the remaining fried spring onion bulbs and the chopped coriander, and serve.

The dish should be accompanied by young cucumbers and *Keng Som* (a sour soup, for examples of which see recipes 18 and 29).

LAO DESSERTS

BIBLIOGRAPHY

INDEX

This drawing, which serves to close the collection of Phia Sing's recipes, depicts a Lao herb garden on stilts, described on page 39.

Lao Desserts

Did Phia Sing leave behind him only the two recipe notebooks reproduced in the preceding pages, or was there a third? The question was posed on page 7, in the Introduction. We have also suggested to Phia Sing's relations that if there was a third notebook it might have contained recipes for desserts, which are entirely lacking in the two we have. These relations have assured us that this is unlikely, and that if there was a third notebook it would have contained recipes similar to those in the first two. Phia Sing would not, they say, have thought it necessary to provide written recipes for desserts.

However, as this book is the nearest approach which has been made so far to a comprehensive collection of traditional Lao recipes, we have thought it appropriate to add this section on desserts. They come from a variety of sources and are mostly associated with the cuisine of Luang Prabang, although known elsewhere. We owe thanks in particular to Mr and Mrs N'guyen Dang, Mrs Thong Samouth Doré, Miss Boon Song Klausner, Mrs Sokprakong Phommavongsa, Mrs Nakhala Souvannavong, Miss Phitsamone Souvannavong, Miss Phouangphet Vannithone and Mrs Kéo Vannithone.

Nam Van Loi Mak Teng

'SWIMMING MELON'

Ingredients
the grated meat of 1 coconut (or the equivalent of desiccated coconut)
200 g (7 oz) sugar
1 melon

Method
Make two extractions of coconut milk. Mix the sugar into the second extraction, and add the melon, cut into small, thin strips. Pour the mixture into individual bowls and top each with a share of the first extraction of coconut milk. Very refreshing.

Khao Niao Thu Lien

DURIAN WITH STICKY RICE

This dish bears some resemblance to the preceding one, but is more substantial and less likely to please everyone; the durian is a fruit whose aroma is notorious, although those who have acquired the taste like eating it very much.

The procedure is simple. Cook some sticky rice in an extraction of coconut milk. Cut up the flesh of a durian and mix it with sugar to taste and with some more coconut milk. Then pour this mixture over the cooked sticky rice, either in a single shallow bowl or in individual bowls.

Nam Van Mak Kuay

BANANA WITH COCONUT MILK AND TAPIOCA

Ingredients
15 dessert bananas (the kind called *mak kuay nam* would be used in Laos)
2 coconuts—grate the meat and make 10 cups of coconut milk in all from it, reserving 1 cup of the first extraction
1½ cups sugar
½ cup tapioca

Method
Peel the bananas and cut each into three.

Pour the 9 cups of coconut milk into a large cooking pot, add the pieces of banana and the sugar, and bring to the boil. Then add the tapioca and continue to boil gently for 20 minutes.

Remove the pot from the fire and add the reserved cup of thick coconut milk. Serve while it is still hot.

Khao Khob

STICKY-RICE 'BISCUITS' OR 'CAKES'

Ingredients (for making 16 to 20)
½ kg (1 lb 2 oz) sticky rice, previously soaked overnight
2 pinches of salt
100–150 g (3–5 oz) sugar

Method
Drain and steam the rice, then allow it to cool a little and form it into round shapes like crumpets, about 8 cm (3") in diameter and fairly thin. Allow these to dry in the sun, which may take 1 or 2 days. They should become completely dry.

After this, deep-fry the biscuits in vegetable oil or pork fat. Meanwhile, heat the sugar until it reaches the 'caramel' stage. As soon as this has happened, 'whirl' the caramel on top of the biscuits. This expressive Lao instruction simply means that the caramel is quickly applied in concentric circles to the biscuits, giving them a sweet topping.

Keep the biscuits in an airtight container for a day or two before eating them.

Khao Paad

RICE-FLOUR, COCONUT AND PEANUT CAKE

Ingredients (for enough for 20 to 30 people)
10 coconuts—grate the meat and make from it 9 soupbowls of the first and second extractions of coconut milk mixed together
2 teaspoonfuls salt
3 soupbowls of rice flour (made from ordinary, not sticky, rice)
1 kg (2¼ lb) sugar, or what the Lao call 'cane sugar paste', which is the same as Chinese 'sugar candy' but comes in large flat pieces instead of smaller lumps
1 kg (2¼ lb) peanuts, roasted and pounded, but not too finely

Method
Put all the coconut milk in a big pot. Add the salt and the rice flour, and put the pot on the fire. Stir it continuously while it cooks. Once the rice flour is cooked (which will take about 10 minutes), add the sugar or 'cane sugar paste'. Continue stirring until the mixture becomes sticky, then add the pounded peanuts and mix them into it thoroughly.

Taste the mixture to check that the sweetness is as you wish it. (If necessary, add a little more sugar or a few pinches of salt.) Remove the pot from the fire and pour the contents into a large platter, with raised sides. Smooth the surface, so that it is all level, then leave it to cool. When it is cold, cut it into pieces of suitable size, transfer them to plates and serve them.

Note
If you are making a small amount, you could use 1 soupbowl of rice flour and 3 soupbowls of coconut milk made from 4 coconuts. You should keep the proportion of 1 to 3 between rice flour and liquid.

Khao Niao Kouane

'STIR-COOKED' STICKY RICE CAKE

Ingredients
3 medium soupbowls of sticky rice
4 coconuts
1 tsp salt
1 kg (2¼ lb) sugar

Method
Soak the sticky rice in water for 3 to 4 hours, then drain it and cook it by steaming.

Grate the meat of the coconuts and use it to make a first extraction of coconut cream and a second of coconut milk. Divide the coconut cream (i.e. the first extraction) into two equal amounts. Place one half in a pot on a medium fire until it separates. Leave this to cool, to form a 'coconut cream caramel'. Mix the remainder of the coconut cream with the coconut milk (i.e. the second extraction).

Put the coconut milk in a wok on the fire, add the salt and bring it to the boil. Then add the steamed rice and the sugar and continue to cook, stirring, until the liquid has almost all been absorbed (which will not take long). At this stage, lower the heat and keep on stirring until the mixture becomes sticky. Then pour it into a suitable platter—large and shallow, but with raised sides—and put the coconut cream caramel on top of it. Make sure that the surface is level, then leave it to cool.

When it is cold, cut it into suitable serving pieces and present these on plates.

Khao Nom Maw Keng

'SOUP-POT' COCONUT DESSERT CAKE

Ingredients (for 10)

3 coconuts—grate the meat and make from it the first extraction only of coconut milk
50 g (6 to 7 tablespoonfuls, or 1¾ oz) flour
500 g (1 lb 2 oz) sugar
10 eggs, beaten
1 teaspoonful salt
1 teaspoonful baking-powder
1–2 spoonfuls finely chopped shallots, fried (optional)

Method

Mix the coconut milk, flour and sugar together thoroughly. Then add the eggs, salt and baking-powder and beat all well together. Sprinkle the chopped fried shallots (if used) on top.

Taste the mixture to check its sweetness, then transfer it to a shallow oven-dish and put it in a moderate oven for 45 minutes or so. Take it out and leave it to cool. Then cut it into suitable pieces before serving it.

Notes

This is a very popular sweet dish in Laos, although the use of baking-powder shows that it is of fairly recent origin.

The great majority of Lao families have no ovens of the western type—indeed these are rarities in Lao households even in the larger towns. Lao cooks have therefore had to use other devices for baking. One method, which presumably accounts for the name of this 'soup-pot cake', is to do the baking in a dry, covered pot.

Another improvised 'oven' is made thus. Having set going a hot charcoal fire in a brazier of the kind shown on page 16, the Lao take the glowing charcoal out of it, put the thing to be baked in it, set a lid on top and put the hot charcoal on the lid.

Khao Tom Mak Kuay

STEAMED RICE AND BANANA PUDDINGS

Ingredients (for 40 servings, or 20 if people have two each)
1 kg (2¼ lb) sticky rice
1 litre (35 fl oz) coconut milk, a mixture of the first and second extractions from 2 or 3 coconuts
500 g (1 lb 2 oz) sugar
1 teaspoon salt
10 bananas

Method
Soak the sticky rice for 3 to 4 hours in plenty of water.

Prepare the coconut milk. Add the rice to it, in a large cooking pot, and cook the mixture, stirring it from time to time, until the rice is half-cooked and still moist. At this point add the sugar and salt. It is important that the mixture should not be allowed to become dry.

Leave it to cool, after stirring well to make sure that the sugar and salt are thoroughly mixed in.

In the meantime slice the bananas into halves lengthways and then cut each half into two across.

Now take pieces of banana leaf or aluminium foil about 6 or 7 inches (15 to 17 cm) square. You will need 40 of these. On to each spoon about 2 tablespoonfuls of the rice mixture. Place a quarter of a banana on top, then wrap the banana leaf or foil over it to make a package, tucking the corners down securely. Reapeat until all the mixture and the pieces of banana have been used up.

Steam the packages for half an hour, then serve them, either warm or cold, leaving the guests to unwrap them and consume the contents.

Note
This is a very popular sweet dish, often used on religious occasions as offerings to the monks at the pagoda.

Vun

A COCONUT DESSERT USING AGAR-AGAR

Ingredients
3 heaped teaspoonfuls agar-agar
¼ litre (9 fl oz) first extraction of coconut milk
1 litre (35 fl oz) second extraction of coconut milk
} made from 2 ripe coconuts or the equivalent amount of desiccated coconut
100 g (3½ oz) brown sugar
100 g (3½ oz) white sugar
3 eggs, lightly beaten

Method

Add the agar-agar to the coconut milk (first extraction only) in a cooking pot, stir thoroughly and bring to the boil. Add the salt and sugar and leave to simmer for 7 to 10 minutes. Then add the second extraction of coconut milk to the mixture. Pour the beaten eggs into a platter with fairly deep sides. Bring the coconut mixture back to the boil, then pour it quickly into the platter, on top of the beaten eggs, and let it set. Do not touch it again until it has set.

This dessert may be prepared the day before it is to be eaten. About 2 hours (not more) before serving it, cut it into small lozenges.

Note

If necessary, the eggs may be omitted, and the quantity of coconut milk (first extraction) increased; but it is preferable to include the eggs, as they make a pleasant contrast with the brown upper layer. This is the advice of Mrs Sokprakong Phommavongsa, from whom the recipe comes. Anyone who has seen and tasted her *Vun* will surely endorse the advice.

Sankhagnaa Mak Phao

COCONUT CUSTARDS IN COCONUT SHELLS

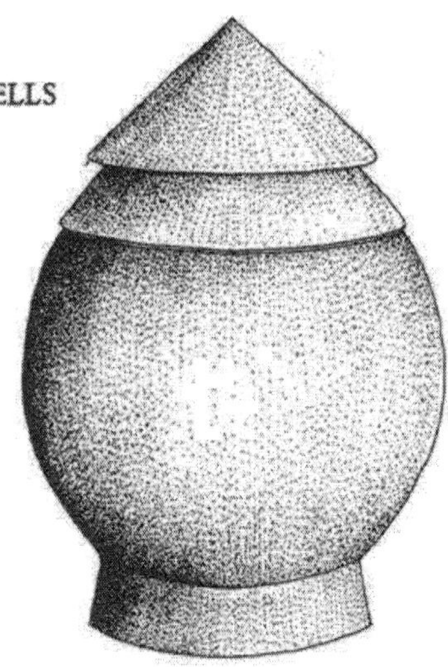

Ingredients (for 4)

- 4 young coconuts, of the small variety
- 6 duck's or 8 hen's eggs, lightly beaten
- 1 cup sugar
- 1 cup of the first extraction of coconut milk from another, larger and mature coconut

Method

Remove the husks from the 4 small coconuts and carve them into the shape shown in the drawing, using a very sharp knife. Cut off the top of each, in the form of a dome-shaped cap, to open the contents. Pour out the coconut water, but do not disturb the meat.

Mix together the lightly beaten eggs, the sugar and the thick coconut milk. Pour the mixture into the small coconuts, set their caps on them and steam them for about half an hour, until done.

Note

This is a particularly pleasing dessert, both in appearance and in flavour.

Kanom Babin (I)

A LUANG PRABANG CAKE OF RICE FLOUR AND COCONUT

Ingredients (for 1 cake of about 8″ diameter and 1–1½″ depth)
300 g (11 oz) sticky rice flour } or increase the proportion of sticky
200 g (7 oz) ordinary rice flour } rice, to achieve a softer cake
400 g (14 oz) grated coconut (or the equivalent of desiccated coconut)
200 g (7 oz) sugar
a pinch of salt
enough water to make the dough

Method
Mix the two flours together on a board and make a well in the middle. Add the coconut, sugar and salt to water in a bowl, mix and then put in the well to make the dough. Use a wooden spoon to mix the dough thoroughly. Pour the dough into a lightly oiled cake tin about 8″ in diameter and put it in a pre-heated oven at 350° F (gas mark 4). It will be ready in about 40 minutes. To prevent it from becoming too dry, sprinkle a little vegetable oil on to it after about 30 minutes of cooking. Note that this is quite a 'shallow' cake. It is similar to the version in the next recipe, but you have one large cake instead of a number of small ones.

Kanom Babin (II)

CAKES MADE FROM STICKY RICE AND COCONUT

Ingredients (for 10 people)
5 coconuts
250 g (9 oz) ordinary rice
1 kg (2¼ lb) sticky rice
1½ kg (3¼ lb) sugar

Method
Grate the meat of the coconuts. Soak the two lots of rice together in water, then drain them and grind them in a *mo* (see drawing on page 312) until fine. Mix together the grated coconut, the ground rice and the sugar.

Select a large cooking pan, preferably circular and without handles but with a lid. Use a clean piece of cloth to coat the inside of it with a thin film of vegetable oil.

Next, you will need some baking rings. The Lao (and Thai) name for this device is *wong kanom*. Each is a metal ring, such as is sometimes used in western kitchens for enclosing and giving shape to fried eggs, about 6 cm (2½″) in diameter and 2 cm (¾″) deep. Set a number of these—there will probably be room for 3 or 4—on the greased pan and ladle some of the mixture of coconut, rice and sugar into them. Sprinkle a very little vegetable oil on top. Put the lid on, with a few pieces of burning charcoal on top of it, and set it on a low to medium fire—just enough to supply a moderate heat below and above.

After about 10 minutes, remove the lid and see whether the cakes are beginning to brown on top. They should be only slightly brown when finished. Once they are done, remove them from the rings and put them on a platter. Repeat the process until all the mixture is used up.

It would not be unusual, if making these cakes just for family consumption, to make 1 or 2 larger ones in the bottom of a wok, using the lid of a cooking pot as the cover. The cakes will then come out with slightly rounded instead of flat bottoms.

This dessert is also well known in Thailand.

Kanom Khao Niao Mak Kuay Jeun

MUNG BEAN FRIED CAKES

Ingredients
500 g (1 lb 2 oz) split green mung beans
250 g (9 oz) sugar
250 g (9 oz) grated coconut (or the equivalent of desiccated coconut)
2 eggs, and flour for coating
oil for deep-frying

Method
Soak the green beans in water for a while, then string them, wash them and cook them by steaming. Once they are thoroughly cooked, pass them through a fine sieve or reduce them to a purée by means of a Moulinex or blender. Mix them with the sugar and coconut, and form the mixture into balls about the size of a hen's egg.

Meanwhile, you have beaten the eggs. Dust the balls lightly with flour, coat them with beaten egg (and with sesame seeds if you wish) and then deep-fry them in hot oil. Drain and allow to cool before serving. (Lao cooks might sprinkle them with powdered fondant; icing sugar may be used in the west.)

Ping Manton

GRILLED CASSAVA

A simple recipe. Take 1 kg (2¼ lb) young cassava roots, peel them and grill them until they are soft. Then remove them from the fire and flatten them.

Mix ¼ cup sugar with 1½ cups coconut milk, dip the flattened pieces of cassava in this mixture and grill them again, for 3 to 5 minutes, over a low heat. (A hot fire will not produce good results.) Serve hot. The quantities suggested should produce 6 to 8 servings.

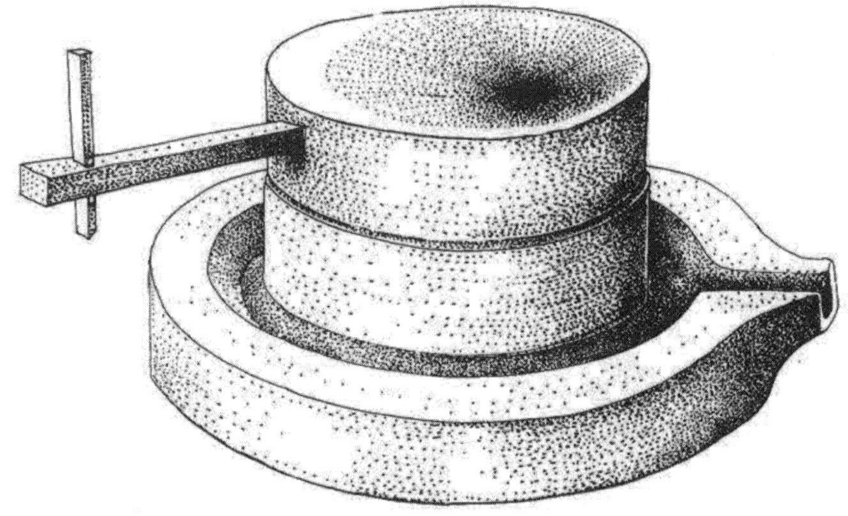

A *mo*, for grinding rice

Bibliography

This short list of books consulted includes some pertaining to the foods and cuisines of neighbouring countries. These often throw light on features of Lao cookery, and are sometimes necessary—given the paucity of documentation on Laos—for the identification of Lao ingredients. Burma, Thailand, Cambodia, Vietnam. The obvious absentee is China, the biggest by far of Laos' neighbours. We have in fact used a number of Chinese reference books (in Chinese) for checking the identity of some plants and similar purposes; but the whole question of Chinese influence on the cuisines of South-East Asia is so complex, and the literature on the cuisines of China itself so vast, that we have not attempted to provide even a selective list. Besides, the frontier region between China and Laos is a mountainous no-man's, or nomad's land, and Chinese influences have not played upon Laos, gastronomically speaking, in the same direct way as, say, Thai influences.

Allen, Betty Molesworth: *Common Malaysian Fruits*: Longmans, Malaysia, 1965

Archaimbault, Charles: *Structures religieuses Lao*: Editions Vithagna, Vientiane, 1973

Burkill, I. H.: *Dictionary of the Economic Products of the Malay Peninsula*: originally published by the Crown Agents in 1935, reprinted by the Ministry of Agriculture and Cooperatives, 2 vols, Kuala Lumpur, 1966

Child, R.: *Coconuts*: 2nd edition, Longman, London, 1974

Davidson, Alan: *Fish and Fish Dishes of Laos*: first commercial edition, Charles Tuttle, Tokyo and Rutland, Vermont, 1975

Giles, F. H.: 'An Account of the Ceremonies and Rites performed when catching the Pla Buk [PANGASIANODON GIGAS] . . .', in *Journal of the Siam Society*, volume 28, 1935, pp. 91–113

Gouineau, Andrée-Yvonne: 'Laotian Cookery' and 'Some Recipes [of Laos]', in *Kingdom of Laos, the Land of the Million Elephants and White Parasol*: English-language edition, France-Asie, Saigon, 1959, pp. 221–34

Grist, D. H.: *Rice*: 5th edition, Longman, London, 1975

Hellei, Professor Andras: *Les coutûmes alimentaires Khmères*, No. 3 of the Etudes Statistiques of the Institut National de la Statistique et des Recherches Economiques, Phnom Penh, 1973

Herklots, G. A. C.: *Vegetables in South-East Asia*: George Allen and Unwin, 1972

Kanchananaga, Suraphong: *Resources and Products of Thailand*: Siam Communications Ltd, Bangkok, 1973

Khaing, Mi Mi: *Cook and Entertain the Burmese Way*: Karoma Publishers, Ann Arbor, 1978

Khin, U San: *Some Medicinal and Useful Plants . . . of Burma*: Rangoon, 1970

Kritakara, M. L. Taw, and Amranand, M. R. Pimsai: *Modern Thai Cooking*: Editions Duang Kamol, Bangkok, 1977

Lan, J.: *Les plantes indochinoises de grande culture*: première partie, 'Plantes alimentaires', et deuxième partie, 'Plantes industrielles et quelquefois alimentaires', Bibliothèque agricole indochinoise, Hanoi, 1928 and 1930 respectively

Lao Women's Association: *Lao Cooking* (in Lao): undated but prior to 1973

Lekagul, Boonsong and Cronin, Edward W. Jr: *Bird Guide of Thailand*: 2nd, revised, edition, Association for the Conservation of Wildlife, Bangkok, 1974

Mackie, I. M., Hardy, R. and Hobbs, G.: *Fermented Fish Products*: FAO Fisheries Reports, no. 100, FAO, Rome, 1971

Medway, Lord: *The Wild Mammals of Malaya*: Oxford University Press, Kuala Lumpur and Singapore, 1969

Miller, Jill Nhu Huong: *Vietnamese Cookery*: Charles E. Tuttle Company, Tokyo, 1968

Ngô, Bạch and Zimmerman, Gloria: *The Classic Cuisine of Vietnam*: Barron's/Woodbury, New York, 1979

Organ, John: *Gourds*: Faber and Faber, London, 1963

Owen, Sri: *Indonesian Food and Cookery*: Prospect Books, London and Washington D.C., 1980

Pongpangan, Somchit and Poobrasert, Suparb: *Edible and Poisonous Plants in Thai Forests* (in Thai): Science Society of Thailand, Bangkok, mid-1970s

Pruthi, J. S.: *Spices and Condiments*: National Book Trust, New Delhi, 1976

Simmonds, N. W.: *Bananas*: Longman, London, 1959

Taki, Y.: *Fishes of the Lao Mekong Basin*: USAID Mission to Laos, Vientiane, 1974

Teng, Ung: *Les aliments usuels au Cambodge*, a thesis published by the Université Royale, Phnom Penh, 1967

Vidal, Jules: *Les plantes utiles du Laos*, 1ère Série, Fasc. I–VI bis: Journal d'Agriculture tropicale et de Botanique appliquée, Muséum National d'Histoire Naturelle, Paris, 1963

Vidal, Jules: *Noms vernaculaires de plantes (Lao, Meo, Kha) en usage au Laos*, Ecole Française d'Extrême-Orient, Paris, 1959

The above works have to do with natural history and cookery. Readers who would like to inform themselves about the political upheavals which took place in Laos between the time when Phia Sing wrote his recipes and the time when publication of this book was set in train will find that the best account is contained in a book by Dr Amphay Doré, *Le partage du Mékong*, Encre Editions, Paris, 1980.

Index

This gives both the Lao and English titles of all Phia Sing's recipes, and of the desserts. For the convenience of the cook there are a few entries representing categories of dishes such as Soups, Fish dishes. The index does not include the various ingredients described in the introductory part of the book. The Table of Contents provides a guide to these by category; and the recipes themselves include specific references to them when necessary.